Enlightenment and Despair

THIS IS A CRITICAL history of social theory in England, France, Germany and the USA from the eighteenth century to the present. Geoffrey Hawthorn begins with the 'prehistory' of the subject and traces, particularly in the thought of Rousseau, Kant and Hegel, the emergence of certain fundamental distinctions and assumptions whose origins – indeed whose existence – are often overlooked in studies of the traditional 'founding-fathers' of sociology such as Marx, Durkheim and Weber. It is a distinctive feature of this book that Hawthorn explains this intellectual history in terms of the very various intentions of the main theorists and the social, political and cultural conditions in which they worked. He is sensitive particularly to the long-standing and important differences in style and character of thought not only between Europe and America but also between England, France and Germany.

The book is itself a contribution to social theory as well as to history. Hawthorn argues that in some striking and important respects the history of sociology has been a failure, and that in some of these respects the failure was inevitable. In a new conclusion to this second edition he argues that, however defensible the project of a social theory once may have been, it is, for theoretical and empirical reasons, no longer so.

The author is Reader in Sociology and Politics at the University of Cambridge.

TO TOM AND DAN

Enlightenment and Despair

A History of Social Theory

SECOND EDITION

GEOFFREY HAWTHORN

Reader in Sociology and Politics, University of Cambridge

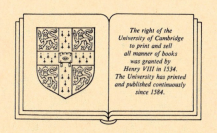

The right of the
University of Cambridge
to print and sell
all manner of books
was granted by
Henry VIII in 1534.
The University has printed
and published continuously
since 1584.

CAMBRIDGE UNIVERSITY PRESS

CAMBRIDGE

LONDON   NEW YORK   NEW ROCHELLE

MELBOURNE   SYDNEY

Published by the Press Syndicate of the University of Cambridge
The Pitt Building, Trumpington Street, Cambridge CB2 1RP
Bentley House, 200 Euston Road, London NW1 2DB
32 East 57th Street, New York, NY 10022, USA
10 Stamford Road, Oakleigh, Melbourne 3166, Australia

Printed in Great Britain by Redwood Burn Ltd., Trowbridge

British Library cataloguing in publication data

Hawthorn, Geoffrey
Enlightenment and despair:
a history of social theory. – 2nd ed.
1. Sociology – History
I. Title
301′.09′03   HM19

Library of Congress cataloguing in publication data

Hawthorn, Geoffrey
Enlightenment and despair.
Bibliography.
Includes index.
1. Sociology. 2. Sociology – Europe – History.
3. Sociology – United States – History. 4. Philosophy, Modern.
I. Title.
HM24.H39   1986   301′.09   86-16703

ISBN 0 521 33101 3 hard covers
ISBN 0 521 33721 6 paperback

A.S.

Contents

Preface

IN THIS BOOK, I try to recover the intentions of those who can be seen to have been proposing what we now think of as social theories. I wanted to understand those intentions as the intentions they were. Of course, I failed. One reason for this, as Bernard Williams puts it at the start of his book on Descartes, was that even if one manages to play old music on old instruments, one cannot hear it with old ears. There is no way of understanding the beliefs of others in terms which are not in some way or another, to some extent or another, ours. There is no escape from translation. And translation, as Quine has made clear, is indeterminate; we can only make it less so by supposing some community of interest between others and ourselves, some similarity in psychology perhaps, or in sociology, by extending, as it has been said, some 'charity'. We understand others and can only understand others by supposing that in one or more respects they are, even as themselves, like us. It may of course be going too far too soon to agree, as Quine and others are reported once to have agreed in discussing the matter, that 'the more absurd or exotic' the beliefs of others seem, the more suspicious we are actually 'entitled' to be of the translations of those beliefs. It will defeat the purpose if we too readily attempt, as Gadamer encourages us to in his *Truth and Method,* a 'fusion of horizons'. But the only perspective on beliefs as the beliefs they are is the perspective of those whose beliefs they are. Ours is ours. Understanding those beliefs in their terms, rather than ours, is pre-empted.

We can nevertheless wish to respect them. We can want to ask of a thought or an argument not, or not immediately, 'what does it mean to us?' but 'what, to those who had it and to those who heard it, did it mean and could it have meant?' Yet to say that we have an interest in 'respect' says too much and too little. It says too much if it suggests reverence. Having played old music on old instruments, we do not have to admire it, much less to like it. But it says too little if it suggests that we can avoid the corruptions caused not only by our interests but also by our hindsight. Some of these corruptions are obvious. We are constrained by what survives and select from it. Others, however, are not. To see the impulse and intention in a past argument, even, sometimes, to see it *as* an argument, is from where we are to see what the impulse in it was not, to see what wasn't said, what might have been said at the time, and what might be said now against whatever was. It's to see what the author and his immediate audience may not have known or been able to know. Having seen all this, of course, we could then try to forget it. We could try instead to see what a writer felt and thought just as he, then, might have felt and thought it, and to describe it in terms that he would have accepted. But even if that were possible, which, as I have said, it is not, it is unlikely to lead to the illumination that difference and distance can bring.

I wanted to get such a distance. I wanted to free myself from a forced intimacy with what Isaiah Berlin, in sympathy with Herzen, once nicely described as the 'symmetrical fantasies' of social theory. I wanted to avoid what John Bayley calls 'the English vice', of pruning the past into a National Trust, and the Soviet vice, of polishing it into 'an instrument of policy and advertisement'. I wanted, as Bayley reports the critic Shklovsky as saying, to 'make it strange', to be able more clearly to see it as a past which impinged on me but in which I was a sometimes irritated, often bemused and always uneasy stranger. In the terms of Richard Rorty's recent discussion of the matter, I realise that I had wanted to avoid 'doxography', 'the attempt', as Rorty puts it, 'to impose a problematic on a canon drawn up without reference to that problematic, or, conversely, to impose a canon on a problematic without reference to that canon'. I had wanted to avoid a history of social theory which treated it as a more or less unproblematic natural kind. I wanted instead to attempt an historical reconstruction of it which had also in part to be a rational reconstruction, and I wanted to make this reconstruction a piece of 'intellectual history', in Rorty's sense, as well; in the spirit of a splendid question that is said to have been set at Oxford before the war, 'why is French music like that?', I wanted to try to answer why social theory too, in the societies in which and for which it was written, was like *that*. But in order even to ask this question, I had to have some prior sense of what this theory was. I had to decide the canon. And in order not to lapse back into supposing that the theory was indeed some sort of natural kind, delivered, as it tended to be delivered when I conceived the book, as an unproblematic and really rather imposing thing, I had to decide what sorts of questions being asked in what sorts of ways made it, for me, that canon. I had, in Rorty's sense of the term, to be a *Geisteshistoriker*.

And *Geistesgeschichte*, as he says, 'is the sort of intellectual history which has a moral'. 'The moral to be drawn is that we have, or have not, been on the right track in raising the questions' that we now do. Ten years ago, I had a sense that something was wrong with the existing track. But I did not know quite what. Now, I am clearer. I am clearer about what, if it has been one project, the project of social theory has been. I am clearer about why I think that it was misconceived. And I am convinced that as that project, it is finished. I have accordingly written a new conclusion which, in what I hope is its greater clarity about the canon, might also, as a late-flying Owl of Minerva, serve as a further Introduction to the book.

I have in addition revised the end of Chapter 10, corrected some avoidable errors and obscurities, and added some more recent items to the Bibliography. I make no apology for the undoubted persistence of what an American reviewer called my 'parochialism'. The book was written from Britain in the 1970s and not from New York then or from some other place at some other time, let alone from that 'point of view (if I may say so) of the Universe' to which Henry Sidgwick, writing a few hundred yards from where I do, once nervously aspired. I do regret not having said more about the diversities of American thought. But I continue to believe that if there is one contrast in this respect to be drawn between Europe and America, mine (that is to say, de Tocqueville's) is it. If I were to write the whole book again, however, I would include something on Italy. Its always more sceptical tradition and its humanist past, so lovingly recovered by liberals towards the end of the nineteenth century, do much to explain the fact that although social thought there, both liberal and socialist, was prompted by some of the same preoccupations as those in the north, it had such a different tone. So too, of course, does Italy's different economic and social character throughout the period. Were I to pursue these differences, I suspect that I might be led to refine some of my accounts of social thinking in the three European countries that I do discuss.

The book began in notes for some lectures that I gave more than twenty years ago in the remarkable department of Sociology that Peter Townsend created at Essex. I owe a great deal to the students I have taught there and since in Cambridge. I remain grateful for an opportunity at Harvard to get things into a perspective with which George Homans, although not quite for my reasons, came to agree. Ruth Hawthorn and John Dunn sustained me in the original writing; many friends took the trouble to comment on the book when it first appeared; Jeremy Mynott did much for the first edition and encouraged a second; Bernard Williams has given me whatever understanding I now have (an understanding which is apparent in the new Conclusion) of what a theory of and for human affairs might be, and of much else besides; conversations in Caracas with Luis Castro, and just before I wrote the new Conclusion, with Richard Rorty, Alan Ryan and Roberto Unger, have left their mark on it; Judith Shklar, in a year of talk in Cambridge, and over a much longer period Stefan Collini, John Dunn, and Anthony Pagden have done more than they know to enlighten me about the past and the point of social and political thought; the last three and Jeremy Mynott have also read and commented on the changes I have made.

Cambridge
March 1986

Introduction

THE SOCIOLOGIST who begins a history of social theories is at once very tempted to stop. To write such a history, he has first to decide what social theories are. If he suggests a sociological answer, he both presupposes the validity of what he is trying to explain and undermines his claim to have taken a decision at all. If he suggests another, he seems oddly to exempt himself and his subjects from the determinations he claims to detect in others. He is caught between circularity, self-cancellation and bad faith. This is a history written in bad faith. It accepts that sociologists have asked important questions. It doubts that they have so far provided very good answers. And this distance between question and answer is nowhere greater than on the issue of what social theories themselves are. None of the existing answers to this question will do, although why they will not makes it clear what might.

One of the first and always the most direct set of answers are the Marxists'. Marxists essentially claim that all social theories, except of course their own, are ideologies, false beliefs promoted and sustained by the extra-intellectual interests of the class which holds them, and explained by those interests. The claim has two obvious difficulties. The first, as Goldmann put it in *The Hidden God*, is that the truth of Marxism, upon which its entire position rests, is no more than a wager on the outcome of history, on the economic, political and intellectual victory of the exploited who by virtue of their exclusion from bourgeois society are uniquely privileged with a total comprehension of that society and its necessary supersession. It has become more difficult to make that wager. Second, however, even if one does, the fact that the variety of ideologies in approximately capitalist societies has been and continues to be so great requires the Marxist either to posulate an equally large variety of bourgeoisies or to concede that the beliefs of the one essential bourgeoisie are so various that the ideological obstacles to that

I

class's supersession are themselves various. Either concession badly weakens the force of the initial wager. It might be said that this is too crude, that the nature of class conflicts, of their infrastructural and superstructural characters, is complex and shifting. But this, while meeting what non-Marxists might regard as more nearly the true state of affairs, concedes too much. If societies do differ so, little or nothing is left of the Marxist philosophy of history but a diffuse teleology, an interesting set of concepts, and a rather roughshod notion of intellectual production.

A second set of answers are those suggested by Durkheim and by those in some way inspired by him. They are implied in accounts of religious belief and of primitive classifications more generally. They point to the similarity of structure between a society and its ideas. Durkheim himself never offered more than a very simple account of how one was to assess such similarities, but even his more sophisticated followers have failed satisfactorily to answer the three obvious questions. First, why should the structure of an idea, the arrangement of its premises and of the contentions derived from or otherwise built upon them, be more fundamental than its content? Second, what is to count as a society? And third, how exactly may one explain the connections between social structures and intellectual ones? Durkheim himself was very high-handed with the heterogeneity of complex societies, which he regarded as a passing phase, and he also exaggerated the homogeneity of simpler ones. This is not a simply scholastic point. If one regards each idea or set of ideas as distinct, which the approach requires, one is faced with the problem of explaining why the heterogeneity of ideas is so great and socially so untidy, of how groups can relate in some ways and not in others, of why a society in one respect is not a society in another. If the reply is that this is exactly the virtue, that the approach sorts analytical order from empirical chaos, then one is back with the first question: why should one sort order in this particular way? It cannot be that it promises more satisfactory explanations. Durkheim's own account of how the homology comes about is notoriously feeble. Where he does not confuse the very faculty of intellectual organisation with particular orderings in particular societies (as in *Primitive Classification*), he resorts (in *The Elementary Forms of the Religious Life*) to the view that the the sentiments engendered in a particular pattern of social relations will cause men to have notions that replicate, reinforce and celebrate that pattern. Others resort to more plausible accounts. Lévi-Strauss takes the more directly Kantian line of suggesting a human mind with certain universal habits of organisation, the outcome of which will depend upon the exigencies of the society in question. Mary Douglas appears similarly to work from a suppressed psychological premise of a need for cognitive order, and also assumes a causal connection between such order and tight social control. But such devices steer an extremely unsteady course between arbitrary declaration and *ad hoc* invention which although in many ways attractive as what Lévi-Strauss himself would call *bricolage* cannot really be sustained as a proper theory of belief, and thus as a plausible starting point for a theory of social theories themselves.

A third answer to the question of what social theories are and how they may be explained has not been proposed as a strictly sociological answer at all, but its ambitions are identical and its promise, at least, is to resolve difficulties raised by each of the first two. It is suggested by Toulmin. Toulmin's thesis rests upon an extension into intellectual history of the Darwinian account of species change. He suggests that one can at any time identify what he calls 'transmits', populations of concepts which are subject always to wide variation and which are constantly being selected, or not, according to their applicability. This has its attractions. It concedes, which most Marxists and Durkheimians do not, that in any society at any time there is a great variety of incompatible or ill-fitting ideas. It also allows the irresistible truth that the ways in which ideas change owe much to what it suits people to believe. But there are difficulties. One is raised by the analogy between mutation and the variety and variability of ideas. The first can be described by models of chance occurrence and explained mechanistically. The second cannot. Another lies in the extension of 'applicability'. In biology, fitness is conventionally and narrowly defined as reproductive success, and although there is in itself nothing wrong with defining the fitness, or success, or applicability of an idea in the same way, such a definition tends to overlook the wholly different ways in which animals reproduce and ideas survive. Indeed, Toulmin's superficially seductive scheme falls apart at every point. At best, it can only provide the basis of a purely statistical description of changing populations of ideas.

Marx and Durkheim and most of those who have looked at beliefs in the ways they suggested have in general looked only at non-scientific beliefs or, in the case of the Durkheimians, at what from a western point of view may be regarded as primitive proto-sciences. Toulmin apparently intends his account to cover beliefs of all kinds. Two others, however, a French philosopher, Bachelard, and an American historian of physics, Kuhn, have talked only of science, and although neither seems to have thought that what he said could also be extended to the social sciences (Kuhn has deliberately denied that it can), others have demurred. Bachelard has been appropriated by Althusser to explain the development of Marxism in Marx himself and in Lenin, and Kuhn has been more or less thoroughly appropriated by others to commend, condemn or merely describe the similarities as well as the differences between natural science and social science. Bachelard wrote from within an uncompromising (but also unorthodox) rationalism. Kuhn writes from within a conventionalism which like the scientists he describes is compromised upon a recalcitrant world. But the outcomes, as history, are remarkably alike. They are also sociological, and unless one presumes that there are no good reasons at all for thinking that the practice of understanding society bears any resemblance to that of understanding nature, they are thus both at least *prima facie* candidates for a sociology of sociology itself.

For each, science is essentially social. It consists of a community within which there is a common view, what Kuhn calls a 'paradigm', a conceptual scheme which defines the objects of investigation and the ways in which they are to be investigated. Bachelard is the philosophically more extreme of the two, appearing to believe that scientists quite literally construct the objects of their inquiry, and equating this at once socially and intellectually displined activity with reason itself. Kuhn does grant an external world, and also grants that it can face any paradigm with eventually intolerable anomalies, so causing a change. Each implies that what scientists believe is the effect of a strictly social pressure, a pressure against imagination and fancy, a pressure which achieves its effect in what are at least partly psychological ways. The paradox of science in their view, therefore, is that its rational constructions are if not always then certainly for long periods independent of the properties of the world and themselves a function of non-rational forces. But for Bachelard, the history of science is necessarily an *histoire raisonée*, a rational history of a rational activity for which because it is entirely exhaustive of reason there can be no rational explanation outside itself. The other history, which *ex hypothesi* cannot be written as a rational and so intelligible history at all, is an *histoire périmée*, a history of the confused and shifting *rêveries* of those who have not yet entered the *cité scientifique*. For Kuhn, the history of science is the history of scientific revolutions, a history of transitions from one paradigm to another, a history which is explained by the recurring fact that rational men, men who are rational by virtue of their being men and not by virtue of their being scientists, encounter facts which their paradigm cannot explain. By extension, and eliding their philosophical differences, the history of sociology implied by each is a history of the systematisation and closure of explanations of social life in clearly demarcated and tightly controlled communities.

As such, it has three difficulties. The first and most obvious, as Kuhn himself has said, is that it is simply not true. The social sciences, and certainly sociology, have rarely been as well institutionalised as the natural sciences, and even where they have, social scientists have seemed much more able to resist the pressure of their peers. There does indeed seem almost to be a qualitative difference. In the one, the deviant is ignored and unrewarded. In the other, at least in Europe, he is praised and respected. It is no doubt indicative of the exceptional professionalisation of modern American sociology that the one thoroughly Kuhnian account of the subject, Friedrichs' *A Sociology of Sociology*, is an account of it as it has recently appeared in the United States. Second, and related to this, there is the difficulty raised by Kuhn's weak suggestion and Bachelard's quite definite insistence that what is not social is not scientific. Bachelard indeed goes as far as to say that the pre-scientific is not only non-social but also non-rational, the result only of unconscious *rêveries*. One could, of course, recast the history of social theorising in this way, but only by stipulation, and it would produce a most bizarre account, an account, indeed, that would itself be vitiated if it were not the product of communal deliberation and official sanction. Third, and most severely, there is in each the difficulty that the rational, whether also social or not, is partly but to that extent paradoxically explained by the non-rational.

This is indeed the most fundamental difficulty in any supposed 'sociology of knowledge'. If beliefs are externally caused, it seems impossible to see how they can also be rational. And if they are rational, it seems impossible to see how they can be externally caused. The solution of arguing that what is rational is also determined, because what is rational is a correct appreciation of the tendency of the external world itself, a world tending towards non-contradiction, universality and so reason, the solution suggested by Hegel and with different emphasis by Marx after him, is, as I suggest in chapters two and three, invalid. Without it, one is forced either to the view that beliefs are sentimental responses to external stimuli, a view that threatens to vanquish them (and itself) as rational, or to the view that rational autonomy exists in a world in which sociologists, above all, insist that it does not. One has to choose.

The choice is clear. If the history is to be rational, it must presume rationality in its subjects, and forswear sociology. It must simply ask what any past thinker thought he was right about, and what his reasons were for thinking he was. But these questions, although necessary, are not sufficient. For in order properly to understand why any thinker thought it important to be right about the things that he thought it important to be right about, and not something else, the historian has also to recover his intentions. This point was made in a general way by Collingwood, and has recently been made again by Dunn and secured by Skinner on the basis of the analytical philosophies of action developed from Austin in England in the 1950s and 1960s. The contention, simply put, is that political philosophies and by extension social theories are to be seen neither as disembodied abstractions nor as the epiphenomenal and implicitly mechanical consequences of social conditions, but instead, as actions. That is to say, they are to be seen as being in part actually constituted by the intentions within them. Thus, properly to understand what a social theorist was saying is not only to understand what he actually said, or his motives for saying it, but also what he thought he was saying in saying it. This is simple, powerful and attractive. Ideas are not detached from their authors and attached instead to social groups or to nothing at all, although it is clear that any author's intentions, in this sense, may be unintelligible without a prior understanding of the social conventions within which he expressed them. The intentions themselves are not prejudged. And the sheer empirical complexity of the provenance of ideas receives its proper due.

As I have said, this does not in any way solve the fundamental problem of the 'sociology of knowledge'. It simply but skilfully avoids it. The intentions and the conventions within which they are expressed have still to be explained, and unless this is done by invoking a potentially endless regress of other intentions and other conventions, any such explanation will still have to face the problem of accommodating apparently external causes. But unlike the other 'sociologies of knowledge' that I have described, this approach no more prejudges these causes than it does the intentions and conventions which they might explain. It ironically allows the most sensitive sociology of knowledge.

It also allows the historian to criticise. Unlike other approaches, of course, and most obviously unlike those which derive from Hegel's Objective Idealism, it does not require him to, and it does not generate any criteria by which he may do so except those of rationality itself, which it presupposes. But because I believe that it is difficult to understand the history of social theorising in western Europe and the United States since the eighteenth century without understanding the extent to which it has been a history of failure, I have taken advantage of this. The approach's final virtue is that it allows one to in a way which does not necessarily interfere with the history itself. My own most firm intention has been to write the history so that others may draw their own conclusions.

1

Enlightenment and doubt

IN MEDIEVAL EUROPEAN THOUGHT, the epistemological authority was the word of God as revealed through the teachings of the Roman Church. There was in this period, it is true, a recognised distinction between natural and divine law, but although the first was held to be distinct from the second and accessible to reason, it was not generally considered to be independent of it. Divine law alone was considered capable of restoring to man that true knowledge lost in his Fall. Reason, therefore, could do more than lead towards, prepare the ground for, revelation.

The Renaissance modification of this epistemology was a radical one, but the radicalism was still one to which the Church could at least in principle accommodate itself, adapting yet maintaining its authority. In medieval thought nature was seen as the creation of God, a realm that was in part intelligible through the use of reason but only in part so intelligible, since a complete understanding of it entailed an understanding of God's purpose in having created it, and that was accessible only to revelation. But towards the Renaissance it came to be asserted, as Bruno put it, that 'it is more worthy for [God] to be the internal principle of motion, which is his own nature, his own appearance, his own soul than that as many entities as live in his bosom should have motion'. That is, there appeared a shift of emphasis, not always clear at the time but nevertheless, and especially in retrospect, fundamental, a shift from a view of God as creator of nature to a view of him as expressed in it. The corollary of this was a shift in the view of the importance of natural law and the power of reason. In the medieval view, reason was always and necessarily subservient to revelation, which alone could reveal God's purpose. But as God came to be seen as expressed in rather than as distinct from and anterior to nature, so the importance of reason grew. God was expressed in nature; nature was accessible through reason; God therefore was accessible through reason. Reason was, perhaps, sufficient.

8

Once this conceptual transformation was accomplished, and despite the persistence of all kinds of variation inevitably disguised in a simple account such as this, it was accomplished long before that period now described as the Enlightenment, it is easy to see how pressure built up towards the state of intellectual affairs that does truly characterise that period. This pressure was the need to know nature better, and it produced a gradual shift from reliance on faith to a reliance on reason and experience. It was this pressure that the Church recognised, ironically, where for example Galileo did not. Galileo strove to reconcile his findings with a framework acceptable to the post-medieval Church and there seems no good theological reason why this should have been impossible or even difficult. Given sufficient will, no theologian would have had any problem in arguing that the Copernican system was any less marvellous an indication and vindication of God than the Ptolemaic, which Galileo's work helped to replace. The Church's hostility rested rather upon what one might call the politics of epistemology. It could see all to clearly that any claim it might hitherto make to a privileged access to the ultimate, divine final cause would be fatally weakened by an alternative institution, science, being able to reveal that divine purpose in nature by describing nature in what we would now call straightforwardly naturalistic ways. It could not tolerate that.

In general, then, it is not difficult to see how the distinctiveness of the European Enlightenment arose and in what it consisted. First, the long-established claims of reason as a means of knowing natural law were strengthened. And second, since it had always been clear that nature was not in itself a wholly metaphysical realm but was an at least superficially physical one, and since an investigation of nature was now of paramount importance, so more attention could and it was thought should be paid to the methods suitable to understanding physical phenomena. Hence the insistence on supplementing the much vindicated faculty of reason by experience and experiment.

If it is clear that nothing in the gradual intellectual evolution from the medieval period to the eighteenth century necessarily implied a challenge to religious faith, it has nevertheless become a convention in the past two hundred years to think of the eighteenth century as the period in which reason triumphed over faith and experience over intuition, a convention that perhaps owes much to the exaggerated reaction of the early nineteenth-century Romantics, a reaction to which I shall return. It is misleading, if not false. Certainly, there was a direct challenge to ecclesiastical authority, in social, political and moral matters as much as in intellectual ones. But this should not be confused, as the Church so long confused it, with faith. Indeed, and ironically, it is largely to differences of religious as well as political tradition within Europe that one can attribute the different courses the Enlightenment took there. These differences have proved crucial to the history of social thought since the eighteenth century.

The Enlightenment is ordinarily thought of as a French affair, with the English having accomplished much of their intellectual revolution with their political one in the seventeenth century, and other people, such as the Germans, remaining in a dogmatic slumber until the next century, when they took somewhat different paths, often in direct reaction to the French. This is an exaggeration. Certainly, two of the architects of the new intellectual radicalism in England, Newton and Locke, did much to inspire the French *philosophes*, and Hume in Scotland and Rousseau in France did much to arouse Kant and so give direction to the train of German Idealism at the end of the eighteenth century. But Hume's scepticism is sufficient evidence of the fact that Scots were not resting in that century, and Kant cannot be described as being in opposition to the ideals of the Enlightenment without grossly distorting his whole philosophy. Much of what followed in Germany was the product, at least to begin with, of a great enthusiasm for the ideals of the French, ideals that were at first thought to have been realised in the revolution of 1789. Nevertheless, there were striking differences between the three countries, and these require explanation.

France was much more rationalist than it was empiricist, in that the *philosophes* tended to rely more upon the deliverances of reason than the evidence of their senses. A corollary of this was that they were more inclined to intellectual systems. D'Alembert asserted in 1759 that 'the true system of the world has been recognised, developed and perfected' and eleven years later D'Holbach described the universe, 'that vast assemblage of everything that exists', as presenting us everywhere 'only with matter and motion; the whole offers to our contemplation nothing but an immense and uninterrupted chain of causes and effects'. This is in marked contrast to the prevailing English view. Locke had implied that man's knowledge can never be more than partial, fragmentary and uncertain. It may well be that an exceptional individual, like 'the incomparable Mr Newton', would be privileged with a revelation of the divinely ordered and harmonious universe. But ordinary mortals should remain content to piece together what fragments they could. In more formal language, if the French in their rationalism inclined more to a view of knowledge as a process whereby true propositons were deduced from a few fundamental axioms, the English in their empiricism inclined more to the view that knowledge was a process whereby truth was induced from experiential observations of particular facts and their connections.

France had been and still was, of course, a primarily Catholic country; England, a Protestant one. To the French the model of intellectual and institutional authority was the hierarchical and absolute Catholic Church; to the English (as to a man of Calvinist inspiration like Locke), it was the individual. To the French, authority was above the individual. He was subject to its decrees but offered no autonomy within it. It is revealing in this respect that the Jansenists, whose theology emphasised autonomous intellectuality and spiritual self-determination, educated some of the most notable *philosophes*, like Voltaire, and no doubt encouraged a predisposition towards intellectual independence. To the English, there was no longer a collective authority which demanded submission. The relationship was in the reverse direction. In principle, a man was his own authority in intellectual matters in exactly the way in which he was his own authority in spiritual ones. His contact with nature was as direct and unmediated as was his contact with God.

These religious and intellectual differences were exacerbated by political ones. In the spreading venality of the years after the death of Louis XIV, the French bourgeoisie could and did buy high office. But it had few rights, and in pressing for more greatly angered the nobility whose own were thereby being threatened. In England, on the other hand, a kind of bourgeois revolution had already taken place. By the beginning of the eighteenth century the English (although not the Scots) were accordingly becoming less concerned about the very premises of their political order, even though, of course, many particular questions of right and obligation still remained to be answered. They had turned their attention to more limited practical matters, to concrete particulars rather than abstract generalities. The contrast was between a society in which the Catholic Church, even while hated, nevertheless provided the model of authority and in which the bourgeoisie had few rights; and a society in which the Protestant model of individual autonomy and independence prevailed, a society in which the bourgeoisie had revised the political system so as to guarantee their rights within it. In the one, the intellectual inclination was towards rationalism and the construction of systems, as thorough, as all-embracing and as monistic as the ecclesiastical and monarchical systems they challenged. In the other, it was towards empiricism and the patient acquisition of partial knowledge, a direct contact with experience which mirrored the direct contact with God in its religion and which was made possible by the liberty and equality of rights at least formally assured in the new state.

Germany was different again, perhaps indeed more different from both England and France than these were from each other. Certainly, as I have said, it would be an exaggeration to say that the ideals of the Enlightenment found no support there. In the eighteenth century, nature was increasingly often invoked as the touchstone of the good, the beautiful and the true, and there was a growing emphasis on the importance of intellecual self-determination. Moreover, Kant's philosophy, the dominating achievement of German thought at the end of the century, even where it qualified them accepted and insisted upon the virtues of rationalism and empiricism. But Kant was a much more isolated figure in his own country than almost any of his English or French contemporaries, and the generation that followed him there rejected precisely that part of his thought which insisted upon these virtues.

The fact remains, then, that although the Enlightenment was by no means an entirely French affair, it was in France almost exclusively (and to a lesser extent in Scotland) in the eighteenth century that theories were proposed which attempted to extend the empirical method of the physical sciences to society while retaining the total view made possible by schematic rationalism. Only in these two societies was there any interest in furnishing a natural account not merely of the individual, his status and his relations with the State, but also of the society in which he acquired that status and was able to maintain those relations. Even then, the two most remarkable theories, the one that had the greatest impact upon contemporaries and the one that led to the most far-reaching revision of the apparent certainties of that century, were by no means mechanical applications of abstract philosophical principles. The most typical *philosophes* were also the least interesting and in the long run perhaps the least important.

The Enlightenment, it is said, was an optimistic time. It is certainly true that the most typical French *philosophes*, men like D'Alembert and D'Holbach and Helvétius who expressed the views of the anti-clerical and literate classes at large, were aggressively confident in their conviction that they had finally solved the riddle of the nature of good and evil. Their solution, as Hume saw so clearly and said so sharply, rested upon a tangle of bad logic and clever puns, but its contemporary force was overriding. To the ancient equation between the good, the right and the true they added the natural and subtracted the divine. If, they implied, the good was the right, the right the true, and, as scientific inquiry was demonstrating, the right was also the natural (since nature manifestly conformed to reason), so the natural must be the good. If this was so, then it seemed clear that what was evil was what was unnatural. Use reason to distinguish the natural from the unnatural, they argued, and you will have at once distinguished good from evil. There was no longer any need to rely upon persons and institutions who claimed privileged access to the good. It was now accessible to all men by virtue of the uniquely and universal human faculties of reason and experience. The logic is transparent and the punning only slightly less so, but it requires little imagination to see how powerful this marriage of the old vocabulary of morals and the new vocabulary of science must have been. 'Men in this country', wrote a contemporary *patronne* of the *philosophes*, 'are like caged lions'. Frustration breeds such ideas, and they in turn relieve it.

Hume's scepticism about them was not widespread, but it was

not the only source of doubt amidst the confidence. For there was still the question of where man stood in relation to nature. 'He hangs between', wrote Alexander Pope, 'in doubt to act or rest; In doubt to deem himself god or beast; In doubt his Mind or Body to prefer'. Whatever comfort the rationalist cosmology gave in other ways, it could not offer an unequivocal or at least an unparadoxical answer to this question. Yet it was clearly a question that had to be answered if there was to be any rational progress in human affairs, and rational progress, it was felt, there had to be. Despite their common adherence to the rhetoric of nature and reason, it is in their various answers to this question that the very considerable differences between eighteenth-century social theories in France mostly lie. The political theory that excited most attention at the time kept within the conventions implied in the rhetoric, and failed to provide a coherent answer to the question at all. The theory that had the most lasting effect on succeeding generations did offer an answer, and in so doing exploded the conventions which it had begun by accepting. The first is Montesquieu's, expounded at greatest length although not always with great clarity in his final treatise *The Spirit of Laws*. The second is Rousseau's.

Montesquieu was unusual among the *philosophes* in several ways. He was an aristocrat, born Charles-Louis, Baron de la Brède, and for most of his active life a member of the *parlement* in Bordeaux. But he was by no means apart from the glittering and turbulent world of the largely powerless *philosophes*. On the contrary, the woman who saw *The Spirit of Laws* through the press and past the censor in 1748, and who was a very close friend, herself ran one of the more famous *salons* in Paris, was said to have given birth illegitimately to D'Alembert, and had even spent some time in the Bastille on the ostensible charge of having caused the suicide of one of her lovers. But Montesquieu spent as much time away from such people as he did with them. He seems to have been a relatively conscientious public man, and even Helvétius, who was to be very scathing about the book, praised his relations with the peasants at La Brède. No doubt the security afforded by his class and his offices and his relations with a wide variety of people all contributed to his reputedly calm temperament and the dry realism of his writing. Moreover, he was, until failing eyesight prevented him, an experimental scientist in an amateur way. Others (like Rousseau, for example, who discoursed on the laws of chemistry) wrote scientific papers, but few of them did any practical work. Inclined, therefore, to empirical investigation, yet as convinced a believer in the power of reason as any; immersed in practical affairs and talking to his peasants in the Gascon accent he is said to have retained all his life, yet widely read and given to abstract speculation; committed to the established political order yet sympathetic to its critics: in all these ways, Montesquieu represents something of a contradiction. It is reflected in his work, is its defect, its virtue, and its historical interest.

The tensions are most clear in his notoriously ambiguous assertions about law and justice. 'Law in general', he explained at the very beginning of *The Spirit of Laws*, 'is human reason, in as much as it governs all the inhabitants of the earth', whereas laws in particular 'should be adapted in such a manner to the people for whom they are framed so that it should be a great coincidence if those of one nation suit another'. Likewise, 'justice is eternal, and depends not upon human conventions, and when it seems to should be disguised from seeming to', yet it is also 'a relationship of convenience to be actually found between two things'. In these apparently contradictory remarks Montesquieu appeared to be groping for a distinction that his own intellectual assumptions could not admit, a distinction between the universal principles which any law has to embody if it is to be just and rational and particular interpretations of those principles which are contingent upon the rules of the society for which the laws are being framed. This is, of course, a very difficult distinction to apply in practice. But what is interesting is that Montesquieu tried to make such a distinction at all. For in doing so, he innocently drove a shaft into the increasingly confident rationalism of his contemporaries. This rested, as I have said, upon an equation between reason and nature: what was rational was held to be natural and what was natural was held to be rational. But if this equation is to be sustained, it requires there to be but one nature. Otherwise, it commits itself to as many rationalities as there are natures. The requirement is easily met in the nature of the physical world. The laws governing the motion of bodies apply equally in Cambridge and the Indies.

But Montesquieu implied that it cannot be met in the nature of the social world. Different societies have different natures. Accordingly, the application of reason will yield different solutions in different types of society.

A growing awareness of different societies was entirely characteristic of the eighteenth century, and Montesquieu was by no means exceptional in his knowledge of the various sources that were circulating in France at that time. But he neither romanticised what he heard and read, nor forced it into a preconceived mould whereby, for example, more primitive peoples were *ipso facto* taken to be more natural. He had no genetic theory of the origin of human error, of unnaturalness. Indeed, and against those who claim to detect in *The Spirit of Laws* the awakening of the historical sense that was to pervade nineteenth-century social theories, it would be more accurate to say that Montesquieu was almost old-fashioned in his conviction that there was one proper form for each society, the one that corresponded most closely to its inner *esprit*. This ancient belief had traditionally been given a metaphysical expression, and in this too Montesquieu was to some extent at one with tradition. But he was also disposed to trust the evidence of his senses, and was very much of his own century in thus attempting to secure an empirical foundation for his thesis.

'One might say of the seventeenth and eighteenth centuries', he remarked in his early, experimental days at La Brède, 'that Nature acted like those virgins who long preserved their most precious possession, and then allowed themselves to be ravished, in a moment, of that which they had preserved with such care and defended with such constancy'. Some of his own most stimulating ravishings were directed to sheeps' tongues. He noticed that cold caused the fibres on the tongues to contract, and in *The Spirit of Laws* explained: 'This observation confirms what I have been saying, that in cold countries the nervous glands are less expanded: they sink deeper into their sheaths, or they are sheltered from the action of external objects; consequently, they have not such lively sensations'. He inferred from this that the markedly different sensibilities of the English and the Italians (both of whom, he said, he had observed at the opera) could be attributed to their climates, and in the rest of this part of the treatise elaborated all sorts of consequences, aesthetic, amorous, religious, political and moral, that followed from different climates in different places.

Again, however, he was no monist. He did not proceed to assert that the physical conditions in every society are the prime determinants of its *esprit*. On the contrary, 'Mankind is influenced by various causes: by climate, by religion, by laws, by maxims of government, by precedents, morals and customs; whence is formed a general spirit of nations. In proportion as, in every country, any one of these causes acts with more force, the others in the same degree are weakened. Nature and the climate rule almost alone among the savages; customs govern the Chinese; the laws tyrannise in Japan; morals had formerly all their influence at Sparta; maxims of government, and the ancient simplicity of manners, once prevailed at Rome'. Accordingly, 'laws should be in relation to the climate of each country, to the quality of its soil, to its situation and extent, to the principal occupation of its natives, whether husbandmen, hunters or shepherds; they should have relation to the degree of liberty that the constitution will bear; to the religions of their inhabitants, to their inclinations, numbers, riches, commerce, manners and customs. In fine, they have relations to each other, as also to their origin, to the intent of the legislator, and to the order of things on which they are established; in all of which different lights they ought to be considered'.

In all this, Montesquieu did not clearly distinguish between the freedom of individuals and the freedom of societies to legislate after their own natures or *esprits*. There is no individual human nature prior to or even independent of society. Men merely reflect, it seems, the *esprit* of their society. The appropriate law for one is the appropriate law for the other. But what of man's place in general in the natural order? In Pope's phrase, is he 'Great lord of all things' or 'prey to all'? Montesquieu gave no answer, for he saw no problem. Nature is everything, and if reason can unravel it that does not mean that we must infer that man, who alone uses reason, is somehow separate from it. On the contrary, if there is a homology or indeed an identity between the two, surely there can be no difficulty? In his classification of societies into four types, monarchy (expressing the spirit of honour), aristocracy (the spirit of moderation), republics (the spirit of *civisme*) and despotism (the spirit of terror), he did not even imply, as some of his other remarks might be taken as doing, that there was an evolution from one type to another, a progression, say, from the rule of physical nature to the rule of will. Correspondingly, he did not urge that men in one kind of society must strive to transform themselves into another. Each society is a self-sustaining, separate and integral whole, men pursue different ends in each, that is their *esprit*, and the only tolerable reform is a reform that furthers an accommodation to rather than a revolution of the characteristic *esprit*. Reason is necessary to effect such reforms, but reason, properly applied, will lead men to adjust and not to overthrow. In his advocacy of a restored nobility in France, countering the slide into a venal and corrupt monarchical absolutism, Montesquieu was thus preaching moderation in a double sense: moderation was the *esprit* of aristocracies, and moderation was the spirit of his own theory.

Moderation, however, was not characteristic of intellectual life in eighteenth-century France, and it is hardly surprising that although the English greeted the book with enthusiasm ('the best book that ever was written', said Walpole), the *philosophes* were more disappointed. 'Ought we then', Helvétius asked, 'to inheret all the errors that have been accumulated since the origin of the human race?'. For anyone who wished for decisive change, the answer had to be no. But Montesquieu did not accept the question, for he did not accept that anything which did not conform to the monistic criteria of the *philosophes* was *ipso facto* erroneous and evil. A distinction had to be drawn between criteria applicable to all men and their societies at all times and criteria applicable to each society by virtue of its unique constellation of circumstances. In one respect, it was a modern distinction. It conceded social and cultural diversity. But this is merely to say that we have since partly returned to the ancient view against which the more uncompromisingly rationalist *philosophes* were defining themselves, the view that a Persian or an Athenian or a Frenchman is to be understood as much as a Persian or an Athenian or a Frenchman as a man independent of any historical or cultural contingency. Montesquieu, far from anticipating the present, was recalling the past, recalling a point that would have been unremarkably plain, say, to a Greek philosopher, the point that the proper ethics and the proper politics cannot be considered apart from the particular *mores* within which they are to obtain. He was at one with the more orthodox *philosophes* only in the superficial respect of his theoretical language. So too, but in quite the opposite direction, was Rousseau.

Rousseau attacked some of the intellectual manners of the day in his first *Discourse* on the arts and sciences, said at one point in *Emile* that he wished to augment Montesquieu rather than reject him, and accepted the conventional rhetoric of reason and nature. But he gave a resoundingly negative answer to Helvétius' question, and as secretary to a M. Dupin prepared an attack on *The Spirit of Laws* in 1748 (which Dupin, persuaded by someone else at the last moment to read it, withdrew from the printer). His revolutionary effect on the world of ideas came after his death, and although he was perhaps justified in his insistent cry that his talents were never sufficiently appreciated, he did not himself ever see quite what these talents were leading to. What exactly this was has been the subject of endless speculation and dispute. Rationalism and emotivism, individualism and collectivism, anarchism and totalitarianism, communism and reaction, Protestantism, Catholicism and atheism, the French Revolution and the retreat from it: all, at some time or another, have been held either to have followed from or to have been strengthened by what he wrote. One thesis may be dismissed at once. Ideas alone are never powerful enough to cause social and political change, and there is no more evidence for Rousseau's having had any significant impact on the events before 1789 than there is for his having affected those that followed. For the rest, only two explanations seem possible: either he was ambiguous and confused to the point of flagrant self-contradiction, so that support for almost any position can be found somewhere in what he wrote, or he was truly original, shifting debate onto a new plane by changing the categories within which it was and still is conducted, and thus confusing his critics. He himself was certainly confused, but no more so than most, and much less so than Montesquieu, who has not suffered to nearly the same extent at the hands of his interpreters. It is, therefore, to Rousseau's originality that one has to attribute most of the debate and dispute. He is indeed a paradigm case of a thinker whose words mean one thing, whose intentions mean another, and whose effects were something different again. Paramount among the last was that his insights, never properly worked through into a sound intellectual defence, gave rise at least in part to a resolution of the problem that the more typical eighteenth-century philosophies had not resolved: that of man's place in nature.

'Readers', pleaded Rousseau in *Emile*, 'never forget that he who speaks here is neither a scholar nor a *philosophe* but a simple man, a friend of truth, without prejudice, without a system'. This was too disingenuous. Simple in origin he may have been, but not so in character; a friend of the truth indeed, but hardly a dispassionate or unprejudiced one; he may have disavowed intellectual systems as D'Alembert or Helvétius or even his friend Diderot understood them, but his theories were as dogmatically all-embracing as any. Even those who see the more typical *philosophes* as relatively straightforward people have not described Rousseau in the same way. His complexity derives in good part from a triple marginality. He was not French, but Swiss, from Geneva. He was neither aristocrat nor bourgeois, but the son of an artisan. And he grew up in a Protestant culture rather than a Catholic one. These three factors would perhaps have been sufficient in themselves to make him more introspective and uncertain than the more confident rationalists raised in the Catholic dogmas they attacked with their own; but this is imponderable, for he was also intensely neurotic, perpetually unable to come to terms with his world, as he put it, 'to square the circle'. Moreover, he was not a political man, like Montesquieu, or Helvétius, or Turgot. He was a political philosopher merely in the sense in which everyone who wrote about society at that time was one. The sense of 'political' in the second half of the eighteenth century was still that implied in the ancient distinction between the domestic and the political, namely, all that which did not concern the private spheres of the 'hearth'. He would have agreed with all those commentators who have since described his political programme as unworkable, but would have meant that if that were so then there was by definition no hope for society either. At the end of his life, bitter and depressed, he did indeed describe what he had proposed as 'less a morality of action than of abstinence'. He remained convinced that his diagnosis was right, but its very radicalism forestalled his taking an optimistic view of such solutions as he proposed.

The diagnosis he set down most clearly in the *Discourse on the Origin of Inequality among Men*, unsuccessfully submitted in a prize competition organised by the Academy of Dijon in 1755. In this, Rousseau started in traditional manner, only half parodying the statement of method in Descartes' own famous *Discourse*. 'Let us then begin', he wrote, 'by laying the facts aside, as they do not affect the question. The investigations we may make in treating this subject must not be considered as historical truths, but only as mere conditional and hypothetical reasonings, intended rather to explain the nature of things than to assert their actual origin; just like the hypotheses which our physicists form daily about the formation of the world'. This was on the face of it an unexceptionable rationalist intent. But the parody sharpened. 'Throwing aside, therefore, all those scientific books, which teach us only to see men as they have made themselves, and contemplating the first and most simple operations of the human soul, I think I can perceive in it [*pace* Descartes] two principles *prior to reason*, one of them deeply interesting us in our own welfare and preservation, and the other producing a natural repugnance at seeing any other sensible being, and particularly any of our own species, suffer pain or death'. 'Sometimes I have good sense', says the Savoyard vicar at one point in *Emile*, 'and I have always loved truth...all I need to do is to reveal what I think in the simplicity of my heart'. These are at once exact summaries both of Rousseau's own philosophy of knowledge and of his view of the essentials of human nature. Reason is not primary but secondary, secondary to innate faculties of self preservation and compassion. To see where man has gone wrong, for gone wrong (Rousseau has no doubt) he certainly has, we must ask what has happened to these two notions in the course of time. This simple idea, the intent of the *Discourse*, came to him, Rousseau says in his *Confessions*, while walking at St Germain with his mistress, his mistress's landlady, and his mistress's landlady's friend in 1753. 'Wandering deep in the forest, I sought and I found the vision of these primitive times, the history of which I proudly traced [in the *Discourse*]. I demolished the petty lies of mankind; I dared to strip man's nature naked; to follow the progress of time, and trace the things which have distorted it; and by comparing man as he had made himself with man as he is by nature I showed to him in his pretended perfection the true source of his misery'.

The root of distortion and the source of misery was civil society. In the *Discourse* Rousseau, in a confessedly speculative fashion, traced four stages in its history to the present. In the first, man, although possessing by virtue of his essential humanity the faculties of self-preservation and compassion, has no desires beyond his physical wants. 'The only goods he recognises in the universe are food, a female, and sleep; the only evils he feels are pain and hunger'. In the second stage, a long one, innate physical differences between men have begun to produce natural inequalities, and these are exacerbated by population growth and the consequent increase in the amount of simple contact between men. 'This repeated relevance of various beings to himself, and one to another, would naturally give rise in the human mind to the perceptions of certain relations between them. Thus the relations which we denote by the terms great, small, strong, weak, swift, fearful, bold, and the like, almost insensibly compared at need, must have at length produced in him a kind of reflection or a mechanical prudence, which would indicate to him the precautions most necessary to his security'. In this stage men learned to compare, and comparison produced language; but they also learned to cooperate in hunting and so formed family groups. Indeed, the weapons of the hunt and the family shelter were the first property, and 'the first man who, having enclosed a piece of land, thought of saying "This is mine" and found people naive enough to believe him, was the real founder of civil society'. The third stage develops from this as the family groups form the basis of the first political structures and become the point of formal ritual. Social organisation becomes more recognisably organised. The fourth stage is marked by the introduction of agriculture and metallurgy. This 'great revolution' ushers in the truly evil present state of affairs. 'From the moment one man began to stand in need of the help of another; from the moment it appeared advantageous to any one man to have enough provisions for two, equality disappeared, property was introduced, work became indispensable, and vast forests became smiling fields, which man had to water with the sweat of his brow, and where slavery and misery were soon to germinate and grow up with the crops'.

It has often been said that Rousseau's morality was very simple: the more distant a society in this history, the better it was. Rousseau, it has been held, glorified the 'state of nature'. But he explicitly says that the very faculty of moral judgement itself is a function of society, a function of the processes of contact, comparison and evaluation that developed in the second and third stages and were intensified with the economic development of the fourth, and that if any stage is to be preferred to the others it is the third, in which evil was by no means absent but which in 'keeping a just mean between the indolence of our primitive state and the petulant activity of our egoism must have been the happiest and most stable of epochs'. The apparent contradiction between arguing in principle that pure virtue lies only in the abstracted, non-social individual and arguing in practice that the closest approximation to virtue lay in the recognisably organised third stage is indeed the clue to the central paradox of Rousseau's theory, separating him both from the *philosophes* who assumed no necessary incompatibility between nature, goodness and society and from those who, while agreeing in the condemnation of modern society, found absolute perfection and unsullied goodness in the primitives, 'guiltless men', in Dryden's words, 'that danced away their time, fresh as their groves and happy as their clime'.

Rousseau's paradox was that although society had been responsible for engendering inequality, dependence and oppression, the greatest evils, it was only society that could eliminate them. This, he said later, was the 'one principle' that connected all his work. Its logic is simple. It was the social relations into which natural man entered that caused him to make comparisons and so to develop moral concepts. Before those relations, he had no sense of evil. But no more did he have any sense of good. In his natural state he was propelled not by moral notions but by mere dispositions of compassion and self-preservation. If, therefore, he was to realise the good and eliminate the evil, this must be through society, since only by continuing to live in society could he retain the moral sense necessary for such a realisation. However, it was patently clear that a society organised on the principles of private property

23

and inequality, as had hitherto been the case, would not do, for
that ensured the continuation of evil.

It was Rousseau's own solution to this dilemma that has given
rise to so much dispute. In principle, it is perfectly clear.
'Everywhere', he wrote in *Emile*, 'that there is feeling and
intelligence there is some moral order. The difference is that the
good man orders himself in relation to the whole, and that the
wicked man orders the whole in relation to himself. The one
makes himself the centre of all things; the other measures the
radius and holds himself at the circumference'. To the question,
how may I, as an individual, maintain my individual integrity
and freedom and yet live in society, Rousseau answered, by
realising that your traditional notions of individuality are
forever incompatible with living in society, and that they must
change. This answer took its famous political form in *The Social
Contract*. As he began to think of a solution in 1756, he believed,
as he later wrote in his *Confessions*, that 'everything is rooted in
politics and that, whatever might be attempted, no people would
ever be other than the nature of the government made them'. In
this belief he reveals his traditional view of politics: it is that
which lies beyond the realm of the domestic, and is coterminous
with civil society. Indeed, he once thought of calling the thesis
that was eventually to appear as *The Social Contract, On Civil
Society*. If, therefore, the answer lies in politics, the question
must be: 'What is the nature of government best able to
create...the best people, taking "best" in its highest sense?
What is the government which by its nature always remains
closest to the law? 'What', finally, 'is the law?'. That there *was* a
law Rousseau never doubted, and his confidence was more
absolute than Montesquieu's. In this, he was squarely within the
ancient tradition.

One traditional argument was that the law had to be premised
on man's nature, and Rousseau did not dissent. Contract theorists had assumed that there was an essential and inviolable
human nature independent of the social relations into which
men entered. To regulate those relations, they argued, individual men must contract with each other to establish a state, the
State, which will ensure a balance between the expression of
individuality and its denial in the name of order. Again,
Rousseau did not dissent. He too hypothesised a human nature

independent of and prior to society. However, the traditional theorists had assumed as basic elements of human nature characteristics which, Rousseau argued, were rather the product of society. Indeed, the very notion of a separate individual whose interests were necessarily at odds with those of other individuals was a function of the particular way in which society had developed. In changing social and political relations, one would also change this notion, and the proper theory and the best government would thus be ones that altered not merely one of the parameters, but both. To maintain the fallacy of a universal and unchanging individualism was to perpetuate wickedness, the ordering of the whole in relation to the one rather than the one in relation to the whole. Unlike Montesquieu, who had also seen the fault in the traditional theories, Rousseau did not however assume that human nature will vary from place to place because societies vary from place to place. He was much less sensible of the differences between societies. For him, all had been and still were set upon the same course.

To change this course, the new contract must entail 'the total alienation of each associate, together with all his rights (as he has customarily come to regard them) to the whole community'. Each gives himself absolutely, and each, 'in giving himself to all, gives himself to nobody'. To do this, the traditional *volonté de tous*, the will of each of the individuals taken together, must be discarded in favour of the *volonté générale*, the general will. 'Let us', concluded Rousseau at the end of the central argument, 'draw up the whole account in terms easily commensurable. What man loses by the social contract is his natural liberty and an unlimited right to everything he tries to get and succeeds in getting. What he gains is civil liberty and the proprietorship of all he possesses. If we are to avoid mistakes in weighing one against the other, we must clearly distinguish natural liberty, which is bounded only by the strength of the individual, from civil liberty, which is limited by the general will; and possession, which is merely the effect of force or the right of the first occupier, from property, which can be founded only on a positive title'. And do not forget, he added, that in submitting himself to the general will man acquires moral liberty, 'which alone makes him truly master of himself', and loses that old liberty which is in fact no more than the 'impulse of appetite', truly a kind of slavery. The highest form of individuality, in which man fully transcends his animal state and so becomes 'Great Lord of all', is also the highest form of society.

It is not difficult to see why this should have been interpreted in so many different ways. Rousseau advocated adherence to a rational law yet said that this will be found to fit with the intuitive sense of what is right. He claimed to have explained how individuality may be perfected yet said that for this to happen each individual must alienate himself entirely to the community. But it is perfectly clear that what he had done was to transform the central terms of the traditional argument, individual and society. Considered naturally, individuals were wholly distinct; considered socially, they were not. It was not that the traditional elements had merely to be rearranged. They had to be redefined. To argue against him on the more conventional definitions may well be valid, but to use those definitions to try to understand what he meant is necessarily to misunderstand him.

It is a long-standing joke amongst Rousseau's critics that he himself saw no hope for the realisation of this ideal anywhere but in Corsica. The joke, however, rebounds. In the same passage in the *Confessions* in which he explains how, in 1756, he had thought that the solution to the dilemma he had explained in the second *Discourse* had to be a political one, he goes on to admit that this later came to seem to him hopeless, that his work, consistently expounding the 'one principle' that society was at once the sole cause and the only cure of man's wickedness to man, constituted perhaps 'less a morality of action than of abstinence'. He had retreated into a solipsistic universe of spiritual isolation. What his conscience dictated, he found intractable. The intractability existed at several levels. He himself had become tired, bitter and depressed, incapable to the last of squaring his personal circle. The society in which he lived, celebrating the long-awaited dawn of full natural liberty, was not sympathetic to a new liberty that seemed to imply its converse. And although he did not admit it (perhaps he could not see it) he lacked the conceptual equipment to explain clearly what he meant. The familiar rhetoric of nature and reason, liberty and law, the individual and the State, had been devised to provide answers he had rejected. All he could do was cry out, and that seemed to his former friends, like Diderot, as to many later commentators, further evidence of confusion, megalomania, paranoia and even madness.

Nevertheless, what remained implicit in Montesquieu as in his less original and perceptive contemporaries in France and Scotland was to become clearer through Rousseau, if not in him. The familiar set of self-sustaining equations, the good is the natural, the natural is the rational, and the rational is the good, could not account for man's place in the scheme of things without either placing him among the beasts, and so seeming to deprive him of reason, or making him akin to God, and so seeming to remove him from nature. They seemed to imply the paradoxical thesis that man was at once the creature and the creator of society.

2

History resolved by mind

KANT WAS the one contemporary who took Rousseau absolutely seriously. Like Rousseau, he saw that 'the one science man really needs is the one I teach, of how to occupy properly that place in creation that is assigned to man and how to learn from it what one must be in order to be a man', and he believed that in Rousseau and Rousseau alone, that 'Newton of the moral world', lay the basis for such a science. Rousseau had shown, most clearly in the second *Discourse*, that what others had taken as the constants of human nature were to a great extent the products of society. In *Emile* and *The Social Contract*, however, he had argued that man did nevertheless have an inviolable moral sense, and that if he were to use it, freeing himself of the contingent contaminations of his social experience, he would be able to discern the correct law. It was this second argument that impressed Kant, who wished to put it on a more secure footing. His achievement was to have done so. In doing so, however, he freed himself completely from Rousseau's first argument. The result was a further dilemma. The Enlightenment's defence of its conviction that man was largely a product of society had been shown to rest on an epistemological muddle. But what then of the conviction? Could it be defended in another way? And could that defence give substantive moral content to Kant's ethics?

These questions, the answers to which essentially define the project of what was later in Europe to be called 'sociology', had already been asked in eighteenth-century Scotland. One set of Scottish answers, David Hume's, although quite different from Rousseau's, attracted and dissatisfied Kant to a similar degree. Quite why there should have been such intensive speculation about moral and political questions in Scotland in the second half of the eighteenth century is still not clear, although part of the explanation must lie in the character of Scots society. Scotland, much more than either England or France, was anomalous. The Act of Union at the beginning of the century had brought it under the jurisdiction of the English legislature, but its institutions were in some respects still very different. Its law was still Roman, whereas English law was not. The Highlands had until recently been essentially feudal, whereas capitalistic high farming had begun to change the already much modified rural social structure in England. The Scottish universities were active intellectual centres, animated by the free and independent spirit of Calvinism, while the English ones remained unreformed and dormant. Yet like parts of England the Scottish lowlands were becoming a live commercial and industrial centre. Such contrasts, within and without, must have had much to do with stimulating the Scots into trying to make sense of the manifestly fast but uneven social development they saw around them. It certainly led them to discuss what the French almost completely ignored, the relations and morality of commercial and industrial activity. Although their assumptions were not unlike Montesquieu's, the fact that they were more directly aware of this activity led them to ask questions he did not.

They did not however all ask exactly the same questions. Ferguson and Adam Smith discussed the problem of the division of labour in past and present forms, and Millar the questions of the origin and nature of 'ranks' in society. Others were more interested in language or law. Nevertheless, they all made similar assumptions. Society, they contended, must be explained not as the outcome of a specific contract but rather as a phenomenon which has in Stewart's phrase a 'natural or theoretical history'. Human nature is everywhere the same but does not appear so, for 'a variety of considerations and circumstances', Ferguson explained, 'lead mankind to vary their forms indefinitely, whether in respect to the number that compose their society, the direction under which a community is to act, or the object to which it is chiefly directed'. This view, 'long received' said Stewart, 'as an incontrovertible logical maxim', owed its contemporary force, as they all acknowledged, to *The Spirit of Laws*, which had appeared in translation in 1750. Like Montesquieu, the Scots believed that an investigation of present circumstances and conditions would reveal the proper morality and the correct laws, but they were more straightforwardly empiricist than he. They traced what they believed to be a connection between 'mental' and 'moral' science. The one would give a correct theory of human nature, the other a programme for action. The connection lay in the effect of experience on men. The capacity for passion and desire, the propensity to have needs, are intrinsic to our constitution, but experience gives them content. Consequently, different types of society stimulate different passions and different needs, different sympathies and different utilities. There is more than a hint of conservatism in this, of course. It can be taken to imply that as a society creates our needs and desires so those needs may best be met and those desires best be satisfied by that society alone. However, the conservatism was not complete, for both Hume and others, more so than Montesquieu, realised that societies changed (quite how, they never decided), and in so doing created new desires. For some, such as Ferguson and Smith, paramount in these changes were the developments of private property and of the division of labour. These encouraged individualistic inclinations and discouraged truly social ones, to which Ferguson quotes Rousseau with approval. In so doing, they facilitated liberty but tended to replace cooperation by oppression, dependence and inequality. 'Liberty is the perfection of civil society', wrote Hume, 'but...authority must be acknowledged essential to its very existence'. Thus, 'the new brood should conform themselves to the established constitution, and nearly follow the path which their fathers, treading in the footsteps of theirs, have marked out to them'. The conservatism thus reappears, in a naturalistic injunction to be cautious. Too rapid a social change is incompatible with the progress of human needs and desires. It satisfies the passion for liberty that it creates, but prevents the satisfaction of more established needs, of the need above all for social cooperation that has its roots in more 'elementary forms' such as the family.

The naturalism is, however, doubly unsatisfactory. It offers no coherent explanation of the 'natural history' of change, and it raises difficulties with the notion of liberty. The first is clear, the second perhaps less so. The problem of liberty lies in the paradox that common experience creates common desires but that one particular common experience, that of having property or a place in the new division of labour, creates individual desires whose satisfaction is potentially inimical to the establishment and maintenance of social solidarity. To solve this dilemma, the Scots generally resorted either to ethical arguments of a non-naturalistic kind, thus subverting their programme of a unified 'moral' and 'mental' science, or to devices like Adam Smith's 'hidden hand', inner regulators that somehow balanced the centrifugal tendencies and so ensured harmony and order. Once again, there had as in contemporary France appeared a tension between a 'natural' account of civil society and a developing sense of the factual importance and moral difficulties of individualism. But whereas the tension was to be solved in France and in Germany, although in very different ways, by the device of redefining the status of the individual in relation to society, in Scotland, and later in England, it was not. There men oscillated between two quite contradictory views. One was that the historical determination of interests was irrelevant to resolving their outcome. The other was that the desired outcome, the greatest good of each and the greatest good of all, lay precisely in recognising the force and indeed the inevitability of the historical determination. The one became defined as utilitarianism, the other less exactly in the notion of a beneficient evolution. In each, the historical, or if one likes, the sociological, insights of the eighteenth-century Scots were to be lost. But their philosophical defence, in Hume's version, was not.

In his philosophical writings (which, he lamented, fell stillborn from the press), Hume had been deeply sceptical of the philosophical conventions of his day, some of which he had begun by accepting. It was Hume's scepticism, together with Rousseau's far less rigorous insights, that prompted the development which was to secure these insights at the same time as it offered an escape from the impasse into which Hume had himself driven empirical philosophy. This development was the philosophy of Kant, intended, despite the fact that Kant gave what appears to have been the first course of lectures on anthropology in Germany, to answer what largely as the result of his own arguments would now be seen as strictly epistemological and ethical questions. Kant himself summarised what he considered to be the essence of his views in 1791, thirteen years before he died. 'I am conscious of myself as myself' he wrote. 'This thought contains a twofold "I", one as subject and one as object. It is altogether beyond our powers to explain how it should be possible that *I*, the thinking subject, can be the object of perception to myself, able to distinguish myself from myself. Nevertheless it is an undoubted fact. It indicates a faculty that goes beyond all visual perception, and it is the foundation of an intellect. It marks the complete separation from all beasts, because we have no reason to attribute to them the faculty of saying "I" to themselves. And this opens the prospect of an infinity of self-made conceptions. But we do not assume by this a double personality: only the *I* who thinks and perceives is the *person*. The *I* as an object, the *I* which is being perceived, is simply a thing like all others which are outside me'. He was quite explicit in attributing the inspiration of this philosophy to Hume, who had woken him from what he called his 'dogmatic slumber', and to Rousseau.

Hume had been adamant. 'To explain the ultimate causes of our mental actions is impossible', he wrote in his *Treatise*. ''Tis sufficient, if we can give any satisfactory account of them from experience and analogy'. It was such an account that he intended. He directed it against what he regarded as the then degenerate state of metaphysical speculation, and rested it upon the principle 'that all our ideas are copy'd from our impressions'. In his view, the proximate cause of 'mental actions' were the impressions made by experience upon a passive intellect and the associations and analogies suggested to that intellect by sets of such impressions. The philosophical question of how one may know something was identical to the psychological question of how one came to believe it. Kant was attracted by Hume's project. He too regarded contemporary metaphysics as degenerate, and wished properly to secure the status of the new scientific thinking that he like others so admired. He was similarly attracted by Hume's arguments. Hume, he believed, had made the most serious of all attempts to solve what he, Kant, regarded as 'the proper problem of pure reason', of how abstract propositions about the world, propositions that were neither purely analytic nor simply synthetic, were possible. Nevertheless, he was not satisfied with Hume's conclusion, most evident in the latter's discussion of causality, that any extension of accumulated impressions into a principle was no more than a delusion, an unwarrantable leap of old-fashioned faith, obscurantism parading itself as 'reason'. On the contrary, Kant argued, 'all my representations in any given intuition (*Anschauung*) must be subject to the condition which alone enables me to connect them, as my representation with the identical self, and so to unite them synthetically in one apperception, by means of the general expression, *I* think'. Thus, even though he was as sceptical as Hume about the possibility of discovering the 'ultimate causes of our mental actions', he did believe that Hume had been too radical in his account of what those actions were. To make sense of what actually happened in one's own thinking as well as in the thinking of the widely-revered mathematicians and physicists, it was necessary to postulate what Kant described as the 'synthetic *a priori*', a class of propositions which were synthetic because their negation was not a contradiction and *a priori* because they were not rooted directly in impressions of the sensate world. 'By means of sense', he argued, 'objects are given to us and sense alone provides us with *perceptions*; by means of the understanding objects are thought and from it there arise *concepts*'. All thinking presupposes concepts to think with, the concepts of space, time, causality and so forth. Without this, our sense impressions would remain sense impressions, and we should not be able to organise them into propositions.

This argument makes Kant's own late description of his philosophy more intelligible. The repository of the concepts is the 'thinking subject', 'the foundation of an intellect', the 'I' as subject. It was towards a firmer conception of the nature of this 'I' that Rousseau directed Kant. Kant was as dissatisfied with existing accounts of the origin and nature of this thinking subject as he was with Hume's account of the genesis and nature of empirical propositions. 'Plato', he wrote, 'took an older conception of the divine being as the source of principles and pure concepts of the understanding, while [Descartes] took a conception of God which still prevails...But a *deus ex machina* in the determination of the origin and validity of our knowledge is the most preposterous device that one can choose; and, besides, the vicious circle in the sequence of inferences from it has the further disadvantage that it fosters every pious and brooding whim'. The vicious circle was clear. God implants our ideas. Our ideas are sufficient for grasping nature. Nature therefore reflects the will of God. To understand nature, I need not therefore investigate it at all. I need merely to introspect and discover what God dictates. The opportunity for pious whimsy is plain. Equally, however, Kant's own philosophy of knowledge prevented him from explaining the thinking subject in a naturalistic fashion, since all naturalistic explanations, he had argued, presupposed the thinking subject. His answer was that in morality as in the making of concepts, man is independent of God and of nature. This simple point, 'the great discovery of our age', he attributed to Rousseau.

What Kant detected in Rousseau was the latter's insistence, never wholly clear and certainly not formulated in a definite way but there nevertheless as a continuing emphasis, upon man's capacity for moral self-direction (what Kant was to call autonomy), upon man's independence of God, of society and of nature, his ability to act rather than be acted upon, his intrinsic quality as a supremely free agent who, when rid of dependence and oppression is clearly able to see by virtue of his reason where his moral duty lies. It lies, Kant argued, where Rousseau more obscurely asserted, in unconditional or categorical imperatives, in directives to action which may be held to apply unconditionally to all men. If they may be held to be universally applicable they may be held to be rational, without inconsistency, and thus to conform to a law, a law, he says at one point, of nature, but a law of course of our own nature. Our morality is our duty, and our duty lies in obeying the rational law that we ourselves create. 'How can it happen', Rousseau had asked in an essay on political economy, 'that men obey without having anyone above them to issue commands, that they serve without having a master, that they are all the freer when each of them, acting under an apparent compulsion, loses only that part of his freedom with which he can harm others? These wonders are the work of law. It is to law alone that men owe justice and liberty; it is this salutary organ of the will of all that makes obligatory the natural equality between men; it is this heavenly voice that dictates to each citizen the precepts of public reason, teaches him to act in accordance with the maxims of his own judgement, and not to be in contradiction to himself'. The answer is Kantian. The affinity is clear.

Kant's formulation, of course, was considerably more exact

than Rousseau's own, and for this reason shows its deficiencies even more clearly. One is that in stipulating conditions that have to be met for a moral injunction, the imperative only stipulates what is unacceptable. It does not point to the ends that we should pursue. A second, related to this, is that Kantian ethics are parasitic. They prescribe a test for injunctions, but no way of generating them. Exactly the same criticisms may be made of Rousseau. The necessary conditions for the law are clear, but what of its content? It remains an abstract solution to the moral dilemma of civil society in general, and does not prescribe a particular social and political programme. Nevertheless, Kant had provided a clear exposition and logical defence of a conception of the individual as partly natural and thus determined but also, and much more importantly, as partly free, independent of God, of nature *and* of society. He had solved the conceptual problem precisely by distinguishing it sharply from any question of men's actual relations in actual societies, although he did suggest that a precondition for the universal rational law was man as a civilised being, bourgeois man, made autonomous by his private appropriations.

Kant's intellectual strength was thus his social weakness. The philosophers who succeeded him in Germany attempted to transcend his austere individualism within the categories he had established to defend it. The question of why they wished to do this, and did not reject it outright, has part of its answer in the state of affairs in Germany itself at the turn of the century. Germany was a largely Protestant country, but it did not exist. England too, of course, was Protestant, but a radical intellectual development of the Protestant conviction that a man is his own authority in spiritual matters had been constrained there by two factors which tended to bring men together. One was the dominantly empiricist temper of English intellectual life. The other was the fact that England was politically coherent and experiencing rapid and radical social change. The empiricist argument ensured intellectual agreement in the very method by which it sought to ensure independence. Each man, by virtue of his senses, was held to be independently capable of forming impressions and ideas of nature, but since nature was the same for all men, all men would form the same impressions of it. I have already suggested how the political coherence of England in the eighteenth century appeared to turn English thinkers away from questions about the very premises of their society and towards more practical matters. What it also did, and in this it was reinforced by the gathering speed of change in town and country there throughout the century, was to make it plain that however independent men may be in one respect they were increasingly interdependent in others. This was the almost unspoken assumption in classical political economy. It was simply unrealistic to maintain otherwise. This was not so in Germany. In that country, there was neither a tradition of empiricism, nor political coherence, nor very much social change. The first remains unexplained, but has perhaps something to do with the fact that in a fragmented country with an archaic social structure, little permeated by trade and commerce, a country moreover in which the intelligentsia were a very separate and unrelated group, thinking men less often encountered practical problems. Nevertheless, it remains true, and Germany had a fragile hold on any notion of the possibility of achieving unified knowledge through experience. It also had a fragile hold on its own identity. In the second half of the eighteenth century it was divided into over three hundred and fifty separate political entities, kingdoms, duchies, prince-bishoprics, free cities and obscure manors, most of which were even by contemporary standards poorly run, feudal backwaters. 'Germany, where does it lie then?' asked Goethe and Schiller in 1796, 'no map of mine seems to show it. Where that of politics ends, that of nature begins'. The only common factor was the German language, and even then, the culture of the courts was French. It is hardly surprising that there was little social change. None of the forces which were transforming France and especially England were evident. There were tight legal restrictions on the sale and possession of land, which remained in the hands of the old *Stände*. There was little trade. And there was no capital flowing in from overseas possessions.

German Protestantism was thus untrammelled. Its theological tenets released man from nature. Kant, in secularising them, freed man from God and society as well. Enthusiastically if crudely interpreted, he had demonstrated the supreme power of the Idea. He had as he put it opened 'the prospect of an infinity of self-made conceptions'. But this was indeed a crude interpretation, and Kant was not slow to say so. It ignored his scrupulous care in maintaining that experience was as essential as reason, and thus ignored the fact that he intended not to reject scientific thinking but to secure it. The liberating power of his philosophy in a country that had only an idea of itself to cling to and in which writers had already begun to laud the spirit and the imagination above all other faculties is hard to exaggerate. 'Sundered from politics', Schiller wrote in 1797 in a draft for a poem, 'the German has founded a value of his own, and even if the Empire should perish, this German dignity will abide unchallenged. It is an ethical greatness, it dwells in the culture and character of the nation, which are independent of any political destiny'. From creature man had become creator. As one, a German was nothing. As the other, he could be everything.

Romanticism, which after A. W. Schlegel's contemporary definition is what most have called this extraordinary movement of artistic and intellectual creativity, is inherently difficult to describe. The spiritual and intellectual freedom that it presumed generated a range of ideas that defy a comprehensive account. It is, perhaps, best characterised as a belief in two propositions: that as one contemporary put it 'we live in a world that we ourselves create', and that the principle of creativity is plenitude, infinite variety. Even so, one has immediately to qualify this, for there was also a conviction, among the poets, novelists, musicians and painters as much as among the philosophers and political theorists, that from the plenitude a unity was possible, although whether merely a unity of the imagination or the senses or a theoretical and practical unity in society remained always in dispute and ever uncertain.

The first attempt to defend the conviction that man is irreducibly social within the Kantian system and thus to solve the dilemma presented by Kant's own ethics was made by Herder. Herder had been a pupil of Kant's at Königsberg and firmly believed himself to be extending his teacher's philosophy. His extension rested squarely on the two principles of Romanticism and was stimulated by some travel. He went to France, which he considered to be mortally sick, and to several of the German principalities, which dismayed him considerably. He saw no possibility anywhere of political reform from above, from a re-ordering of the existing society by the State, and instead formed the conviction that change must come from below and within, from the people and a realisation of their inner direction. Herder expressed his views in several works, including some *Ideas for a Philosophy of History of Mankind* that upset Kant when he read what was being argued in his name, but in some respects the most revealing was the prize essay he wrote in 1770 on the origin of language. This was Herder at his least unsystematic, dealing with a question that had exercised other thinkers but none so much as the Germans. 'If I were as eloquent as Demosthenes', wrote Hamann to Herder in 1784, 'I would do no more than repeat one sentence three times: Reason is language, logos. On this marrow-bone I gnaw, and I shall gnaw myself to death on it'. Herder agreed.

In the *Essay*, he proposed four 'laws of nature'. The first was was that man 'is predisposed for language'. 'All processes of the mind of which we are consciously aware', he asserted in Kantian fashion, 'involve the use of language. The former is indeed inconceivable without the latter'. The second law, however, resorted to what had become a truism of eighteenth-century thought. 'Man is by nature a gregarious creature, born to live in society; hence the development of language is both natural and essential for him'. Herder was careful to distinguish the 'natural' instinct of birds to build nests from the 'natural' development of language, although the second of these two senses blurred the distinction that Kant had himself insisted upon at the beginning of his *Anthropology* in his remark that 'Anthropology, treated physiologically, describes what nature has made of man; treated pragmatically, it states what a freely acting being can and shall make of himself.' Herder's third law was that 'since the whole human race is not one single homogeneous group, it does not speak one and the same language. The formation of diverse national languages, therefore, is a natural corollary of human diversity'. This appeared to abandon the Kantian scheme altogether, but Herder then argued in the fourth and last law that 'since mankind in all probabilty forms one progressive totality, originating from one common origin within one universal order, all languages and within them the whole chain of culture, derive from one common source'. This was his confusion. He accepted the Enlightenment assumptions that human nature is constant although everywhere manifested differently according to circumstances and that essential to this nature is the capacity for reason. To this, he added the Kantian conclusion that reason operates within certain fundamental categories and his own insight that these categories are embodied in language. He then observed that languages vary, 'a natural corollary of human diversity'. Having done this, and apparently socialised Kant, by conceding that language is a social fact, he was then required by his own assumptions to maintain that a necessary condition of universality, what he called the human essence, *Humanität*, was a universal language. But to expect such a language was to emphasise not human diversity but human unity, a 'common origin within one universal order', and to have to assume a universal society. Herder was too much of a naturalist (albeit of the apparently non-natural) to abandon the pre-Kantian assumption that unity would come about not by will but by a predetermined process (he postulated the mechanism of contact between cultures). Not to abandon this, however, as Kant himself pointed out in an angry review of the *Ideas*, was to fail to recognise the crucial importance of the exercise of will and reason for the realisation of the Kantian universality that Herder had taken to be possible. To be consistent, Herder would either have had to argue that the two facts, that categories and reason are embodied in language and that languages vary, together refute Kant's philosophy, or that the categories of reason are universal despite the variety of languages. To have held both beliefs was contradictory, for one implied different rationalities and the other a common one.

Herder's historical significance is ambiguous. On the one hand, as most modern commentators imply, he is important neither for the development of Idealist philosophy nor for the elaboration of Rousseau's political problem. He contributed only confusion to the first and intuition to the second. He neither clarified the Kantian separation between what nature had made of man and what his will could make of him, nor showed how this separation could be resolved in a law for civil society. This is the conclusion of hindsight and is perfectly correct. But in another respect Herder is both interesting and important. He is interesting precisely because he was so naive. In his naivety he clarified what other Germans were beginning to see as the problem without then at once obscuring it in a solution of his own. He is important because he exemplifies a recurring phenomenon in the history of social theory over the past two hundred years, someone who while sensitive to the terms within which the intellectual fashion of the moment asks the recurring questions about man's relation to nature and his place in society is equally if not more sensitive to social reality, its intractable diversity and undeniable tenacity, and sensitive to the fact that the social problem cannot be solved by a few abstractions. Such persons are almost always second-rate theorists and first-class observers, and often unaware of the tension between their self-imposed theoretical unity and their practical sense.

However, Herder illustrates very clearly a crucial transformation that the German Idealists did much (although not all) to bring about: a transformation in the importance attached to history. There is much dispute still as to whether the Enlightenment was a historically-minded movement, if indeed it can sensibly be called a movement at all. Some argue that since the philosophers' ideal was a rational harmony between all elements of nature (including society), and since they believed that this was an immediate practical possibility, they were unhistorical. Others argue that they nevertheless developed a strong sense of how circumstance transformed men, and that this sense is historical. After all, did they not in Stewart's phrase often describe what they were attempting as 'natural, theoretical history'? Montesquieu, Rousseau and many others are invoked to justify both sides, and the more obviously historical historians, like Gibbon, are separated from the Enlightenment to justify the first or included within it to justify the second. Here it is sufficient to state the obvious. Men in the eighteenth century did not conceive of historical study as we now do, but that in so far as they held that man was subject to natural causes they were bound, in tracing this connection, to inspect changes in society and human nature over time. This is evident in Herder. But also evident in his work is the German transformation of this truism, that as 'we live in a world that we ourselves create' so we create a succession of worlds. History not only happens to us. We also make it.

Kant himself had sketched an 'Idea for a universal history' in which he saw man having hitherto been the product of natural circumstance, brought to the edge of Enlightenment in modern civilisation, and only then to a state in which he could use his reason to construct an ideal of a fully free, law-governed State. This sketch was not a sketch of the history of reason. That came later, from others. It was rather an attempt to historicise his philosophy in the way in which he had also in lectures at Königsberg 'anthropologised' it, to point to the force of nature in the past and the task of reason in the future. His theoretical conviction was that the rational will could construct the rational law. It was not that it would inevitably do so. It was a teleological view only in the sense that it argued that if man were to be rational (in this sense) then and only then would history result in the universal law. Kant was very cautious about committing himself to saying not only when but even if this would ever happen. He had no faith in the ability of men to perceive their duty (or his philosophy). His philosophy of history remained an abstract temporalisation of his ethics, but unlike Rousseau's similar exercise, the greater soundness of the ethics had given a more secure base to the history, and thus effected a transformation in the force of time in human affairs. The transformation is plain in Herder, who tried to give it substance while at once rescrambling the natural and the non-natural and the pre-determined and the self-determined.

By the end of the century, therefore, Kant had established three crucial doctrines to his own satisfaction: that the science of nature, to be put onto a sound footing, requires the postulate of the synthetic *a priori*; that the exercise of the rational will may bring about a universal law; and that history is the process by which man exercises this will to transcend his natural determination. But in *Die Horen* in 1798 Schiller, a vortex of Romantic brilliance and enthusiasm, had said that Kant must not be taken too literally. It is what he had implied that was so important. This, contended Schiller, was that a transcendental unity of knowledge and sensation which would incorporate history was the supreme possibility of human comprehension. 'Each people has its day in history', he wrote later, 'but the day of the German is the harvest of time as a whole'. Kant was roused by this sort of poetic licence to issue in August 1799 a formal repudiation of all those who pretended to understand him better than he did himself. 'May God preserve us from our friends', he expostulated, 'regarding our enemies we will take care of ourselves...[my] critical philosophy, by virtue of its inexorable tendency towards the satisfaction of reason, both historically and morally-practically, must feel the calling that no change of opinions, no improvements, nor any doctrinal edifice of another form are in store for it'. Such edifices, however, were in store, from Fichte, Schelling, Hegel, Marx and many more, now forgotten. The most amazing, to succeeding generations as well as to their own, were those of Hegel and Marx.

Both Hegel and Schiller had the same vision. It grew from their common perception of classical Greece, that 'paradise of the human spirit', as Hegel called it, with its 'mythical integrity'. It was a vision of a society in which politics, art and religion were at one with themselves and each other. Greece was, in Hegel's description, a world of harmonious *Sittlichkeit*, a world within which all the customs or *Sitten* fused into a coherent and satisfying whole, an *ethos*, a world which manifested fewer contradictions than any before or since, historically determinate evidence of the possibility of reconciliation, a world of the practically possible in contrast to Kant's forever unattainable injunction to a rational moral autonomy in *Moralität*. Herder too had seen Greece in this way, as an integral culture reconciling the ideal and the sensuous in perfect harmony, a model for the modern German mind and soul. It was a view that permeated almost all the Romantics, and which presented a striking contrast to the perceived formalism of classical life which had furnished a model for the French a century earlier. 'Give birth to a Greece of your own from within', urged Schiller to Goethe in 1794, 'by substituting in your imagination through the power of thought the element of which reality has deprived it'.

Hegel too was an imaginative thinker. His closest friend at the turn of the century was the poet Hölderlin, in whom he sought 'the rapture of assurance' until Hölderlin went mad and he went to Jena. Hegel's first substantial book, the *Phenomenology of Mind*, which he finished in Jena as Napoleon was marching into the city in 1806, is written in an allusive, elusive and complex style far removed from what has been described as Kant's bureaucratic prose. Nevertheless, Hegel made it ever clearer in this and subsequent lectures that a new *Sittlichkeit* cannot be realised in art and he thus began to diverge, intellectually and personally, from the Romantic artists. His unwavering belief was that the task was a philosophical one, in the broadest sense a task of reason, and his arguments became perceptibly more formal. He described the *Phenomenology* as a 'recollection of the spirits' of the past, a necessary preliminary to 'absolute knowledge or spirit knowing itself as spirit'. The recollection had two aspects: 'as free existence appearing in the form of the accidental, [it] is history; as comprehended organisation, it is the science of the appearance of knowledge', or phenomenology. This view spread into later lectures on the history of philosophy, the philosophy of history and aesthetics, and in all these he emphasised two crucial transitions, the decline of the Greek *Sittlichkeit* and the Protestant Reformation.

The harmony of ancient Greece was, he said, one of 'felt reason'. It was thus entirely appropriate that it represented itself in art. Art 'is immediate and therefore sensuous knowledge, knowledge in the form and body of the sensuous and the objective themselves, in which the absolute announces itself to the perceptions and sensations'. With the Greeks, 'art was the highest form in which people imagined the gods and gave themselves a consciousness of truth'. It was not, Hegel argued in his *Aesthetics*, that there were abstract ideas which were then aesthetically expressed. The ideas were what they expressed. Similarly, 'the peculiarity of this state was that *mores* were the form of its existence, that is to say, thought could not be separated from cultural life'. But just as 'art has within itself a limit and hence passes over into higher forms of consciousness' so the Greek *Sittlichkeit* was sundered. Appropriately, the break first appeared in Greek art itself, in the tragic dramas, tragic precisely because resolution was impossible. The image of Sophocles' Antigone dominates this section of the *Phenomenology*. But then the contradiction also began to appear in philosophy. 'Socrates, by assigning the determination of men's actions to insight and conviction, posited the individual as capable of a final moral decision, even of one opposed to his country and its mores'. The citizens had to kill him, and so doing they killed themselves. 'Felt reason' had been transcended. The transcendence took shape at first in classical philosophy but there again, Hegel argued, the unity was more apparent than real. 'The Greeks and Romans...knew nothing of [the] concept that man as man is born free, that he is free...although it is the basis of their law. Their peoples know it even less. They knew indeed that an Athenian, a Roman citizen...is free, that there are free and unfree. Just because of that they did not know that man is free as man – man as man, that is, man in general, such that thought comprehends him and as he himself comprehends himself'.

The transcendence then passed to the Christian religion. With Christianity, 'the doctrine arose that all men are free before God, that Christ has freed men...for Christian freedom'. Christianity itself, Hegel contended, had passed through three stages in history, the 'realms of the Father, the Son and the Spirit (Holy Ghost)'. The first, up to Charlemagne, was without 'any great interest'. 'The Christian world at this time presents itself as Christendom, one in which the spiritual and the secular are only different aspects'. In the second, to Charles V, separate states came into being 'so that every relation becomes a firmly fixed private right, excluding a sense of universality' and the Church vacillated between spiritual universality and secular partisanship. Conflict, uncertainty, confusion and chaos were rife. It was in the third, which extended from 'the Reformation to our times', that Christian freedom was properly restored. In Protestantism 'the principle of free spirit is...made the basis of the world, and from this principle are evolved the universal axioms of reason'. 'From that epoch', he continued, 'thought began to gain a shape properly its own; principles were derived from it which were to be the norm for the constitution of the state. Political life was now to be consciously regulated by reason. Customary morality and traditional usage lost their validity. The various rights had to prove that their legitimacy was based on rational principles. Only then is the freedom of spirit realised'. 'Protestantism had introduced the principle of inwardness...[and] the furthest reach of inwardness, of subjectivity, is thought. Man is not free when he is not thinking'. The freedom of Protestantism, however, like that of Romantic art which had developed within it, was illusory. It retained a conception of 'otherness' in divine infinity, and this was in contradiction to the individual spirit. In it man thus only knows infinity in the recognition of his own finitude. That, for Hegel, was an intolerable contradiction. In Romantic art, on the other hand, the free individual in attaining what Hegel called his 'formal independence' becomes capricious. He rewrites himself and external circumstances in a myriad different ways, and any possible unity 'falls asunder'. 'It thus appears that the necessity which argues consciousness on to the attainment of a complete comprehension of the truth demands higher forms than Art is able to produce'. With this extraordinary history, of philosophy, of religion, and of aesthetics, Hegel thus arrived at the point he wished to make. Greece, Protestantism and Romantic art all pointed towards the 'absolute' but contradicted themselves in attempting to comprehend it. And so, finally, did Kant.

Although Hegel's argument is best approached as he first approached it, historically in the *Phenomenology*, the other historical lectures came later, at Berlin. By 1817, when he went to his chair there, he had already articulated a more formal defence of the argument in the *Science of Logic* and the *Encyclopaedia of the Philosophical Sciences*. Here was the crux, and the flaw. It consisted in part of an argument against Kant. Kant had argued that we could never know the essence of things, things-in-themselves. We could only know them as they presented themselves to us through our sensations, and as we ourselves conceived and connected them through our reason. Our reason, therefore, was strictly our reason, and not the world's. But, Hegel contended, this must mean that 'reason is incapable of cognising that which is reasonable'. Our reason could not justify itself. It could not show itself to be necessary, and thus could not show itself to be rational. Kant had conceded this. Hegel would not. Accordingly, he attempted to show that one did not have to. His attempt was formidably complicated, but rested ultimately upon an undefended assertion about things themselves which insisted that things-in-themselves were also things-*for*-themselves. The realm of things, of what he called 'determinate being', evidently consisted he agreed of particularity, separateness, in his word, 'finitude'. As such, it was disconnected and in contradiction with itself. It was not coherent. But, he went on, this was merely contingent. What was by contrast necessarily true of the world of 'determinate being' was precisely that it was indeed necessary. As such, it is potentially coherent, and so everywhere in flux. It is in flux towards not-finitude, not-contradiction, towards infinity and rational unity. Therefore, a rational appreciation of the world is an appreciation of its potential unity which is rational, because it is without contradiction, and for that reason, also necessary. Thus, reason, *pace* Kant, is justified in the 'real' world of infinite necessity. The real is the rational and the rational the real. Hence the truth of 'objective idealism', of the philosophy of the necessary connection between the necessity of subjective reason and the necessity of objective fact. But it is an illusion. There are no grounds for thinking that because any finite thing may be annulled or transformed, it must necessarily be. If there are no such grounds, then there are no grounds for the further belief that the world of things is 'really' not-contradictory, destined to infinity and necessity. If it is not destined for necessity, then our reason cannot be justified within it. And we are back with Kant.

Nevertheless, the promise of necessary reconciliation gave Hegel an olympian perspective on all past and present 'contradictions', and this had enormous value in itself, a value quite independent of whether or not he was right about necessity. His histories are in many ways unsurpassed in their insight, power and command. The promise, however, also prompted him to explain how the reconciliation in philosophy could be situated in the real world. Such a situation, in social and political affairs, was the purpose and subject of his political theory in *The Philosophy of Right*. In this, as well as in variously scattered and more partial accounts, he accepted Montesquieu's belief, as he put it, that one should regard law as necessarily 'related to all other aspects of a nation and a period', and accepted Rousseau's principle that the will must be the principle of the State. But Montesquieu was far from resolving the question, even on his own terms, and Rousseau always maintained that the construction of the State depended upon the conjunction of individual wills, pure wills, divorced from the *Sitten* of the civil society and thus potentially destructive, realising a partial and illusory freedom that was its own contradiction. Witness, argued Hegel, the 'terrible and shrieking' aftermath of the French Revolution.

Hegel's own political theory was entirely consistent with his philosophy. What is revealing for this history is his conception of civil society. Kant had sketched the *bürgerliche Gesellshaft* in which existed, in his view, 'the external conditions' for *Moralität*. It was a society of individuals upon whom lay the duty of fashioning the universal law which would transform what he called the society's 'unsocial sociality'. Kant's particular kind of dualism implied a distinction between the society and the State, but he did not develop it. Hegel did, and perhaps for the first time the two became sharply distinguished. He accepted that there can be no question but that private property is necessary. 'In order that a person be a fully developed and independent organism, it is necessary that he find or make some external sphere for his freedom'. This is achieved by possession, which objectifies the individual in society. 'The rationality of property does not lie in its satisfaction of wants, but in its abrogation of the mere subjectivity of personality. It is in property that person primarily exists as reason'. 'It is more than fifteen hundred years since, under the influence of Christianity, personal freedom began to flourish, and became, at least for a small part of the human race, recognised as a universal principle. But the freedom of ownership has only since yesterday...been recognised...as principle. This is an example...of the length of time required by Spirit for its advance into self-consciousness'. As so often for Hegel, the contrast was with Greece. There men were given free status, but the rights of status were not the rights 'of a person *as such*'. Dependent, then, upon property, 'the concrete person which is an end for itself as a particular person, a totality of needs and a mixture of natural necessity and arbitrary will, is the *one principle* of civil society'. But in the Hegelian scheme neither needs, natural necessity, nor arbitrary will were adequate as a basis for the realisation of the absolute. The exercise of that will, for instance, would merely lead to specific contracts, as emphasised by Rousseau and Kant, in which the totality of the society would still present itself as otherness, in contradiction to the contract between the individuals which by virtue of its dependence on individual wills would be arbitrary. 'The State', he continued, conceived quite independently of specific contracts between individual men or even putatively universal contracts between all men, 'is the actual reality of the ethical (*sittlich*) idea'. 'This substantial unity is an absolute, unchanging end-in-itself in which freedom gains its supreme right, just as conversely the final end has the highest right *vis-à-vis* the individuals whose highest duty is to be members of the State'. It is a wholly separate realm. Rousseau, and more sharply Kant, had distinguished nature from law and predicated the State upon the second. Hegel contended that their law was not universal since it failed in practice to achieve what the philosophy upon which it was founded had failed to do in principle, namely, to resolve all contradictions, remove 'otherness' or alienation, and thus achieve true universality in the absolute.

Conceptual unity, however, is one thing, social and political unity quite another. Hegel's mechanism for getting from civil society to the State was based more upon faith than practical politics. Constitutions cannot be made, he argued, they must be left to arise out of the consciousness of persons in society. It is important to educate those persons, but no more can be done. In fact, in an early unfinished essay on the German constitution, he did concede that 'if Germany were to become one State, it should be remembered that such an event has never been the fruit of reflection, but only of force, even if it corresponded to the general development and the need were felt deeply and distinctly'. The concession was revealing. He faltered before the paradox that it is precisely in a society in which individuals come to realise their concrete individuality through the private ownership and use of property that one may, on his own premises, expect those same individuals as subjects to subsume their separateness and achieve a true freedom 'in the actual reality of the ethical idea'. His remarks upon education (he was a professor employed by the Prussian monarchy) were naive and offer little insight, and this part of the argument indeed puts great strain on the concept of 'freedom' itself.

If Hegel was weak in his account of how his State was to be realised, he was nevertheless reasonably clear about what its structure would be once it was. In previous epochs, notably that of the greatest political unity achieved so far, in the Greek *polis*, the *Sittlichkeit* had been expressed through the institution of the family, 'the substantial whole which cares for the individual both as concerns his means and [his] aptitudes'. 'But civil society tears the individual from this context, alienates the members of the family', he argued, 'and recognises them as autonomous persons'. 'Thus the individual becomes the son of civil society'.

What he explicitly referred to as 'a kind of second family' becomes necessary to mediate between the individual and the State. This will be found in the *Stände* or corporations. However, the idea that all individuals should participate equally in these corporations was 'superficial thinking', for it forgot that if the State exists then by definition each individual representative will represent at once the particular and the general. The State itself, to which the corporations would be the mediators, would be represented in the monarch. 'In a perfect organisation all that is required is the end point of formal decision making; [of] a monarch all that is needed is a man who says "yes" and who puts the dot on the "i"'. It has been said that this appears to be a justification of the Prussian monarchy that employed Hegel and that he was therefore a reactionary totalitarian who grotesquely betrayed freedom and reason for the sake of his immediate political interests. But he expressly stipulated conditions which were not all met in contemporary Prussia, and in the 1820s it was indeed far from clear to someone of a liberal disposition that Prussia was not already among the more enlightened of States. England had the apparatus of freedom but its parliamentarians were scandalously venal and its institutions in conflict (Hegel is not remembered as a wit, but his description of the English upper classes is one of the funniest things he wrote). France had retreated to absolutist terror. Russia was despotic. American democracy appeared to rest on slavery. Where Hegel was and is culpable is in the thinness of his argument for how the State, as he sees it, was to be established.

Nevertheless, he considered that he had effected in Kant's own terms the 'transcendence' (which, when effected, was not such) which Kant could not; that he had extended this in the realm of ethics by showing that Kant's universal was not so; and that he had shown that Kant's 'universal history' was in fact but one point on the successive, generally progressive and wholly necessary history of Thought's attempts to realise itself by overcoming the contradictions that lay in each successive finite solution. The *Sittlichkeit* of the properly constituted State was the instantiation of that *Moralität* which Kant, irremediably dualist, had supposed to be both autonomous and independent of things-in-themselves, and probably unattainable. By the end of the 1820s, when Hegel had become rector of the University of

Berlin, he was the most famous philosopher in Germany. Yet by 1840, nine years after his death, virtually no-one accepted his conclusions as he would have wished them to. Some rejected his argument for the necessity of non-finitude. Others rejected his argument for its realisation first and above all in philosophy itself.

History resolved by men

HEGEL'S IMMEDIATE AUDIENCE, like that of Kant and the other German philosophers at the end of the eighteenth century and the beginning of the nineteenth, consisted of university students. The contemporary German universities were relatively isolated from the rest of the society. Only Halle trained men for practical careers. For the rest, they were avenues of mobility to which the society offered no destination. They were thus a furnace of youthful bourgeois frustration. Up to the time of Hegel's death in Berlin in 1831, this frustration had expressed itself largely in the realm of ideas. Events changed this. After the rebellion in the July of 1830, liberal demands for a constitution and greater freedom of the press became more urgent, and the creation of the *Zollverein* heightened the contrast between increasing economic liberty and the continuing political repression. And repression, at least in the Prussian State, the State that Hegel had appeared to defend in *The Philosophy of Right,* did continue. The students began to feel the need to protest. It was into such an atmosphere that Karl Marx moved when he came to the University of Berlin in 1836.

This 'black lad from Trier', as a friend described him, who 'rages without compare, as if ten thousand devils had him by the hair' ignored the more formal parts of his education in favour of philosophy, and during an illness in 1837 'got to know Hegel from beginning to end'. He joined a post-graduate club of like-minded students in Berlin. These 'Young Hegelians' were orthodox in their thinking if radical in their style. They were largely absorbed in extending Hegel's criticism of Christianity or, like Marx in his own doctoral dissertation, in dicussing those more distant 'philosophers of self-consciousness' as he called them, the Epicureans, Stoics and Sceptics. They were, however, explicit in drawing parallels between the periods of critical thought Hegel himself had identified and their own time, and began to argue that Hegel's own method could be turned against him. Since Hegel had produced his least satisfactory arguments in defence of his own position, this was not difficult. With characteristic exaggeration, Marx was later to remark that 'during three years, from 1842 to 1845, Germany went through a cataclysm more violent than anything which had happened in the previous century. All this, it is true, took place only in the realm of pure thought. For we are dealing with a remarkable phenomenon, the decomposition of the Absolute Spirit.'

Marx left Berlin in 1841, and in that year one of the Young Hegelians, Feuerbach, published a treatise on *The Essence of Christianity*. Marx read this at about the time that he began to work on a radical newspaper in Cologne, and together with this experience it crystallised his particular objections to Hegel's conclusions. Feuerbach was an unsubtle thinker, and his thesis would have been unremarkable to another audience. It was, simply, that 'the true relationship between thought and being may be expressed as follows: being is the subject and thought the predicate. Thought is conditioned by being, not being by thought'. Hegel, he said, had got it the wrong way round. The Absolute Spirit was nothing other than 'man's essence outside man, the essence of thinking outside thinking'. Had Feuerbach dealt with Hegel's political theory rather than with his discussion of Christianity, he might have produced a better criticism than he did, for in that remark, that Hegel takes 'the essence of thinking out of thinking', lies the most obvious question to ask of his philosophy in general and *The Philosophy of Right* in particular: how is a supra-individual *Sittlichkeit* to which individuals subscribe of their own free will possible? Working on the newspaper, the *Rheinische Zeitung*, Marx found himself in the predicament of having to join in the discussion about so-called 'material interests' as they affected practical politics. Infected by Feuerbach's 'transformative criticism', he realised, as Feuerbach had not, that its conclusions had political implications, and he accordingly sat down in the early months of 1843 to work out his ideas on Hegel's conception of the State. They were relatively straightforward, and of great importance in crystallising his own intellectual dissatisfactions, but in some respects their greatest interest lies in what he did not question.

'Hegel', argued Marx, 'turns the moments of the idea of the

State into a subject and makes the old political arrangements into a predicate, while in historical reality things always work the other way round: the idea of the State is always a predicate of these arrangements'. The State is an illusion of self-determination. Of course, this was not quite fair to Hegel. Although Hegel had produced very poor arguments to explain how the State as Absolute *Sittlichkeit* could emerge, these were, nevertheless, arguments which assumed that it would arise from the consciousness of men in civil society. What was at issue was how. Hegel did not assume that the State had to be created *a priori*, in Marx's terms, as 'the subject', although on one interpretation of *The Philosophy of Right* it certainly looks as though Hegel thought that this was possible, despite the lack of the proper consciousness amongst some individuals in civil society. Nevertheless, neither interpretation of what Hegel meant can rescue him from materialist criticism, and in this respect Marx's points were sharp and just. They were directed to the relationship between property-holding individuals in civil society, the mediating *Stände*, and the property-less. Marx pointed out that Hegel was forced to assume a radical contradiction between the individual as a member of civil society and the individual as a member of the State; and that from a materialist standpoint it was the State (as Hegel conceived it) rather than the individual and his interests which had to be criticised. He was equally scathing about Hegel's very poor arguments for supposing that the *Stände*, the landed gentry, the guilds, and the bureaucracy, could mediate between the individual and the State. He then proceeded to argue that Hegel's own view that the ownership of property determined a man's private status as an individual must be inverted; that from the materialist standpoint property must be seen as determining an individual's public status. And if that was so, then divisions based upon property were at the foundation of the State, and it was 'the class differences of civil society [that] become political differences'.

Marx's comments on the property-less in civil society appeared in the *Introduction* to the critique of Hegel's philosophy which he wrote late in 1843. These comments reveal that although he rejected Hegel's Idealism, he did not reject the assumption that had persisted from Rousseau and Kant into Hegel, albeit transformed, of a 'universal' solution. As with the other philosophers, it was at once the principle and the flaw of his theory. To resolve the class differences and thus the political ones, he argued in the *Introduction*, 'a class must be formed which has radical claims, a class *in* civil society which is not a class *of* civil society, a class which is the dissolution of all classes, a sphere of society which has a universal character because its sufferings are universal, and which does not claim a *particular redress* because the wrong which is done is not a *particular wrong* but *wrong in general*. There must be formed a sphere of society which claims no traditional status but only a human status, a sphere which is not opposed to particular consequences but totally opposed to the assumptions of the German political system; a sphere finally, which cannot emancipate itself without emancipating itself from all the other spheres of society, without, therefore, emancipating all the other spheres, which is, in short, a *total* loss of humanity and which can only redeem itself by a *total redemption* of humanity. This dissolution of society, as a particular class, is the *proletariat'*. 'When the proletariat', he continued, 'announces the *dissolution of the existing social order*, it only declares the secret of its own existence, for *it* is the *effective* dissolution of this order. When the proletariat demands the *negation of private property* it only lays down as a *principle for society* what society has already made a *principle for the proletariat*, and what the latter already involuntarily embodies as the negative result of society'. Marx clearly retained the central assumption of Hegel and the Young Hegelians alike. Each phase in history eventually reaches its contradiction. At that point, a new synthesis becomes necessary. The final synthesis is final because it is universal and thus also rational and so beyond contradiction.

Why Marx should have been so attached to Hegel is plain. Few men entirely reject the assumptions of their culture or their teachers, even when seeming to, and when that culture furnishes the means for its attack its attraction to an angry man is assured. For the same reason, it is clear too why he should have been so excited by Feuerbach's transformative criticism. There has been more argument (often of a very pedantic kind) about why he should have become especially interested in the working class; but the course of events seems plain. Marx's father was, at least at home, a forthright free-thinker. Trier had been the home in the 1820s of Ludwig Gall, a reformer who subscribed to the views of the early socialists like Owen, Fourier and Saint-Simon, and Marx's future father-in-law appears to have discussed these views with him. Marx's early letters home display a radical nature concerned with abstract justice. His experience on the *Rheinische Zeitung*, as he said, had brought him into direct contact with practical affairs. And he almost certainly read von Stein's account of socialism and communism in Paris, a work which had been commissioned in 1840 by a Prussian government considerably alarmed by what was happening across the Rhine. Von Stein examined the roots of discontent in the French capital and explained the 'science of society' (in fact a heterogeneous collection of ideas derived from various sources) that the workers declared to justify their politics. Marx was not at all impressed by this spurious 'science', but was moved by the political reality that lay behind it. He experienced it at first hand when he himself went to Paris in November 1843 after the *Zeitung* had been suppressed. 'When the communist artisans meet', he remarked, 'they seem to be meeting for the purpose of propaganda. But in the process they also acquire a new need, the need for society, and what seemed to be a means has become an end in itself...the brotherhood of Man is no idle phrase but the real truth, and the Nobility of Man shines out at us from these faces brutalised by toil'. But he was appalled by the naivety of their theories and indeed by virtually all the radical ideas that were bubbling in Paris then. They seemed to him unhistorical and utopian, to display an insufficient appreciation of the way in which the new bourgeois order had to be entirely superseded. He thus set about developing his own.

He fashioned them out of two sources. One was Hegel. 'The greatness of Hegel's *Phenomenology*', he wrote in some private drafts in 1844, 'and its final product, the dialectic of negativity as the moving and creating principle, is on the one hand that Hegel conceives of the self-creation of man as a process, objectification as loss of the object, as externalisation and the transcendence of this externalisation. This means, therefore, that he grasps the nature of *labour* and understands objective man, true, because real, man, as the result of his own labour'. This greater generosity to Hegel, however, in no way meant that Marx had abandoned his earlier inversion in the criticism of *The Philosophy of*

Right. 'The only labour which Hegel knows and recognises is mental labour', he said again, and this was a defect in so far as Hegel did not see that mental labour was also part of practical labour in nature. But this did not alter the fact that it was Hegel nevertheless who first grasped the point that 'labour' in the broadest sense was man's essence in the world, that man was not merely, to Feuerbach as also to the old punning German proverb, what he eats, but also what he does, what he creates in and for himself.

Marx's second source of inspiration was the political economists. Indeed Marx went as far as to say that 'Hegel's standpoint is that of modern political economy' and his discussion recalls the few remarks Hegel himself made about this subject in *The Philosophy of Right.* The intellectual achievement of these economists, Adam Smith, Ricardo, Say and others, had been to show, against the older mercantilist conceptions, that wealth could be produced by labour. In the notes he made in 1844, Marx seized upon this insight and reinterpreted it in terms of his Hegelian conception of the nature of labour. He agreed that the analytical scheme of the classical economists was perfectly correct. 'We have accepted its terminology and its laws'. But he argued that it did not go far enough. It accepted as assumptions what needed to be explained if the nature of the system was to be properly understood. 'Political economy provides no explanation of the basis for the distinction of labour from capital, of capital from land...it does not show how [economic] laws arise out of the nature of private property'. At this point, however, Marx did not take up the whole of his own challenge. He concentrated upon developing his Hegelian assumption that man 'was the result of his own labour'. In producing goods in the market, he argued, which are then sold, man becomes alienated from himself, as labour. His product, exchanged for money which circulates in the economy, thus becomes independent of him, and oppresses him. He is the victim of the laws of motion of his own product. Correspondingly, he becomes separated or alienated from his own self and from other men, from his natural 'species-being', as a productive, therefore conscious, therefore social and therefore potentially 'universal' being. And 'if the product of labour is alien to me and confronts me as an alien power, to whom does it belong? To a being *other* than myself. And who is this being? The gods?... Not the gods, nor nature, but only man himself can be this alien power over men.'.

In these deservedly famous arguments, which he did not apparently intend to publish and which indeed only appeared in print after 1927, Marx had developed his theory in two important ways. The first was to have shown that a proper extension of Hegel's insights in the *Phenomenology* (and not a mechanical inversion which like Feuerbach merely stressed the way in which ideas reflected material activity), could provide an at once historical and theoretical explanation of the premises of the political economists, and thus a reinterpretation of the laws they had derived from these premises. The second, implied in this, was to have shown that the concept of property had to be redefined. The mercantilists, the political economists and even Hegel (like Kant and Rousseau) had seen property as possession. So did Marx. But his theory required a reinterpretation of possession. On the one hand, what he called 'appropriation' was necessary to man for him to realise his 'species-being' as something which creates itself through practical labour. But on the other, as soon as this 'truly human and social property' was estranged from him by other men, thus alienating him from his very 'being', it became someone else's property, of a different kind. It was this alienated true property which was private property. In arguing this, Marx thus achieved a most extraordinary conceptual connection between two hitherto unconnected parts of political economy and between these and Hegel. 'All wealth', as he put it, 'has [now] become industrial wealth, the wealth of labour; and industry is accomplished labour, just as the factory system is the essence of industry – of labour – brought to its maturity, and just as industrial capital is the accomplished objective form of private property. We can now see how it is only at this point that private property can complete its dominion over man and become, in its most general form, a world historical power'.

Communism, therefore, had to be the negation of this negation of man. 'Crude' communism, Marx argued, 'has not yet grasped the positive essence of private property'. It either advocated an equal amount of property for everyone or proposed the abolition of property altogether. In the first case, it misunderstood the distinction between 'true' and 'private' property. In the second, it would take away even 'true' property and alienate it to the State, which then becomes the capitalist. Real communism would have to transcend private property and thus effect 'a complete return of man to himself as a social (i.e. human) being'. It would be 'the genuine resolution of the conflict between man and nature and between man and man – the true resolution of the strife between existence and essence, between objectification and self-confirmation, between freedom and necessity, between the individual and the species'. All wealth has now become industrial wealth, private property has completed its dominion over man and has become a world historical power. But this world historical power negates man's 'species-being' which thus secretes its own negation of the negation. In so doing, it prepares the final resolution. 'Communism', argued Marx, 'is the riddle of history solved', but 'as such' he added 'it is not the goal of human development, which goal is the structure of society'. The ideal of the *volonté générale*, the universal law, the true *Sittlichkeit*, had taken a conceptually more powerful and historically more immediate form. It thus pointed even more directly to practical politics.

Marx's subsequent dedication to radical politics was not, however, the straightforward outcome of his abstract theoretical conclusions. These had themselves been galvanised by his experience on the *Rheinische Zeitung* in 1842 and still more by the ferment of radical ideas and activity he encountered later in Paris. Having become clear about the proper course of action in 1844, he accordingly proceeded to contribute to it by mounting a series of blistering attacks upon the 'crude communists' and other as he saw them well-intentioned but dangerously futile and wholly uncomprehending apostles of reform and revolution. In this he was greatly helped by his new friend Engels, who had in the same year published an article on economics that impressed Marx greatly by what he regarded as its comprehension of the true state of affairs.

Marx had himself by this time contracted to develop his economic theory of history, and Engels encouraged him. 'Hurry up and get your book on economics finished', Engels urged early in 1845, 'even if there are parts you are still not satisfied with, that doesn't matter. People are ready for it and we must strike while the iron's hot'. But the middle 1840s were in Germany not a time for reflection, and instead they together struck at other theorists. These long polemics, not all of which were published in their lifetime, seem tedious now, but in some, and especially in the first section of *The German Ideology*, which was written in 1846, Marx continued to develop his own ideas. After 1844, he had become convinced that he had to elaborate a history of European and Asiatic societies to show in more concrete fashion how it was that the new capitalist system had necessarily to be succeeded by communism, and in the first section of *The German Ideology* the bare bones of this historical theory appear for the first time. 'Every new class... achieves its hegemony only on a broader basis than that of the class ruling previously, in return for which the opposition of the non-ruling class against the new ruling class later develops all the more sharply and profoundly'. The dominance of each ruling class rests upon its control of the forces of production and is maintained by a set of ideas or an ideology which although appearing to be the ruling ideas of the society as a whole are nothing other than the 'mental productions' of that class itself; and from stage to stage the division of labour, which is at once the division of man's 'species-being' and of society, becomes ever more marked. 'I do not deserve', he wrote to a correspondent six years later, 'the credit for having discovered either the existence of classes in modern society or the struggle between them... What I did that was new was prove: 1. that the existence of classes is only bound up with particular phases in the history of the process of production; 2. that the class struggle necessarily leads to the dictatorship of the proletariat; and 3. that this dictatorship itself is only a transition to the abolition of all classes and the eventual classless society'. He continued to work away at his history for the next twenty years, and although much of it eventually appeared in *Capital* much more of it remained in notes and draft. It was and is, nevertheless, an extraordinarily impressive attempt to explain the nature and in some cases the transformation of ancient, oriental, medieval and modern societies in terms of their economic relations which, while always recognisably Marxian, does not often fall into mere dogmatism. But at many points (notably in his inconsistent accounts of what he once called the 'Asiatic' mode of production) it reinforces the conviction that his theory was at its most powerful in explaining modern capitalism.

This power was at the time most graphically expressed in a

short manifesto that he and Engels were asked to write in 1847 for the new Communist League in London, a bitter, brilliant pamphlet that remains one of the greatest of all socialist declarations. In it, they together summarised their theory of history and outlined a strategy for Germany, where revolution seemed imminent. The workers were at first to unite with the bourgeoisie and only then, when 'the absolute monarchy, the feudal squirearchy and the petty bourgeoisie' had been defeated, turn against the bourgeoise itself. However, various sympathetic radicals in Germany, bourgeois and worker, pointed out both before and after the *débâcles* of 1848 that the bourgeoisie were apathetic and the workers cautious and disorganised, and that the strategy had little chance of success. Nevertheless, Marx continued to advocate it when he returned to Cologne in 1848 to work on a *Neue Rheinische Zeitung,* but in the growing disillusion after the revolutions in that year, he eventually abandoned it, together with his support for the Democratic Union, and turned instead to a philosophy of proletarian attack and the Brotherhood of Workers. This brought another expulsion order and now, Marx had little choice but to move to England. He went there in August 1849, and stayed until he died in 1883. The first twelve years of this long stay were demoralising. Where the European radicals had not disintegrated they were being led by men of whom Marx disapproved, and few people in England were interested in his ideas one way or the other. Moreover, he was virtually penniless, and he and his family were forced into barren and often desperate circumstances. But Marx continued to work: at his economics, which he pursued with prodigious industry in the British Museum reading room, at newspaper articles, for which he received small fees, and at encouraging what few radicals he could find. A relatively casual meeting between French and English socialists in London in 1863 at last led to something, the creation the following year of the Working Men's International Association. This gave him new hope. He dominated its Council and almost alone willed its fortunes until it collapsed in 1872, torn by a dispute with Bakunin and his followers and vilified by outsiders after Marx's support of the supposedly revolutionary Paris Commune. During the same period, his financial situation improved, and he was at last able to finish the first section of his economics.

The first volume of *Capital* was published in 1867. Although Marx continued to work away for the next decade, he did not manage to finish another manuscript to his satisfaction. It has been suggested that he was dismayed by the possible refutation of his predictions by rising profits and wages and new factory legislation in the 1860s. The second, third and fourth volumes were put together from his voluminous and chaotic notes by Engels and Kautsky after he died. Together, they constitute nearly three thousand formidable pages of a closely argued and minutely illustrated if sometimes repetitive and obscure moral, historical, and analytical condemnation of capitalism. The theory starts from the proposition that 'the value of a commodity is determined by the quantity of labour spent on it'. At the very beginning of the first volume, Marx distinguished between 'use-value' and 'exchange-value'. The first is independent of the labour spent in producing the useful object (for there can be useful objects which require no labour at all). The second is not. This, exchange-value, is a function of what he called 'abstract labour' in the sense that the value is not that of any specific labour but rather the value of the labour time 'socially necessary' for its production. Two products may be incommensurable in their use-value, and may be produced by people with very different skills over very different periods of time, but they may be theoretically compared and practically exchanged according to the socially necessary labour time put into them. 'The labour time socially necessary is that required to produce an article under the normal conditions of production, and with the average degree of skill and intensity prevalent at the time'. This is the essence of value, and thus of exchange and of the unit of exchange, or money.

In capitalist society, which dissolves all pre-existing social ties, the labourer is free, but free only to sell his labour power (or himself), for that is all he has. He therefore needs the capitalist's money in order to be able to realise his labour power, not merely to survive but also, from the capitalist's point of view, to be able to work effectively and reproduce himself through his children. Marx assumed that 'in a given country, at a given time, the average quantity of the means of subsistence necessary for the labourer is practically known'. However, for it to be worth the capitalist's while to buy labour as a commodity (for that is what it becomes under capitalism), he must be able to extract more value than he returns. 'This surplus value is the difference between the value of a product and the value of the elements consumed in the formation of that product, in other words, of the means of production and the labour-power'. It is the source, indeed, the very constitution of profit.

Marx agreed with the political economists that capitalists were disposed to accumulate, but disagreed with them about the consequences of this fact. They held that it increased what Smith called 'stock' which in turn made for higher productivity, which raised wages. Marx, on the other hand, argued that the increase in stock meant an increase in the proportion of what he called 'constant capital' (in materials and machinery) and a corresponding decrease in the proportion of 'variable capital' (labour power) devoted to production, and that since profit derived from surplus labour value the greater volume of production made possible by the increasing constant capital would mean that the *rate* of profit would therefore decline. It may well be, he continued, that the accumulation of constant capital would occasionally create an increasing demand for labour so that wages would rise, but the pressure to maintain the rate of profit against its inevitable long-term decline would serve to depress them again or even to encourage capitalists to lay men off. If they were laid off, an 'industrial reserve army' of the unemployed would appear. Various short-term steps could be taken to stop the fall in the rate of profit, and the cycle might start again, but the long-term tendency, he was convinced, was towards a concentration of constant capital at one extreme and a progressive unemployment of labour at the other. This tendency would be aggravated by the results of competition between capitalists. Such competition would serve to concentrate capital and in larger concentrations the proportion of constant capital would be higher. Moreover, the concentration into larger units would bring labourers together and make them more aware of their common fate. In these ways, the structure of post-capitalist society is foreshadowed in the final stages of capitalism. 'The knell of private property sounds'. 'Its integument is burst asunder' in the inescapable contradiction between the propensity to accumulate and the falling rate of profit. Capitalism may stagger from crisis to crisis, but it is bound as a matter of necessity to be superseded by the only society which can resolve its endemic contradictions.

Marx was not specific about the organisation of this society. In *The German Ideology* he and Engels sketched a romantic picture of a free community without division of labour. In the first volume of *Capital* he indicated an arrangement in which 'the total product of the community is a social product', where 'one portion serves as a fresh means of production and remains social but another is consumed by the members as means of subsistence', the distribution to the producers depending, he suggested, upon the amount of labour time that they put into the social product. In such an arrangement, one assumes both a directive central organisation and a division of labour, but he did not elaborate.

Marx considered his theory to demonstrate the necessary collapse of capitalism, but it itself has proved defective in two crucial respects. The first lies in the notion of 'labour time'. This is conceptually straightforward but practically intractable. No one has succeeded in defining a unit of labour time, and for this reason it has proved impossible to explain, to predict or (in the Soviet case) to arrange prices in terms of it. The second problem lies in the fact that (partly as a result of Marx's own views) labour has organised to maintain its wages and capitalists have organised to maintain employment. This has meant that although the rate of profit in the more advanced economies may indeed have been falling, demand has not fallen with it, creating a crisis of underconsumption. With the help of the State, which has come to assume the task of the general manager of aggregate demand, the system has so far managed to maintain itself. In assuming that nothing and nobody would intervene to dampen the oscillation of the market, Marx made exactly the same mistake as the classicists. In this respect, crises such as that which developed after 1929, far from vindicating his theory, imply in their consequences a striking refutation of it.

Nevertheless, it has been plausibly maintained that if only the industrial working class had accepted (or would accept) Marx's diagnosis, his prognosis would have been fulfilled and capitalism would have been (or would be) overthrown. The obvious question has therefore been why they have not. Part of the answer clearly lies in theoretically peripheral factors. Capitalism may have eroded many traditional ties, but one that it has not is the tie of national identity. Thus, workers of one nation have been happy to fight workers of another on behalf (as Marxists would put it) of the ruling class of each. Another part of the answer lies in the historically more damaging point that divisions within those who sell their labour have multiplied over the past century to the extent to which few groups, despite the concentration and centralisation of capital, feel a common identity with any other. But perhaps the most important part of the answer, and certainly the theoretically most damaging one, lies in Marx's theory of the possible relationship between men and property.

Like Hegel, Marx accepted that particularity, separateness, finitude, 'determinate being', would necessarily be transcended. This was the rational justification in the Hegelian sense of his entire system. For him, however, the most important source of particularity and separateness was private property. It was this above all which divided men from themselves and from each other. It was this therefore which had necessarily to be destroyed and so transformed. Then men would be rationally, necessarily, finally united. This was doubly mistaken. First, Marx was no more justified than Hegel, whose argument in this respect he used, in thinking that 'finitude' would necessarily be transcended. Second, even if as private property it were to be, he was not justified in believing that this would produce a unified society. If he was right in thinking that it was only private property that divided men, then he was required to believe that all that we understand by individuality, by the notion of a distinct human being, was a function of private property. This, however, would mean that the abolition of private property entailed the abolition of anything that we understand as human beings, finite, particular, separate people. Socialism in this sense, therefore, is not a society of human beings at all, and so not a society for us. If on the other hand he was wrong in thinking that it was only private property that divided men, then the abolition of private property would not transcend all finitude, particularity, separateness, human individuality, and its consequence would not be wholly rational and without contradiction, at rest in some eternal unity.

This was a strictly theoretical failure, but it was severe. Like Hegel, Marx argued from premises that were either incoherent or false. It meant also, however, and again like Hegel, that he argued from premises that gave him an extraordinarily clear view of past and present 'contradictions' and thus furnished a powerful history. And even though he did fail in this strict sense, it does not follow even on his own terms that the abolition or at least curtailment of private property would not go some way towards resolving the kinds of conflict and 'contradiction' to which he pointed. Nevertheless, the failure does perhaps suggest why it is that the kind of society which he imagined and for which he worked is more conceivable in societies which have *not* first experienced what he could have regarded as a properly capitalist mode of production.

4

History resolved by laws I

'IN GERMANY', announced Destutt de Tracy to a meeting of the
Institute in Paris on 7 *floréal* in year X, 'one is a Kantian as one
was a Christian, a Mohammedan, a Brahmin, as one was a
Platonist, a Stoic, an Academician, and as one was later a Scotist
or a Thomist, and as finally in the seventeenth century we were
all Cartesians'. In France, on the other hand, 'in the ideological,
moral and political sciences there is no head of a sect. One does
not follow anybody's banner. Each one has his personal and
completely independent opinions; and if there is agreement on
several points, it always takes place without people making a
plan for agreement, often without knowing it'. But, he continued, the French did have a method. 'It consists in scrupul-
ously observing the facts, in deducing consequences when they
are completely certain, in not giving to simple suppositions the
quality of facts, in trying to bind together only such truths as are
linked naturally with one another and without *lacunae*, in admit-
ting ignorance and always preferring it to any assertion which
lacks verisimilitude'. While conceding at once that de Tracy was
naive, or disingenuous, or simply misinformed, and probably all
of these; that even if it were true (which it was not) that all
French thinkers subscribed to this ideal, very few came anywhere near realising it, even in the sciences of nature; it was
nevertheless the case that Frenchmen did remain at this time
almost completely unaffected by German philosophy. France
had none of the pietistic Protestantism and provincial isolation
of the German states: neither the intellectual traditions nor the
social and political conditions that prompted the theories I have
already discussed. Moreover, the Germans had not hesitated to
be very rude about the immediate consequences of the revolution in 1789.

This 'shrieking aftermath', however, as Hegel had called it,
was not overlooked in France itself. To one section of society, it
seemed plain that the Terror, and then the establishment of the

Directorate and the Consulate on the morrow of the 18 *brumaire*, in which Bonaparte declared himself First Consul for life and proclaimed his right to name his successor, were but new embodiments of the old oppression. Accordingly, they continued to reassert the old ideals of liberty and equality. It was their successors that so excited and frustrated Marx when he came to Paris in 1843. To a second section, the events after 1789 merely revealed the savage and wicked nature of man, the inevitability of perpetual slaughter, the truth of the view that it was the passion for self-immolation and not that for liberty and justice which created armies and civil societies. These events showed beyond all doubt the need for absolute authority, for punishment and continued repression if civilisation and order were to be secured. They proved beyond question that intellectuals were a pest, corrupters and deluders of men, sirens whose voices had to be silenced in favour of the re-establishment of the authority of the Pope and Roman Catholic Church. This bleak and dark reaction had its theoretical justification. 'Man only exists for society', argued de Bonald, 'and society only educates him for itself. He should therefore employ in the service of society everything which he has received from society, everything which he is and everything which he has'.

Each of these views is readily intelligible. Each can be justified by a simple, if partial, inspection of what did in fact happen after 1789. This is not to say that either should be dismissed, either for its intrinsic interest or for the effect it has had on the interpretation and indeed the direction of events in nineteenth- and twentieth-century France. Nevertheless there was a third reaction, more complex than either, of equal intrinsic interest and of considerable importance for the subsequent history of social theorising, although not, perhaps, for the history of immediately subsequent social and political events themselves. In essence this consisted of the view that the aftermath of the revolution had shown that both the Jacobin slogans and the cries for traditional authority from beyond the mountains were inadequate guides to the proper realisation of a good society, the one because it abandoned order for liberty and the other because it abandoned liberty and reason for order. By far the most prolific and enthusiastic proponent of the third view, a man who has often been described as he was by very many of his contemporaries as a muddled and deluded utopian, a megalomaniac madman with a pathetic faith in every social change, in the phrase of a sacked secretary a 'depraved juggler', was Henri, Comte de Saint-Simon.

That Saint-Simon was an opportunist is hard to deny. From a family of the old *noblesse*, he went as a young officer to fight with the French against the British in America, where, as he later claimed, 'I first conceived the desire to see [liberty] this plant of another world flower in my country', a boast rather belied by his private letters home at the time. He was detained for 'the purposes of general security' in 1794 and was actually sent to the Luxembourg, from which few men came out alive, yet a year or two later he was making a considerable fortune speculating in land in northern France. He enthusiastically embraced the renaissance of the Directorate, but when it fell, at once transferred his hopes to Napoleon, to whom he sent extravagant plans for social reconstruction long after it had become clear to others that the first Consul was merely passing such submissions directly to his police files. And he courted by turn scientists and industrialists, in whom he saw the promise of the new order, but who received his profuse enthusiasms with passing bemusement and lasting disdain. Saint-Simon's opportunism was a direct consequence of his indestructible idealism. Everywhere, except in the old order and the what was to him vapid libertarianism, he saw a promise of the good society. Everyone, except the reactionaries and the Jacobins, was thus at the some time or another the inspiration of his hopes and the target of his ambitions. These were for order, but not the order of a re-established theocracy. In his view the revolution in 1789 had been brought about by the 'bastard classes': the lawyers and metaphysicians, the non-noble military men, landowners and rentiers who had overthrown the nobles in the name of a third class, the *industriels*, those who worked, whether as employers or as workers, in the new economic order. But the consequence of 1789 was that both the old class and the 'bastard' class had established themselves on the shoulders of the third. The new nation was largely financed by the new order, but that order had no say. For Saint-Simon, this was not merely a question, so to speak, of adjusting the mechanisms of representation. It was also a question of the class in whom the future of France and of Europe more widely lay being suffocated by the interests of the past.

Saint-Simon's enthusiasm for the *industriels*, however, came somewhat later in his spectacular, sad career. At first, in the years around the turn of the eighteenth and nineteenth centuries, he urged 'no more honours for the Alexanders; long live the Archimedes', a characteristically seventeenth- and eighteenth-century ideal of a rational, progressive society directed by a college of scientists. There was to be a new social order, the work towards which would be financed by an international fund established at Newton's tomb and the theory of which would be designed 'to so situate man that his personal interest and the general interest are always located in the same direction'. 'I wanted to try', he wrote later, 'to systematise the philosophy of God. I wanted to descend in sequence from the phenomenon universe to the phenomenon solar system, from there to the terrestrial phenomenon, and finally to the study of the species considered as a dependency of the sublimer phenomenon, and to deduce from this study the laws of social organisation, the original and essential object of my research'. This was, as he conceded, a conventionally rationalist ambition, but he did not simply see himself as doing the same sort of thing as the pre-revolutionary *philosophes*. 'The philosophy of the eighteenth century was critical and revolutionary', he insisted, 'that of the nineteenth will be inventive and organisational'. 'The crisis in which the European peoples are involved is due to the incoherence of general ideas; as soon as there is a theory corresponding to the present state of enlightenment, order will be restored, an institution common to the peoples of Europe will be re-established, and a priesthood adequately educated according to the present state of knowledge will bring peace to Europe by restraining the ambitions of peoples and kings'. The religion of Rome was to be replaced by the religion of Newton. Priests would give way to scientists.

Saint-Simon never articulated a clear, let alone a persuasive theology for the new religion. But it is plain in which direction he believed it should be sought. In his *Treatise on Systems*, Condillac, an eighteenth-century populariser in France of what he believed to be Locke's epistemology, had explained that 'elements which explain others are called *principles*, and the system is the more perfect as the principles are smaller in number. It is even desirable that they may be reduced to one'. The sensationalist psychologists, like Condillac himself, had argued that the origin of ideas was in matter, and since Newton had shown that matter obeyed a single law, it seemed clear to Saint-Simon, as he wrote in 1808, that 'universal gravity is the sole cause of all physical and moral phenomena'. Such a bizarre simplification was unacceptable even to Saint-Simon's scientific contemporaries, who were much more interested in their particular investigations, but their disdain characteristically drove him to renewed fervour. A 'positive' social science which he variously referred to as 'the science of man', 'the science of society', 'physiology', 'social physiology' and 'the science of politics' (it was one of his secretaries, Auguste Comte, who in 1838 invented the ugly neologism 'sociology'), would reveal the developmental laws which had always determined the course of human history but which only now, in the new positivist dawn, would be known, so that men could henceforth order their lives rationally, in accordance with the revelation. The explanations which these laws would provide would be materialist, grounded in turn in the fundamental laws of matter, and would show in their systematic and harmonious inter-connectedness the blue-print for the new order, at once necessary, rational and desirable. The 'epoch of the positive system' was about to begin, celebrated with the first rites of the religion of Newton. Saint-Simon explained this new epoch by an extrapolation to history of his general materialist principles. Just as mind could be explained in terms of the motion of matter, so history, and more particularly, the history of ideas, could be explained in terms of the motion of material production. Hence his enthusiasm for the *industriels*. They were directly engaged in the transformation of production. They were the motor of the new positivism.

The general drift of the political theory of the Enlightenment, whether it began from empiricist premises or from rationalist ones or from some combination of the two (as did Saint-Simon himself), had been towards insisting upon what men had in common, either by virtue of their common experience or of their universal capacity for reason, and in this sense at least had been potentially egalitarian. Saint-Simon rejected this. The work of the 'physiologists' had shown to him that men differed in their nature. At one with the *philosophes* in his belief that social reconstructions had to begin from what was natural (and therefore rational, and therefore good), he differed in his conception of what the natural was. It was not equality, but inequality.

Saint-Simon combined these two notions, that the history of society was to be explained by its material base and that men were by nature unequal, into the general proposition that the good society would arise from the leadership of the natural élite of the historical moment: the *industriels*. In the second volume of his *Industry* which was published in 1817, he asserted that there had so far been two apotheoses of 'universal' (that is to say, European) history: the polytheistic period, in the third and fourth centuries A.D., and the theological, coterminous with eleventh and twelfth century feudalism. Feudalism, however, had begun to crumble in the face of new economic pressures after the twelfth century, pressures that had their origin in the institution of free communes and individual property rights and in Arab science, and the positive epoch was born. The present period was the last gasp of the medieval order. The third apotheosis, of industry and positive science, a rational order explained and supported by scientific laws, was about to begin. This was the path of history. The new élite must thus seize their rightful and necessary position. The remnants of the old order and its mistaken antithesis, the libertarians, had finally to be relegated and surpassed. The cry was not 'workers of all lands, unite' but as it were '*industriels* of all classes, unite'. This alone was the proper path for a truly civil society.

Saint-Simon's marriage of what was by the time of the Consulate a conventional rationalism with his premise of natural inequality and his sharp observation of the economic roots of political wrangling thus produced an intriguing and persuasive twist of Enlightenment social theory. The *industriels* had produced the new society, the scientists had explained it. Together, they would direct it in the interests of all progressive classes. By the 1830s, the slogan of his numerous and exuberant followers had become 'à chacun selon sa capacité, à chaque capacité selon ses oeuvres', to each according to his capacity, to each capacity according to its work. The final battle was not between the oppressed and the oppressors, but between the workers of all

classes and the idlers, the lumpenproletariat, the aristocracy and
the officers of old religion, bastards of all classes and the bastards
among classes. Right, in all its senses, was on the side of the
positivists. 'The philosophers of the nineteenth century will
make people feel the necessity of submitting all children to the
study of the same code of terrestrial morality, since the similarity
of positive moral ideas is the only bond which can unite men in
society'.

Finally, however, Saint-Simon allowed the inference from his
own account of 'universal history'. 'It is no longer a problem',
he wrote in the third volume of *Industry*, 'of discussing endlessly
how to know which is the best of governments. There is nothing
good, there is nothing bad, absolutely speaking. Everything is
relative, that is the only absolute. Everything is relative above all
to the times in so far as social institutions are concerned'.
Positivism was the apotheosis of the nineteenth century. It was
not the apotheosis of all history. Yet ironically, it is Saint-Simon's
model of society which insofar as any general model can do so
accounts for the nature of twentieth-century industrial society.
It is the supersession of this society that others, like Marx,
predicted from different and indeed opposite premises, which
remains for the future. The irony is sharpened when one sees all
too clearly that Saint-Simon arrived at his conclusions by a set of
transparently bad arguments, Marx by a set of exceptionally
brilliant ones, and sharpened still further when one discovers
that in disclaiming his having discovered the existence of social
classes Marx almost certainly had Saint-Simon in mind. The
history of social theory is littered with bad histories supported by
superficially persuasive abstract systems. Saint-Simon is someone whose passion for system never, despite himself, quite
cancelled his historical sense, or his opportunism. This cannot
ultimately be said of Auguste Comte, the obscure intellectual
from Montpellier whom Saint-Simon hired as his secretary in
1817 and sacked in a torrent of mutual recrimination in 1824.

The immediate cause of the breach was Comte's view that
Saint-Simon had published a piece of his without due acknowledgement. But this was merely a straw, for they were also
temperamentally antagonistic, the one ebullient, extravagant,
impetuous and opportunistic, infused with aristocratic con-

fidence, the other withdrawn, severe, contemplative and moralistic, at times almost paralysed by *petit bourgeois* anxiety. And this difference of temperament was reflected in, if it did not cause, Comte's impatience with Saint-Simon's desertion of his more systematic work in the interests of courting influential *industriels*. Even in his later, more spiritualist utterances, Comte never lost his passion for system. Nevertheless, he did acknowledge his debt to Saint-Simon, however much it may have pained him to do so after the break. The debt is plain in all his work. Like the older man, he abhorred what he called the 'two opposed and equally vicious conceptions' of absolute monarchy and libertarian licence, conceptions, he believed, which 'by their very nature tend reciprocally to strengthen each other and in consequence to maintain indefinitely the source of revolutions'. 'The destination of the society now maturing', he wrote, 'is neither to inhabit for ever the old and miserable rut which its infancy created, as kings suppose; nor to live eternally without shelter after having left it, as the people imagine. Its destiny, rather, is this, that aided by acquired experience it should with all its accumulated materials construct an edifice fitted for its needs and enjoyments'. 'Such', he believed, 'is the great and noble enterprise reserved for the present generation'. Like Saint-Simon he was convinced that this edifice should be one in which there was one goal, pursued by all. Only then could one talk of society, as distinct from mere agglomeration. 'The true Organic Doctrine can alone produce the harmony so imperatively demanded by the condition of European civilisation'.

Again like Saint-Simon, he believed that this doctrine could only be established 'scientifically', in a positive spirit. 'The fundamental condition which must be fulfilled in order to treat politics in a positive spirit', he argued, 'consists in determining with precision the limits within which, by the nature of things, the combinations of social order are contained. In other words, it is necessary in politics as in the other sciences, that observation and imagination should be rendered perfectly distinct and the latter subordinated to the former'. These programmatic remarks come from 'A plan for reorganising society' which Comte had sketched in 1822. He set out his ideas on the exact nature of and relations between the sciences between 1830 and 1842 in the six dense and extended volumes of the *Course of*

Positive Philosophy, and these ideas (although not their intent) constitute his difference from Saint-Simon.

The *cours* was at once formal and historical. Comte wished to secure a thesis about the relations between the sciences, and did so in part by arguing that the progression of this relationship was a historical one. The sciences, he argued, differ in the complexity of the subject matter with which they deal. There are two broad classes of science, the abstract and the concrete, the former consisting of laws upon which the existent phenomena, the subject of the latter, depend. The order is from the abstract sciences of mathematics, astronomy, physics and chemistry to the concrete sciences of biology and sociology. The laws of the concrete sciences subsume the laws of the abstract sciences, but this is not to say that the concrete particularities of the laws which they reveal can be decomposed without loss into the abstract terms of the abstract sciences. Similarly, although the laws of the social science or sociology subsume the laws of biology, social phenomena cannot be decomposed without loss into the terms of biology. Comte did not however appear to wish to argue that the respective realms were in any sense essentially different. 'The positive *esprit*, recognising the impossibility of discovering absolute notions, renounces the search for the origin and destination of the universe and the fundamental cause of things in favour of the search, by means of reason and observation, for their laws, that is to say, for the invariable relations of similarity and succession between them'. This seeming scepticism was unusual. In the rationalist constructions of the eighteenth century there had been virtually no suggestion that 'science', however understood, was anything other than a different, if superior, way of grasping the real properties of the world. Even Saint-Simon, of course, by his own account a positivist and dedicated to exactly the same project as Comte, had recklessly declared that there was a 'sole cause of all physical and moral phenomena'. Such declarations, Comte believed, were not merely misrepresentations of the positivist spirit; they were thoroughly metaphysical and so characteristic instead of the stage from which positivism was painfully but triumphantly emerging.

The historical thesis of the *cours* consisted in the simple view that the sciences had developed in historical progression, from mathematics in the ancient world to sociology with Comte himself. Europe was now ready, but only now ready, for the application of the positivist method to its social and political reconstruction. The present therefore represented the full flowering and final triumph of the positivist spirit. Comte elaborated this last point into a general characterisation of what Saint-Simon would have called 'universal history' as a whole. But whereas the older man had distinguished as the three apotheoses of this history, the polytheism of the third century, the theology of the eleventh and the positivism of the nineteenth, Comte talked of the theological, lasting in one form or another to the Reformation, the metaphysical, just then ending, and the positive. He thus collapsed Saint-Simon's first two into his first, and inserted the metaphysical which Saint-Simon had not recognised, in himself any more than in others. Such schemes were not peculiar to the positivists, or even to Frenchmen. They were by then part of the general currency of historical assertion. Comte indeed devoted much of his early energy to reviving and correcting the speculations of others. His own scheme, however, has a peculiar interest. At the time, it constituted by far the most systematic attempt to secure such a thesis, more systematic even than Hegel's, and seen retrospectively, it crystallised a French tradition. Like many thoroughgoing systematisers, Comte has been grossly oversimplified, and the resultant banalities, when combined with the evident subversion of his own thesis in his later work, have led many to dismiss him. Yet at the time he was taken very seriously even by those who suspected and indeed derided his particular moral and political ambitions.

The simplest version of Comte's view of history would have it, as I have already suggested, that a coherently theological stage was followed by a coherently metaphysical one, and that this in turn had just been succeeded by the emergence of a coherent positivism. Yet the historical aspect of his argument for the relations between the sciences immediately reveals that Comte's scheme was by no means simple, since the foundations of the positive *esprit* could be discovered even in the polytheistic phase, the dawn of the theological. And quite apart from the gradual progression of the changes, as Comte characterised them, changes which were no sooner secured than they generated their own supersession in an almost dialectical fashion, they were not simply changes of mental attitude. In an early essay, 'A brief appraisal of modern history' written in 1820, he set out what could almost be described as a materialist thesis: an account of social transformations in Europe from the eleventh century to the nineteenth in terms of economic activity, military policy and changing legitimations of power. He argued that no sooner had the Catholic Church established its spiritual and temporal power in the eleventh century than two processes began to undermine it. One was the introduction of science to Europe by the Arabs, and the other was the development of 'industrial' production by free labour, the 'Commons', being gradually freed from the military obligations of feudal dependence. These two forces co-existed with the theocratic powers until the religious reformation in the sixteenth century, the bourgeois challenge to the existing temporal powers in the seventeenth, and 'the general and decisive attack' on both in the eighteenth. Only then were the productive, political and intellectual characters of the European societies (in reality, of course, France) coincident; and only then, therefore, was a coherent plan, a proper system, possible. But this possibility was being squandered by the 'opposed and equally vicious conceptions' of absolutism and libertarianism, an historically regressive and socially debilitating squabble which required the active intervention of men of positivist spirit.

Ex hypothesi, the 'Organic Doctrine' could not be expected to arise spontaneously. The rabble were still deluded by destructive Jacobin nonsenses, and the lawyers, one of Saint-Simon's 'bastard classes', were still peddling metaphysical notions. Thus 'the nature of the works to be executed of itself sufficiently indicates the class on which their execution must derive. Since these works are theoretical, it is clear that those whose professed aim it is to form theoretical combinations, in other words *savants* occupied with the study of the sciences of observation, are the only men whose capacity and intellectual culture fulfil the necessary conditions'. So, 'in the system to be constituted the spiritual power will be confined to the hands of *savants*, while the temporal power will belong to the heads of industrial works...on the *savants* devolves the task of undertaking the first series of works and on the leaders of industry that of organising, on the bases thus established, the administrative system'. 'Such', concluded Comte in a somewhat metaphysical lapse, 'is the nature of things'. Productive, political and intellectual characters had coincided. The coincidences, or system, constituted a vindication of the possibility of systematic apprehension and application. To realise these possibilities, men with a grasp of the system must be allowed absolute discretion, yet no discretion was possible. The 'nature of things' was evident. The *savants* had merely to explicate it. And the explication would be a sociological one, sociology being the science that subsumed the laws of all worldly phenomena. It was perfectly clear, to Comte, that scientific and historical necessity required the rule and supervision of the new social physicians.

This rule, as Comte made clear, was not temporal but spiritual, analogous to the rule exercised by the medieval Papacy at its height and to the rule sought but in his view never effectively achieved by the metaphysical political philosophers. Instead of invoking supernatural authority, or the authority of the individual with his natural rights, his interests and his conscience, it would invoke the demonstrable (and not *fictif* or imaginative) organic social unity of which it was itself the mid-wife and guarantor. Comte's apparent clarity on this matter, however, reveals a considerable confusion. To understand its force, one has to recall that although he despised the intellectual basis of the medieval papacy, he greatly admired its achievement. He has with good reason been called a 'Catholic atheist'. He was a theologian by temperament and a theocrat by inclination. This is all too evident in a later work, the sad, often mad and certainly interminable *System of Positive Polity* which appeared between 1851 and 1854. This was the realisation of only one of four projects Comte had set himself at the end of the *cours*. The others were systematic treatises on morals, industry and the philosophy of mathematics or 'positive logic', of which he attempted only the last before he died in 1857. 'Others may laugh', wrote J. S. Mill of this later work in 1865, 'but we could far rather weep at this melancholy decadence of a great intellect'. Looking back over his work, Comte considered himself in the *Course* to be engaged upon an Aristotelian task, but in the *System*, a Pauline one. Paul, 'the real founder of what is improperly called "Christianity"', had been the prime mover towards the spiritual power of the theological state. Comte, the real founder of what (one might say) is improperly called 'positivism', saw himself as the prime mover in the establishment of the spiritual power of the positive stage. Accordingly, from his bourgeois apartment in the rue Monsieur le Prince, he proclaimed himself High Priest of Humanity.

The decisive turning point had been 1845. In that year, Comte met a Madame Clothilde de Vaux, for whom he at once formed a strange and wild passion. Their affair was apparently never consummated, and this, with Clothilde's early death, drove Comte quite mad. But instead of rejecting Clothide, he idealised her, declared her to be the Virgin of the positivist faith and established her tomb as a place of pilgrimage. 'Since 1845', he wrote towards the end of the *System*, 'under her holy influence, I have come clearly to see the whole of my career, the second half of which will transform philosophy into religion as the first transformed science into philosophy'. The central tenet of the religion, and so the new spiritual power, was altruism. 'Love your neighbour', Comte enjoined, 'live for others'. He watched the civil strife in the Paris streets in the June of 1848 with a kind of demented detachment. The regressive forces were battering themselves to death, failing to appreciate the possibilities of unity so passionately evident to the High Priest. 'It is to this salutary disturbance', he had once written of the 1789 revolution, 'that we owe the struggle and the audacity to conceive a notion upon which rests the whole of social science and consequently the whole of positive philosophy of which this final science alone could constitute the unity'. Now, faced with further futile and destructive disorder, he inclined to the view that only a spiritual change could save France, although he never seems actually to have abandoned his conviction that this was merely the sentiment necessary to secure men's commitment to the positive polity. Nevertheless, it is plain that positivism and the altruism to secure it against the egoism of the mob had become purely metaphysical slogans. In these awesome delusions, Comte had effectively undermined his own project. His final lunacies indeed exceeded even Saint-Simon's own, from which he had tried to escape in 1824. Yet in all respects, save in his early distinction between theological and metaphysical notions, the differences between his theories and those of the old aristocrat were slight. Had he lived to write his promised treatise on industry, they would have doubtless seemed even less marked. Ridiculed as they have both been by the beliefs of their sectarian followers, however, who linger still in Brazil and died only recently even in England, their spirit persisted.

Nor was it without immediate impact. Harriet Martineau, who abridged and translated Comte's *Course* into English, remarked in 1853 that 'my strongest inducement to this enterprise was my deep conviction of the need of this book in my own country'. 'We are living', she continued, 'in a remarkable time, when the conflict of opinions renders a firm foundation of knowledge indispensable, not only to our intellectual, moral and social progress, but to our holding such ground as we have gained from former ages ... In close connection with this was another of my reasons. The supreme dread of everyone who cares for the good of the nation or race is that men should be adrift for want of an anchorage for their convictions. I believe that no one questions that a very large proportion of our own people are now so adrift ... The work of M. Comte is unquestionably the greatest single effort that has been made to obviate this kind of danger'. Such sentiments recall Saint-Simon's own conviction that 'the crisis in which the European peoples are involved is due to the incoherence of general ideas'. Hinting at fear of the consequences of excessive liberty and uncontrolled social change as much as at a distaste for the refusal of conservatives like Burke to concede ground to 'utility' and general ideas at all, Harriet Martineau perhaps expressed the appeal that Comte had for all of the rather small group of intellectuals in England who were attracted by what he wrote. It was the appeal that he initially had for John Stuart Mill.

Looking back in his celebrated and moving *Autobiography* to the time at which he first encountered the work of the two Frenchmen, Mill remembered that 'the chief benefit which I derived from the trains of thought suggested by the Saint-Simonians and Comte was that I obtained a clearer conception than ever before of the peculiarities of an era of transition in opinion, and ceased to mistake [in utilitarianism] the moral and intellectual characteristics of such an era for the normal attributes of humanity'. 'I looked forward', he went on, 'through the present age of loud disputes but generally weak convictions, to a future which shall unite the best qualities of the critical with the best qualities of the organic period; unchecked liberty of thought, unbounded freedom of individual action in all modes not hurtful to others; but also, convictions as to what is right and wrong, useful and pernicious, deeply engraven in the feelings by early education and general unanimity of sentiment, and so firmly grounded in reason and in the true exigencies of life; that they shall not, like all former and present creeds, religious, ethical and political, require to be periodically thrown off and replaced by others'. The language and in certain respects the sentiments too, the longing for a 'general unanimity of sentiment' and for convictions 'firmly grounded in reason and the true exigencies of life', were Comte's own. Like him, Mill wished to secure moral progress with a thorough and thoroughly scientific analytical case. Yet Mill's view of the constituents of the progressive state was very different. Comte would never have agreed that 'unchecked liberty of thought' and 'unbounded freedom of individual action' were anything but the most pernicious inheritance of the critical period, dangerous metaphysical nonsenses. This is Mill's interest. It lies not merely in the fact that he was Comte's most perceptive and systematic critic, indeed perhaps the best critic that Comte has ever had, but also in the fact that his criticism and the confrontation it brought about are to a great extent representative of the differences between English and Scots empirical practicality and 'the mania for system and regulation', as Mill put it, 'by which Frenchmen are distinguished among Europeans, and M. Comte among Frenchmen'.

Mill could not have been more firmly placed in the tradition of British analytical philosophy. His famous and awesome childhood was a strict apprenticeship to the cauterising utilitarianism of his father. James Mill, recalling the Scots of the preceding generation, held that ethics and thus political prescription had to be based not upon abstract and fictional notions such as those of natural rights but instead upon the real, determinate wants of individuals, what gave them pleasure and saved them from pain, wants that were conditioned by the pleasurable and painful aspects of their experience. His son had two objections to this. First, although this scheme could in principle account for feelings of sympathy and altruism ('All those to whom I looked up', he wrote later, 'were of the opinion that the pleasure of sympathy with human beings, and the feelings which made the good of others...the object of existence, were the greatest and surest sources of happiness'), the ruthless analysis by which it did so in practice dessicated feeling altogether. Second, and more damagingly, it was as Macaulay had so wittily shown in his demolition both of Bentham and of James Mill, either trivial or false: trivial, if every motive was to be translated as pleasurable self-interest, and false, if the attribution was in any way restricted, for many known motives would then be excluded.

J. S. Mill rounded upon Macaulay himself, however, in an attack that in fact went somewhat wide, for Macaulay agreed with much of what Mill said. If his father had been guilty of applying the methods of geometry to human affairs, Mill argued, Macaulay was guilty of applying those of chemistry. He was guilty of restricting himself to the empirical peculiarities of unique situations and thus being able to draw no more than the most limited conclusions. He had also been guilty, Mill added, of asserting the validity of the analogy between combinations of chemicals producing an entity different in kind from its constituents and combinations of men producing an entity different in kind from its constituents. Since Mill was even more critical of the intuitionist case, which had received powerful support in Whewell's *History of the Inductive Sciences*, published in the year in which Mill set about his own logic of what he called 'the moral sciences', a case that supported 'false doctrines and bad institutions', he might appear virtually to have closed his options. But Comte offered an alternative.

The Frenchman had proposed a method of what he had called 'inverse deduction', owing nothing to intuitionism, the resort of conservatives and metaphysicians, but combining the virtues, in Mill's terms, of both chemistry and geometry. Superficially, it was straightforward. Empirically-derived generalisations were to be tested against deductions from the twin premises of human nature and a particular set of conditions. Carried forward, these generalisations would become the laws of what Mill called 'ethology', the science of character, of the modifications of psychological disposition by circumstance. In practice, the method is difficult to use, largely because it is not clear where the premises are to come from if not from the empirical observations. And since as Mill more than once conceded these observations will more often than not suggest the great complexity of behaviour, it seems that one is back more than he would have liked to the 'chemical' position.

The second source of Mill's attraction to Comte's work was his appreciation of the Frenchman's hierarchy of the sciences. Where Comte, however, had argued that although the laws of the more fundamental sciences, like chemistry, were subsumed in the laws of the higher ones, like sociology, they could not alone generate the latter, Mill inclined to the more atomistic view that they could. For him, social science was not like chemistry, in which combinations produced entities different in kind from their constituent elements. On this matter, Comte would appear to have been the more sensible. There is a crucial difference between saying that sociological laws (if such there be) should be consistent with psychological, or physiological, or even physical and chemical ones, and saying that they may be inferred or deduced from them. Mill insisted, even in his later and somewhat tempered appraisal of Comte in 1865, that although one could produce many different classifications of the sciences Comte's was adequate because it was useful, yet he seemed to fail to see that the uses to which he put it were rather different.

Thirdly, and most enthusiastically, Mill approved of Comte's history. He was, it is true, sceptical of Comte's extension of the empirical generalisation of the three stages to the status of a law. 'His predictions and recommendations with respect to the future of society...appear...greatly inferior in value to his appreciation of the past', he said. 'We fail to see any scientific connexion between his theoretical explanation of the past progress of society, and his proposals for future improvement'. Nevertheless, as an account of the history of the past to the present, Mill considered Comte's scheme to be of the highest class. It avoided all the usual exaggerations of historians, and above all it showed clearly the increasing causal importance of states of belief and knowledge upon events. This conclusion, he argued, 'deduced from the laws of human nature, [is] in entire accordance with the general facts of history. Every considerable change historically known to us in the condition of any portion of mankind, has been preceded by a change, of proportional extent, in the state of their knowledge or in the prevalent beliefs'. Inspected closely, of course, the conclusion turns out to be virtually tautologous. If men do what they do not know, or do not know how to do, then they are either acting unconsciously, or history is a series of accidents. Mill intended neither of these conclusions, errors characteristic of the historians whom Comte had exposed. But it is on this principle that the two men agreed so well. States of belief were the determining principle in the past. They were both guides to and guarantors of the future. It was their laws which provided the foundation of a positively rigorous attempt to secure the historical and moral convictions in a properly constructed social science.

However, Mill's recollection in his *Autobiography* of what he looked forward to as a younger man, 'a future which shall unite the best qualities of the critical with the best qualities of the organic period, unchecked liberty of thought, unbounded freedom of individual action in all modes not hurtful to others', itself recalls the moral distance between the two men. Mill was most explicit about this in his *Auguste Comte and Positivism*, which he wrote nearly thirty years after the sixth (in reality, the first) book of his *Logic*, the programmatic argument for a social science which, put together in 1837, was naturally innocent of Comte's magnificent imaginings in the *System*.

First, Mill was unlike Comte, and it may be said, unlike almost all other architects of sociological systems in being clear about the difference between what might in principle be possible by way of a comprehensive and successful social science, and what he and others might in practice achieve. Comte appears to have assumed that the establishment of investigative and corroborative procedures was *ipso facto* a demonstration of the science itself, which thus sprang imposing and fully-formed from the mere expression of its possibility. Free of Comte's certainty, Mill could readily concede that since 'personal or class interests and predilections interfere with impartial judgement, the hope of...accordance of opinion among sociological inquirers as would obtain, in mere deference to their authority, the universal assent which M. Comte's scheme of society requires, must be adjourned to an indefinite distance'. After all, circumstances, and thus characters, and thus interests, varied. This was itself a supposition of 'ethology'. 'It is because astronomers agree in their teaching', he said, taking what now seems a somewhat unfortunate example, 'that astronomy is trusted, and not because there is an academy of sciences or Royal Commission issuing decrees or passing resolutions'.

Mill was thus firmly set against intellectual coercion, the

'mania for regulation' that he rightly detected in Comte. The distinction between coercion and other causes of belief was indeed fundamental to both his theory and his ethics. It was the second decisive difference between the two men. Theoretically, Mill wished to argue that although all behaviour was caused, and could thus be shown to be subject to deterministic laws, not all behaviour was coerced; and it was the absence of coercion which constituted freedom, freedom from the material, or moral, or intellectual, or political subjugation of others. Mill's argument, to put it somewhat simply (for it was a brave and complex attempt), was that an uncoerced man could have done other than he did, yet of course, that he did do what he did was the result, in Mill's account, of determining causes, and if that is true, then there is a sense, the only sense consistent with the kind of determinist account that Mill wished to secure, in which he could not have done other than he did. Nevertheless, the point is that Mill did wish to secure a compatibility between a causal account of all behaviour, in the mechanical sense, and the possibility of choice. And this was because it was of supreme ethical importance to him that he should have been able to do so. 'Though our character is formed by circumstances', he insisted, 'our own desires can do much to shape those circumstances; and what is really inspiriting and ennobling in the doctrine of free will is the conviction that we have real power over the formation of our own character; that our will, by influencing some of our circumstances, can modify our future habits or capabilities of willing'. We should not therefore underrate 'the importance, to man and society, of a large variety of types of character, and of giving full freedom to human nature to expand itself in innumerable and conflicting directions'.

It is, in short, in his scepticism and his insistence upon the importance of an open future that Mill differs so sharply from Comte. The difference was not peculiar to these two men. In its essentials, it represented the more general difference of purpose and temper between French and English political philosophers which had already been evident by the eighteenth century. Mill himself was clear about one of the most fundamental reasons for this. In *Auguste Comte and Positivism* he criticised Comte for the latter's failure to appreciate or at least to concede that England was both Protestant and orderly and so an exception to the vaunted connection between the 'vicious conceptions' of liberty and revolution. 'He does not seem to be aware that Protestantism has any positive influence, other than the general ones of Christianity; and misses one of the most important facts connected with it, its remarkable efficiency, as contrasted with Catholicism, in cultivating the intelligence and conscience of the individual believer'. Not content, Mill continued, talking now of Comte's insistence in the *System* upon the devotional apparatus needed to ensure the positive polity, 'with an equivalent for the Paters and Aves of Catholicism, he must have one for the sign of the cross; and he delivers himself'.

Exactly like the more orthodox eighteenth-century rationalists in their own country, both Saint-Simon and Comte took as a model of intellectual and moral authority the very theological framework they considered themselves to have superseded. The incomparable Mr Newton was for them at once an intellectual inspiration and a symbol for the religion of the directing class. For Mill, uninterested in his tomb or in anything else at all redolent of High Priests and spiritual coercion, Newton was simply a model of analytical excellence, an entirely secular figure. If Comte was a Catholic atheist, Mill was a Protestant one. For the one, the secularised Catholicism of a positive sociology was a force for unity and order through obedience to an intellectually invincible and spiritually privileged class. For the other, the secularised Protestantism of ethology allowed independence and variety, requiring obedience to reason and experience but allowing conscience and compassion too, and in that way, in liberty, ensuring order and perhaps (for Mill remained sceptical) even progress.

In enlightened eighteenth-century circles, it was widely agreed that the good was the natural, the natural the rational, and the rational the good. This was never a precise set of axioms, however superficially lucid it may have seemed. Having traced its vicissitudes through the less orthodox *philosophes*, the German Idealists, the putatively positivist philosophies of reconstruction in France and the younger Mill, it becomes clear that it can be invoked to support a large and mutually inconsistent variety of descriptions and prescriptions. It cannot serve to characterise any distinctive thesis at all. Nevertheless, as I have implied in previous chapters, it does serve as a point from which to approach a set of questions whose answers do enable one more nearly to distinguish, describe, and explain the divergences. What is man's status in the natural world? Is he creature or creator, or both? If it is his reason which, as most argued, distinguishes him from nature (even though its application may return him there), how does its extension and application serve to distinguish one man from another as an individual? What is the connection between this distinction and the claim, again made very generally, that the application of reason also serves to secure a basis upon which individuals may come to act together? If it is the application of the naturally human faculty of reason that can secure a coherent society, can one then say that there is a natural social state, to be defended against the unnaturalness of other states? These themselves are scarcely the most lucid of questions, but they are the ones that were asked, and it was the answers to them that provided at once a theory of the errors and contradictions of the past and a plan for their supersession in a morally defensible future.

The simplest way in which to understand how they were asked and answered, however, is to return to the interests behind the equations from which they derive and ask of each of these men, what was his conception of the good? What exactly did he consider as a defensible social, political and moral order? For it is that which most directly informed analysis. Montesquieu, Rousseau, Hegel, Marx, Saint-Simon and Comte, even Herder (and in a much more complex way Kant too), despite their plainly multifarious and obviously incompatible differences, were of the view, which Mill was not, that however constituted, explained and maintained, the ideal order was one without interior contradiction. Kant put the case most abstractly, and so most clearly. Man had a duty to a morality established by his own reason which, once perfected, would unite all men, for being rational it would be without contradiction. It is clear why this abhorrence of inconsistency should have been so strong in France and Germany. Each in its different way was incoherent, the one torn by wholly opposed ideologies, the other existing merely as an idea with no structural cohesion at all.

Mill in particular and most, but not all, Englishmen in general were a fascinating and instructive foil to the French and Germans. On the one hand, Mill was as committed as any to a rational science of society, and indeed outlined a programme for it that was unexcelled in its remorselessly atomistic, mechanical determinism. Yet on the other, he rested his science on a set of laws which emphasised not merely the effect of varied circumstances on past states of belief but their continuing effect into the present, so that he committed himself to a persistent variety of opinions. This was not mere scepticism. He was convinced that variety was the essence of progress. It was both the condition and the expression of freedom, the 'unchecked liberty of thought' and 'unbounded freedom of action in all modes not hurtful to others' that he so cherished. His eighteenth-century spirit led him to try to reconcile this view with a determinist account of human behaviour, and more plausibly to pursue a rational defence for it in *On Liberty*. Yet the lack of passion in his account is crucial. It reveals not merely an austere temperament but also a set of circumstances in which passion and urgency seemed uncalled for. English society between 1830 and 1870 was hardly without dispute and even contradiction, but these were not of the extent, for example, of the contrast between the German intellectuals' sense of their integrity and the somnolent fragmentation of the reactionary German states, or of the battle between the conservatives and radical liberals in immediately pre- and post-revolutionary France. They certainly did not appear to call the very moral and political foundations of the society into question, however great the apparent divergence of interests and instability of opinions. This difference, indeed, is perhaps more fundamental even than the differences of religious tradition to which Mill himself drew attention. The origins of German idealism can after all not implausibly be traced to that country's pietistic Protestantism, yet the brooding introversions of this pietism there nourished the Romantic desire for the true *Sittlichkeit*, for complete and perfect harmony between men. Although the epistemological authority of 'the knowing subject' in this philosophy owed much to Protestantism, the conviction that in knowing fully the individual subject would cohere into a social subject was due more, as I have already argued, to the seeming impossibility at that time of any more practical kind of unity in the German provinces. One thus returns to the economic, cultural and political differences between England and the two European societies. In so doing, one becomes clearer about two general conditions for distinctively sociological thinking, for theories or interpretative schemes or what might more accurately, if somewhat pejoratively, be called secular cosmologies which, by invoking merely one or two principles of social organisation, claim to explain both the ills of the present and the necessary basis for a coherent future.

The first of these conditions is fundamental doubt about the very premises of the society. It is only Mill among the men I have so far discussed who lacked any such doubt. Nothing in his moral and political philosophy questioned the basic structure of English society. On the contrary, there is a case for regarding it as an exceptionally sophisticated articulation of the ideology of the liberal bourgeoisie in a society in which, unlike both France and Germany, this class was already secure and in the ascendant; but this is too crude. Certainly, Mill took his society for granted in a way that the Continental intellectuals did not. But to say that he was confident of the status of the individual in this society is to make his entire project unintelligible. It was precisely an unease about this status that propelled it. Although he felt no need to offer a comprehensive account of the principles of English society, and instead took them largely for granted (as he could expect his audience to do), neither did he consider that this society could be left at rest. Accordingly, he proposed not wholesale reconstruction or revolution but instead piecemeal changes, the redressing of inequalities through the redistribution of wealth, the raising of the status of women and extended and improved education, changes that would allow more room for individual determination in an evidently established structure. If it was not just a philosophy of anxiety, no more was it one of calm confidence.

Mill also lacked the second condition for comprehensive sociological conceptions, the monistic moral confidence of the rationalists, the conviction that there was one principle which if established would ensure a society at once just, coherent and enduring, a principle which, once the intellectual and institutional errors of the past could be swept away, would be evident to all reasonable men. It is the vision of revolution and reconstruction proposed in the name of such principles that we inherit as classical sociological theory. From the more pragmatic liberals we inherit instead the more modest conviction that circumstances affect men, and the sense that there are many causes, many effects and many futures. This too may be called 'sociological', but the moral and analytical purposes and premises that inform it are quite distinct. Nevertheless, such are the paradoxes of the history of social theorising that it was from the liberal, pragmatic and Protestant English middle class that there was at the same time emerging a theory which appeared to unite these two quite separate convictions, and so seems completely to subvert the point. Its author was Herbert Spencer.

History resolved by laws II

SPENCER'S REMORSELESS RATIONALISM was uncharacteristic of English intellectual life. He thus raises difficulties for those who wish to propose sociological explanations of social theories. Is he best seen as a limiting case, the extreme instance of the confident mid-Victorian moralist and man of science, the least doubting apologist of his class? Or was his apparent confidence, as I have just said of nineteenth-century English liberal thought more generally, the answer to doubt, a reflex of Calvinist anxiety in the midst of extraordinary social changes? Or was he merely odd, a neurotic upon whom the assumptions of the time worked to produce a quite untypical and even perhaps pathological dogma? The most sensible conclusion, if perhaps the least interesting, is that there is truth in all three. He was indeed confident: no other psychologist or sociologist has dared to proclaim that his work 'will ultimately stand beside Newton's *Principia*'. He was also anxious: the most casual inspection of his correspondence reveals an almost pathetic need, quite absent, for instance, from Marx's letters, or Mill's, or even Saint-Simon's, to be properly understood and duly respected. And he was odd: even close and well-disposed friends were bound to agree that toward the end of his life he inspired pity more than any other feeling, and in his *Autobiography* he dwelt at length upon personal difficulties. Perhaps typical of his time and place, he nevertheless parodied it. He expressed what some of his contemporaries would have liked to believe, but what most of them, wiser and more secure than he, found it unnecessary to believe.

In common with other architects of what we selectively inherit as sociological systems, Spencer, who was much more than a sociologist, declared that his 'ultimate purpose, lying behind all proximate purposes', was that 'of finding for the principles of right and wrong in conduct at large a scientific basis'. Amongst its many features, his attempt has three of particular historical interest: its claim to derive a theory of social development and moral necessity from a more general theory of the cosmos as a whole; its emphasis both upon the analytical and (although he would have rejected the description) the historical importance of individual character and upon that of what (largely because of him) we now think of as social structure; and the extent to which it was subsequently misunderstood. His social theory was not, as it has often been said to have been, derived from a biological one (and he certainly owed almost nothing to Darwin); he was by no means an unqualified apologist for unrestrained competition; and although a necessitarian, he was not an unequivocally optimistic one. He would have been the first to agree that he was a more than usually misunderstood man, but he would have naturally resisted the equally plausible view that a proper appreciation of his work shows it to be much more superficial than many have supposed.

Spencer came from the ranks of provincial parsons, doctors, solicitors, and engineers, self-taught men of comfortable and occasionally independent means, subscribers to reviews, energetic organisers of small philosophical and scientific societies, radicals in their religion and politics, men who contributed so much to English provincial life in the first two quarters of the nineteenth century. He was born in Derby in 1820 and educated by his father and an uncle in scientific rather than humane subjects. He worked for a time as a railway engineer (in that extraordinary burst of enterprise whose spirit was so well caught in his friend Marian Evan's novel *Middlemarch*), moved to the *Economist* as an assistant editor and then, made independent by a legacy from his uncle in 1853, devoted himself with characteristically Victorian single-mindedness to his writing until he died in 1903. Except in those who mistook him, he seems always to have inspired respect rather than enthusiasm. Towards the end of the century he became in England a living monument to vanished assumptions.

Despite their prolonged although never unfriendly dispute, these assumptions were in general not dissimilar to Mill's. Spencer set them out first in 1850, in *Social Statics*. They were that the utilitarian commitment to the empirical and moral principle of the pursuit of pleasure quite overlooked the variability of mankind and its accordingly multifarious ideas of what happiness was (although as he proudly explained to Leslie Stephen in 1899, he had hardly read a utilitarian word); and that a thoroughly determinist account could be given of human nature and the consequently proper morality. He was not as exercised as Mill by the problem of defending the compatibility of determinism and free will. He had his own easy solution which revealed a teleology to which Mill, always more judicious, never subscribed. 'Assuming happiness is an end to be achieved', *Social Statics* was to show it 'as dependent on fulfilment of conditions; conformity to which constitutes morality...and a cardinal doctrine...is that Man has been, and is, undergoing modifications of nature which fit him for the social state, by making conformity to these conditions spontaneous'. Fit for the social state, which it was the purpose of the *Statics* to describe, man will be free, and will have been caused, indeed pre-determined, to be so, for evils 'perpetually [tend] to disappear' and so 'surely must man become perfect'. Spencer also directly recalled his evangelical roots by invoking an additional authority. 'God wills man's happiness. Man's happiness can only be produced by the exercise of his faculties. Then God wills that he should exercise his faculties. But to exercise his faculties he must have liberty to do all that his faculties naturally impel him to do. Then God intends he should have that liberty'. Mill had no place for such a brisk and cheerful deism.

Spencer himself soon abandoned it. In the early 1850s, he concentrated more upon his still fragmentary notions of evolution, a doctrine he first enunciated in something approaching the final form he was to give it in the early 1860s in his *First Principles*. In the meantime, however, as soon as he was able to leave the *Economist* and devote himself as far as his already uncertain health would allow to writing, he published some *Principles of Psychology*. He conceded in the preface to this book that 'as may be supposed, the analytical divisions are much less readable than the synthetic ones'. They are of little interest here. What is, is the synthesis which, with his commitment to universal causality and to a teleology, and his hostility to the arguments (although sympathy with the spirit) of Benthamite utilitarianism, is the bedrock of his system. The most remarkable and quintessentially Spencerian aspect of this synthesis was its attempt to secure as a scientific conclusion the premise on which it rested. 'It is a dominant characteristic of Intelligence', he wrote in agreement with Comte (whom he had not then read) and with Mill (whom he had), 'that its processes, which, as originally performed, were not accompanied with a consciousness of the manner in which they were performed, or of their adaptation to the ends achieved, become eventually both conscious and systematic'. Consider, he continued (parting with both men), 'the canon of belief . . . to be used in testing every premise, every step in an argument, every conclusion which men have from the beginning used to these ends; that beliefs which are proved by the inconceivableness of their negations to invariably exist' are true. The step that remained to be taken 'was simply to apply this test consciously and systematically'. 'It will also be seen that the like may be said of the second canon . . . viz. that the certainty of any conclusion is great, in proportion as the assumptions of the Universal Postulate made in reaching it are few'. The *Psychology* began with the Universal Postulate, defended against what Spencer saw as the errors of others; and it was with the Universal Postulate that it ended, not as a methodological point but as a substantive one, the conclusion, with the second canon, of his analysis of the progress of intelligence.

Mill always respected Spencer, but more than either Spencer's initial theism, or his teleology, the Universal Postulate divided them. To Mill, Spencer seemed in his subscription to 'obviously indisputable' propositions to have embraced Whewell and so precisely the more common-sense philosophy of science (as we might now call it) that Mill's *Logic of the Moral Sciences* was directed against. But Mill did realise that unlike others Spencer had no wish to use such a philosophy in the service of a mystical and conservative reaction to rational, scientific progress. Quite the contrary. In spirit, if not method, they were united. Nevertheless, Spencer took his second canon perfectly seriously, and the single assumption he thereby arrived at, carrying the principle of parsimony to its farthest extreme and so disdaining a properly empiricist foundation, was the one from which he claimed to derive his various substantive theories. It seems to have come upon him rather suddenly. 'Within the last ten days', he wrote to his father on the 9 January 1858, 'my ideas on various matters have suddenly crystallised into a complete whole. Many things which were before lying separate have fallen into their places as harmonious parts of a system that admits of logical development from the simplest general principles'. Setting these principles down was not easy. To stave off 'cerebral congestion', he even at one point took his amanuensis on to the pond in Regent's Park so that he could alternately row for five minutes and dictate for fifteen. Nevertheless, the *First Principles* soon began serially to appear.

In them, he pursued three main arguments. The first was an attempt at the very height of the debate about the matter to show that science and religion could be reconciled by a clear demarcation between the knowable and the unknowable. 'Is it not possible', he asked, 'that there is a mode of being as much transcending Intelligence and Will, as these transcend mechanical motion? Doubtless we are totally unable to imagine any such higher mode of being. But this is not', he continues, very much against the more uncompromising agnostics of the time, 'a reason for questioning its existence; it is rather the reverse. Have we not seen how utterly unable our minds are to form even an approach to a conception of that which underlies all phenomena? Is it not proved that we fail because of the incompetency of the Conditioned to grasp the Unconditioned? Does it not follow that the Ultimate Cause cannot in any respect be conceived because it is in every respect greater than can be conceived? And may we not rightly refrain from assigning to it any attributes whatever, on the ground that such attributes, derived as they must be from our own natures, are not elevations but degradations?' Spencer could not tolerate an unexamined premise and it is perfectly comprehensible that he should directly have faced the most hotly-disputed intellectual question of the day. The logical difficulties of his doctrine of the Unknowable, to which he returned after they had been revealed by others, are both more obvious and less interesting than the historical fact that he set himself against the view that an interventionist account of the world could replace a causal one, and instead consigned the Unknowable merely to the first place in a scientifically accessible causal chain.

The second and more extended argument in *First Principles* was for the general properties of this chain, and the third for its motor. The chain itself he chose to call 'evolution', and in so doing, he introduced the notion that was to pervade putatively scientific accounts of social development until the First World War. 'Evolution', he had decided by 1900 (although the decision is clear even in the first edition), 'is an integration of matter and concomitant dissipation of motion; during which the matter passes from an indefinite, incoherent homogeneity to a definite, coherent heterogeneity; and during which the retained motion undergoes a parallel transformation'. This described the chain of events. 'Manifestly', Spencer continued, 'this community of result implies community of cause'. Perhaps though, he wondered somewhat rhetorically, 'it may be that of the cause no account can be given further than that the Unknowable is manifested to us after this mode'. No so, 'Analogy suggests' that just as Kepler's laws could be shown to be special cases of the 'law of gravitation', 'so it may be possible to interpret the foregoing empirical generalisations as necessary consequences of some deeper law'. Indeed, he said, revealing his life plan, 'unless we succeed in finding a *rationale* of this universal metamorphosis, we obviously fall short of that completely unified knowledge constituting Philosophy'. He elaborated thus. 'It has to be shown that the re-distribution of matter and motion, *must* everywhere take place in those ways, and produce those traits which celestial bodies, organisms, societies, alike display. And it has to be shown that in the universality of process, is traceable the same necessity which we find in each simplest movement around us, down to the accelerated fall of a stone or the recurrent beat of a harp-string. In other words, the phenomena of Evolution have to be deduced from the Persistence of Force'. This was Spencer's universal motor.

The idea was essentially very simple. Force persists through time. In so doing it constantly bombards things. This constant bombardment, moreover, is always a differential one, affecting one part of the thing more than another. Therefore, homogeneity is an unstable state, and the tendency is inexorably toward the differentiation of things, of matter into more definite forms, of organisms into species, of societies into more differential structures, and of 'motions' into more specialised functions. And the consequent heterogeneity tends not to chaos but towards a systematic, equilibrating order. By the time he came to revise the final edition of *First Principles*, however, Spencer was clearly perplexed by the implications for his cosmology of the discovery and generalisation of the fact that in any system energy tends to become dissipated and order to dissolve, the second law of thermodynamics, a generalisation that seemed to him (as it has seemed to others) to controvert his thesis. He duly retreated to the empty and pathetic assertion that 'phenomena going on everywhere are parts of the general process of Evolution, save where they are parts of the reverse process of Dissolution'.

Spencer's perplexity, however, did not discourage him from embarking upon an extended account of the evolution of his own ideas, and in this obsessively meticulous *Autobiography* he provided a clear account of their origin. In his early manhood, he recalled, he had gradually abandoned his belief in special creation, and inclined towards 'a belief in evolution at large' that was 'doubtless...then latent'. As he quite reasonably said, 'anyone who, abandoning the supernaturalism of theology, accepts in full the naturalism of science, tacitly asserts that all things as they now exist have been evolved'. 'The doctrine of the universality of natural causation, has for its inevitable corollary the doctrine that the Universe and all things in it have reached their present forms through successive stages physically necessitated'. 'No such corollary, however', he continued, with characteristic seriousness, 'had....made itself manifest to me [in the late 1830s]; and I cannot recall any definite belief then entertained about the origin of the Universe or the origin of living things. The first pronounced convictions on these matters were...due to the reading of Lyell's *Principles of Geology* when I was twenty: his arguments against Lamarck producing in me a partial acceptance of Lamarck's view'. Spencer's recollection of having but partially accepted Lamarck was no doubt coloured by an interval of sixty years and the increasing acceptance during this time of Darwin's theory of natural selection, for it was by Lamarck's views that Spencer remained convinced, as indeed in a curious way did Darwin himself. Subsequent arguments have tended to vindicate Darwin's own thesis in *The Origin of Species* 'that individuals having any advantage, however slight, over others, have the best chance of surviving and of procreating their kind', and Darwin is frequently invoked against Spencer as an instance of the superiority of careful observation and limited inference over extravagant generalisation. But this retrospective judgement overlooks Darwin's own adherence to the rhetoric of 'great laws' and his puzzle over the causes of the variation from which he believed nature selected. Lamarck's vaguer view that acquired characteristics were inherited allowed a wide variety of environmentalist and hereditarian positions and for those, like Spencer, who were interested more in grand designs than in the details of natural history, it could better be absorbed into a cosmological conception of the mutual dependences of 'natural' phenomena and their environments over time. As Spencer went on to explain in the *Autobiography*, he early added to Lamarck the conclusion of von Baer, a German anatomist, that organisms become more complex and differentiated from youth to maturity and from generation to generation, and the popular notion of the 'conservation of force', and so arrived by the late 1850s at the synthetic system he expounded in the *First Principles*. In an historically exact but analytically misleading sense, Spencer did derive his synthesis from a biological theory. But to say so overlooks, first, his prior disposition to system and second, his own insistence that the synthesis came not from the extrapolation of biological evolution to other forms but rather from the deduction of all particular evolutions from a Universal Postulate about the progress of the cosmos as a whole.

Spencer set out his sociological ambitions in a series of articles in the *Contemporary Review* in the early 1870s, almost immediately published as *The Study of Sociology* in 1873. He had with help begun to assemble a vast list of facts about various societies, and these appeared from 1874 as *Descriptive Sociology*. Between 1876 and 1896 he published his monumental *Principles*. Altogether, it was an extraordinary amount of matter; and it was very confused. Spencer's central intellectual failing, which was not his alone but the failure of all those eighteenth- and nineteenth-century thinkers who asserted the processual uniformity of the Universe, was to run together as one developmental processes that appear now to be quite different. He seems always, for instance, to have thought that the development of kinds of organisms over time (what we now call 'evolution') and the development of one organism over its lifetime were aspects of the same process. Similarly, he appears to have equated the succession of types of society over time with the internal development of single societies. His general thesis, which has since passed in one form or another into the largely vacuous currency of much modern sociological generalisation, was that over time societies exhibited a differentiation of structures and a corresponding internal specialisation of functions. Earlier societies which, Spencer suggested after a conventional contemporary distinction, could be called 'militant', were characterised by a relative lack of differentiation in the face of a hostile environment: a hard exterior and an undifferentiated interior, like the most primitive organisms. Later societies, 'industrial' ones, were like the higher organisms characterised rather by a relatively great internal differentiation, a differentiation that economists had called the 'division of labour'. The transformation from the one to the other, he believed, was facilitated by an increase in 'mass' operating as a predisposition toward individuation. The conjunction of mechanical causality and teleology is plain. Spencer was not quite so resistant to facts as some of his contemporary critics said. He did in the 1870s and 1880s become perceptibly less certain about the steadiness of the evolution and more willing pessimistically to concede that there could be temporary reverses. He was forced to conclude that structurally complex 'militant' societies, like those in pre-Imperial Australia, could only be explained as regressions from more advanced forms. Nevertheless, he no more abandoned his general sociological scheme than he did the Universal Postulate from which, like his biology, his psychology and his ethics, it derived.

Quite apart from his elision of various sorts of development, however, Spencer was badly confused about three other aspects of social evolution: the place of competition, the significance of specialised political institutions, and the analogy between organisms and societies. He is often recalled as an enthusiast for the benefits of social struggle, and although this is certainly not true, it is unclear just what importance he did place on it. Critics often point to an early essay on 'A principle of population', to which he himself often drew attention (while regretting that he had not seen in Malthus the engine of generational succession that Darwin saw), and in which he argued that an increase in numbers favours the survival of the more adaptable through their successful competition with the less so. They point also to his phrase 'the survival of the fittest', and to his reception in the United States. But this is selective perception. The early essay was only an early essay, and not as significant to Spencer himself at the time as others. He was largely misunderstood in America. In the *Principles of Sociology*, where one would expect to find many references to struggle and competition, there are in fact extremely few. And where he did discuss them, he anyway contradicted himself. At one point, for instance, he talked of competition within even more advanced societies stimulating activity and individuation (and so evolution and progress), at another of competition between societies increasing the mass and heterogeneity of the victor and so doing the same, and at yet another of the decline of such struggles with the evolution of 'civilised' societies. Indeed, Spencer was required to contradict himself at some point, since he wished to argue both that competition had facilitated evolution to the present and that the future would be marked by altruism as the individuated parts recognised their dependence upon each other in the complex structure of the fully 'industrial' society. Wallace rightly doubted after reading *The Data of Ethics* 'that evolution alone...can account for the development of advanced and enthusiastic altruism'.

Other contemporary critics pointed to Spencer's political ambiguity. It was clear that he abhorred all forms of regulation and wished individuals to have as much liberty as was consistent with their not inhibiting the freedom of others. Yet he also argued that 'a compound regulating system characterised by a dominant centre and subordinate centres, is accompanied, in both individual organisms and social organisms, by increasing size and complexity of the dominant centre'. Individual organisms develop elaborate brains; societies, the analogy seems to imply, develop politics. To preserve his political preferences, however, Spencer simply overrode this inference from the Universal Postulate by asserting that in the industrial societies (which were the larger and more differentiated ones) 'a corporate action subordinating individual actions by uniting them in a joint effort is no longer requisite'. He appeared to think (although the argument is decidedly opaque) that each individual's spontaneous recognition of what his individuality owed to the preservation of the individuality of others would be adequate to social order, a belief contradicted by several of his strictures about the exchange of one kind of slavery for another by the lower class.

This second confusion points to a third. This arises out of Spencer's relentless comparison between the structure, the functioning and the evolution of individual organisms and of societies. Indeed, the very terms 'structure' and 'function', which later became so popular in American sociology and British social anthropology, almost certainly derive from this comparison. The scholastic confusion that they have caused, however, at least in sociology, is of a different kind from that induced by Spencer. For him, the comparison was not merely metaphorical, as it has often been called, too gently, an 'analogy', but direct. All phenomena followed the same course of development, as a result ultimately of the same cause, the constant persistence of force. This meant, Spencer was bound to suggest, indeed to assert, that they had therefore to be described in identical terms. In so doing, he was unable to steer a course between empty absurdity and self-contradiction. He was committed either to quite unilluminating and really rather comic parallels, such as that between nerves and telegraph wires, or to a tangle of exceptions which made nonsense of the comparison and the theory upon which it rested, such as the fact that whereas individual organisms had one centre of consciousness societies had as many as they had members. The resultant nonsense was not, of course, surprising, for it derived directly from his assuming that some superficial similarities between the two kinds of phenomena, such as those displayed in their respective evolutions, were indications of more fundamental ones, whereas the truth seems to be that the similarities were indeed superficial, the fundamental fact being rather of the striking differences between them. In short, this confusion, like the previous two, was but a special case of his basic muddle about evolution in general.

If, in the 1850s and 1860s, Spencer expressed what some of his contemporaries would have liked to believe and what others found it unnecessary to, by the 1880s he was in saying the same things expressing what the first group could no longer accept, what the second had come definitely to reject, and yet what a new if somewhat heterogeneous third group was coming gradually to realise it required.

Among the first was T. H. Huxley, an ardent evolutionist who while always sympathetic to Spencer's project ('The Universe is one and the same throughout', he once obscurely proclaimed) did not himself set about matching it with a similar one of his own until the end of the century. Then, without mentioning his old friend's name, he attacked him. He did so in a much-discussed lecture in Oxford in 1893, the point of which was that 'the ethical progress of society depends, not on imitating the cosmic process, still less in running away from it, but in combating it'. Social progress, Huxley said, has as its end not 'the survival of those who may happen to be the fittest, in respect of the whole of the conditions which exist, but of those who are ethically the best'. And so as to dispel any suspicion that he was merely proposing a variant of evolutionary moral naturalism, he explained that 'the practice of that which is ethically best, what we call goodness or virtue...is directed, not so much to the survival of the fittest, as to the fitting of as many as possible to survive'. This lecture, Spencer wrote angrily to an acquaintance, 'is pervaded by the ridiculous assumption that, in its application to the organic world, [the general doctrine of evolution] is limited to the struggle for existence among individuals under its ferocious aspects, and has nothing to do with the development of social organisation, or the modifications of the human mind that take place in the course of that organisation...[it] is practically a going back to the old theological notions, which put Man and Nature in antithesis'. He published a retort, a paper on 'Evolutionary Ethics', in which he declared that he found it strange that Huxley, who had had his work beside him, should not have realised its point. Yet Huxley's interpretation of this work, given Spencer's confusion about the status of competition and the feebleness of his argument for the necessary emergence of altruism, was not wholly unreasonable, and is also historically interesting, for it was the way in which Spencer was interpreted by virtually everyone whether, like Huxley, they had read him or not. It was partly the result of the impression his theory gave. But it was also in part the result of a popular equation, fostered by the ambiguities of both men, between his views and those of

Darwin, who, while usually resisting moral inferences, did put competition at the centre.

Huxley, Wallace and others, biologists who were interested in Spencer's theoretical ideas if resistant to what they took as their ethical corollaries, were perhaps the most wounding of Spencer's later critics. But a second group, of men who had no direct interest in natural history and biological evolution but were more concerned directly with the progress of individualist, laissez-faire society, was larger, and shifted from a tacit approval of what were taken to be Spencer's intentions in the 1850s and 1860s to a decisive rejection of them, unchanged as they were, in the 1880s and 1890s. In the middle of the century it was still possible to believe in good faith, and, without too evident a contradiction with the facts, that liberal capitalism was pregnant with moral goodness. After the recession in the 1870s, however, and the accumulating evidence of the horrors of urban industrial life and their articulation by the working classes themselves, all but the most insensitive considered there to have been a miscarriage. 'It is the sense of helplessness that tries everyone' said Charles Booth. Those, therefore, committed to progress, the self-consciously enlightened intelligentsia, saw such progress lying not so much in rational intervention to maintain the system as in rational intervention to control it and ameliorate its effects. Few of Spencer's earlier contemporaries in fact survived into the later 1880s and 1890s, for Spencer was even by then an unusually old man, and this second group consisted less of the same individuals who had tacitly approved his purposes than of their moral, intellectual and even literal descendants, of people such as his old friend Potter's daughter Beatrice who, with her husband Sidney Webb fairly typified this movement towards the end of the century. The various ideologies of liberal laissez-faire, including not only what was taken to be Spencer's notion of social evolution but also the prevalent political economy were seen to fail 'from want of reality', to rest upon 'a series of assumptions very imperfectly connected with the observed facts of life'. They were thus discarded in favour of schemes for the more active rational administration of progressive (but still gradual) reform. Such schemes entailed a more active role for government, a role the government had already been assuming even if by default, yet Spencer had insisted that the 'form of society towards which we are progressing I hold to be one in which the government will be reduced to the smallest amount possible'.

This particular rejection of Spencer's conclusions did nevertheless retain his spirit and that of most nineteenth-century English social analysis, a commitment to what were taken to be scientific procedures, to what was then and is even more now loosely referred to as 'positivism'. But another, of similar moral and political intent, did not. For there was also what has sometimes been called a revival, but which was really an introduction, of Idealist conceptions into social and especially political analysis, conceptions which in England had hitherto been fashionable only among literary men. The dissolving futility of classical political economy, the repugnance at Spencer's and other's apparent justification for competition, a conviction that the empirical and rationalist tradition was epistemologically and morally bankrupt, as well as a reaction especially in Oxford to orthodox theology, all stimulated an interest in Idealist philosophy in general and in Kant and Hegel in particular. Spencer misdiagnosed its attraction. Writing to various correspondents at the turn of the century about this 'old world nonsense' as he called it, so 'dramatically opposed' to his own views, he asserted that it was 'really the last refuge of the so-called orthodox'. 'As I have somewhere said', he wrote, 'what could be a better defence for incredible dogmas than behind unthinkable propositions'. In fact, Kant's ethics and Hegel too were deployed in England and Scotland in arguments for the proper purposes and actions of a progressive state in the name not of reaction, but of liberal reform.

A third reaction to Spencer, however, also based upon what he would have regarded, and did, as a misunderstanding of both his theory of social evolution and his ethics, was enthusiastic rather than critical. For some, like Francis Galton and Karl Pearson, the general doctrine of survival through competition indicated that those whose misery was being widely proclaimed towards the end of the century were manifestly unfit, and despite his protestations some of Spencer's own remarks clearly committed him to this view too. 'Give educational facilities to all, give a minimum wage with free medical advice', Pearson warned, 'and...you will find that the unemployables, the degenerates and the physical and mental weaklings increase rather than decrease'. 'The quality of a society is lowered morally and intellectually', Spencer had written thirty-six years before, 'by artificially preserving those who are least able to take care of themselves and to behave well'. For others, like Ferri, Marx and Engels, the doctrine of progress through competition appeared to provide a more general and solidly scientific basis for the socialist programme of class conflict. For others again, a collectivised competition could be generalised still further to explain and justify international predation in general and imperialist expansion in particular.

The filiation of these views in the years between 1870 and 1914 is thus quite bewildering. 'Social Darwinism' owed little to Darwin himself, who had largely restricted his remarks to the development of species and who anyway partially retreated from a faith in the differential natural selection of variations to a belief in the inheritance of acquired characteristics. Spencer, 'our great philosopher' as Darwin had called him, popularised the term 'evolution' and asserted the ultimate necessity of altruism in social life, said that natural selection was an inadequate explanation of evolution, yet partly because of his own muddles was taken to be lauding competitive struggle. By the turn of the century, in fact, both men had become little more than symbols for a set of often inconsistent and always very general theories which were used either to explain and justify a vast array of natural and social phenomena or to provide a large if ill-defined target for those whose interests were often close to those of others who were defending some version of evolutionary doctrine. 'Evolution', indeed, came to mean as much and as little as 'liberalism'.

It was from the second of the three sorts of reaction to Spencer and what he was supposed to stand for that emerged what came to be taken as 'sociology' in Britain. The first reaction was essentially defensive, and after the criticisms of Huxley and Wallace in the 1890s and the advances in biology itself immediately after 1900 the biologists devoted themselves to species other than man. The third group, with the exception of the self-styled eugenicists like Galton and Pearson, either had a no more than incidental interest in evolution as the English saw it or soon lost interest in anything that was then seen as the 'progress' of English society itself. The eugenicists were indeed the most coherent of the several sets of contributors to the establishment of a self-styled 'sociology' in Britain, but their effect on the subject (except as objects of hostility to the more compassionate, those of 'maudlin sentiment' as Pearson called them) was a delayed one. In their advocacy of a progressive interventionist state which would alleviate the injustices and miseries of industrial capitalism, the Webbs were not untypical of the second reaction. But they devoted their formidable energies to the Fabian Society, the Labour Party, their new London School of Economics and other practical activities. As their later injunctions to social inquiry revealed, they would anyway have had little to contribute, for they inhabited a pragmatic vacuum between bland liberal confidence and properly socialist theories. Nevertheless it was at the London School of Economics that the first British chair of sociology was established in 1906, and its first occupant, Hobhouse, defines the second reaction. Indeed, his interest lies less in the simple fact that he was the first formally to profess sociology in Britain than in the fact that what led him slightly unwillingly and certainly unintentionally to his chair was the intellectual pursuit of a moral purpose that was generally shared by many sensitive liberal thinking men but which led very few of them to sociology.

Hobhouse began as a classical scholar in Oxford, where it was said at the time that 'it is an article of faith with nine out of ten of us that the world is constantly growing better and happier, and that the future is sure to see the dawn of a general social prosperity'. Hobhouse, however, could not take progress for granted. 'If progress means anything which human beings can value or desire', he wrote in 1913, reviewing his opinions, 'it depends on the suppression of the struggle for existence, and the substitution in one form or another of social co-operation'. Describing 'The Career of Fabianism' in 1907, he argued that 'the policy of a progressive state' would be to use its 'corporate power to support, strengthen and enrich individual life by affording that security and those opportunities which lie beyond the reasonable limits of individual self-help'. Put so, his views would seem essentially similar to Huxley's in *Evolution and Ethics*. But where Huxley, like Wallace and, had he thought much about it, Darwin too, separated 'cosmic' and 'social' evolution, Hobhouse, like Spencer, sought to unite them. The old man's project, Hobhouse thought, was admirable. It was its outcome that was morally so appalling. 'I was convinced', he remembered, 'that a philosophy that was to possess more than a speculative interest must rest on a synthesis of experience as interpreted by science, and that to such a synthesis the general conception of evolution offered a key. The immediate question was whether it was possible to overcome the contradictions of that theory as applied to human progress.'

The academically most accessible philosophy to Hobhouse was the adapted Idealism of T. H. Green and his circle in Oxford. 'This method, however, to speak quite frankly and personally', Hobhouse said, he 'could never accept'. To conceive of everything as 'spiritual', as he put it, emptied this morally valuable term of all meaning, and he was sure that 'the philosophy of the future must make its account with science'. Hobhouse was not sceptical of grand systems, but was critical of attempts to derive them exclusively either from experience or from metaphysical preconceptions. 'In this respect', he said, 'Mr Spencer, whatever the defects of his method, seems to have been justly inspired'. Nevertheless, he continued, 'it seemed to me that, details apart, the Hegelian conception of development possessed a certain rough, empirical value. There were grades or degrees of consciousness and self-consciousness, and as personal self-consciousness was distinctive of man, so there was a higher self-consciousness of the human spirit, which would represent the term of the present stage in development. Further, if this conception was interpreted in terms of experience, it indicated a point of union, where one would not expect to find it, between the Idealistic and Positivistic philosophy. This higher self-consciousness would be the Humanity of Positivism, regulating its own life and controlling its own development'. In short, 'the factor of consciousness...would influence the course of development', something which Spencer had always denied (although it can be argued that his theory of altruism required him to believe it). Lévi-Strauss has said that in any society at any time there is a variety of often inconsistent notions, combinations of which are selected according to the prevailing purposes of its members. Hobhouse's theory was just such a *bricolage*. Out of the morally serious upper middle-class English air he took empiricism and Idealism, the assumption of pre-determined progress and a belief in benevolent intervention, the general English notions of biological evolution and a Comtean conviction in positive altruism and put them together in the service of a liberal socialist ideal. It is not surprising that against the intellectual muddle of the new Sociological Society, he urged a view of sociology as the truly synthetic social science. Nor is it surprising that his own synthesis was always bland and frequently hollow.

He began by making observations of animals, to assess their mental operations. He published his conclusions in *Mind in Evolution,* and one cannot help but feel that like Spencer before him (whose empirical work, however, was limited to cursory geological inspections on Scottish walks), they prefigured the analysis. They were that 'mind' evolved from being driven by instinct to being driven by reason, as he put it later, that 'it was possible to conceive of evolution in general as a blind and even brutal process, dependent on the anarchical struggle for existence, but to maintain that in the course of this struggle there had arisen among other species one which owed its survival to mind'. Hobhouse was well aware of the difficulty of making inferences from animal experiments, of the absence of any need to tie, indeed the danger of tying, his account to 'any theory of the ultimate nature of reality', and of the problems involved in tracing an historical, let alone a causal, path from the existence of mind, of reason and self-consciousness to the existence of collective altruism. This last difficulty, however, the most obviously worrying one for his moral purposes, he resolved with the dawning conviction that 'by mechanical reasoning from a purely empirical starting point a candid thinker would be led to admit an element of purpose in the system of Reality', a conviction that belied his respect for observation and revealed a closer affinity with his more optimistic Oxford associates than he himself conceded. The complete circularity into which it led him is most evident at the end of a later 'essay towards a philosophy of evolution', as he called it, *Development and Purpose,* his reply to Spencer's *First Principles.* 'At the highest known phase of development', he wrote, 'we say that the mind comes to realise itself, that is, to realise what are the fundamentals of its structure as it has been all along. In this new consciousness it discovers a unity underlying the differences of life and a plan containing the possibilities of a future self-realisation. It does not invent this unity and this plan. It discovers them. It finds that they are already there, and have been among the conditions operating to determine its growth from the earliest stages. Its own purposeful activity is merely the continued operation of these conditions completed by the unifying link of the consciousness of their significance.' Unlike Hegel, Hobhouse had no philosophical time for the importance of contradiction in his 'phenomenology' (as he also called it), for he had no moral time for conflict. But like the German, he did have to presuppose the ends of his history in order to write it at all.

The sociology that Hobhouse developed from his philosophy shows its origins very plainly. 'The factor of consciousness...would influence the course of development' he had written in 1913, and in his final book in 1924, *Social Development*, he tried to show that it had. This was not remarkable. What was was his only slightly faltering optimism after an awful war and in conditions of distrust and conflict that had demolished almost everyone's confidence. 'The actual structure of society', he wrote, somewhat blandly, 'is conceived as the tentative or partial solution of the problem of living together under the conditions of the environment, and Development as the effort after a better solution'. 'Fundamental institutions', he continued, more interestingly, '...exhibit a development corresponding in vital points with the development of thought', so that 'the development of society in its completeness is conditioned by the available fund of moral wisdom'. The thesis depended upon a correlation between social and intellectual development, and Hobhouse failed to convince. He clearly wanted to show that the 'efficient organisation of a great community resting on free acceptance and energetic support by the ordinary citizen', the indicator of 'high moral and mental endowment', was becoming more common, yet was forced to concede that liberty had frequently been more secure in older and smaller societies, and was driven shakily to argue that the depressing facts of post-war Europe were but temporary reversals.

In their conviction that progress lay in increasing altruism, later nineteenth-century English liberals were thereby assuming that it lay in a society comprised largely of people like themselves. This raised a difficulty. The supersession of the appalling consequences of laissez-faire had to be shown to be a gradual, natural, 'evolutionary' one, for the alternative, of a more sudden, revolutionary change, would almost certainly entail the supersession of the presently small but crucial altruistic class itself, of themselves. Yet the change from egoism to altruism was clearly a qualitative one, and evolutionary rather than revolutionary arguments for such changes seemed hard to secure. Spencer had inadvertently made this very clear. Despite his later protestations to Huxley and others, he had completely failed in what he himself regarded as his central moral purpose, to show the evolutionary necessity of altruism. Indeed, the failure was so total as to make it seem to most that he was commending competition and struggle instead. Revolutionary socialists, had the liberals read them, would have made the difficulty even clearer. But in England they did not, not least because there were almost none of them to read.

Hobhouse's response to the difficulty was an unusual one. It lay in facing it. More usual were one or other of two sorts of escape, one purely intellectual, the other more practical. The first was simply, but as it transpired effectively, to denounce the possibility of there being a 'natural' and so scientifically accessible demonstration of moral right at all. In the course of a withering and quite justified attack on what he regarded, in 1885, as three representative sociologists, Comte, Spencer and a German evolutionary socialist Schäffle, a Cambridge philosopher, Sidgwick, accused them all of finding in the tendencies of social life the evolution of that which they variously wished to see. It was plain, Sidgwick argued in the plainest language, that the putative science was in a very rudimentary state, for there was so little agreement about what it showed, and it was plain too that all three men erroneously believed that if there were agreement on what would happen there was bound to be agreement on what should happen, which was logically fallacious. Their opinions had fatally infused their work and the work itself was quite falsely held to justify them. The more formal attack on the so-called 'naturalistic fallacy', however, came several years later, again from Cambridge, but from G. E. Moore, who had Mill, Spencer and Green particularly in mind. Moore simply argued that there were no grounds for believing that what ought to be bore any logical relation to what was, an argument which perhaps rested upon an excessively optimistic view of the possibility of dispassionately discovering what the facts actually were, revealing a confidence in 'science' even among those decrying its place in moral discourse, but an argument that at once had vigorous support. It led to the view that moral statements were merely the expression of intuition or taste. But it is also possible to infer from the argument against naturalism that if moral argument owes nothing to science and moral progress owes nothing to a determined course of natural evolution then they must both depend instead upon the exercise of Will. This inference, not made directly from Moore, but arising in people in the same moral culture as Moore's from the disillusion with political economy and schemes like Spencer's, when combined with a diffuse belief in progress, had made a way for Idealism and an anglicised Hegel. Hence the circle into which the young Hobhouse had moved at Oxford, but whose arguments he refused to accept.

The second avenue of escape from the difficulty of providing a plausible 'natural' explanation for the development of altruism lay in simply not bothering to. This was a peculiarly English possibility. By comparison with the situation in other European countries, and in France and Germany in particular, political power was not in the hands of the illiberal. Liberal reformers were not associated with anticlericalism and lack of patriotic loyalty and entangled in unstable administrations, as in France. Nor did they find no avenue of access between an old and intransigent nobility, a threateningly strong socialist party and an active, industrialising State and its bureaucracy, as in Germany. Instead, they appeared to be able to articulate the distresses of a relatively incoherent working class to a receptive élite, from whose ranks many of them came, without really threatening any powerful vested interest at all. They were taken, as in fact they were, to be committed to the preservation and improvement of the *status quo* rather than to its destruction or deflection. In particular, they found a State willing to listen to proposals for more active intervention. Accordingly, they concentrated less upon grand designs for wholesale reform, the resort of the impotent, and more upon particular practical proposals. The concern which they expressed and did much to articulate and transmit had the effect of rapidly increasing the extent of State administration and of doubling public expenditure on social services between 1905, when the liberals first took office, and 1914. Hobhouse, who had written leaders for several years for the liberal *Manchester Guardian*, was sympathetic to them.

Between the dogmatic anti-naturalism of the moralists and the pragmatic energies of the reformers, therefore, there was virtually no room for sociology as the architectonic science of social progress. To the first it was absurd, and to the second, unnecessary. In directly facing the difficulty of providing a comprehensive natural account of the evolution of altruism, Hobhouse was thus assured of virtually no audience at all, and since, as he himself somewhat belatedly came to realise, such a purpose essentially defined the task of general sociology, it is easy to understand why the subject itself excited little interest in England. The Sociological Society, to which Hobhouse devoted a good deal of energy from its establishment in 1903 and which under other conditions might (like its analogues in France and Germany) have become a real intellectual and moral force, merely comprised a small group of rich visionaries, academic eccentrics and the (not wholly welcome) social biologists. The London School of Economics, in committing itself to a grand, evolutionary conception of the subject, committed the subject itself to lasting intellectual oblivion in England, the object of indifference and even scorn. The lack of attention to Hobhouse was not due to his failure to produce anything other than a wholly bland and largely circular account of the evolution of altruism. It was due rather to a relative lack of interest in the attempt. In England by 1914, Spencer was not merely dead, but doubly buried.

6

History resolved by laws III

TO SAY THAT the history of sociology in Europe to 1870 or so is the history of attempts to secure a comprehensive morality and a moral polity upon the principles of social life, rather than upon theological precept or an abstracted human nature, is correct, but of course far too simple. Unqualified, it suggests that neither religious tradition nor *a priori* notions of man played any part, whereas it is the parts that they did play, and their connection to various social and political circumstances and purposes, which explains both the nature of each attempt and the differences between them. As I have already suggested, the most striking difference is that between English and German thinkers, both insisting upon the constructive powers of the individual yet producing what have come to be seen, as they were at the time, as an asocial individualism in the one case and an anti-individual holism in the other. The common insistence doubtless derives from the Protestantism that they shared, the assumption of the spiritual, moral and cognitive autonomy of the individual. The difference, however, derives from the wholly opposed social and political conditions in the two countries. England was established, Germany was not. In the one, the social structure was so clear that it could be taken for granted. In the other there was not merely no clear structure but really no structure at all, simply a pathetic chaos of local arrangements. In the one, the individual had to define and defend himself against the society. In the other, he had to define the society. In the one, he had to realise the Protestant promise of autonomy against other men. In the other, he could only realise it through other men. In the one, he was constituted by his experience of others and in that sense determined by them. In the other, he had as it were to constitute himself from within. The irony of these differences was that in England the force of society was so pervasive that it went largely unremarked, whereas in Germany it was so feeble that it became the object of all attention. To describe the intellectual outcome of the one as asocial individualism and of the other as anti-individualistic holism is almost entirely to misdescribe the presuppositions and motives of both.

After 1870, however, circumstances changed in each country and with them, the motives of the social philosophers. As I have already said, sensitive liberal Englishmen found it more and more difficult to take their society for granted, rejected the philosophies that rested upon the assumption that one could, and began to consider intervention. In so doing, some of them turned to earlier German ideas. Germans, on the other hand, were rather suddenly confronted with a coherent and energetic Reich. The problem of constructing a society had been solved, but by von Bismarck, not the liberal intellectuals; and in trying to come to terms with the new order, some of these men turned perceptibly if temporarily to some of the assumptions that the English themselves were beginning to qualify.

Bismarck's unification of Germany in 1871 was facilitated by the Prussian victory in the war with France. One would expect France's defeat to have had as profound an impact upon that country as victory did on Prussia and through it, on Germany as a whole. Yet although in one sense it did, in another it did not. There is no doubt that 1871 was a disastrous year for France. The emperor had surrendered to the Prussians at Sedan in September 1870. At once, a crowd invaded the Chamber in Paris and declared a 'Government of National Defence' under the hastily improvised leadership of some republican deputies. There was no opposition. Paris was as delighted at the overthrow of a regime it detested as it was hostile to German occupation. Unable to halt the German advance to the city, however, the new government decided to defend it. Paris was besieged for four months, but at the end of January 1871, entirely worn out, the Parisians capitulated. Defeat was complete. It was the greatest humiliation the country had suffered since the Hundred Years' War. Elections were held in February, but were inconclusive. Royalist deputies outnumbered the republicans, but were divided between themselves. Nevertheless, they combined against Paris when in Paris, always the seat of republican ambition, several factions angered by the siege, the result of the elections and the peace terms with Prussia rebelled, and in the following month established a Commune in the name not merely of the ideals of the republic but also of the socialism that had so fascinated Marx and so appalled Comte in 1848. The Communards, however, were defeated by Thiers' government in the May, but Thiers, acting on his subsequent declaration that 'the Republic is the regime which divides us least', was censured by the monarchist majority in the Assembly in May 1873. Not since the Terror, not even in 1848, had the monarchists' fears of incipient revolution been so apparently justified, and so they installed a soldier as president for seven years to give them time to establish a monarchy. Unfortunately for them, the man they chose was an intransigent Bourbon who refused to make any concessions at all to republican sentiment, with the result that a republican constitution was after all soon passed, albeit by a majority of one. The elections of 1877 were at last decisive. The republicans won and the Third Republic was established. But the opposition was far from silenced, and there were to be fifty-five successive ministries to 1914.

In one sense, then, the defeat in the war with Prussia did indeed have a profound impact, for it exacerbated the old divisions of French society: the perpetual rancour between republicans and monarchists that had begun with the revolution itself, had flared after Napoleon's ill-fated hundred days in 1815, again in the late 1820s, in 1847 and 1848, and in 1851, and had been complicated by the Church's determination to retain its power; the Jacobin enthusiasms, crushed in 1794, revived in 1848 and all the while absorbing the developing notions of nineteenth-century socialism; and the persistent bitterness, resentment, and contempt between Paris and the provinces. In the broadest sense as well as the narrowest, the very constitution of France was still in question. Yet precisely because the new battles were largely the old ones, the crisis of the 1870s, although profound, raised no new questions. It merely revived the old ones. What seemed important to the intellectuals in the 1870s was remarkably similar to what had seemed important to Saint-Simon and Comte in the twenties, thirties and forties. Despite the partial, fragmented and battle-torn development there of what everyone was by then calling 'socialism', which had anyway been seen to discredit itself in the Commune, France, by 1880, had in this respect experienced far less change than either England or Germany.

In the eighteenth century the poorer French *philosophes* lived largely by tutoring. Saint-Simon, at the beginning of the nineteenth, had managed to secure considerable private means for himself. Comte, although he gave a few occasional lectures at the Ecole Normale, lived at first on a salary from Saint-Simon and then, more precariously, on royalties and on subscriptions raised by respectful admirers like J. S. Mill. But at the end of the century, more and more French intellectuals were able to obtain secure and salaried posts in the newly reformed and at last properly financed institutions of higher education. This was important. It not only meant that they had students, Berlin in the 1830s is testimony to the possible effect of that, but also that they were required to defend to their colleagues as respectable disciplines whatever ideas and activities they were attempting to promote in the society outside. One such discipline was sociology, which soon became as fashionable among the republicans as it was detested by their opponents. 'The word is on everyone's lips' wrote one republican, 'and it is even used abusively; the thing has become popular. People's eyes are fixed on the new science and they expect much from it. There has thus emerged at the end of the century an intellectual movement altogether analogous to that...at its beginning which, moreover, results from the same causes'.

Depending upon quite how one defines them, there were anything up to two dozen sociologists teaching in various institutions in France in the first years of the century and an at least equal number of scholars in other disciplines, in philosophy, law, history and geography who were sympathetic to the subject. At that time, it was conceived as Comte had in general conceived it, as the positive science of society, the attempt to discover laws of social life formally analogous to those of nature, although no-one outside the Positivist Church, not even his faithful biographer, Lévy-Bruhl, was uncritical of Comte's later excesses. The empiricism of the English and the idealism of the Germans after Kant had made a little impact, but it had been almost entirely absorbed into the native rationalism and in this form popularised by men such as Hyppolite Taine and Ernest Renan who each, to different degrees, recalled Comte in their metaphysical enthusiasm and, in Renan's case, in the suggestion that positivism could form the basis of a new faith that 'can resolve for man the eternal problems to which his nature imperi-

ously demands the solution'. Spencer too, who had been translated, and Schäffle were read, and enthused. There were of
course differences between the sociologists. There were the
followers of the empirical investigator Le Play, who paid attention to the dislocations of peasant and urban working-class life in
the nineteenth century, and made recommendations for their
amelioration in the spirit of a conventionally Catholic concern
for stabililty and order. There was René Worms, whose sociology was propelled by a fear of the consequences of individualism
and who founded his own *Revue internationale de sociologie* in
1893. But a majority were in some way committed to reason and
the republic, and none was more explicit about this than Emile
Durkheim, who rapidly became the most noticeable of them all.

Durkheim was born in Lorraine in 1858 of a rabbinical
Ashkenazi family. He entered the Ecole Normale Supérieure in
1879, where he was remembered for his republican enthusiasm
and his distaste for what he regarded as the frivolous dilletan-
tism or sheer mysticism of much of the teaching. He appears to
have been a morally serious young man, and to have adopted
the cause of republican nationalism with all the fervour of a
convert to Parisian intellectual life. His ideological convictions
together with his moral seriousness inclined him to a faith in
intellectual rigour, in the virtues of an uncompromising
rationalism and a nominal empiricism in the French manner,
and away from the spiritual fopperies of more literary men,
whom he always scorned. He is said to have disliked Renan's
thesis, but he had much of his spirit.

Not all the teaching at the Ecole dismayed him, however, and
two philosophers there, Renouvier and Boutroux, affected him
deeply. Boutroux taught the history of philosophy. He urged a
respect for science and the view that each of the sciences dealt
with a distinctive and irreducible realm. Durkheim, as he later
explained, was 'very impressed by this idea' and 'applied it to
sociology'. Renouvier was clearly an extremely impressive man,
one of those university teachers in an élitist educational system
whose intellectual and moral example has a wide effect upon the
politicians, lawyers, administrators, and academics that his
pupils become. He was a neo-Kantian, a rather new phenomenon in French philosophy, insisting upon the importance of
morality and the dignity of the individual, the priority of reason

and the need to use it to reconcile autonomy and order in a just society yet also, as Lukes suggests perhaps very significantly for Durkheim, upon the subordination of theoretical to practical reason, with the implication that the *a priori* categories of the former are subject to a choice dictated by a will grounded in the latter, a connection that points towards Durkheim's own later thesis that such categories are founded in practical social life.

The rationalist, progressive, liberal or (in the non-Marxist sense) socialist republican intellectuals, among whom the sociologists counted themselves, had already scored a considerable political victory in the Third Republic, a victory in which Renouvier had had a part and a victory that Durkheim was to devote a good part of his professional life to consolidating. This was to have severely limited the influence of the Church in the syllabus and staffing of the schools and universities (a name that could not henceforth be used for exclusively Catholic institutions). Not unnaturally, the Church was displeased with this, and so were its increasingly frustrated allies in the 1880s and 1890s, the army and the monarchists. The ideological lines were most sharply drawn, however, in the later 1890s, in the course of the celebrated Dreyfus affair. Dreyfus was a Jewish army officer accused, it appears wrongly, of spying by a rascally fellow officer, and convicted. The resultant storm did not shake France to its foundations, as has sometimes been said (in the election in 1898, most people appear to have been much more concerned about the rising price of bread), but it unleashed the latent fury between the two camps of ideologues in Paris. Predictably, Catholic apologists took the opportunity of attacking the 'ignoble race of...academics...who spend their lives teaching error and in corrupting souls and, in due course, society as a whole'. Maurice Barrès, an irrational, nationalistic writer who had begun his revealingly titled trilogy *Le Roman de l'énergie nationale* in 1897, doubtless expressed the views of many when he asserted that 'the great culprits, who should be punished, are the "intellectuals", the "anarchists of the lecture platform", the "metaphysicians of sociology". A band of arrogant madmen. Men who take a criminal self-satisfaction in their intelligence, who treat our generals as idiots, our social institutions as absurd and our traditions as unhealthy'. Others, with more attention to what they took to be the principles at stake, identified the enemy as 'individualism', 'the great sickness of the present time'. Durkheim was one of those who replied to such charges, and in so doing, inflamed the debate. His reply, an essay on 'Individualism and the Intellectuals', shows as clearly as anything that he wrote his moral position and his view of the way in which sociology could serve it, the force of his thesis and its evident faults.

He began by agreeing with the opposition that the questions were indeed those of the moral status and political consequences of individualism. He distinguished two variants. The first was the 'utilitarian egoism of Spencer [whom he too misunderstood] and the economists'. He recognised that in its origins, this view had a certain justice in that 'our fathers were concerned exclusively with freeing the individual from the political fetters which hampered his development'. He recalled the euphoria of the 'men of my generation...when [with the establishment of the Third Republic] twenty years ago we finally succeeded in toppling the last barriers which we impatiently confronted'. But he also remembered his subsequent dismay at the internecine strife the new liberty 'that no one knew what to do with' had caused, and cleverly agreed with the anti-Dreyfusards that 'nothing is more just than that such doctrines should be treated as anarchical'. The second variant was the individualism as he described it 'of Kant and Rousseau, that of the *spiritualistes*, that which the Declaration of the Rights of Man sought, more or less successfully, to translate into formulae, that which is currently taught in our schools and which has become the basis of our moral catechism'. In terms which foreshadow his subsequent argument in the essay itself and reflect his developing sense of the place of ideas in society generally, and which were also perhaps meant to strike a sympathetic chord in the opposition, Durkheim summarised this second conception as 'a religion of which man is at the same time both believer and God'. By pointing to the philosophical development of this view, in Kant himself, in Rousseau, in Fichte and in Marx, Durkheim attempted to dispel the belief that it also had socially divisive implications. 'Doubtless, if the dignity of the individual derived from his individual qualities, from those particular characteristics which distinguish him from others, one might fear that he would become enclosed in a sort of moral egoism that would render all social cohesion impossible. But in reality he receives this dignity from a higher source, one which he shares with all men', one which points to an 'impersonal and anonymous end' that 'soars far above all particular consciences' and can thus serve to unite them.

At this point, Durkheim came to what he candidly conceded to be 'the great objection': 'if all opinions are free, by what miracle will they then be harmonious?' His answer was the plank upon which he erected his entire sociology, and it is not secure. He argued that only rational opinion could be allowed in moral argument, and then implied that such opinion had *ipso facto* to rest upon 'expert knowledge', those without such knowledge being required to defer to the authority of those who had it. He immediately proceeded to claim such authority for himself. Individualism, he declared, 'is henceforth the only system of beliefs which can ensure the moral unity of the country'. This is because 'all the evidence points to the conclusion that....the natural course of things...[is]...the increasing growth of the division of labour'. 'One is thus gradually proceeding towards a state of affairs, now almost attained, in which the members of a single social group will no longer have anything in common other than their humanity, that is, the characteristics which constitute the human person in general'. Durkheim explained his conviction that the sociologist was the person uniquely able to provide the rational basis for a common morality. 'Individualism itself is a social product, like all moralities and religions. The individual receives from society even the moral beliefs which deify him. This is what Kant and [he mistakenly asserted] Rousseau did not understand. They wished to deduce their individualist ethic not from society, but from the notion of the isolated individual. Such an enterprise was impossible, and from it resulted the logical contradictions of their systems'. Durkheim himself avoided self-contradiction, but his argument was weak in at least two other respects. The first and more obvious of these was his apparent equation between rational and empirical support. It is clear that someone with privileged access to the facts, a Durkheimian expert, might have a certain authority in the matter of means to a certain end or set of ends, or that he might legitimately interfere in a discussion of ends by pointing out that some were unrealisable, or mutually contradictory or otherwise impractical, but it is far from clear that by virtue of his empirical knowledge alone he could adjudicate on the moral validity of such ends. In the preface to the first edition of his main doctoral thesis, published five years earlier, Durkheim had in fact set himself against exactly this. 'The moralists who deduce their doctrines...from some propositions borrowed from one or more of the positive sciences like...sociology call their ethics scientific. We do not propose to follow this method'. Yet the impression left by 'Individualism and the Intellectuals', as well as by a more deliberate paper which he gave to philosophers in 1906 on 'The determination of moral facts' (where he said that 'it is impossible to derive a morality other than that endorsed by the condition of society at a given time'), is quite the reverse. The second and less obvious difficulty of Durkheim's argument in the earlier essay, a difficulty that pervades his whole sociology, lies in the ambiguity of his use of the terms 'morality' and 'society', and of his view of the connections between them. The positivist tradition in which he deliberately placed himself was not one in which the language of moral analysis had been made at all precise. He cannot, therefore, be blamed for his terminological confusions, although neither can he be quite absolved from their consequence. This is that one is never quite sure when he is talking about the status of moral arguments, the contents of the moralities themselves, or their causes. When he talked of 'moral unity', did he mean agreement about how moral arguments were to be conducted and secured, or agreement on the premises of moral arguments, or agreement about particular substantive ends? It would seem that he was more concerned with the first and second than with the third. He did not, in 'Individualism and the Intellectuals', specify the ends men were to pursue beyond hinting indirectly at the three catchwords of the republic; but he did deal directly with the need to ground moral arguments in the facts of social life, and from what he took these facts to show, he did insist (it was the main point of the essay) that the premise of contemporary moral arguments had to be the morally autonomous individual, exercising the right society had granted him to pursue what he alone took to be his moral duty. And, which was crucial to his sociological view of morality (as to his moral view of society), he not merely repeated the Kantian view that to be moral was to obey a rational law towards which one thus had a moral duty, and that to be free was to use one's reason to construct such a law (in his version, to derive it from the social facts), but drew the additional inference that if the law were rational it must be the same for all men, and that if it were the same for all men then it transcended each individual man and so constituted itself as a distinctively social phenomenon. In this respect, society itself had authority. For Durkheim, 'society' was therefore the source of morality in a double sense. It was a set of facts-in-the-world from which correct moral inferences could be made and it was the authority for moral judgements. Being a moral naturalist, however, the two senses were for him scarcely distinct. His naturalism aside, there are still two difficulties. The first, to which I have already alluded, is that even if 'reason' establishes as a moral premise the rights of the individual, it does not, in Durkheim's view at least, establish how the individual is to exercise those rights, what end or ends he is to pursue. The answer that he must defend individualism merely restates the problem. The second difficulty is that if society is the source of morality in the double sense in which Durkheim intended, it is not exactly clear how it is to be defined independently of morality. This weakness became more evident as his ideas developed and as he paid even less attention to the morphological or structural basis of societies.

From his argument in this Dreyfusard article, Durkheim produced two conclusions that went directly into the enemy's camp. One was that the danger to society did indeed come from those who threatened its moral basis, but that these were the enemies of individual rights; the other was that if a religion was necessary then it was the 'religion of individualism'. The essay ended with a call to action in the name of the faith to restore the 'moral patrimony' of France, the republican ideals. In its schematically rationalist pursuit of a morality anchored firmly in the purported facts of social life, its commitment to a progressive order between the absolute reactionaries on the one hand and the heirs of the Jacobins on the other, and its vision of an intellectual elite inspiring literally religious allegiance, Durkheim's moral and intellectual programme clearly recalled Saint-Simon's and Comte's. It differed from theirs, however, in its recognition not of the empirical pervasiveness of individualism but of its positive moral importance. And through Renouvier, Kant had entered French social theory.

Durkheim had taken his *agrégation* from the Ecole in 1882. He taught in three *lycées* and in 1885–6 went on a public scholarship to Germany to study the state of philosophy and the social sciences there. It was then that he first read Marx, but he was more impressed and affected by the less determinist, organically-minded 'socialists of the chair', like Schäffle, and by Wundt's putatively scientific conception of the distinctively social nature of moral ideas. A year after his return, Durkheim took a post as *chargé de cours* of social science and pedagogy at the University of Bordeaux. He stayed until 1902, when he at last realised his ambition of a similar appointment at the Sorbonne. In his years at the two universities between 1887 and 1916 he lectured on a wide range of topics, on education, morality, 'social solidarity', suicide, the family, crime, religion, the history of sociology and of socialism, the social structure of France (in the most general terms), and pragmatism. He started and continued vigorously to edit a new journal, the *Année Sociologique*. He wrote books on *The Division of Labour, The Rules of the Sociological Method, Suicide* and *The Elementary Forms of Religious Life*, as well as a pamphlet on the German war mentality and over four hundred articles and reviews. All the while, he played a most active part in intellectual and academic, but not political, affairs in Bordeaux and especially in Paris. It was a full life, one which virtually defined the establishment of professional sociology in France, and which because of its moral point drew ever more venom as it appeared to have more effect.

According to the practice of the time, Durkheim prepared two doctoral theses, one on the relations between the individual and society and the other on Montesquieu. The first appeared as *The Division of Labour*. It was an extended exposition and defence of the thesis that he later set out more briefly and with sharper moral and political point in 'Individualism and the Intellectuals'; yet in a strict sense it was a conventional work. Durkheim accepted without question that the most evident characteristic of contemporary society was its high division of labour (which he scarcely bothered to define); that this had been caused by increasing population pressure and the consequent increase in the density of social or moral life; and that the moral issue was whether to accept the law of its evolution (that was to say, its evolution) or not. None of these theses did he defend. They would have been as commonplace to his audience as the term 'solidarity' itself, which was as much part of the everyday currency of moral and political conversation as its despised opposite, 'individualism'. Instead, he directed his energies against Spencer, Comte and a German contemporary little appreciated in his own country at the time that he first published, Tönnies. As Durkheim read him, Spencer had argued that accepting the law of evolution would ensure 'a harmony of interests', whereas it was plain to Durkheim that it could 'only give rise to transient relations and passing associations'. Comte and Tönnies had seen this too, but drew the mistaken conclusion that society could only be preserved by a strong, directive central authority, an authority, however, Durkheim argued, that could be effective only if based upon a consensus, in which case it would be unnecessary. (In fact, Durkheim parodied Tönnies and presented more the views of his vulgarisers than his own, for Tönnies, indeed rather like Durkheim, saw the greatest hope in occupational associations.)

Durkheim's point in *The Division of Labour* was to show that consensus was possible. He argued that the increase in the division of labour had transformed the basis of social solidarity from individual likeness (called, in a sarcastic inversion of Tönnies, mechanical) to individual dissimilarity or 'individual personality' (called organic), and that this transformation was reflected in a change of *conscience collective*, itself reflected in a change of morality (toward greater respect for the rights of the individual) which was in turn reflected in a change in the character of penal law from 'repressive' (forcing errant individuals back into the undifferentiated and uniform mass from which they had deviated) to 'restitutive'. He crystallised the thesis by affirming that 'social life comes from a double source, the likeness of consciences and division of labour'; that the first is not destroyed by the second but merely re-established by it on different principles, on the grounds that 'society does not find the bases on which it rests fully laid out in consciences' but 'puts them there itself'. Yet Durkheim's defence of the whole argument was extraordinarily poor, both in its logic and in its purported empirical 'proof'. The logical failure was pointed out by his most tenacious and institutionally authoritative contemporary critic, Gabriel Tarde. Tarde was a magistrate, criminologist, statistician and sociologist, who from 1894 had directed the criminal statistics office of the Ministry of Justice. He was intellectually committed to the view that the facts of social life could be derived from the properties of individuals, which were themselves a function of autochthonous creation and its imitation, and many of his criticisms of Durkheim's work stem from this conviction. His most persuasive criticism of *The Division of Labour*, however, owed little to it. It was simply that the argument for a transformation of the basis of solidarity presupposed that some form of solidarity would persist, for there was nothing in Durkheim's book to show why it should. This was fair, and devastating. Durkheim had assumed that by virtue of being a general fact individualism was *ipso facto* a social one; and since he assumed that social facts had a constraining authority over men, he simply inferred that men were, or at least could be, thus constrained into mutual solidarity by virtue of their common individualism. His main thesis, therefore owed nothing to 'scientific' proof. The defence against Comte, Tönnies and Spencer rested instead upon a wholly *a priori* argument. What he had set out to prove he had assumed in his definitions. Moreover, as more recent commentators have said, the 'proof' that Durkheim did offer (and believed himself to have secured) was exceedingly thin. There were six crucial terms in the argument, the division of labour, solidarity, individual personality, *conscience collective*, morality and penal law; but apart from purely casual asides, in the book itself he only offered evidence for the values of the first and last. These were the morphological features of the two kinds of society (their internal differentiation), and penal law. The values of the other terms, and the connections between them, were assumed. Durkheim's description of the morphological and structural differentiation of the 'lower' societies was fuller than his account of its nature and extent (as the division of labour) in 'higher' ones; he seems to have taken the latter for granted. But it was his attribution of 'repressive' penal law to the former and of 'restitutive' law to the other that was seriously defective. It now seems (if one wishes to use such a distinction at all) that the relation is the other way round.

The original purpose of the thesis that eventually became *The Division of Labour* had been to examine 'the relations between individualism and socialism'. Although Durkheim was attracted to socialist thinking in Germany in the 1880s, and especially to Schäffle's conception of the State as 'an organ which concentrates and expresses the whole of social life' (rather than a deliberate counter to the dispersive effects of occupational specialisation), he was less enthusiatic about socialism in France. After the *débacle* of the Commune in 1871, many French republicans regarded socialism as a recipe for conflict and disorder and so not an acceptable candidate for the establishment of solidarity. Many of the socialist factions, euphoric still that the Commune had even been possible, were committed to various forms of direct action, and even the more orthodox, led by the bitter and ascetic Guesde, seemed in their very orthodoxy, in their ideology of class, to be committed to division and disruption. Yet it was Durkheim's own influence upon socialist thinking, especially through his old friend from the Normale, the brilliant and attractive if somewhat opportunistic Jaurès, that played some part, although no doubt a very small one, in the establishment of a greater unity of the left in 1905. Durkheim explained himself very clearly in a review of an Italian work on socialism in 1899. It would be a great advantage, he wrote, 'if socialism finally ceased to confuse the social question with the working class question. The first includes the second but goes beyond it. The malaise from which we suffer is not located in a particular class; it is general throughout the whole of society...it is not simply a question of diminishing the share of some so as to increase that of others, but rather of remaking the moral constitution of society. This way of putting the problem is not only truer to the facts: it should have the advantage of divesting socialism of its aggressive and malevolent character with which it has often, and rightly, been reproached'. Nevertheless, and in striking contrast to his followers (some of whom were among the founders of the left-wing newspaper *Humanité*), Durkheim remained aloof from day to day political activities, perhaps coming nearest to them in the restrained Dreyfusard polemic of 'Individualism and the Intellectuals' in 1898, and instead lectured on socialism in 1895–6 and on law, custom and politics more generally between 1896 and 1900.

He did not complete his historical survey of socialist thought, and merely reached a general definition and an exegesis and discussion of some eighteenth-century thinkers and of Saint-Simon. 'We define as "socialist"', he said, 'every doctrine which calls for the connection of all economic functions, or', he added significantly, 'of certain among them which are currently diffuse, to the directing and conscious centres of society'. He distinguished this, for him, commendable doctrine from the reliance of the classical economists upon unregulated competition on the one hand and the view that the State had to impose order and integration on the other, in exactly the way in which he had distinguished his own thesis in *The Division of Labour* from Spencer, Comte and Tönnies. He also drew a sharp line between socialism and communism, the one concerned with organised production, the other with organised consumption and as such impractical and utopian, of no interest to modern men. Saint-Simon, he argued, had had an essentially correct vision of the socialist order and of the positive method by which it should be determined, but his belief that it could be achieved simply by giving the *industriels* their head, excusable in the 1830s, was evident seventy years later as precisely the wrong prescription unless these economic forces were also and in addition subjected to moral forces which surpassed, contained and regulated them. Although Durkheim never realised his plan to lecture on Marx, one of his arguments against the 'communists' of 1789 (among whom he included Rousseau) is a clear indication of the fundamental difference between the two men, much more fundamental than Durkheim's own description of it as a disagreement about the causal importance of economic factors and about whether economic class conflict could establish a new order. He agreed that it was quite natural that in their intense desire for social justice the 'communists' should have looked with particular compassion on 'the working classes' as evidence of the lack of liberty, fraternity and equality in the *ancien régime*. Like Marx, he agreed that the problem of the working classes was the problem of society as a whole, but against him, did not consider that they therefore constituted an alternative society and could by themselves solve the problem they represented. In this he was prompted by the history of the Commune as much as by the intellectual tradition of organising rationalism in which he worked, as was French socialism itself after 1905. Despite his theoretical respect for Kautsky in the German Social Democratic Party, Jaurès was of the same view.

If the function of the State was to organise upon the *conscience collective* of the new economic order, however, exactly how was it to do so? Durkheim attempted an answer to this in his lectures on law, custom and politics, and summarised them in a new preface to the second edition of *The Division of Labour* in 1902. In both, he departed from his earlier view of the State, influenced by reading Schäffle, as doing little more than reflecting and articulating the *conscience collective*, and argued that it should more actively intervene. He was even prepared to concede 'that decisions taken by the government...may be valid for the whole community and yet...not square with the state of social opinion'. This no doubt reflected a growing impatience with the lack of progress in the Third Republic, a dawning realisation (also coming upon Marxists in France, Germany and even Russia) that the predetermined course of social evolution could take an irritatingly long time to work itself through. Like most of the Marxists, moreover, Durkheim did not wish to alter this course, that was theoretically inconceivable, but merely to hasten it. The State, therefore, was to intervene to guarantee the security of individualism as he defined it. He even supported his case by insisting that recent governments had already achieved this to some degree. Consistent, however, with his argument in *The Division of Labour*, he was at pains to distinguish himself from the purely negative view of the functions of the State proposed by liberals, both utilitarians and (as he saw him) Kant as well, and the too positive view of the Hegelians, in which individuals were required to subordinate themselves to a 'mystical solution' of solidarity that promised to vitiate their autonomy. Instead, he insisted that, properly constituted, the State should plan 'the social environment so that the individual may realise himself more fully', and aim 'at an ideal which [individuals] pursue peacefully and in common', protecting them from forces that bore heavily upon them while at the same time upholding an ideal to which they could aspire. He did not however consider that the State could achieve this directly. It was 'too remote'. There was need for a more 'fundamental political unit', to incorporate men 'into the current of social life', and since men were now primarily distinguished by their occupations (for occupational specialisation was the most evident fact of the 'higher' society), it seemed most obvious to him that corporations of men in the same industry (cutting across what others would have regarded as social classes) could serve this purpose. Characteristically, he reviewed the history of such institutions from economically homogeneous family groups in ancient societies through to the medieval guilds that were appropriately dissembled after the revolution, set himself against the 'narrow subordination' into which the guilds had sunk, and then tentatively expressed the hope that the new corporations would not merely regulate economic life but also provide a proximate moral community for their members. Yet although they were desirable for these reasons, they could he thought well comprise exactly the anti-individualist forces that the State had itself to combat, and he concluded the argument by insisting that it was precisely in such tensions that liberty could best be guaranteed. It was a socialist vision in the literal sense. But it was very different from the sectarian politics of class. Since it was not, however, by his own insistence, a fresh attempt to solve the formidable if conventional problem of freedom and obligation by assuming a natural tension between the two (although it frequently reads as one), it raises exactly the same difficulty as do *The Division of Labour* and 'Individualism and the Intellectuals'. Can the stipulation of a morally authoritative *conscience collective* of individualism remove the tension without at the same time emptying the notion of individual autonomy of its full force? Or conversely, can the stipulation of individual autonomy remove the tension without allowing the possibility of political conflict in its name? In this respect, the ironically similar encyclical *Rerum Novarum*, issued in 1891 and addressing itself to the same problem, was more consistent.

Durkheim saw clearly that his case for the proper moral and political constitution of France would be greatly strengthened by his being able to show that the much remarked social maladies of the time were the effect of either unbridled egoism, the suppression of true individuality, or the lack of moral regulation. One such malady was the disorder and conflict of capitalist industrialisation. Another was suicide. He discussed the first in the third part of *The Division of Labour*, and the second in a monograph that has since become a classic of sociological analysis.

He distinguished three 'abnormal forms' of the division of labour in the 'higher' societies: 'industrial or commercial crises' and 'conflict between labour and capital', inequality, and 'lack of co-ordination' of the 'functions' in commercial and industrial enterprises. By the second, which he referred to as the 'forced' division of labour, Durkheim meant those situations in which individuals were prevented by virtue of their caste or class position from realising their talents, and in which they were forced to exchange services for inappropriately low rewards. Since he considered that 'harmony between individual natures and social functions cannot fail to be realised, at least in the average case', that the normal state of affairs was in this respect at least much as the classical economists and Spencer had conceived of it, he rejected the view that these inequalities were more than a temporary aberration. By 'lack of co-ordination' Durkheim appears to have meant situations in which the use made of specialisation was not commensurate with its possibilities, and he argued from a characteristically Spencerian, and specious, organic analogy that as functions became more continuous men would work harder and as a result of both become more dependent upon each other and so exhibit greater solidarity. More distinctive of his later concerns, however, was his diagnosis of crises and class conflict. These were due, he considered, to the development of economic activities in general and the division of labour in particular outrunning their proper regulation, a state of affairs he described by the then already familiar term 'anomie'. 'Contrary to what has been said', he wrote, 'the division of labour does not produce these consequences because of a necessity of its own nature, but only in exceptional and abnormal circumstances', and these could be rectified (as could 'lack of co-ordination') by better planning, clear procedural rules, and, he concluded, by giving the worker 'the feeling that he is serving something', giving him a conviction that 'his actions have an aim beyond themselves'. Like the forced division of labour and the lack of co-ordination, industrial anomie was a passing disruption, a literally abnormal state.

Durkheim's analysis of these, as of other consequences of the division of labour in the 'higher' societies revealed his extremely slight acquaintance with the facts and in particular his poor sense of the complex realities of crises and conflicts. This was not so with *Suicide*. In preparing lectures on this subject in 1889–90 and revising them into the manuscript that was published seven years late, he combed with the help of his nephew Mauss the European official statistics and used some unpublished ones that Tarde had let him have. Perhaps as much as any kind of human action, and more than most, suicide is a problem from virtually every ethical standpoint. With the sense of growing antinomies between the individual and his spiritual, moral, social and political relations that characterised the seventeenth, eighteenth and nineteenth centuries, it was especially so, and was discussed at length according to the various intellectual conventions of the time. In the nineteenth century, it had attracted the attention of the moral statisticians, and analyses of the connections between the suicide rate and prevailing states of civilisation and morality were common. Although Durkheim set himself against 'the common theories of the moralists', both his analysis and his conclusions were firmly in that tradition.

As he had to, he defined suicide as the intention to kill oneself, but carefully avoided any attribution of reason or motive. This he reserved for his classification of suicides, a classification which he made at the beginning, a classification entirely to be expected from his previous work. It consisted of a fourfold distinction between egoistic and altruistic suicides and anomic and fatalistic ones. The first two were distinguished by what he called the degree to which society attracted the sentiments of indiviuals, the second two by the degree to which individuals were 'regulated'. The first two were endemic respectively to insufficiently and excessively integrated societies, societies which either gave individuals no 'aim beyond themselves', as he put it in *The Division of Labour*, or which put that aim beyond the individual's capacity. The second two were not necessarily endemic to any society, but rather contingent respectively upon too little or too much discipline in the normal type (which is why Durkheim restricted the description 'anomic' to those suicides that occurred in moments of economic or familial crisis). He said that he could find no substantial number of cases of fatalistic suicide, and accordingly relegated this type to a footnote.

Many commentators have pointed out the weaknesses of the book (although curiously enough, no single satisfactory assessment of it has ever been published): the *petitio principii* involved in the prior classification of the types of suicide, the possibility

that the distinction between egoistic and anomic suicides owed
more to a wholly *a priori* distinction in Durkheim's mind than to
any (more than trivial) empirical differences he was able to show,
the obscure relation between social 'forces' (to use one of his
own mechanical metaphors) and individual states of mind, the
unqualified (although perfectly comprehensible) reliance upon
official statistics, and the inferences about individual behaviour
from correlations between aggregates. From the point of view of
Durkheim's central purpose, however, the purpose of establishing a rational foundation for a coherent society in which individualism could properly be secured, the most interesting of
these weaknesses is that surrounding the notions of egoism and
anomie. 'Both', he argued, 'spring from society's insufficient
pressure in individuals. But the sphere of absence is not the
same in both cases. In egoistic suicide it is deficient in truly
collective activity, thus depriving the latter of object and meaning. In anomic suicide, society's influence is lacking in the
basically individual passions, thus leaving them without a check-
rein'. The distinction has a superficial lucidity, and was certainly
drawn sharply. In the one case, individuals are not attached to
society, in the other they are, but the attachment is not sufficient
to regulate their 'passions'. Durkheim appeared to be advancing
an argument for two successive conditions of solidarity or (as he
called it in *Suicide*) 'integration', the first of which is necessary to
the second but not in itself sufficient. It recalled *The Division of
Labour* and his suggestion there of a causal progression from
moral density to solidarity. The difficulty with that, however, was
that each term appeared to have a purely internal, logical
connection with the next so that the arguments rested more
upon purely conceptual connections than upon a determinate
series of empirically distinct phenomena. At first sight, this
would not seem to be a difficulty with *Suicide*, for Durkheim
adduced copious evidence for each of the three types that he
discussed at length, including the egoistic and anomic. But the
evidence compounds rather than resolves the difficulty. For
example, he argued that the relatively high rate of suicide
among Protestants was an instance of the pathology of egoism.
According to the conceptual argument, this should have meant
that they were not attached to society and so not regulated. Yet
on Durkheim's own terms one can just as easily argue that

Protestants, even if not attached (and that is dubious, for they formed a Church), were nevertheless regulated by their 'religion of individualism'. If they were not, then Protestant beliefs did not have the moral authority Durkheim was prepared to ascribe to others, including his own secular religion. Yet if they were, then either Protestants were regulated but not attached (which destroys the distinction he drew between states of egoism and anomie) or they were both attached and regulated, in which case they could only be prone to the 'suicidogenic currents' of altruism or fatalism. The point is not that any of these interpretations is more satisfactory than Durkheim's own, but that each is as likely as his own on his own theoretical terms. It suggests that he was not clear about exactly how individuals were, were not and could be attached to and integrated with society, not clear, that is, about his main sociological thesis.

In 1898, Durkheim had said in reply to the anti-Dreyfusards that if, as they maintained, a religion was essential to the order and stability of France it should henceforth be the 'religion of individualism'. This was not simply a debating point. He had lectured on religion in 1894–5 and 'that course...marked a dividing line in the development of my thought'. In preparing it he realised that 'religion contains in itself from the very beginning, even in an indistinct state, all the elements which in dissociating themselves from it, articulating themselves, and combining with one another in a thousand ways, have given rise to the various manifestations of collective life'. By this time, there had been in European thought a simple but profound and somewhat ironic change in the way in which religion was regarded. In the eighteenth and early nineteenth centuries, social philosophers, especially in France, had set their own views of the proper explanation and justification of human affairs against religious ones, the 'positive' against the 'theological'. By the end of the nineteenth century, their convictions were so secure that they were beginning simply to treat religious ideas and practices as social phenomena like any other, objects for rational explanation. Durkheim himself was predisposed to this view, and convinced of it in his early thoughts on religion by Fustel de Coulanges, an ancient historian at the Ecole, and by a very sociologically-minded English Semitic scholar, Robertson

Smith. In these early thoughts, he became convinced of two propositions in particular, that religious ideas were obligatory in the societies in which they flourished, and that what was obligatory was of social origin. These were developed in *The Elementary Forms of the Religious Life*.

This book, which appeared in 1912, was a secondary analysis of Central Australian totemism. Durkheim considered totemism to be of a piece, and falling back upon a residual evolutionism (for the book itself was not directly concerned with change) described it as the most primitive and for this reason the most simple of religions in the most simple of societies. He has been rightly criticised for these views, but they explain why he took Australian totemism as his 'one...experiment', the simplest case which would in its simplicity furnish a 'universally' valid proof of the nature of 'religion in general'. Durkheim characterised this nature in a celebrated definition: 'a religion is a unified system of beliefs and practices relative to sacred things, that is to say, things set apart and forbidden, beliefs and practices which unite into a single moral community called a Church all those who adhere to them'. Starting from the premise 'that the unanimous sentiments of the believers of all times cannot be illusory', which prevents one dismissing religion as an epiphenomenal error of pre-scientific men, he defended three main theses: that religious beliefs and practices have their source in the 'effervescence' of everyday contact between men who stand in certain definite relationships to each other; they they are a cognitive and expressive 'representation' of these relations; and that they have the effect or function of delineating, delimiting, cementing and regulating them. In short, they are the 'simplest' *conscience collective*, with all except one of the properties attributed to such *consciences* in *The Division of Labour* twenty years before.

The exception was their cognitive properties. In an essay he had written with Mauss in 1903, on 'Some primitive forms of classification', he had argued that there was a central connection between social and conceptual structures so that even the most basic of concepts, such as those of space and time, had their sole origin in society. As contemporaries were quick to point out, this thesis failed to make the elementary distinction between the prior propensity to think conceptually and the socially variable content and arrangement of concepts. It was also ethnographically deficient. Nevertheless, when developed as it was in *The Elementary Forms* it raised an obvious question about sociology itself. Since as Durkheim had often said, sociology was in its account of the proper relationship between individuals and society 'the religion of today', and was *ex hypothesi* derived from contemporary social facts, could it not therefore be said to have undermined its own claim to be scientific? He dealt with this question in some lectures on pragmatism and sociology in 1913–14.

Not surprisingly, his answer to it was no, and he expressed it in a combative but tenuous defence of his rationalism. He made two points against William James, his main adversary, who as he saw it had argued that what was deemed to be logically and empirically true at any time was what it was considered useful to believe to be true. The first point was that this claim itself, to be true, required a criterion of truth outside itself, and the second was that the claim that logic could vary removed the possibility of rational discourse and so in this way too a rational defence of any position (including the pragmatists' own). James had presented a very exaggerated version of what he took to be pragmatism, including the pragmatic determination of logical procedures as well as of empirical facts. For this reason, and because they were also rather unsubtle, Durkheim's arguments against him have little intrinsic interest. Moreover, they were contradicted by the concessions which he himself made: that beliefs about truth had a social origin, that they derived their obligatory character from being social, that they had the effect or function of constituting societies even while deriving from them, and that 'they are in no sense arbitrary, being based upon realities, and in particular upon the realities of social life'. That rational criteria of truth have a social origin like any other, he appeared to be claiming (like some Marxists after him), does not make them any the less valid for everyone. Nevertheless, in a rare moment of self-awareness, Durkheim was moved in these late lectures to grant, quite against his earlier claims, that the 'concepts which describe social phenomena in a truly objective way are still very rare' and so to concede that 'in the absence of objective knowledge [society] can only know itself from within and must discern the sentiment it has of itself and be led by it. That is to say, it must be led by a "representation" of the same kind as those which constitute mythological truths'. It was a fitting description of his own sociology, an *a priori* system of internally related concepts whose validity, separately and together, rested less upon any empirical determination that upon a prior and intuitive sense of the necessary basis of a morally justifiable social order in the Third Republic.

Durkheim nevertheless promoted this sociology with flair. In 1896, he broke off his lectures on the history of socialism to start the *Année Sociologique*, each issue of which he edited, each issue of which contained a large number of his own contributions, especially reviews, and each issue of which was a definite intellectual event. Throughout his professional life, as a *chargé de cours* in education, he lectured to intending school teachers, and his conception of what education should be, the systematic implantation of the socially correct, the Durkheimian morality, in the spirit of Jules Ferry's reform in the earlier years of the Republic, had considerable practical effect and in so doing drew the hostility of right and left alike. Perhaps most importantly, his repeated, polemical insistence upon the intellectual distinctiveness and exhaustive power of sociology, an insistence most evident in *The Rules of the Sociological Method* but rarely absent for long in anything that he wrote, has served as a veritable professional charter. That it has so, explains, perhaps, why subsequent sociologists have often been reluctant to criticise him or at least, if they have, why they have always softened their appraisals by pointing to the immense fertility of his ideas. Some are fertile, and especially those which comprise *The Elementary Forms of Religious Life*, yet the fact remains that in his central purposes, a characterisation of morality, a defence of the compatibility of individual autonomy and social order, a causal account of structural and ideal features of societies, and the practice of a viable scientific method, he failed.

The final irony of his reputation, perhaps, is that his sociology is in intention what Wolin has called the 'purest restatement of Rousseau', and that where he criticises Rousseau, as he does, he does so from the very weakest points in his own theory. Durkheim seems not to have read Rousseau properly until towards the end of the 1890s. His early references to Rousseau reveal a crude and superficial understanding, very much in accord with the popular if somewhat contradictory misconceptions in France at the time of the aberrant *philosophe* as both anarchist and repressive authoritarian, the harbinger of the Terror. Indeed, one may suppose (for there is no evidence) that when he eventually did read him he played down the extraordinary similarities between them precisely because Rousseau had exactly the moral and political reputation that he, Durkheim, wished to avoid. Yet in one of his two extended commentaries on Rousseau, on *Emile*, he offered no criticisms at all (and defended the philosopher against exactly the kinds of criticism that he himself had made earlier). In the other, a commentary on the *Second Discourse* and *The Social Contract*, he concluded by criticising Rousseau for failing 'to explain how social life, even in its imperfect historical forms, could come into being' and of having 'great difficulty in showing how it can possibly cast off its imperfections and establish itself on a logical basis', criticisms that were doubly odd in that they are ones which can be made of his own arguments in *The Division of Labour* and the lectures on law, custom and politics and which, in the case of the first, he had just previously disallowed of Rousseau himself. In fact, Durkheim's main point against Rousseau's argument in the *Second Discourse* and *The Social Contract* was that in insisting that although natural causes may permit the creation of societies the exercise of reason is necessary to the establishment of the good society, Rousseau posited a faculty of reason that was independent of 'natural' or social causes. Yet it was precisely Durkheim's inability, or perhaps refusal, to see the need for such a device that so badly flawed his own theory. Where Rousseau reserved certain dispositions and the faculty of reason as truly individual traits, logically prior to society, while suggesting that a properly moral sense was a product of social relations, Durkheim reserved only certain non-rational dispositions as logically prior, and by conflating the individual's ability to reason and his moral sense, and declaring them both to be social products, produced a theory at once less plausible and less interesting: less plausible in its account of reasoning, and less interesting because the solution to the moral problem was given by definition in its cause, the cause also of the reasoning necessary to secure it. His was, in short, an entirely hollow victory.

7

History resolved by will

SCHILLER HAD DECLARED that Germany's greatness was an ethical one, 'dwelling in the culture and character of the nation' and 'independent of any political destiny'. By the middle of the nineteenth century, the German middle classes, as a contemporary journalist put it, were 'sick of principles and doctrines, literary greatness and theoretical existence'. Faced with apparently established nation states to their west and even eventually and humiliatingly to their south, eager for identity, security and prosperity, and anxious about revolutionary disorder, they demanded power. The history of Germany between 1848 and 1919, however, is not so much the history of the acquisition of that power as the history of the political failures of the middle classes in the course of growing national power and then, at the end of the period, of a faint success amidst national defeat and renewed humiliation.

In their manifesto for the Communist League in London in 1847, Marx and Engels had realised that the agitation in the German states, and especially in Prussia, was a liberal one, and that if the workers were to defeat the bourgeois liberals, their 'true' enemy, they would first have to join them against 'the absolute monarchy, the feudal squirearchy and the petty bourgeoisie', only afterwards declaring their hand. But Marx and Engels did not merely over-estimate the strength and commitment of the workers. They were also too confident of the liberals. These men did not do what Marx expected. They wanted not revolution but simply a place, and unable to act independently of socialists or of the monarchy and aristocracy, had no hesitation in siding with the latter, as Marx himself later came to see. In any event, the German National Assembly that was called in the free city of Frankfurt in 1848 could do nothing. Germany was torn between Prussia in the north and Austria in the south. The only practical possibilities were a 'greater Germany' with Austria or a 'lesser Germany' without it but with the directing influence of Prussia and its aristocratic *Junker* estate.

The Prussian delegate to the Frankfurt parliament had derided the liberals' demands as 'a hybrid of a timorous thirst for power and tame revolution'. With the more clear-sighted liberals, he saw that it was only 'power, power, power' that could effect unity, that the power was with Prussia, and that Prussia could only use it if Austria were neutralised. This man, von Bismarck, became Minister of State and acting Chairman of the Cabinet in Prussia in September 1862. He engineered a war with Austria in 1866 and against most expectations (including Engels') won it with his overhauled Prussian army in one short battle. As a result, Austria relinquished its influence in 'lesser Germany' and Prussia incorporated the principalities of Hanover, Schleswig-Holstein, Hesse-Cassel, Nassau and Frankfurt, thereby establishing and directing a North German Federation. The south German states, Bavaria, Württemburg, Baden and Hesse, were formally independent still, between Austria–Hungary and Prussia. But Bismarck had already concluded secret mutual defence pacts with them and brought them into rudimentary economic union with his Federation. In 1870, he engineered a second war, this time with France, and the southern states were at once drawn into it. Bismarck won, and the new Reich was proclaimed on 1 January 1871.

By that time, seven main political parties had established themselves: the Conservatives, the Free Conservatives, the National Liberals, the Progress Party, the Centre Party, the General German Workers' Association and the Social Democratic Workers' Party. The Free Conservatives (who became the Deutsche Reichspartei) and the National Liberals had broken with the Conservatives and the Progress Party in 1866 to support Bismarck's unconstitutional aggression against Austria. Both also accepted his plan for universal suffrage, which he wrongly thought would ensure stability and conservative rule, and it was upon them that he relied in the early years of the Reich. The relatively ineffective Progress Party consisted largely of constitutional legalists and as such drew Bismarck's wrath, although it did not, paradoxically, support the universal suffrage that he himself claimed to. The Centre Party, brilliantly led by Windthorst, the one man in the country who could consistently outwit Bismarck, was above all Catholic. Windthorst was a skilled opportunist, but in the absence of clearly structured interests outside the traditional *Stände* and the new working class even opportunists had to have an ideology. His was at once conservative, liberal and socialist, an ideology of order and community, of individual rights and of the dignity of all classes, mercurial, adaptable and remarkably successful. It was an ideology closer to that in Jaurès' and Durkheim's blend of liberal republicanism and solidarism than to anything else in Germany. It infuriated Bismarck, and outlasted him, but its Catholic base consistently vitiated its national strength. The General German Workers' Association had been founded by Lassalle in 1863 and led by him until his death a year later. Lassalle, to Marx's professed disgust, wanted universal suffrage and the establishment of Production Associations, of industrial enterprises run by the workers and financed by state credit. He was not, in any clear sense, a revolutionary, or in Marx's sense even a socialist. A majority of the increasing number of workers still supported the liberal parties as did Lassalle's successor, von Schweitzer. A more sharply anti-Prussian left inclined to the view that the proletarian cause could better be furthered from a greater Germany than a lesser one. This was put together in 1869 by Liebknecht and Bebel into the Social Democratic Workers' Party. But their purposes were almost immediately frustrated by the establishment of Bismarck's 'lesser' Reich in 1871, and in 1874 they joined with the General German Workers to form the Social Democratic Party. Lassalle had been a good organiser, and the Party was initially dominated by the Association he had begun, but he was not a distinctive or powerful ideologist. The Party thus came to acquire more rather than less of a nominally Marxist character, and its Erfurt programme of 1891 was more orthodox than the one with which it had begun in Gotha in 1875 and which so enraged Marx. Its excellent organisation and increasingly clear ideological commitment ensured its progressive consolidation up to the declaration of war in 1914, yet precisely because it was nominally revolutionary, and because (despite its steady electoral success) successive chancellors would not accommodate it and other parties would not deal with it, it remained powerless, the largest and most coherent yet the least effectual political force in the country.

As Marx said in his *Critique of the Gotha Programme*, Bismarck's Reich was 'a military despotism...with parliamentary trimmings [and] an admixture of feudalism, influenced by the bourgeoisie, constructed by the bureaucracy and protected by the police'. It remained so until 1918. The parliamentary trimmings consisted of the national assemblies, increasingly liberal and socialist, and the Prussian chamber, which was conservative. The Reichstag was powerful, but only in a negative way. It applauded the Kaiser's dismissal of Bismarck, now very old, in 1890, but it could not effectively direct William II's policy afterwards. This policy, as it had been since 1871, was in the hands of secretaries of state formally responsible only the Kaiser. Before 1890, Bismarck had managed to control the state bureaucracies. Afterwards, however, they increasingly became laws unto themselves. None were more independent than those controlling the navy and army, with the result that by 1914 the navy was second only to Britain's and the army second to none. Both, like the other offices, were run by Prussians. And the Prussian leaders were *Junkers*, members of a rural aristocratic *Stand* or status-group, who presided as virtually feudal lords over their estates in the east.

The French aristocracy had at last begun to retire from active political interference, and so had the British, but both were rich. The *Junkers* were not. They were thus presented with the simple choice of extinction or of trying to retain power in an enlarged Germany without a secure economic base. That they managed to achieve such power was due to their actually promoting, through the state apparatus, the industrial growth and prosperity which was the bourgeoisie's interest, and so undermining what might otherwise have been a strong and independent middle class. This prosperity was considerable. The value of German production had exceeded that of France in the late 1870s and by 1900 was equal to that of Britain. By 1910, it was second only to that of the United States. The population was increasing steadily and in 1900 two-thirds of it, thirty-five million, consisted of industrial wage-labourers. Thomas Mann later referred to the 'power-protected inwardness' of Germany before 1914. It was a fitting description. The bourgeoisie was generally satisfied (as it had been after 1848) to pursue profit and culture in the security provided by the Prussian state apparatus. It was the succulent and civically enervated centre of the mollusc that von Tirpitz (whose metaphor this was) had set out to protect with the shell of his navy.

In France, the intellectual reaction to the disjunction between the forces of economic change and political development after the Franco-Prussian War owed its character to the fact that the intellectuals themselves, especially in the universities and the Grandes Ecoles, were committed to the bourgeois cause. The Ecoles, after all, had been instituted to facilitate the administration of France. The universities were decisively detached from the Church in the early years of the Third Republic and so from the one substantial source of conservative ideals. It was quite the reverse in Germany. Although the then new University of Halle had in the eighteenth century been expressly devoted to 'cameralistics', the science of administration and statecraft, the other universities had set themselves against practicality. The intellectuals at Göttingen, Berlin, and elsewhere were instead devoted to the cultivation of *Bildung* and *Kultur*, to the ideal of individual development in its purest senses, an ideal that owed much to the native Pietism and expressed itself in Romantic conceptions and Idealist philosophies and carried a deep contempt for the worldly. It reached its most extreme expression in Schelling and Fichte and in some respects in Hegel, and in some ways its most extreme reaction in the professedly materialist Young Hegelians in the 1830s and 1840s. By the end of the nineteenth century, German philosophers and historians were agreed that it had gone into decline, and this was for them a matter of deep regret. They were convinced that Germany's greatness, indeed its very character, lay in the cultivation of knowledge for its own sake, more exactly in the pursuit of the *Geisteswissenschaften*, the humane disciplines. To relapse into mere practical education for everyday life would be, as the economist and historian Sombart put it in a piece of First World War propaganda against England, to forsake the ideals of the hero for those of the trader. These intellectuals were hostile to what they regarded as the crass materialism and egoism of their burgeoning economy and its products, the bourgeois and the proletarian, with their practical ambitions and their superficial positivist philosophies of mere technique. In so far as they were interested in the social and political changes in Germany at the end of the century, they tended to reinforce the old Idealist conception of the State as not merely the arbiter and administrator of society but as the institution which defined its ends and so transcended it. In this, they were at least the tacit allies of the

Prussians, whose bureaucracies their pupils staffed. Thus the Reich had little to fear from its intellectuals, and because of their status as a virtual estate, a separate *Stand*, with defined privileges and considerable prestige, even the bourgeoisie itself was proud to send its sons to them to acquire the cultivation of a gentleman. This mandarin ideology, however, as it was described, was neither clear nor unanimous. It was at most a general attitude whose exact articulation and application was much disputed. The disputes were philosophical, economic, political and methodological. Out of them emerged for the first time a distinctive and self-styled German sociology.

Simply put, the Germans' view at this time of the history of their philosophy in particular and of their *Geisteswissenschaften* in general was that it had succumbed in the middle years of the century to the corrosion of positivism and practicality. This was not entirely true. Certainly, by comparison with the unbridled Idealism at Berlin under Schelling, Fichte and Hegel, German philosophy did later become rather quiescent and ceased to provide much clear intellectual direction, and psychologists and historians turned more to empirical work. But there was scarcely a single German scholar in any humane subject who dealt with his material in a way that a contemporary Englishman or Frenchman would have regarded as properly 'scientific'. The one exception, or so it seemed, was Marx. We have recently become accustomed to point to the intellectual connections between Marx and Hegel and so to brand him as something of an Idealist. But Marx himself suppressed his more philosophical work and deliberately cultivated the view that his theories were scientific in the more ordinary sense. They were, however, theories of a social change the mandarins deplored leading to a revolution they abhorred, the horrendous experience of another 1848. Even Hegel, whom German intellectuals very well knew had been intellectually responsible for the reaction against him, suffered from Marx's reception. Nevertheless, the philosophical confrontation with Marx in the latter years of the nineteenth century in Germany, as elsewhere, was curiously indirect. For most, he was too appalling or simply too contemptible to face.

Instead, the German philosophers returned directly to Kant, to resurrect and refine both his critical philosophy and his ethics.

Their intentions were clear. 'Knowledge of the forces which prevail in society', wrote Dilthey, the doyen of this later generation of thinkers, early in the 1880s, 'of the causes which have brought about its instability, and of the resources available in it for progress on sound lines, has become a vital question for our civilisation. Therefore the importance of the social sciences in comparison with the sciences of nature is growing'. The task, he had said in his inaugural lecture in 1867, 'is clearly marked out for us: to follow Kant's critical path to the end, and establish an empirical science of the human mind...to get to know the laws which govern social, intellectual and moral phenomena...[ultimately] to be active in the moral world in accordance with a clear knowledge of its great system of laws'. This purpose, so described, would have been as acceptable in France, or England, or Italy, or even the United States as in Germany. Like Comte, Mill, Spencer, Hobhouse and Durkheim, Dilthey inclined to the view that 'those who devote themselves to the [humane] studies are apt to approach them from the standpoint of the practical needs of society, for the purposes of a professional education which equips the leading members of society with the knowledge requisite for the fulfilment of their tasks. Yet this professional education will fit the industrial for the higher functions only in proportion as it goes beyond the limits of a technical training'. Dilthey confessed his failure, however, to have provided a satisfactory basis for the general psychology that he believed to be necessary, a basis that seemed to him to be independent of the particular historical conditions of his own and Kant's thought. He thus moved from his earlier and more naturalistic ambitions towards what was essentially a transcendence of Kant, towards the view that our understanding of ourselves (and of our art, our politics, our society, our philosophy itself) consists in a perpetual reappraisal of our own lives and the extension of these appraisals into 'every kind of expression of our own and other peoples' life'. This, however, against Fichte, Hegel and the others, 'disposes of the view which sees the task of history in the progress from relative values, obligations, norms or goods to unconditional ones', and replaces it with the realisation that in comprehending the past from one's own synthetic but peculiar vantage point one is merely providing material for an endless series of such reappraisals. Any agreement will be temporary, the question of absolute standards lying in 'the ultimate depths of transcendental philosophy, which lie beyond the empirical circle of history, and from which even philosophy' (which 'seeks the solution of the riddle of the world and life') 'cannot wrest an answer'. Somewhat to his surprise, Dilthey ended his career lecturing in the largest hall which the University of Berlin could provide. He had begun his work in the period and the style that the generation after him were to revile, yet in pursuing it with an evident integrity, in the very best tradition of *Wissenschaft,* he had appeared to come to the conclusion that the possible contribution of a natural science of man to the problem he had set himself was much less than he had originally thought. In so doing, he helped undermine what was elsewhere in Germany being redefined and applauded as the Kantian tradition.

Yet it is not wholly surprising that Dilthey should have followed the course that he did, for the connections between psychology and philosophy are uniquely close, and his philosophical culture had always been that of the Lutheran Church (for which he had initially prepared) and the University of Berlin. The power of this culture in Germany revealed itself rather more remarkably in the study of economics. Marx's awareness of English and French classical economics was by no means exceptional among German economists, and in his insistence that what purported to be universal and timeless laws of economic behaviour were but expressions of the particular values and interests of a particular group at a particular stage in the history of economic activity, he was at one with Roscher, Hildebrand, Knies and others who were more acceptable to their academic successors. Moreover, although he did not put it in quite the same terms, Marx realised that the science of economics had ethical implications, that it reflected and by default commended a certain sort of relationship between men, and this too was a view shared by others. However, he replaced the laws of classical economics with scientific 'laws of motion' of his own and was taken to be firmly committed to the thesis that a society's economic organisation decisively determined its character. In these respects he differed, and was rejected by all except the Social Democrats.

The notion that economic life should serve and not determine the character of the society and the nation lay behind the creation in 1872 of the Verein für Sozialpolitik, the Association for Social Policy. Marianne Weber later said that the members of the Association were united by a 'common search for compromise between the economic demands of particular groups, and by the determination to secure the supremacy of ideal interests over material ones', but they became increasingly divided. One faction continued to believe that the Prussian State bureaucracy was the appropriate agent of such ideal interests but another, which became increasingly vocal (although never dominant), argued that the interests of this bureaucracy were as partial as those of any other group, a source of national weakness and conflict rather than of strength and cohesion. (Durkheim, who visited Germany before the second faction made itself felt, was enthused by the ideas of the first, the disparagingly and rather inaccurately named *Kathedersozialisten*, and although his own ideology had independent causes it did somewhat resemble theirs). The first faction was led in its political convictions to underemphasise the importance of the forces of 'capitalism' and so the relevance of Marx; the second, although scarcely sympathetic to the Social Democrats, was not.

It was to some degree each of these trends, but especially Dilthey's philosophy and the stand of some of the older members of the Verein, that provoked the methodological disputes. The issues that were raised in these disputes were not merely academic, for although they took place within and between the universities, they derived their considerable force from the passions that surrounded the question of how one should regard the fundamental economic, social and political changes in Germany itself, a question that also raised that of the proper position, duties and philosophy of the mandarins. The protagonists were many and the arguments, as so often in the history of German dispute, frequently opaque, but virtually all revolved around two connected issues, of how one should in general pursue the *Geisteswissenschaften*, and of the particular place of values in this pursuit.

The argument began in the 1890s. Two philosophers from the University of Marburg, Windelband (whose history of German philosophy later crystallised the distaste many of his generation felt for the middle of the nineteenth century) and Rickert, confronted the ever more evident ambiguities of Dilthey's heroic attempt to establish a basis for the *Geisteswissenschaften*. In a self-styled declaration of war against positivism, Windelband struck indirectly at Dilthey's attempt to effect some sort of methodological connection in a revised psychology between the 'positivist' and 'idealist' approaches. He did so by elaborating upon Dilthey's own distinction between nomothetic and idio-graphic disciplines, the one having an interest in the particular only in so far as it constituted an instance of the general, the other having an interest in the particular for its own sake, for its irreducible uniqueness. The one, Windelband maintained, was characteristic of the sciences in the English and French sense, including psychology; the other of those disciplines concerned with grasping the concreteness, the *Anschaulichkeit*, of things, above all of things to which one might ascribe meaning, and it was these disiplines, Windelband contended, that the fashions of the mid-century had perverted. Rickert, a clearer and altogether more powerful thinker, drove this distinction further toward an equation between the scientific and nomothetic on the one hand and the cultural and idiographic on the other, although he was sensitive enough to realise that many disciplines, including psychology and economics (which he conventionally regarded as a branch of history), were committed to some sort of compromise. Most distinctive about Rickert's argument, however, was his view of the condition which made any subject a candidate for an idiographic approach, a condition which he described as that of 'having a reference to cultural values in order to distinguish between the meaningful and the meaningless'. The argument was one that has since become commonplace in philosophical discussions of the status of the human sciences (although it should be said that Rickert's own defence and extension of it is still one of the best). It was that our selection of subjects for study and our conceptualisation of them out of all the possible conceptuali-sations each depend upon culturally given criteria of importance, so that 'there are', in his words, 'as many different historical truths as there are different spheres of culture', in contrast to truths about nature which (whether yet discovered or not) are timeless and unconditional. Indeed, Rickert drew the inference that 'there is no longer any sense in speaking of truth' in the classic senses at all in the cultural sciences. Yet he did want to claim (after Dilthey and his notion of 'objective *Geist*') that in so far as the culture which informed the selection and conceptualisation was an objective fact so the resultant history (or psychology, or economics) could also be said to be 'objective'. He hesitated over the question of whether or not a universal culture was likely, furnishing a *Kulturwissenschaft* about which all men could agree, but he had no doubt in concluding that 'the point of view of the historical sciences that deal with cultural phenomena is altogether superordinate to that of the natural sciences'. 'Not only are the natural sciences an historical product of civilised man, but also "nature" itself, in the logical or formal sense, is nothing but a theoretical value of cultural life . . . And it is precisely the natural sciences that must always presuppose the absolute validity of the value attaching to this conception'. It would be too vulgar to see this philosophy as a simple rationalisation of the traditional status of the German mandarins, yet the fact that they considered such issues important is clear evidence of their social and political anxiety.

The methodological dispute in the Verein für Sozialpolitik itself smouldered throughout the first years of the century and came to a head at a meeting in January 1914. Two of the most conspicuous and tenacious protagonists were the Weber brothers, Alfred and Max, although it was Max who pursued its more abstract aspects. The paper in which he did so has since become a classic in the philosophy of social science, and although its arguments are not entirely clear, Weber's purpose in it is. It was to distinguish between that which is relevant to values and that which is valued, between the inevitable and indeed entirely desirable circumstance of selecting phenomena according to what Rickert would have described as their 'reference to cultural values', and the reprehensible activities of infusing one's personal values into an analysis or of purporting to derive them from it. Weber's target was the group of older economists in the Verein who by making what seemed to them obviously sensible proposals for the organisation and control of German economic life, between the extremes of the conservatives and the Marxist socialists, were in fact merely parading compromise as disinterested economics. The intensity of his hostility was not unconnected with the fact that like his brother and several other younger economists he strongly disapproved of the actual programmes the older group was proposing. In an earlier essay he had considered the possibility of 'objectivity' in the social sciences in a way very reminiscent of Rickert, with whom he was at the time engaged in a mutually enthusiastic private dialogue. It seems clear that he meant by the term just what Rickert did, namely the condition of selecting and describing a phenomenon from the point of view of the prevailing culture and not of doing so independent of any such bias, which he seems not to have considered as a plausible possibility. 'The *objective* validity of all empirical knowledge', he concluded in this article, 'rests exclusively upon the ordering of the given reality according to categories which are *subjective* in a specific sense, namely, in that they present the *presuppositions* of our knowledge and are based on the presupposition of the *value* of those *truths* which empirical knowledge alone is able to give us'. More bluntly, 'in the cultural sciences concept construction depends on the setting of the problem, and the latter raises the question of the content of culture itself'. It was the culture (as distinct from purely personal values) which was objective, not, in the sense which is intended by Weber's more recent empiricist critics, the judgement itself. To secure the distinction between the value-relevant and the valued ('the exact wording', he wrote to Rickert at the time, 'is of secondary importance'), Weber borrowed from a contemporary, Jellinek, the device of the 'ideal type', of a description, as he put it, 'which is thought to be perfect on logical grounds only, yet by no means as a normative pattern', a description which would embody (from the 'objective' point of view) the necessary features of a phenomenon, shorn of the contingent characteristics it possessed in any particular historical instance. In this way, Weber believed that he could more firmly establish a working procedure for the class of intermediate sciences mentioned by Rickert, and the latter seems to have agreed. The ideal types would make absolutely clear the presuppositions with which the historian was working, and because they did not anywhere perfectly correspond with actual cases, would thus enhance and perhaps secure the objectivity of his analysis. They would not, however, constitute the analysis. This, Weber claimed, would have to be causal, although a complete causal account (let alone one which successfully imputed a single cause) was so unlikely as to be in practice unrealisable. Thus, not only can we not rest content in the historical sciences with enunciating general laws (if any there be), but neither can we be sure even when taking particular cases that we will have provided a complete explanation. Weber was not a philosopher and set these arguments down in the practical interest of promoting good history and 'social-economics' in Wilhelmine Germany. Nevertheless, they served to characterise his conception of sociology, which was a description of his work that he only came often to use in the later part of his working life. This was not so much as an activity distinct from history, but as history made explicit to itself, most especially in its analytical preliminaries.

In his inaugural lecture as professor of economics at Freiburg in 1895, Weber agreed that he was 'a member of the bourgeois classes'. 'I feel myself as such', he said 'and have been brought up in their opinions and ideals'. In one of the last pieces that he wrote before his death in 1920, as an introduction to his essays on religions, he explained that 'a product of modern European civilisation, studying any problem of universal history, is bound to ask himself to what combination of circumstances the fact should be attributed that in Western civilisation, and in Western civilisation only, cultural phenomena have appeared which (as we like to think) lie in a line of development having *universal* significance and value...The central problem for us is not...the development of capitalistic activity as such, differing in different cultures only in form,...It is rather the origin of this sober bourgeois capitalism with its rational organisation of free labour. Or in terms of cultural history, the problem is that of the origin of the Western bourgeois class and its peculiarities, a problem which is certainly closely connected with that of the origin of the capitalistic organisation of labour, but [which] is not quite the same thing'. The subsequent interpretation of Weber's work, where it has not been concerned with the purely philosophical implications of his methodology or the purely analytical and empirical aspects of his history and sociology, has revolved around the consequences in it of this evident bourgeois interest and interest in the bourgeoisie. Was he a bourgeois in the most general and familiar sense, committed to the market and its corollaries of freedom and rationality? Or was he a peculiarly German bourgeois, committed to the demand of his class since before 1848 for a coherent and powerful Germany? Or was he less for any particular cause than against socialism in general and Marxism and the Social Democratic Party in particular? And if he was committed to all or any of these positions, and if the commitments affected his scholarly work, then what of his own precept that the value-relevant and the valued could and should be kept distinct?

Weber was born in Erfurt in 1864. His father, who was than a magistrate, had previously worked for the city of Berlin and returned there with his family in 1869 to take a seat as a National Liberal in the Prussian House of Deputies and (for a shorter period) in the Reichstag. He was an active and intelligent man, but despite his views would never accept that he had to oppose Bismarck or the Prussian hegemony. Weber's mother was a withdrawn and spiritual woman who became increasingly estranged from her husband and his life of worldly satisfactions. Much has been made of the effect of these two and of their relationship upon their eldest son, but the psychology of knowledge is even less determinate than its sociology, and it is sufficient here to say that Max was tormented, a man of exceptional gifts and passionate convictions, yet painfully aware of what he thought of as his failures (especially in practical matters), and with a strong and at times almost crippling sense of duty. He read law at Heidelberg and Berlin, and practised it intermittently in between some teaching and writing until Freiburg offered him a chair in *Nationalökonomie* in 1894. It did so on the basis of two theses, one on medieval business associations and one on Roman agrarian history and its significance for public and private law, and on the basis also of an extensive analysis of rural labour in eastern Germany which he had done for the Verein für Sozialpolitik. He moved on to Heidelberg in 1896, but had a nervous collapse in 1897, and although he was able to begin writing again a few years later he did not return to a university until 1918, when he taught briefly in Vienna. He accepted a chair in Munich in 1919, but died a year later.

The work which has since established Weber's reputation was therefore done largely outside universities, although between 1907 and 1918 he kept up with the Verein, joined the new German Sociological Society, maintained a wide range of acquaintances and affiliations, and eventually took a tentative, tormented and unsuccessful step into politics. His output in the last twenty years of his life was prodigious. In his pursuit of the distinctive features of the western bourgeoisie he wrote about Protestantism, Confucianism, Taoism, Islam, Hinduism, Buddhism and Judaism. In his attempt to establish a basis for sociology he wrote not only several methodological essays but also a monumental but unfinished compendium of 'ideal types'. In his attempt to comprehend and to some extent influence the course of politics, he wrote a large number of often very substantial articles on contemporary events in Germany and Russia. His last intensive work was on a course of lectures at Munich, which were later reconstructed from the audiences' notes and published as a *General Economic History*. It is as misleading to distinguish between the scholarly and polemical in this work as it is to take it as one. Its difficulty and its interest lie in the complexity of the relationships in it between analysis, commendation, condemnation and prescription. These are most close in the various commentaries he wrote toward the end of the First World War on events in Germany and Russia, least so in the compendium of ideal types, but nowhere are they straightforward.

In 1886 and again in 1890 the Verein für Sozialpolitik had discussed the problems created in Germany by the fall in world grain prices in the 1870s. Cheap grains from abroad were displacing the native crop, and as German farmers turned for survival to other cash crops their labourers began to leave the land. In the east, on the large *Junker* estates, Poles, willing to work for lower wages, moved into replace them. This Slavic 'invasion' was taken to be a potential threat to the integrity of German civilisation, and at its second discussion, in 1890, the Verein decided to investigate the whole issue by sending out questionnaires to landowners all over the country. Weber was asked to analyse the results for the most sensitive and problematic areas east of the Elbe. The difficulty here was both economic and political. Unlike the areas to the west and south, the eastern farms were large. Since the beginning of the century they had been able to support relatively large numbers of labourers on annual contract, a contract that in practice gave them consider-

able security and by including some payments in kind incorporated them into the total local society and so involved them,
Weber reasoned, in the economic future of the farms. The
Prussian landowners were thus able to maintain both a viable
agriculture and a modified but secure form of patriarchical
domination. But with the pressure to produce cheaper crops
there came a corresponding pressure to abandon long contracts
for short ones, and so there emerged a class of day labourers
whose interest was more narrowly material and whose connection to the farms was strictly instrumental. The *Junkers* could not,
however, pay high wages, and even where they could (as in parts
of the south-east) the workers, detached from their customary
dependence and subordination, were impatient for independence and upward mobility. Unable to achieve it, they left.
Weber drew two conclusions from this. The *Junkers* were losing
their traditional authority with the advent of what he later came
to call 'the rational organisation of free labour', or capitalism;
and the workers, once freed from patriarchy, were preferring
individual independence to socialist collectivism. Both pleased
him, despite the anxiety he shared with the other members of
the Verein over the immigration of poor Poles. What displeased
him, however, was that although the *Junkers* had 'dug the grave
for [their] own social organisation' they persisted anachronisti-
cally to staff the State and set the social standards for the society.
The bourgeoisie, whose economic practices the *Junker* landowners were being forced to adopt, persisted in aping them in
sending its sons into their bureaucracy and in seeking ennoble-
ment and estates on which to enjoy its prosperity; and the
proletariat, who at least in the case of the eastern rural day
labourers had shown commendable energy and independence,
were prevented from giving it social and political expression by
the Social Democratic Party whose revolutionary rhetoric kept it
apart and drove the bourgeoisie more firmly still into collusion
with the Prussian aristocracy. 'We want to cultivate and
support', he said in 1895, 'what appears to us as valuable in man:
his personal responsibility, his basic drive towards higher things,
towards the spiritual and moral values of mankind, even where
this drive confronts us in its most primitive form. Insofar as it is
in our power we want to create the external conditions which
will help to preserve, in the face of the inevitable struggle for

existence, with its suffering, the best that is in man, those physical and emotional qualities which we would like to maintain for the nation'. The implication was that the 'external conditions' in Wilhelmine Germany were stifling it, and in Weber's view, they continued to do so until his death.

It was clear from his approval of the motives of the day labourers and his disapproval of the attitudes and actions of the bourgeoisie (whose 'cowardice', as he called it, was plain in his own father's position), that Weber valued the conventional liberal virtues of independence and freedom. It was even clearer in his essays on Russia and on socialism. These were written in 1905, 1917 and 1918 and although prompted by the revolutions carried a deeper implication, for he saw alarming similarities between the two countries. In each, capitalism had been imposed from above and had pre-empted the establishment of economic individualism, the proletariat had asserted itself before the bourgeoisie, and the Church had provided no ethical basis for individualism. By 1918, he was castigating the perpetrators of the soviets in Berlin and Munich as fantasists, the tragic effect of the resolute isolation of the Social Democrats, and pointing out that the Bolsheviks in Russia were military dictators who 'had preserved, or rather re-introduced, the highly paid entrepreneur, piece-work, the Taylor System, military and industrial discipline, [had] instituted a search for foreign capital', who in short had had 'to take on again absolutely all the things they had fought as bourgeois class institutions in order to keep the State and the economy going at all'.

Weber's commitment to freedom, however, to economic independence, civil and political rights and to the condition 'in which the soul...chooses the meaning of its own existence', was most apparent of all in his attitude to bureaucracy, the modern debate about which indeed he established. Formally, bureaucracy was a technically efficient instrument of administration, 'the most rational known means of exercising authority over human beings,...superior to any other form in precision, in stability, in the stringency of its discipline, and in its reliability', and as such 'completely indispensible'. But in practice, Weber argued, pointing repeatedly at Germany but also at Russia before and after 1917 and at other societies, it tended to exceed its purely administrative functions and become a political force, expressing the interest of the class which ran it and in its inherently restrictive effects thus inhibiting the freedom of others. This attitude was perhaps Weber's most decisive difference from the more conservative members of the Verein who, like the Russians and like Hegel in Germany before them, saw in the bureaucratic state the very transcendence of particular interests that could alone unite and direct their nation. Weber and his brother confronted the conservatives at a meeting of the Verein in 1909, although each differed in his remedy, Max wishing to reduce the State bureaucracy and all others to their technical, executive functions, Alfred believing that the problem could instead be solved by persuading the bureaucrats of the virtues of liberal values. But both lost the debate, and once war broke out, the Prussian bureaucracy increased its power. This bureaucracy, however, and the similar organisation of the Tsarist State, were not Weber's only targets. He was if anything even more horrified by and so scathing towards the incipient bureaucracy of the Social Democratic Party and a future socialist State. 'If private capitalism were abolished', he warned, 'the State bureaucracy would rule *alone*. Where now the bureaucracies of government and private industry can at least in principle counterbalance each other and hold the other in check, they would then be forged together in a single hierarchy'. The worker would have no redress at all. Freedom, in all senses, would be stifled. In his passion, Weber even deployed his wide reading to argue somewhat tendentiously that the decline of Egypt and Rome provided a precise and terrible historical lesson.

From these political analyses, one might infer that Weber believed that a second late antiquity could be avoided in Germany simply by encouraging the bourgeoisie to assert its interest. But although he believed this to be necessary, he thought it by no means sufficient, for it did not seem that this bourgeoisie had a clear or correct view of what its interest was. In his inaugural lecture at Freiburg he asked 'whether they are politically mature: that is to say, whether they possess respectively the understanding and the capacity to place the political power interests of the nation above all other considerations'. Of course, he argued subsequently, 'personal relationships of dominance' were being replaced by 'the impersonal dominance of class', and this new conflict of class had to be brought into politics. It was as foolish to believe that it could be ignored as it was to believe that it could be abolished, and in this respect the conservatives and National Liberals were as blind as the Social Democrats. But the conflicts of class were by definition conflicts of material interest, and even if properly politicised could not themselves direct the nation. 'The absence of great national power instincts, the restriction of political goals to material ends or at least to the interests of their own generation, the lack of any sense of responsibility towards the future', were all reprehensible, and to be deplored. Weber's justifications for an assertive nationalism for Germany acting imperialistically beyond its frontiers were essentially three. It would facilitate capitalist development, as it had in England. It would secure liberty for the smaller states in Europe by giving them some security in a balance of tension between the great powers. And perhaps most importantly, it would enhance the honour, integrity and vitality of German *Kultur*.

Taken by itself, the successful promotion of this nationalism required as Schmoller put it 'men who stand above party and class'. For Schmoller, on the more conservative wing of the Verein für Sozialpolitik, such men were to be found in the Prussian bureaucracy. Weber rejected this. Instead, he turned to England, to the administrations of Gladstone and Lloyd George, instances, he believed, of what he wanted: an elected leader who nevertheless stood above conflicts of material interest and who, by virtue of his personal vision, was in critical issues able to secure the allegiance of the whole nation and so furnish a truly national policy, but a leader who was nevertheless subject to electoral recall. 'The elected member will conduct himself entirely as the mandated representative of his master the electors, whereas the leader will see himself carrying sole responsibility for what he does. This means that the latter, so long as he can successfully lay claim to their confidence, will act throughout according to his own convictions and not, [like] the member, according to the expressed or supposed will of the electorate'. Parliament would negotiate the claims of the various economic classes and guarantee the individual rights of the electorate. The leader would lead. But by 1919, Weber had become disillusioned with the German parliaments, and was advocating a presidential system in which the leader (more necessary than ever in defeat) would be wholly independent of the compromises and material preoccupations of the representatives.

To the question, therefore, of whether Weber was a Manchester liberal, or a German liberal (in a sense which his father would have resisted), or simply a bourgeois who was hostile to Marxism and the Social Democrats, the answer is that he was both of the first and much more than the third. In a view of politics that was remarkable for its brutal realism, he combined a recognition of the necessity in an industrial society of class conflict and bureaucratic administration with an unremitting hostility to the view that any class but the bourgeoisie could lead; and then insisted that it could only successfully do so if it were able to transcend its strictly class interests.

Weber's purpose in these political writings was firmly to assert what, in his view, Germany required, and to show how to achieve it. The question of objectivity did not arise. Politically, his presuppositions rested upon the belief that the 'peculiarities' of the bourgeoisie were the only ones appropriate for contemporary conditions. In that context, they had no 'universal' significance. Yet in his introduction to the collected essays on the world religions, he referred to 'the origin of...sober business capitalism', 'the origin of the Western bourgeois class and...its peculiarities' as phenomena which lay 'in a line of development having *universal* significance and value', and explicitly declared that it was this significance and this value which informed the essays. There was, therefore, a coincidence between what he himself valued in politics and what he considered universally relevant for historical and sociological analysis. This coincidence suggests that like more orthodox philosophers of history (whether sociologically inclined or not), his entire work derived from and was intended to secure a definitive view of the meaning of events and the desirability of a particular end. But he himself seemed to dispute the validity of any such connection. 'We must realise', he wrote, 'that the general views of life and the universe can never be the products of increasing empirical knowledge', that we can never in that way 'learn the meaning of the world', that such meanings arise only 'in the struggle with other ideals', in the course of purely moral debate. However, as he readily agreed, the topics and terms of his historical explanations and sociological typologies were chosen in the light of their relevance to 'universal' values, and although no value was logically entailed by the subsequent analysis the very fact that this analysis proceeded within such value-related terms meant that in a non-logical sense it inevitably commended and condemned without at all impugning what Weber himself would have described as its validity. 'An attitude of moral indifference has no connection with scientific objectivity', even though no morality may properly be deduced from an objective analysis. But as a result, the line between the 'value-relevant' and the 'valued' was and is more difficult to draw than Weber was willing to concede.

His first and always most famous academic essay on the distinctive characteristics of the western bourgeoisie, 'The Protestant ethic and the spirit of capitalism', appeared in two parts in the journal of the Verein in 1905. It was, he said, a purely 'preparatory' piece, intended not to explain the development of capitalism (that had its roots in more mundane and distant circumstances) but rather to describe its *Geist*, its spirit, and the 'elective affinity' between this spirit and the distinctive ethic of the Protestant sects of the Reformation. In it, he argued that there was an affinity between on the one hand the conception of economic activity as a 'calling' (*Beruf*), as an obligation to work, save and invest as an end in itself, denying all hedonism, an obligation that put economic activity at the centre of life and did not relegate it to the moral margins, the conception that defined the distinctiveness of capitalism against other forms of accumulation; and on the other hand the psychological consequence of the Calvinist doctrine of pre-destination which, in asserting that nothing men could do in this world affected the decision God had already taken about their fate in the next, was that to assure themselves that they were graced in the next world men were driven to ascetic industry in this. The affinity was causal in so far as it was psychological, but Weber's point was less to establish a causal thesis than to argue, against the prevailing materialist interpretations of capitalism (among conservatives as much as among Marxists) that what was most distinctive about it, what crucially distinguished it from other forms of appropriation and accumulation, was its moral character. In that sense, the essay was an attempt to establish an 'ideal type', the pure and necessary characteristics of western bourgeois capitalism.

This purpose becomes clearer when the essay is compared

with another on 'The Protestant sects and the spirit of capitalism' which he wrote after a visit to America in 1904, and with his
extensive survey of urban life. In these (and again in his later
summary in the lectures on *General Economic History*), Weber
attributed the development of bourgeois capitalism to the
absence of ritual demarcations and taboos between the
heterogeneous groups of inhabitants in the cities of the west, to
the associated disappearance of separate and opposed moralities
within and between groups, most especially kin groups, and to
the absence of domination from outside. By this argument, he
arrived at a similar position to Marx. What distinguished western capitalism was the remorseless intrusion of money-making
into all social relations, the thoroughgoing rationalisation of
social life, which tended to subordinate everything to the material conflict of interest between capital and formally free labour.
But neither Marx nor the conservatives, Weber insisted, recognised the moral significance of this process, the fact that the
western bourgeoisie was not merely one more group dedicated
to material accumulation but the one group for whom this end
had at once religious and thus moral significance. Other groups
had either separated the moral life from the material, or had
been so dominated by moral proscription that their accumula-
tive energies were altogether inhibited.

Weber at first intended to go further into the social history of
Protestantism, but because his friend and colleague Troeltsch
was doing so, decided instead to reinforce his argument for the
distinctiveness, the 'uniqueness', of the western bourgeoisie by
turning to a study of other religions: hence the essays on Confucianism, Taoism, Islam, Hinduism, Buddhism and ancient
Judaism. In each it is clear that Weber was pursuing his insight
into the crucial importance of the relationship between the
worldly implications of religious ethics, of the ways in which they
did and did not distinguish between moral and material life, and
of the extent to which they prescribed accommodation to, rather
than conquest of, the world. Since Christianity, and thus Protestantism, derived from it, and since some contemporaries (like
Sombart) were insisting upon its significance for the development of capitalism, the essay on Judaism is perhaps the most
illuminating. The turbulence and insecurity of Jewish life from
the twelve hundred or so years before Christ, Weber argued,

had had the effect of inducing in the Jews a defensive ethnic solidarity and a fatalistic conception of the will of God. 'An ascetic management of this world', he put it later, 'such as that characteristic of Calvinism, was the very last thing of which a traditionally pious Jew would have thought...It was incumbent upon the individual Jew to make peace with the fact that the world would remain recalcitrant to the promises of God as long as God permitted the world to stand as it is...[his] responsibility was to make peace with this recalcitrancy of the world, while finding contentment if God sent him grace and success in his dealings with the enemies of his people, toward whom he must act soberly and legalistically...This meant acting toward non-Jews in an objective or impersonal manner, without love and without hate'.

Thus, although there was material accumulation in non-western societies, it was rarely if ever capitalistic, at the most marginal to the ethics of social life and so not valued, and at the least altogether constrained. Similarly, the evident accumulation of Jews and Catholics in Europe itself, although often called capitalist, was not so, for it too was morally epiphenomenal and thus had little or no effect upon the fundamental values of either group. Only the Protestant sects, in reinforcing their hope of election to grace in the next world by material accumulation and investment in this, caused this truly capitalistic activity to take a central place in social life. Only through them did the characteristic rationality of capitalism come to pervade all social relations. Only through them did the western bourgeoisie acquire its distinction, which was both practical and moral. In defending this argument, however, Weber was indulging in nothing so simple as special pleading. Of course, he had himself always valued and so regarded as of general importance the drive in any group 'towards higher things, towards the spiritual and moral values of mankind' and was thus led to value the historic distinction of the western bourgeoisie, particularly since its values were the ones he shared. And he regarded the outcome of capitalist rationality in the formal discipline of organised administration as unavoidably necessary for the efficient management of modern societies. But to accept is not to commend, and as his political polemics clearly reveal, he condemned the 'disenchantment' of the world that this formal rationality had produced, the denial of 'spiritual and moral values' in the dead if efficient hand of bureaucratic administration and the purely material squabbles of elected politicians.

All of Weber's essays before his nervous collapse in 1897, and most of his subsequent political ones, were pieces of history, directed to 'the causal analysis and explanation of individual actions, structures and personalities possessing cultural significance'. The studies of the world religions, although prompted by the historical claims of others, were intended more to define the ideal-typical characteristics of each as they related to economic activity, although the vigour of the debate about them since, and especially about 'The Protestant Ethic and the spirit of capitalism', has largely rested upon the assumption that in them Weber was making only causal claims. However, in the terms of Weber's own later distinction, they were rather sociological, seeking 'to formulate type concepts and generalised uniformities of empirical process'. Between 1910 and 1914, he worked upon another similarly 'sociological' enterprise, albeit one that also contained much causal imputation, which he called 'The economy and normative and *de facto* powers'. Only in the last two years of his life did he turn, somewhat hesitantly and with misgivings ('people', he said, 'will shake their heads'), to a purely ideal-typical task, an elaboration of some 'basic sociological terms'. The lack of enthusiasm with which these were greeted, however, prompted him to abandon them and turn back finally to a general economic history. It is these definitional chapters, together with the far larger work on economies and power, which make up the two parts of what we take as his *Economy and Society.*

When he was preparing 'The economy and normative and *de facto* powers', Weber described it as a study of 'economic development...[conceived] as part of the general rationalisation of life' and as 'dealing with the structure of...political organisations in a comparative and systematic manner'. This is what it is, an analysis of types of economic action and organisation, of types of norms and values and political domination, and of the relations between them. In this sense, it is both typological and propositional. Its distinctions and propositions cut across the 'basic terms' he added after the war, although (as he himself of course believed) at least one of these sets of terms helps explain their point. It is the one intended to distinguish 'types of social action'. Weber distinguished four such: instrumentally rational, 'value rational', affective and traditional. The last two are straightforward and self-explanatory, actions distinguished by their emotional or habitual character; but the first two are not. He defined them respectively as actions determined by the rational consideration of alternative means to an end and actions determined by convictions of 'the value for its own sake of some ethical, aesthetic, religious or other form of behaviour, independently of its prospects of success'. Relying upon what may be apocryphal asides by Weber himself, commentators have seen something of Nietzsche in the second, but it is perhaps better understood in Kantian terms, as a moral imperative whose social expression is an overriding sense of duty to an ideal. In itself this is readily comprehensible. What is not is Weber's description of it as *Wertrationalität*, since it is clear that it is neither rational in the Kantian sense, furnishing a binding because rational law (for Weber never accepted such a possibility), nor 'irrational' in any sense except the dubiously useful one of not corresponding to facts. It is, more simply, non-rational.

However, whether *Wertrationalität* is rational or not, the contrast Weber drew between it, *Zweckrationalität*, and traditionalism serves to elucidate his purpose in 'The economy...' although not, perhaps, the work itself. The purpose was to classify the types of power consequent upon types of economic action. Weber never seriously doubted the very general Marxist tenet, as he read it, that men's interests, and especially their material ones, were almost always to be found at the root of their political claims. What he did resist was that this was always and in every instance true, or that even where it was, that it was the sole and uncomplicated motive. What he resisted most strongly was the view that it should be, which is why he devoted so much energy to the exceptions and complications. It had been the motive, he agreed, in the cities of late medieval Europe, 'in which power [had] its source in a formally free interplay of interested parties such as occurs especially in the market'. But it had not been true in almost all other instances, either because traditional considerations had played a part (and in some places, such as India and China, a dominant part), or because, even if they had not, material interests had been complicated by those who were seeking to secure their power having appealed to ethical justifications, something, indeed, which had happened in the early modern period in Europe itself.

Weber thus distinguished two broad classes of domination, the legitimated and the unlegitimated. Within the first, he distinguished between legitimations in the name of tradition, legitimations in the name of the personal qualities of a leader ('charisma'), and legitimations in the name of established and wholly binding rules, formalised as law. This cut across his typology of action in two ways. First, although 'charismatic' domination corresponded to *Wertrationalität* and traditional domination to traditionalism, both legal and non-legitimate domination were forms of *Zweckrationalität*. But second, the distinct status of 'traditionalism' in the typology of action looks peculiar in view of that fact that an appeal to tradition is a way of securing allegiance, and in that way *zweckrational*. Indeed, in his description of it, it seems less of a pure type than a contingent mixture of *Zweckrationalität* and appeals to emotion. One is indeed tempted to ignore the typology of action altogether, for it seems to confuse rather than to clarify what Weber says about everything except the free-for-all of the late medieval European city and the historically intermittent appearance of charisma. Yet precisely because of the unique historical coincidence, so central to Weber's entire view, of the appearance of capitalism in the late medieval city and the emergence there of charismatic Protestant sectarians, the confusion clarifies. It clarifies not the actual typologies of *Economy and Society* but instead Weber's purpose in constructing them, which was by more formal analysis once more to reveal the uniquely 'value-relevant' double paradox of western bourgeois capitalism: the paradox of its origins in an extraordinary conjunction of relatively unconstrained material possibility and an overriding *Wertrationalität*, and the paradox of its development, only comprehensible by reference to its origins, into a most remorseless and far reaching *Zweckrationalität*.

Weber is the least easy of sociologists to assess. To assess him by sociological criteria alone is indeed to ignore his value, and his 'value-relevance'. He proposed no logically complete method and set himself against the elaboration of a general, formal and definite theory. To criticise him, therefore, for technical inconsistency or for incompleteness, while perhaps helpful to oneself, is by implication to attribute to him intellectual intentions he never had. It is in his substantial realisation of the intentions that he did have that his enduring value lies. He is quite alone in the history of social theorising in western Europe and North America in having set himself against the classical sociological project of furnishing comprehensive typologies and complete causal accounts yet in having managed at the same time to produce an interpretation of the singularity of western capitalism which carries more weight than any but Marx's, and in its historical sensitivity, more weight than any. In good part he overcame the moral and analytical disadvantages of both historical particularity and sociological generality. But in doing so, he did subvert two of his own principles. He did not in general maintain the distinction that he drew in the methodological debates in the Verein between the 'valued' and the 'value-relevant', and, which was related to this, he did not entirely escape his own injunction against imputing a meaning to history. It is true that he spurned teleology. But his commitment to what was for him at once the uniqueness and universality of western capitalism was a commitment which led him to impute a meaning to the future of past events. Nevertheless, one must concede that if he did fail in these two respects, it did not matter. Had he not, he would not have produced a comparative history of such value. And had he not tried to succeed, he would not have so clearly revealed the extraordinary difficulties of writing such history.

In his formulation of his problems, Weber was very much a member of the Wilhelmine *Bildungsbürgertum*, albeit an exceptionally politically aware one. In his solution of them, however, he was much less so. Indeed, he is in this respect not typical of anything. It is particularly ironic that especially in the country which after his visit there in 1904 he praised for its forthright and critical individualism, he has since been taken to be a paradigmatic sociologist. No-one stands in sharper contrast to the intellectual sterility and moral fatuity of much modern professional sociology. And no-one stood in sharper contrast to the intellectual arrogance and moral and political irresponsibility of the *Bildungsbürgertum* itself.

8

History doubted

IT IS CONVENTIONALLY assumed that the 1914–18 War was in Europe as decisive a turning point as the revolution of 1789. It perhaps marked the clear beginning of the end of pure industrial capitalism as both its apologists and Marx had described it, and yet also the beginning of institutionalised communism as virtually no-one (not even Lenin) had quite imagined it. It marked the beginning of the refutation of all the progressive social theories of the nineteenth century. But this is hindsight. It would have been remarkable if in 1918, or in 1920 or even in 1930 many had realised this, and few did. Accordingly, social theorising between the wars displays a greater continuity with the pre-war period than does the history of the societies themselves, a continuity not only in its most general assumptions (which one would not anyway expect to change so suddenly) but also in its intentions and expectations.

Nowhere was this more marked than in England, victorious in the war and not seriously threatened by revolutionary socialism. Sociology there, such as it was, like sociology in France and Germany, had before the war been a stalking horse of those whom one can now see as 'modernists', men who wished to solve the problems of capitalist change as they revealed themselves in the particular social and political disjunctions of their society without resorting either to irrelevant reaction or to revolutionary change. But unlike their contemporaries in France and Germany, such men in England had no lasting need theoretically to justify this solution, and no need to organise themselves outside the political parties to promote it. The growing realisation that classical laissez-faire could not by itself be expected to increase the welfare of all had, in the 1870s and 1880s, been marked by a revulsion towards those theories which had earlier been proposed to explain and justify it, a revulsion particularly towards various sorts of utilitarianism. But this was relatively short-lived. By 1914, the arguments of those like the Oxford Idealists who wished to see the State intervene more actively to redress the miseries and iniquities of unbridled capitalism had been so widely accepted, by governments as well as by the intelligentsia, that their theoretical foundations had ceased to be necessary and so ceased, to most, to be interesting. Hobhouse, for example, was already an anachronism. This success had a profound and paradoxical effect upon English intellectual life. It was to make the country's intelligentsia relatively indifferent to the theoretical changes that were occurring on the continent and to allow them to work once again within the assumptions that in the period of guilt and disillusion in the 1870s, 1880s and 1890s they had begun to reject. The result was theoretical muddle amidst relatively rapid social reform.

Those assumptions are nowhere more clearly revealed than in Henry Sidgwick's *The Method of Ethics*, the Sidgwick who had so sharply exposed general sociologies to the British Association in 1885. Painfully abandoning his youthful Christianity, Sidgwick had attempted to combine a long-standing view that moral goodness was immediately knowable through intuition with utilitarianism which, like most of his contemporaries, he believed to be insufficient as a basis for a properly moral philosophy but essential to any decision as how best to compromise between private and public welfare. It is at once apparent that his attempt was doomed. Unless one intuits that moral goodness lies in a direction that itself happens to coincide with a coincidence between private and public happiness, there is no way of ensuring a compatible outcome and thus of avoiding three possibly conflicting ones. Sidgwick ceased for a time to be taken seriously by many philosophers, many of whom either, like Moore, abandoned utilitarianism and indeed any attempt empirically to calculate the good, or, like T. H. Green and Hobhouse, had turned to Hegel. Had the arguments towards the end of the century for benevolent intervention been unsuccessful, it is possible that the middle-class intelligentsia more generally would have accepted the need for a fundamental reconsideration of the premises of their liberalism, and that the working class and the new labour parties would have embraced Marx. But the arguments were not unsuccessful. Most (including most of the working class) were able to convince each other that there were feasible policies to guide the structure of capitalism and the society it had created in more acceptable directions without affecting the basic structure of either, and were thus able to persuade each other (without invoking his professionally somewhat discredited name) that Sidgwick's project was an entirely reasonable one. The assumptions of those concerned with the social question in England after 1918, as already before the war, were those of a technically incoherent ethics.

This ethics, in its implication that capitalist development was compatible with active social reform, was also in the most general way the philosophy of the French and German sociologists. Shorn of their native rationalism, Durkheim's beliefs (and their weaknesses) are remarkably like Sidgwick's, and Max Weber explicitly invoked Gladstone and Lloyd George as men who had been able in ways of which he entirely approved to rise above the sordid materialism and evident injustice of unfettered economic competition to guide the nation towards the higher ideals of which he believed the bourgeoisie was capable. But because the Liberal Party and the gradually coalescing labour parties in England began early to pursue such a course, there was no need, in England, for the kind of academic bridgehead that the *Kathedersozialisten* had tried to establish in the Verein für Sozialpolitik (and that Tönnies and Weber had later attempted in the German Sociological Society), or for the kind that Durkheim and his associates had tried to establish in the *équipe* of the *Année Sociologique* and later in the *écoles normales*. Hobhouse's pre-war isolation is entirely comprehensible. It was not that he was going against prevailing views. It was that he was so much with them that few required him (and thus his conception of general sociology) to point them out. He was unique among European social theorists of his generation in drawing no native polemic at all. Nevertheless, there were groups in England who believed that within the broad liberal and liberal–socialist consensus they could best further their particular ambitions in the name of 'sociology'. One consisted of Hobhouse himself, his successor Ginsberg, and a few friends. A second consisted of Branford, Geddes and their immediate circle, who had organised the Sociological Society before the war and persuaded Martin White to pay for the chair of sociology at the London School of Economics, and who continued to edit the *Sociological Review* until the early 1930s. A third, much the largest and much the least connected, consisted of the considerable number of people who believed that rational reform required facts and who accordingly instituted a large number of empirical surveys to discover them.

Branford and Geddes were eccentrics with extremely diffuse beliefs. Branford had acquired a broad Scots education in scientific subjects, written poetry, organised the railways in Paraguay and set up a Cuban telephone service before devoting himself to what both he and Geddes called 'civic sociology'. This was broadly inspired by Le Play. Branford set himself against an analysis purely in terms of a supposed antagonism between capital and labour, and argued instead that all successful civilisations had consisted of a co-operation between 'chiefs', 'people', 'emotionals' and 'intellectuals', a co-operation whose contemporary expression and guiding force was to be the synthesis of all science, philosophy and aesthetics in the 'more vital doctrine' of sociology. He also invoked the attitudes of Le Play, and it was Le Play in particular who inspired Geddes' much less elaborately articulated and more practical vision of communities in which all aspects of life would be in harmony both with each other and with the physical environment, a vision that recalled much earlier arcadias of rural life but which for Geddes was to be realised in the more realistic compromise of planned 'garden cities'. This conception had some impact in England (and was to be revived after 1945 in the establishment of 'New Towns' in England and Scotland), but the civic sociology upon which it rested died with its proponents, with Branford in 1930 and with Geddes a year later. Their friend, Farquharson, continued as an editor of the *Review*, but the periodical almost immediately changed its character and by 1934 there was no sign in it at all of the romantic effusions of those who had begun it.

Despite the fact that Branford and Geddes had together secured the funds for the first chair in sociology at the London School of Economics, neither Hobhouse nor Ginsberg paid them any further attention. They were evidently an embarrassment. Like Hobhouse, Ginsberg came to sociology from philosophy, first as Hobhouse's assistant at the School and then as a temporary replacement for Attlee and Tawney there during the war. But Hobhouse had come from an Hegelian Oxford, and although he was never a conventional Hegelian, even a conventional English Hegelian (he had too much respect for Spencer for that), there was always a discernibly Hegelian teleology in what he wrote. Ginsberg was greatly affected by Hobhouse (who quite apart from his views was clearly a man to be loved and respected), but not by Hegel. His direct inspiration, as he later recalled, was Sidgwick, and Sidgwick's ambitions and failures are exactly his. Unlike Hobhouse, he had no teleology, but he did have faith in an historical progression towards the universalisation of morals, towards a greater influence upon men of their consciences (and thus of their own independently critical rationality), and towards a clearer distinction between individual and collective responsibilities (evident in the steady separation of morals, religion and law). If moral progress was not, as for Hobhouse, pre-ordained, it seemed nevertheless to be occurring. But Ginsberg realised that it was a conditional matter, and the task of sociology as he saw it was to discern and specify the conditions under which it could continue. This of course was exactly Durkheim's view, and Ginsberg did indeed once say that had Sidgwick lived he would have done so to eat his words about general sociologies in the face of what was to Ginsberg the evident agreement between Durkheim and Hobhouse (and, he was too modest to add, himself). It was plain to him that general sociology, thus conceived, had justified itself. He was right, and he was wrong. He was right in that most liberal Englishmen, even into the depression of the 1930s, continued to share Sidgwick's faith; but wrong in that precisely because they did so they had no need to secure and defend it by anything as distinctive as a separate intellectual and academic pursuit. He did indeed identify others as being in accord with the spirit of the subject as he and Hobhouse had defined it, men such as J. A. Hobson, Lowes Dickinson, R. H. Tawney, G. D. H. Cole and Harold Laski. But what is interesting about such men is that they felt able to articulate their views in economics, economic and social history, the new political science, the Labour Party or even, in Hobson's case, quite independently. No-one, except a few pupils, needed or heeded Ginsberg's sociology.

'The prevailing disposition' amongst sociologists in England, Hobson remarked in the 1930s, 'is to deny the existence of a social mind, a collective consciousness, and to regard all social activities and institutions as contributions to the life of the individual persons who join in these co-operative processes'. The inverse of this disposition, to avoid talk of abstractions like structures and consciousnesses and to concentrate instead upon the effects of economic and social circumstances on individuals, recalling J. S. Mill's recommendations nearly a century before, exactly describes the intentions of those, much the most numerous among all who ever described themselves as 'sociologists', who believed that effective reform depended upon a detailed knowledge of what had to be reformed. And the recollection of Mill is not merely academic, for like him these people took for granted in a way that European theorists almost never did that their audience would have a generally agreed picture of the society as a whole and how it should be reformed, and needed only to be told about the details. Hence the enthusiasm for particular, often local surveys, of which nearly two hundred had been completed by the middle of the 1930s, in which the intention was as precisely as possible to document the effects on the deprived of the circumstances in which they found themselves.

The moral, intellectual, and political conditions in which this work was done are well revealed by the treatment in it of the notion of 'class'. In Germany, the economic classes of capitalism had cut directly across a pre-industrial social structure that had itself lasted almost intact into the nineteenth century. For this reason, German social theorists (of whom Marx and Weber are only the most conspicuous examples) were much exercised by them, and it is indeed to them still that one returns for a proper discussion. In France, economic classes had been evident much earlier (Saint-Simon, after all, had discussed them), but after the Commune to talk of classes was to concede the analytical scheme of the more revolutionary socialists and the concept dropped away from liberal sociology. In England, however, it was possible to concede what elsewhere only the most determinedly blind, like Durkheim, could not, that capitalism was in one sense or another about the development of clear and potentially antagonistic classes, for there was no danger of thereby conceding too much to the revolutionary cause. There were no revolutionaries. Indeed, there was such agreement in England, where the language of class pervaded all discussions, that their existence and nature could be taken for granted. They were simply part of the scenery. Accordingly, 'class' was mentioned everywhere and analysed almost nowhere in discussions of the social question in England between the wars. A rough classification had been officially established by the Registrar General in 1911, and although it was afterwards altered in minor ways it was generally accepted right up to the beginning of the Second World War, and indeed for several years afterwards.

There is therefore no need to be especially surprised by the lack of a flourishing self-styled sociology in England before 1939. And there is no need to invoke the 'empiricist temper of English thought' or to invent conspiratorial enemies like the old universities at Oxford and Cambridge to explain it. After all, Hegel had, for a time, swept through both these universities; Weber and to a much lesser extent Tönnies had not been entirely unsuccessful in impressing 'idealist' Germans with the need for empirical inquiry; and Durkheim had successfully stormed the heart of the French educational establishment. The proper explanation starts rather from a redescription of what has to be explained. Sociology was virtually absent in England as an intellectually and academically distinctive pursuit because it was virtually everywhere present as part of the general liberal and liberal–socialist consciousness. There are good historical reasons for the frequent English complaint that sociology is mere commonsense.

If the continuity of English social and political thought throughout the nineteenth century and into the first four decades of the twentieth is most simply understood by the absence both of any threat of revolution from the left and of any concerted resistance from the right, the continuity of French thought over the same period is most simply understood by the perpetual presence of such threats, not always real, but always perceived, after 1789, after 1848, after 1871 and finally after 1920. Saint-Simon's enemies were Comte's, Comte's were Durkheim's, and Durkheim's were those of his less assertive but nevertheless evident disciples in the 1920s and 1930s, although by this time they were as a result of Durkheim's tactical successes in the French educational system more academic than they had been in the years immediately before the war.

The rationalist republicanism of the group around Durkheim,

directed against both the right and the revolutionary left, an ideology of orderly evolution to be directed by an informed intelligentsia, had before 1914 had only a fleeting representation in French political life. This was in the Parti Socialiste Français, led by Durkheim's fellow *Normalien* Jaurès, a party which despite its name took a quite different view from the collection of Blanquists and men from the old Parti Ouvrier who made up Guesde's Parti Socialiste de France in rejecting faith and hope in the deliverances of capitalist collapse and in insisting instead that reform, democratic reform through the parliamentary system, could produce a progressive order in which all classes (and not just the bourgeoisie) could enjoy the fruits of liberty, equality and fraternity. But Jaurès' orthodox political ambitions drove him first into temporary alliances with the radicals and then, seeking a wider base, into a more deliberate collaboration with Guesde, the outcome of which was the creation in 1905 of the Section Française de l'Internationale Ouvrière, a party that he and Guesde led together until 1914 when he was assassinated and the party joined the Union Sacrée of all groups to fight the war. Not surprisingly, the S.F.I.O. in this first, short period of its existence was an ideologically and politically heterogeneous organisation, uniting very disparate groups on the left between the staunch defenders of the spirit of Babeuf and the more radical syndicalists on the one hand and the more liberal than socialist and almost wholly bourgeois moderates on the other. It was generally although not always Marxist in its analysis, although not at all radical, in any usual Marxist sense, in its recommendations. Durkheim could no more belong to it than he could to the anarchic syndicalists or the equally anarchic although more moderate Radicals.

After the war, the S.F.I.O. preserved a precarious unity until 1920, when one faction split to promote the dictatorship of the proletariat in a new communist party and the other remained, under the old name and the leadership now of Léon Blum, to pursue a socialism that although still loosely Marxist in inspiration set itself against what it regarded as the communists' willingness to place the interests of one class and even of Soviet Russia above those of France. Two years later, the unions split similarly into a communist federation and one retaining the more ancient ambitions of the Jacobin cause. On the right were parties both of the industrial and commercial bourgeoisie and of the more traditional conservatives and reactionaries against whom self-consciously progressive men had fought over Dreyfus in the 1890s. The centre was held, although that is hardly the right word, by the Radicals, the party of the petit bourgeoisie and, in the 1920s, of lawyers, doctors and teachers, a party whose base was almost entirely outside Paris, in small towns and the rural areas, whose ideology was essentially negative, against the Church, the army, and the communists, and whose pivotal political position was almost entirely vitiated by its distrust of the kind of power that of all parties it stood most chance, by being in the middle, of securing. The result of this fragmentation was markedly ineffectual government, relieved only temporarily and very belatedly by the Popular Front between 1936 and 1938. Its cause was the extremely complex pattern of interests still in France, between industry and agriculture, Paris and the provinces, and the Church and the laity. Its reflection was ideological confusion.

The confusion most relevant to the history of sociology between the wars was that between the Radicals and Blum's socialist party. In what it was against, the rationalist republicanism which had before the war affected the *Normaliens* like Jaurès and Durkheim found its most natural expression outside Jaurès's own party in the Radicals. In the 1920s, indeed, most of the intelligentsia belonged to this party. In what it was for, this republicanism would appear to have been more at home with Blum. But Blum always declared a faith in Marx, and this was incompatible with the view of the republicans (in this respect very much like the views of the progressive liberal socialists in England) that although much difficulty had been caused by the antagonism between capital and labour everything would be lost by the issue being decided in favour of one or the other. It was not until the 1960s that this political vacuum, the lack so to speak of a forum for the spirit of Saint-Simon, was to be filled. As a result, the theoretical tradition that Durkheim had so quickly and so skilfully revived found no ready practical outlet, and instead remained a purely academic force, although in France that meant much, since also at issue as before the war was the proper training of teachers and so also the proper education of children.

It was, however, an academic force in one respect not unlike that of the liberals and liberal socialists in England. Writing of the period before the war, Lévi-Strauss said that 'French sociology does not consider itself as an isolated discipline, working in its own specific field, but rather as a method, or as a specific attitude towards human phenomena. Therefore one does not need to be a sociologist in order to do sociology'. This was also true before 1914. Of the *professeurs agrégés* engaged with Durkheim in the production of the *Année Sociologique*, a majority were *agrégés* in philosophy, and their leader's inspiration was as marked afterwards in psychology, linguistics, history, law, geography and even economics, for long under-developed in France, as it was in sociology, so named, itself. The spirit of the *équipe* of the *Année* had been above all an *ésprit de système*. The circle had been convinced that Durkheim's conceptions were so fundamental and all-embracing that it was perfectly natural that those infected with them should attempt to apply them elsewhere. That these applications went formally under the name of other subjects was simply due to the organisation of French faculties, in which sociology found no ready place. By the end of the 1930s, there were still only three chairs of sociology itself, at Bordeaux, Paris and Toulouse, but it was significant that Bouglé, one of the original circle, was by then director of the Ecole Normale Supérieure. As he himself declared in 1938, Durkheim's sociology stood for humanism against individualism and specialisation, for the intellectual unity of the country in a spirit of rational progress, as a cohesive force, a force whose power was conceded even by the old ecclesiastical enemy who in the 1930s was still declaring that the proposal to teach Durkheim's sociology in the two hundred *écoles normales* was the greatest danger facing France. It is perhaps testimony to the myopia of the Durkheimians as much as to that of the Church that each should even then, as France drifted through the depression, have identified this, of all things, as the issue.

Many of the original *équipe*, including Durkheim's son, were killed in the war, and of those who were left the succession passed most naturally to his nephew Mauss. Mauss tried, unsuccessfully as it turned out, to revive the *Année* in the 1920s, and the few issues that did appear indicate the conservatism of his direction. After extensive tributes to Durkheim himself, Mauss set out 'la division et les proportions des divisions de la sociologie' in a way directly reminiscent of the original scheme of the magazine, and his own subsequent work as well as that of other Durkheimians pursued not only the same notions but also the same subjects as had Durkheim himself. Bayet and Halbwachs published separate works on suicide which, although making more concessions than did the original to psychological factors, were still polemically sociological. As such, they drew the fire of psychologists and psychiatrists. Fauconnet published a book on the concept of responsibility, in which he argued that this notion was a product of a long course of social differentiation, in which there had developed a high degree of individuation and a corresponding respect for the individual such that 'society' was led to attribute responsibility for crime to individuals. Davy and Moret in *From Clans to Empires* argued for the importance of the totemic group in early Egyptian society. And Mauss continued the more general attack on 'psychologism' as well as Durkheim's concern with simpler societies. However, in Halbwachs and in Davy and Moret, at least, one can discern some softening of the original intransigence towards both psychology and the dogma that religion is an entirely social product, and Mauss concentrated more upon the inverse of the method of concomitant variation, upon the residues that such variations could not explain, with the result that he came in the 1930s to recommend more empirical work and so to train a number of ethnographical fieldworkers. Moreover, the criticisms continued to come, not only from psychologists, themselves of course just as *parti pris*, but also from those in other subjects who resented the Durkheimians' ambitions and those like Lacombe who saw clearly that this putatively scientific sociology was indeed nothing more than a marvellously sustained tautology in defence of the classical bourgeois interest of orderly change.

Although, therefore, the intellectual situation of French sociology after 1918 resembled that of sociology in England, the resemblance was entirely superficial. Sociological notions were, as in England, diffused among many who were not primarily and who would certainly not have called themselves sociologists, but the notions were abstract and their diffusion was an almost wholly academic one. Even by the 1930s, there was virtually no sustained consideration of social reform between the mechanical parrotings of Thorez's communists (who were increasingly dictated to by Moscow) and the resolutely backward-looking individualism of the Radicals, and even if the responsibility for this lies as much with the intellectuals as with anyone else the fact was that the sociologists had no forum beyond the seminar and arguments about school curricula. For this reason, there was outside the interests of Mauss's anthropological pupils no corrective to the established tendency of French intellectualism towards extreme generality. Durkheim's intellectual victory before the war had been a purely verbal one. His pupils made virtually no advance. Despite the economic and social changes in French society, nearly half-rural as it still was, French sociology had almost the same intellectual character in 1940 as it had had in 1914, and less moral and political force.

The German intellectuals' appreciation of the changes brought about by the First World War were altogether more acute than those of the English or the French. But the comparison is pointless, for the changes they perceived were changes quite different from those which in hindsight one can see as having taken place to the west. It was not merely that Germany had suffered what all agreed was in Max Weber's words a 'terrible defeat and violation'. It was also, and much more importantly, that the defeat had appeared finally to destroy the pre-industrial order and so propel the country into exactly the sort of state that all had managed to unite in fighting in the war itself. It signalled not the end of a bourgeois order but its beginning, the final collapse of honour and ideals and the long-feared arrival of materialism, 'interest-mongering' and scepticism, the autumn, as Spengler described it in *The Decline of the West*, of Faustian culture, the victory of what Sombart had called the 'utilitarian–mercenary' values of hated England. It is in this context that one has to understand Max Weber's attempt politically to secure what he believed to be the altruistic idealism of the bourgeoisie at its best. By 1919, nothing more was possible, and to him as to almost all Germans except those in the Social Democratic Party, anything less spelled capitulation to *Zweck-rationalität* and perhaps even to socialism.

The socialist threat did indeed seem considerable in 1919.

Already in the election in 1912 the Social Democrats had emerged as the largest single party with thirty-five per cent of the votes and twenty-eight per cent of the seats in the Reichstag, much more formidable than the socialist parties in England and France. But their impact on events to August 1914 was reduced by their insistence on the establishment of full parliamentary rule, the government's refusal to concede it, and the disinclination of the bourgeois parties to help them press it. The Social Democratic leaders were also internationalist in outlook and against war, and this served further to estrange them from others. In 1914, however, fearing that if they refused they would lose many of their own members and be cast once more into the wilderness by others, they accepted the Kaiser's invitation to join a Reichstag united for victory. In the later summer and autumn of 1918, when it was clear to ordinary people (including soldiers) as well as to the government that the war had been lost, but before the government had taken any steps to re-establish what before the war had passed for normal political life, people took events into their own hands. Sailors mutinied, there was a revolution in Munich, strikes were declared, and workers and soldiers set up their own directive councils. The Social Democrat Ebert was hastily appointed chancellor 'in order', as von Hindenberg telegraphed to the army commanders, asking them to support Ebert, 'to prevent the spread of Bolshevist terrorism in Germany'. But Ebert was not merely a pawn. He too wanted order, although unlike the army and other conservatives, the order of full parliamentary democracy. Accordingly, when Liebknecht proclaimed a Soviet state on the 9 November, two hours after Ebert's colleague Scheidemann had proclaimed a republic, Ebert moved against the extreme left and the people's commissars. The final revolt was put down in Munich in the following May, but already, in the January, there had been elections for a new national assembly.

These were contested by the Social Democrats, the more radical Independent Socialists, the old Catholic Centre and three new associations, the Democratic Party, the German People's Party, and the German Nationalist People's Party. The Democrats stood for individual freedom and social responsibility and sought the support of those who wished for parliamentary democracy without either socialism or reaction. They absorbed the Progressives and the more liberal members of the old National Liberals. But Stresemann, the most prominent National Liberal, could not accept the moves to the left that the Democrats appeared to be making, and he set up the German People's Party into which he brought most of the rest of the National Liberals. The German Nationalist People's Party was a coalition of various conservative and largely monarchist groups each of which realised that in the circumstances of 1919 it alone stood little chance. Combined, however, they were a formidable organisation and secured support not only from the old aristocracy and industrialists but also, through the old Christian Socialists, from several employees' unions. Both the 'people's' parties were cool, if not hostile, to the very idea of the republic, but supported it for want of a plausible alternative, and because it did at least appear to set its face against 'Bolshevism'. In the elections, the Social Democrats received thirty-eight per cent of the vote, and altogether three-quarters of the electorate (of whom eighty per cent, now including women, voted) declared themselves unequivocally for the republic. The new constitution, which had been drafted with the active intervention of Max Weber and which was ratified soon afterwards, gave more power than previously to the Reichstag, although it also allowed the president to retain emergency powers to override parliament, a provision that was in 1932 to prove disastrous.

By 1928, the Social Democrats and the Communist Party (almost entirely dictated to by Moscow) had increased their share of the vote at the expense not only of the Nationalists (and even the new National Socialists, who lost seats in that year) but also of the centre. This, however, merely served to accentuate what had already been clear at the turn of the decade, the power of the right, of the industrial trusts as well as the old aristocracy and the army. Much has of course been said about the failures of the republic that ruled so ineffectually from Berlin and gave way to Hitler, and much blame has been laid. The left accuses not only the right but also the Social Democrats, for not realising that they alone were firmly committed to the idea of a parliamentary democracy and (somewhat inconsistently) for not more vigorously using the power that they had been given in the election in 1919. Liberals blame the centre parties for not having supported the Social Democrats because of their inability to see the difference between social democracy and revolution. The right blames the conservatives for not having realised that they could never return to the glories of the empire. But consistent with each accusation, and correct, was Max Weber's observation that the most crucial structural fault in German society was the absence of a secure and progressive middle class, which led the country in 1919 to inherit a ever-larger and dispirited proletariat balanced only by the old *Stände*, the army and highly concentrated capitalists. England was the most obvious contrast, but even in France the communists and the militaristic, monarchist and Catholic right were insignificant beside the groups in the middle.

Most academics supported the German National People's Party and a few were conspicuous in the Democratic cause, but only four or five professors can be found to have belonged to any of the Marxist parties. Although two of these were sociologists, Karl Mannheim and Tönnies, and although the Weber brothers were prominent in the Democrats, the majority of social theorists, like the majority of their colleagues, were either on the right or held themselves above politics altogether, a position that in the Weimar republic was tantamount to supporting its enemies. This was a unique state of affairs. No substantial group of social thinkers in Europe, before or since, have rejected what in each context might reasonably if somewhat loosely be thought of as 'progressive' views. Yet the explanation is relatively clear. Before 1914, virtually all social theorists in Germany had belonged to the *Bildungsbürgertum*, that section of the middle class which upheld what it regarded as the traditions of *Bildung* and *Kultur*, the unique and quintessential (if somewhat romanticised) essence of German humanism. Yet almost all, even men like Schmoller and Sombart, were in their way also modernists. During the Empire, they thought it quite possible to combine these beliefs and seek a distinctively German path towards what is now called 'modernisation'. But the war shattered this faith. Wartime propaganda had portrayed the battle as an heroic struggle between culture and civilisation, between the high ideals of Germany and the crass materialism and superficial egalitarianism of England. The defeat appeared to mean that culture and with it the whole humanist *Weltanschauung* had apparently gone down not merely to 'civilisation' in England but even more horrifically to a parody of materialism and 'interest-mongering' in the new republic in Germany itself. The despair which this induced accounted immediately after 1918 for the extraordinary popularity of Spengler's *The Decline of the West*, in which the distinction between culture and civilisation was most dramatically drawn and in which the transition from one to the other, from the summer to the autumn of Faustian culture, was projected in a way that even now one has to admit, for all its faults, is remarkably plausible. There was a choice: should one throw in one's lot with democracy and the appalling mediocrity and socialism that it appeared to bring with it? or should one strive still for the ideals of high culture? and if, as almost all did, one chose the second, how was this to be combined with the evident tendency of social and political change? There were essentially four replies. The first, and most common, was simply to evade the question, to argue that the pursuit of ideals had henceforth to be a private matter, divorced from the sordid realities of practical life. The second, and most rare, was squarely to face it and to argue, with Max Weber, for a stoic acceptance of the inevitable which might in certain small and possibly quite ineffectual ways be countered by a supreme effort of will. The third was simply to concede that material progress and cultural excellence were entirely incompatible, and to argue that the first must at almost all costs be sacrificed for the second. The fourth was to insist that far from preventing the realisation of all that was most desired in the idealist dream, modern tendencies were uniquely capable of realising it. Hardly anyone, of course, falls easily into one or other of these groups, but most leant more clearly to one than to any other. What is most striking is that virtually no-one, after Max Weber's death, was much interested in the actual facts of the new society.

Evasion is evasive, and can lead in many directions. In the thinking of the humanist intellectuals in Germany, however, it led generally to an exacerbation of the inwardness and the divorce from practical matters that had long been a tendency there. This was nowhere more marked than in the arguments of the new phenomenological philosophy. These began in reaction to the revived Kantianism of the years before the war, to the view that our knowledge of the world is constituted out of experience by the formal categories of reason, categories that are common to all men simply by virtue of their being men. To begin with, the phenomenologists argued that the constitution was not a formal matter, but a practical one, the consequence of the actual intentions of an empirical ego. Accordingly, there could be as many constitutions as there were thinking men. Later, to avoid the threatening solipsism of this view, some, and most especially Edmund Husserl, attempted to return to Kant, to return not to Kant's categorical formalism but to return to the transcendental security that his categories had provided. Husserl himself did this by maintaining that the constituting ego was not contingent (and thus various) but itself transcendental (and thus one). The difference from Kant, so Husserl appeared to believe, lay in the insistence that the transcendental ego was an actively thinking substance, instantiated in intending men, and not as it were a formal grid prior to active intention; and in the belief that by what was often described as 'free imaginative variation' this instantiated transcendental ego could penetrate beyond the phenomenal appearances that its activities delivered to it to an apprehension of the phenomenal essences that lay behind them. By the 1930s, most of those who were attracted to Husserl's project had returned to the more radical, but also more threateningly solipsist and relativist, earlier view, that the constitution was a variable matter, dependent upon the various intentions of various empirical egos. But this was evident even before the war, and quite markedly so after 1919. The spirit of the more radically anti-Kantian phenomenological contentions was a spirit of retreat, an apparent denial of the possibility of secure public knowledge, an exhortation instead to each man privately to discover and pursue his intentions. It promised the intellectuals a liberation from the dreadful regularities of a hitherto supposedly external world, and thereby allowed them to preserve their ideals against what others might have regarded as the facts.

Not only does such a view allow evasion by retreat. It also permits a dissociation from others and their claims by an appeal to the relativity of their intentions. This in turn suggested a 'sociology of knowledge', which also after 1918 became an expression of those who could only come to terms with the dilemmas presented by Weimar society by in some degree evading them. It was most clear in Karl Mannheim. Mannheim was a Hungarian who had gone to study in Germany under Simmel and Alfred Weber and been affected by many of the intellectual fashions of the time (including Husserl's phenomenology) before returning to Budapest at the outbreak of war. He had also been attracted to Marxism, but in the brief communist revolution in Hungary in 1919 he realised that unlike most of the rest of his circle there he could not fully commit himself to it. When the revolution failed, however, his associations required him to leave Hungary and he once more returned to Germany. The outcome there of his pre-war education and the experience of events in Budapest in the spring of 1919 was to incline him to the view that although there was an irreducible incompatibility between various claims to truth and right, and although such claims were at least in part a function of men's social situations (of which Marx had given the most plausible account), the intellectuals could nevertheless claim to be able to formulate views that were as *situationsgerecht*, as free from social influence, as any. Quite apart from the obvious instabilities in this view, pointed out then and since by many critics, and quite apart from the fact that he never approached a resolution to the very difficult question of the relation between internal and external interpretations of ideas, his solution was no solution at all since although the intellectuals may well be able to see more clearly than others (a barely permissible exaggeration of a Weimar mandarin), they would by virtue of the thesis itself be prevented from persuading others to do so. Caught between his nostalgia for the classical German conception of intellectual possibility and a more than usually honest appreciation of what was happening to society in central Europe, Mannheim in the end evaded all claims.

Two others, however, who also devoted themselves to a *Soziologie des Wissens*, and who also believed that it was impossible to combine the idealist promise with the mundane interests of modern societies, were able in rather different ways more satisfactorily to reconcile the claims of each. But they did so by arguing that they were claims of quite different kinds. The first and more profound of these was Max Scheler. Scheler had a complete and despairing contempt for what he regarded as the banalities of *Gesellschaften* and an almost inconsolable sense of the relativity of any possible counter to them. Before the war, this inclined him to a bleak authoritarianism and an attraction to Nietzsche, and during the war he found some release in writing propaganda about the 'cant' of English thought and the glories of militarism. Afterwards, he returned to his early Catholicism. But both before and afterwards he also devoted himself to intellectual justifications of his views which, like his own despair, were directly related to the more general sense among intellectuals of the crisis of German culture, and show plainly the attractions of phenomenology (to which Scheler had been introduced by meeting Husserl in Jena in 1901) to someone in such a predicament. Yet such was Scheler's sense of the variety of human intention, of the various ways in which men strive to know, that his reflections led him implicitly to relativise the phenomenologists themselves. He distinguished three kinds of knowledge. The first was that understood in the west as 'scientific', pursued in order to be able to master and control, a knowledge of the contingent nature of things which accomplished itself in classifications and laws and eventually in technologies. This man shared with the animals. The second, which he did not, was a knowledge of being, of essences (*Wesen*), in which 'love replaces control as the motive', a knowledge of phenomena which men seek for the sake of apprehension itself, phenomenological knowledge. The third, to Scheler the most important, was knowledge of a metaphysical reality of eternal values, a knowledge to which men come (as he argued in his later sociology of knowledge) with a multitude of subjectivities that are dependent upon their limitlessly varying social situations but which when rarely achieved is grasped as in some sense transcendental, independent of social and material contingency. The philosophical difficulties in Scheler's vision are of course immense, but if understood as a vision and not as a technical philosophy (which was no part of his intention), it recalls Max Weber's austere and desperate contrast between the realm of practicality and the realm of ultimate values. Like Weber, Scheler, having soon again abandoned the Catholic Church, was interested in what he called 'the foundation of cultural politics', and he believed his sociology of knowledge to be a contribution to it. And like Weber again, he put his faith in a leader who, informed by such a sociology, would unite the disparate and partial perspectives of the population into a coherent and acceptable political philosophy. But unlike Weber, he was able to believe in some permanent and immutable although only intermittently and dimly perceptible absolute. He was disenchanted, but not wholly so. Moreover, he did not believe that enchantment had been granted solely to men in past societies. In a way reminiscent of Hegel's contrast between the 'felt unity' of classical *Sitten* and the rational unity of absolute knowledge, he looked back from the superficiality and chaos of his own society to what he idealised as ancient communities (*Gemeinschaften*) bound together by love (and, he now believed, Catholicism) and forward to a universal communion in which once again a collective personality (*eine Gesamtperson*) would in a supreme effort come to know and share perfect solidarity. Such was the effect even upon politicians and the army of eight years of the Weimar Republic that in 1927 Scheler was asked by the chancellor to expound this philosophy in lectures to officers and the public in Berlin, which he did (sometimes speaking for four hours without interruption) with what appears to have been considerable success.

Less profound, and quite without Platonic conviction, was Alfred Weber. Weber's career illustrates more clearly than any the shift of concern in the humanist intellectuals before and after 1918. Before the war, he trained as an historical economist, wrote a treatise on the economics of location, and took part in the more political arguments within the Verein für Sozialpolitik. In 1919, he made an unsuccessful attempt to secure the leadership of the new Democratic Party which he, his brother and others had begun. Disillusioned by this and the subsequent charade of politics in the republic, he resumed his chair at Heidelberg and proceeded systematically to develop his new sense that what Germany required was a cultural revival. His *Kultursoziologie*, as he described it, recalled Scheler, but although he read Scheler's work in the 1920s and defended him against criticism from the Marxists it can equally easily be understood as an extension of his brother's concerns and like those, as well as Scheler's, as a more general reflection of the concerns of most of the intellectuals. Drawing upon the contrast that Spengler had thrust into everyone's minds, Alfred Weber distinguished between the 'social' process, the 'civilisation' process, and the 'culture' process. The first two, to do respectively with the simple physical growth and extension of societies and with the development within them of instruments of control, were subject to laws that applied across all cultures. The third, however, was not. It was a matter of historically unique 'immanent transcendances' in each society. It followed no simple progression, and could not be predicted. But without it, societies merely followed the predetermined path of quantitative growth, material accumulation and technical improvement without any sense of overall purpose. Again like many other intellectuals, Alfred Weber was unclear about the political consequences of his analysis. He recommended a form of free socialism, as he called it, a curious mixture of liberalism and syndicalism more directly reminiscent of Tönnies than of anyone else, but seems never to have addressed himself to the problem that his brother faced, of how to combine in this (or any other political arrangement) the dictates of civilisation and the promise of culture, the need for both organisation and direction. It remained true that Max Weber's response to the problem in the few months of the new republic that he saw established in 1919 was unique, at least among professional intellectuals. Virtually alone among them, he faced the fact as Kant had earlier, that the condition of freedom in Kant's positive sense was *bürgerliche Gesellschaft*, however much of a threat this society was to the very values that had inspired it yet which, properly run, it alone could secure. It is almost entirely idle to guess how he would have reacted to events between 1920 and 1933. But even if he had entered politics, and brought his exceptional realism to bear upon the other liberal politicians (some of whom by no means lost their heads in the 1920s), he could not have created the large and secure middle class that he and subsequent historians have argued was necessary.

The right, of course, did not agree that it was. For them it stood for individualism and competition, and was itself responsible for the degrading chaos. Indeed, like Marxists rather than like more liberal conservatives to the west, conservatives in Germany laid the blame squarely with the bourgeoisie rather than with the proletariat. Hence their reply, the third kind, to the dilemma created by the defeat in 1918 and the new republic: simply to suppress modern tendencies. This was evident in the deliberately didactic and polemical theory of Othmar Spann, who although he taught economics and sociology in Vienna gained a considerable following in Germany itself. Spann insisted that 'empirical' investigation would reveal that of the two ways of conceiving the individual, as an entirely self-sufficient rational subject who derives nothing from society and owes nothing to it beyond what his own interests dictate, or as a subject who derives his subjectivity as an object of society and can only realise it through the society which has granted it, the first leads to anarchy and destruction and the second to responsibility, community and fulfilment. The first is characteristic of a society of social classes, the second of a society of *Stände* arranged in a hierarchy of reciprocal interest, mutual obligation and friendship. Accordingly, Spann argued, society had to be reconstructed as an organic and unchanging unity of estates, from manual workers at the bottom to spiritual creators at the top, with a *Ständhaus* to replace parliaments and Machiavellian manipulators. At the time, this theory was compared in France with Durkheim's, but although it is more direct than his, and on its own premises more plausible, it derived from a quite different intent. Where Durkheim had tried to rescue the individual in a solidaristic community, Spann wished simply to suppress him. His theory had almost all the features that Rousseau and Hegel's liberal vulgarisers have attributed to them. But it was frankly unhistorical. Spann appears to have believed that change could simply be stopped. The more plausible alternative would have been to argue that *bürgerliche Gesellschaft* would itself be transcended in an order that restored the old values, and this was in fact suggested by Hans Freyer, one of the few Weimar sociologists who continued to be active in Germany after Hitler assumed power in 1933. Freyer claimed that as civil society had superseded older communities based upon ties of kinship, so a strong, integrating and directive State would supersede civil society, an argument similar to those in what passed for National Socialist political theory, and an argument that even before 1933 was congenial to the army and to the industrialists who resented the constraints placed upon their activities by democratic parties. But although there were such social theories in the 1920s, and although they did gain a certain currency, they were not the most general expression of conservative dislike. This remained unpolitical.

The fourth sort of reply, however, could not. If one was to

use, if not exactly to accept, social changes to realise the integrated consciousness that bourgeois society had so far denied, then one had presumably to act upon those changes. Since *ex hypothesi* one could not act with the bourgeoisie, or with the patriarchical right, one had to take the side of the proletariat. Knowing, now, the ideas that Marx set out before 1847 about the way in which the revolutionary practice of the working class could realise Hegel's universal, the answer seems theoretically plain. But in 1920 no-one knew Marx's early writings, Hegel had been discredited by both the neo-Kantians and their critics, and the prevailing Marxist view outside reformist circles was that the inevitable triumph of the working class was the prediction of a resolutely materialist theory. Moreover, the Bolshevik triumph in backward Russia had cast some doubt upon the possibilities of class, as distinct from party, action. In short, Marxism in theory or in practice did not seem to be the solution to the question of how to replace bourgeois civilisation, whatever it might achieve by way of economic and political change. Not, then, known, Marx's youthful theory had therefore to be re-invented, and it was such a re-invention by a German philosopher, Karl Korsch, and a Hungarian intellectual, Georg Lukács, that constituted the fourth reply. Of these, Lukács's is the more interesting in having arisen directly from the kind of despair shared by most other intellectuals in Germany immediately before the First World War.

Lukács, like Mannheim, had studied in Germany, under Georg Simmel in Berlin and Emil Lask and Max Weber in Heidelberg, and returned to Budapest to experience and in his case take part in the brief revolution in 1919. Simmel was a brilliant and mercurial man who although unsystematic in his thinking and extraordinarily diverse in his interests persuaded Lukács, who was then absorbed in questions of aesthetics, that culture consisted in a multitude of forms whose content and original impulse derived from the actions of individuals but which then took on a life of their own, as independent objects, and that contemporary societies constituted the most extreme divorce so far between these objects and the creative individual. Lask's views were rather like Scheler's, in that he used the weapons of the new phenomenologists to argue against the neo-Kantians that there was a metaphysical realm of absolute value. The two together gave Lukács a conception of the nature and object of culture, and of the crisis into which it had got itself in bourgeois society. Unlike most philosophically-inclined persons of the time (except, significantly for him, Dilthey) Lukács also went beyond the various reactions to neo-Kantianism to read Hegel. At first, the result of all this was a belief that the cultural crisis required as it were a purely cultural solution, a belief of course shared by many of his contemporaries. But Lukács was also enthusiastic about syndicalism, and although he rejected Max Weber's own politics Weber did make him think that the solution might after all have to be political. This suspicion crystallised in Budapest in the summer of 1919, and henceforth Lukács began to take revolutionary socialism very seriously. The result was a series of essays that were collected together and published in Berlin in 1923 as *History and Class Consciousness*. Although they are in fact more ambiguous than has sometimes been suggested (and certainly more ambiguous than the Soviet Communist Party suggested at the time), they do imply, and were taken to imply, not merely that 'materialism' as espoused by Engels and Lenin was an essentially pre-Kantian and thus bourgeois philosophy, but also that the party as a revolutionary vanguard was at most a temporary necessity, to be inevitably superseded by the class in whose name it ruled as that class acquired its pre-determined capacity, in the Hegelian sense, to abolish all classes and so realise the intellectual, moral and political totality promised in Hegel's philosophy. This was an intolerable deviation to the official communists, who were at the time desperately trying to impose a Leninist orthodoxy upon parties outside as well as inside Russia, and Lukács's subsequent wish to remain in the party forced him for the next thirty years to recant much of what he had said. Nevertheless, his own much later assessment of what he had done, implied in a diatribe against German thinking from Schelling to the Weimar years which contained a section on German sociology in 'the imperialist period', was correct. Almost all Germans, and almost all German sociologists, reacting to the crisis of the Empire and its collapse in 1918, had in their purely theoretical attempts to solve it failed to realise the Hegelian truth that the path of reason encounters practical problems that require practical action, with the result that they had ended up justifying the *status quo* they mostly hated. Thus was Simmel for instance condemned, although it was he who had originally given Lukács the idea that appeared in *History and Class Consciousness* as the objective 'reification' of civilisation which only the proletariat as historical subject could transcend. Yet like all the others, except, again, Max Weber and perhaps Tönnies, Lukács was himself guilty of a theoretical solution which although it pointed towards practice itself paid remarkably little attention to what was actually happening in central Europe in the 1920s. In that, he was a characteristic Weimar intellectual.

So too were many of the other theoretical Marxists of the time. The group which established the Institute for Social Research in the new university at Frankfurt, for example, in 1924, and which had previously included both Lukács and Korsch (each of whom later departed in more directly political, although different, directions) from the beginning refused to commit itself to the view that the sort of reconciliation envisaged by Lukács was possible. Although its members also began from the characteristically Weimar premise that bourgeois culture was an abortion, and although they each in various ways believed that what was called by some a 'left Hegelian' stand was the appropriate one from which to appreciate this fact, none of them could accept that a triumph of the party in the name of the working class, of the kind that was represented in Soviet Russia, promised any sort of solution at all. In that respect, they were perhaps more realistic and certainly more honest than Lukács. It meant that they came to argue in one or other of two rather different directions. The first was to insist that a more specifically German socialism was still possible, although the increasing paralysis of the Social Democrats, the divisions between the Social Democrats, the Communists and other left-wing groups, the continued interference of the Soviet Party and the accumulating muddles and despair of the Weimar Republic itself all made such an insistence progressively less plausible. The second was to concede that working-class action was after all perhaps entirely irrelevant to the problems of German society, even to the problems as Marxists saw them, and to suggest instead that a more purely cultural criticism, with no particular political programme, was all that was possible. In their assumptions, their inclinations and even their solutions (of which there were few), the second group was much more closely akin to those other intellectuals who had sought refuge in other more purely philosophical criticisms than to any practical Marxist. And by default, it assumed direction of the Institute before the assets were moved to Holland in 1931 and then, in 1934, to the United States.

Thus, although German intellectuals in the years immediately before and after 1918 generally had a more acute sense of what was happening to their society than did most of the intellectuals in England and France of what was happening to theirs, this sense derived from and continued to serve a situation that was itself part of the very problem they saw. The native cultural tradition in combination with the social separation of intellectuals from all the main classes and vestigial *Stände* in the country (a combination in which it is very difficult to assign cause and effect) produced a diagnosis of the collapse of the empire into the republic that merely served to maintain the tradition and the separation of the institutions within which it was maintained. Social disarray and disorder actually reinforced the intellectual continuities. This was so despite a deliberate effort in 1919 by the Prussian Ministry of Culture to introduce more sociology in the universities in order to break down the barriers between faculties and to make students more responsive to social and political change. Although this helped the establishment of sociology at two or three new institutions, like Frankfurt and Cologne (where it was encouraged by the mayor, Konrad Adenauer), it also produced a burst of polemic from the more orthodox (including those, like Sombart, who in the pre-war Verein had by precept and practice attempted to encourage the analysis of contemporary changes), and the kind of sociology that the Ministry intended was never conspicuous. Even Tönnies, who had published his best-known book, *Community and Society*, in 1887, who came from a provincial agricultural background in Denmark, remote from Prussia's intellectual life, who had avoided the ideologically-charged methodological disputes in the pre-war years, and who had deliberately started the German Sociological Society in 1909 as a forum for progressive views (which is why Max Weber joined it), was unable to counter the belated reception that his book received in the years after 1918.

Where he had intended it as an argument for the establishment of occupational associations to combine the organisational virtues of *Gesellschaft* with the solidarity of *Gemeinschaft*, it was taken as a simple plea for the virtues of love and community over the divisive desiccation of bourgeois society. The only way, indeed, that a sociologist could if he wished altogether escape such arguments was like von Wiese to redefine the subject as the purely formal analysis of the elements of social interaction, but even von Wiese drew the wrath of those who saw in what he was doing yet more evidence of the insidious success of alien methods.

In England, France, and Germany, therefore, although in very different ways, sociological thinking between 1918 and 1939 (in Germany, to 1933) consisted largely of a response to evident changes in the nature of capitalism and the possibility of socialist change that in its essential intellectual continuity in each country from the period before the First World War ensured that these changes were not fully grasped. Such a conclusion, of course, has little critical interest, for it comes only with hindsight. But what it does help to explain is the distaste in all three countries after 1945 for historical speculation and even for historical discussion, and the marked enthusiasm, at least in England and Germany, for American thinking. For by then, European societies did seem completely to have changed, and one had only the assumptions of the 1890s to help one understand how.

9

History ignored

LOOKING BACK IN 1916 at 'fifty years of sociology in the United States' Albion Small, the chairman of the new department at the new University of Chicago, lamented that the subject had become established in his country without a distinctive intellectual content, a distinctive method, or even a point of view. Like many of his contemporaries, Small's comparison was no doubt with Germany, where he had studied for two years, and he exaggerated. But the academic establishment of the subject had indeed been remarkable. Only about six colleges or universities were teaching what they described as 'sociology' at the end of the 1880s; by 1894 there were nearly two hundred, by 1909, twice as many; and the number of full-time professors of sociology had risen from twenty-nine to fifty. By 1916, twenty-six textbooks had appeared to meet the demand, and although the very first sold only a few hundred copies the sales of some of the subsequent ones came to be reckoned in thousands and even in later decades in millions. When asked by the American Sociological Society in 1909 to explain the new demand, teachers across the country replied that it was overwhelmingly for instruction of practical use in reform. Most students were uninterested in theoretical matters. Yet the texts that they bought paid little attention to the facts of life in America. They consisted more in long and loose elaborations of principle. They did have a point of view, and even, although not perhaps in the European sense, a distinctive intellectual content. Indeed, it is only in comparison with European ideas that this content becomes clear, for they were not what would then and would now be regarded by Europeans as 'intellectual' at all. This apparent paradox is the paradox of American thinking more generally. It has meant that social thought and sociology there has always been very different from similar thinking in Europe, so much so, indeed, that European thinking seems by comparison to be of a piece.

This at once raises another paradox, for it has often been said that the prevailing assumptions of Americans have been those of Locke, and while it has been said that Locke's direct effect upon the promoters of the new republic has been much exaggerated, the point has a certain force. The paradox is resolved, however, by the fact that the conditions under which this kind of thinking came to pervade America were quite different from those under which it was first proposed in England. The Americans' intentions in using Locke and other Whig theorists to the extent that they did were quite different from the theorists' own. Like the younger Mill in the nineteenth century, Locke in the *Two Treatises on Government* was taking for granted the dense and complex structure of constraint and obligation that existed in his own society. He was merely, although of course on one view subversively, insisting that such a structure did not give any man the right to dispose of any other, that on the contrary, each man, whatever his station, was epistemologically free to decide for himself the limits under which he would live. He was arguing against the restoration of an absolute monarchy, and against the absolutely hierarchical and immutable paternalism of Robert Filmer. But as de Tocqueville implied in the 1830s, Americans had been able to take such intentions as descriptions. There was no native feudalism, no patriarchy, no Filmer to defend it. The American revolution was not a revolution against the kind of old order that was being criticised and attacked in Europe. It was a revolution to secure what had already been begun in an historical vacuum. The radical rhetoric of the European Enlightenment was there deployed for what were literally conservative ends.

This had three profound effects. The first was that the only social institutions of which Americans were aware were property and the State. There was nothing in the new country to correspond to the European estates and there was no established Church. There were merely individuals, with or without property, and government. Of course, there was slavery, and in the attempt by Southerners later in the nineteenth century to maintain it the slaves were compared to a traditional European estate, but they were more usually conceived as just an extension of the property of individuals. The prevailing religious mode (and America was then, of course, as it has uniquely remained, a very religious country) was a pluralistic sectarianism in which the most prominent, the New England puritans, were entirely at one with the Calvinism implicit in Locke himself. This history meant and has continued to mean that Americans had no firm grasp of what from England to China has always been taken for granted, the notion of what sociologists would now call 'social structure', the notion that there are if not immutable then certainly enduring complexes of institutions; institutions that do not merely as in the radical liberal view serve to constrain individuals, but by virtue of the individual's membership of them from birth to death serve in good part to constitute and define him as a person. The language of institutions, of course, pervades American thinking as it does that of other societies; but there, the meaning has always been more restricted.

The second effect of the conservative consolidation of an apparently un-conservative liberalism in America was an inducement to conformity. This was and has continued to be both practical and ideological. Practically, no man could dare to consider himself or could bear to consider others as in any way above or below any other. Ideologically, there could after the abolition of the property franchise be no grounds for any man claiming by virtue of any characteristics whatsoever that he was privileged with exceptional insight, or that he was by virtue of experience or affiliation intrinsically or by right qualified to direct others. The radically egalitarian spirit of Protestantism, which had done much to affect philosophical and political thinking in England and Germany, in America met no opposing institutions or ideologies by which it had to be tempered or on which it had to compromise. In the name of liberty and equality there thus developed there a most persistent pressure to conform, a pressure that on occasion has amounted almost to a panic about those who do not and produced popular persecutions in the name of ideals they appear to deny. This has made Americans characteristically vulnerable and anxious. Unable to flee into any institution and thereby pass to it responsibility for his beliefs or actions, a man is there exposed to the pressure of popular opinion and so forced to examine himself as an individual, alone, to a degree that he is not in any more highly structured society.

The third effect of the uniquely unhistorical consolidation of a liberal society in America has been to produce a very special sense of time. The characteristic European sense of the arrangement of events had derived from the Christian view that in one way or another improvement, perhaps indeed, perfection, lay in the future. The notion of progress dates in its secular form from the Enlightenment, but the hope that lies beneath it is an ancient one. It was such a hope, indeed, that informed not only the puritans in the New England settlements but also the many other sects that spread across the country and came to constitute the distinctive character of American faith, the character that so impressed Max Weber when he went to America in 1904. Yet in the break from England and the establishment of the new republic, in part inspired by these sects, America seemed already to have reached perfection. The past had been consolidated in a future whose integrity lay in remaining as much like the present as possible. This in Hofstadter's phrase has been the 'nub of the intimate American quarrel with history': 'how can a people progress if they have started near to perfection?' A simple answer, but an answer that many Americans have implicitly given, is that although the society itself may have no distance to progress, there have been and continue to be virtually infinite possibilities of material improvement and technical advance within it. If such progress was not in fact necessary to the society, no more was it inimical to it. Indeed, it could be held to be a natural concomitant and consequence of its liberty. This firm faith in one of the residual principles of European progressive thought has, however, generated one of the most persistent of all dilemmas in American society, the dilemma of how to reconcile the effects of spectacular material accumulation and technical advance with the established ideal of a perfect society in a state of markedly primitive innocence. It was a dilemma already evident in the 1840s, it became a matter of absorbing concern in the years before 1914, and it reappeared in the 1960s. All the while, it has driven the primitive populism of the south and west against the trusts and banks and politicians of the east.

Each of these three effects of early American history has itself affected intellectual life. First and most importantly, philosophical, social and political thinking has proceeded within what are by comparison with Europe extremely narrow bounds, the bounds of an established liberalism. In Europe, liberalism was at first a critical principle, and no sooner had it become established (even then, in arguments against patriarchy) than it itself began to be undermined by what has there generally been understood as socialism. In the United States, on the other hand, liberalism was only ever a critical principle in arguments against Europe. It was established with the new republic, ideologically, if not in fact, and criticisms of the progress, or not, of that republic have always been made in its own terms. Not only was patriarchy in any form exactly what the country had set itself against, but also, because of the absence of any nostalgia for the virtues of its reputed solidarity and mutual obligations, socialism, which in Europe has always drawn strongly upon such nostalgia, has seemed at best irrelevant and at worst an insidious stalking horse for the kinds of collective restraint and institutional domination evident, to liberals, in patriarchy itself. This is the paradox of American intellectualism. In Europe, as Durkheim, for instance, and his opponents saw (it was in Europe at that time that the word acquired its modern sense), to be an intellectual was to criticise, to criticise not merely the ways in which various groups sought to achieve their ends but also, and much more importantly, to criticise the ends themselves. In America, the ends have been given, given both in the ideological sense and also, and much more forcefully, in the very constitution of the society itself. To mount an argument against them has been to mount an argument against America and thus, to mount an argument that immediately disqualifies itself from serious consideration as a relevant argument at all. At issue only have been means, the means of recalling the society to its original and unquestionable inspiration, original in the historical sense and unquestionable in the sense that to question it is to question not merely one view, and one group, in the society, but the very society itself. Second, therefore, American intellectuals have been deprived of part of the normal theoretical apparatus of modern European thought, the assumption that one may locate one's critical principles in some more or less imaginary future state, a state yet to be realised but nevertheless conceivable by virtue of the inexorable passage of the past into the future that since the Enlightenment all Europeans have been able to take for granted. In Europe the once-vaunted promise of salvation in the next world was translated, with much confusion and dispute, it is true, but without great intellectual difficulty, into the promise of salvation in this. In America since 1776 such translation has been impossible. With the old sectarian faith, the colonists could still hope. Without it, the citizens of the new republic could not. Secularisation has there had an ironical twist. Moreover, and third, even in such criticisms as they have made, American intellectuals have been persistently crippled by the dogmatic and fearful egalitarianism of their native liberalism. Although European intellectuals have been troubled by just this sort of attack, as were ecclesiastics before them, they have been able even when they have been defending what they have taken to be the side of the oppressed and the uninformed to exploit the deference that the latter have always grudgingly if mistakenly given to their spiritual betters. The peculiar difficulty of the American intellectual, on the other hand, is that his very status has been in question. His own criticisms have usually come from within the native liberalism, and it is from within that liberalism that he himself has been challenged. No-one has ever shown that anti-intellectual sentiments are more common in America than elsewhere. It is simply that they have more often been expressed, for they have always been more legitimate. The intellectuals themselves, aware of and indeed often defending this legitimacy, have thus often been driven into agonised impotence. Where they have not been undermined by others, they have themselves furnished the grounds for their own immolation.

This is the heritage and character of American social thought, often vigorous and critical and even radical, but in its very radicalism literally conservative and definitely unhistorical, leaning always to more technical prescriptions than to truly intellectual ones. It bristles with tension. The professional sociology that developed with such extraordinary speed after 1890 was at once a consequence, an instance and eventually an exacerbating cause of that tension.

The first self-consciously sociological ideas in America, however, emerged not after but before the Civil War, in defence of the southern interest in slavery that the war itself defeated. This in itself, when set beside the common purpose of sociological theories in Europe, is ironic. One's sense of the somewhat topsy-turvy world of American social thinking is increased when one realises that in one expression these ideas replicated Marx's interpretation of the classical economists and did so a full ten years before he himself arrived at this interpretation. They were prompted by events of the 1830s. Southern planters were then becoming increasingly angry about what they regarded as their exploitation by northern capital. Not only were they at the mercy of northern commercial interests, having failed to develop any banks, industries or shipping companies of their own, but the federal government had imposed a stiff tariff on their agricultural products. There was growing talk too in the north of abolition. This presented acute difficulties which were most brilliantly if eccentrically resolved by the proposals of John Calhoun, a senator for South Carolina, a man of whom it has been said that he could do wonders with a premise but usually showed an extraordinary lack of judgement in choosing it. 'Let those who are interested remember', Calhoun declared to the Senate, 'that labour is the only source of wealth, and how small a portion of it, in all old and civilised countries, even the best governed, is left to those by whose labour wealth is created'. This could only result in revolution, and for that reason, he continued, the owners of wealth, that is to say, of labour, should combine to preserve what they had. Northern politicians should combine with the southern planters who presided over a 'condition of society' 'vastly more favourable' for 'free and stable institutions' than anything in the north, where revolution would undoubtedly occur in the next generation. His consistency only faltered before the inference that the free workers of the north should also therefore be enslaved.

This did not deter others. A decade or so later, George Fitzhugh and George Frederick Holmes used much the same arguments to insist that the supposed 'free society' of the north was not such at all. Surprising an America that had been used to welcoming changes in the name of liberty in Europe, they pounced with glee upon the disorders of 1848 in Paris and Berlin and elsewhere and waved them in the face of the north, many of whose citizens, Fitzhugh pointed out, were themselves already acceding to calls for reform to ameliorate the conditions of the northern 'free'. To resolve its hypocrisy and banish the threat of socialism, Fitzhugh argued, the north, like the south, required a society of estates, a truly conservative society of established and enduring hierarchy in which the higher orders should take responsibility for the lower and the lower toil for the higher. Fitzhugh, indeed, although not Calhoun, who appealed for a conservative society in the name of a liberalism that that society appeared to deny, is one of the few American thinkers to have completely abandoned the prevailing assumptions of his society. But even he agreed that the southern poor whites should be given some stake in a modified market economy. In any event, and like Calhoun and Marx, he misunderstood the genesis of socialism. It was not the product of capitalism alone, but of the discrepancies created by the moves to capitalism from feudalism. And like Calhoun, he also mistook the force of the Ricardian point about the effect on wages of the ratio of population to resources. In America, resources were not limited. On the contrary, there were enough, as yet unexplored and unexploited, for everyone to become his own capitalist. The facts of the American economy, booming just at the time at which he resorted to the desperate strategem of conceding that America was in this respect 'abnormal and anomalous', defeated Fitzhugh as much as the liberal ideology he so hated but so badly underrated. This brilliant if bizarre attempt to introduce the notions of a de Bonald or a de Maistre into American long after they had ceased to be taken seriously by most Europeans received its final *coup de grace*, of course, in the Confederate defeat in war in 1864.

The prevailing philosophies of the north in the period before the war were those of Unitarianism and transcendentalism, diffuse Christian theologies of an idealistic sort which permitted, if they did not actually encourage, conventional liberal thinking. After the war, their complacent pieties began to be undermined by a freshly critical biblical scholarship, but already many men had been affected by the popularisation of English science. Lyell's *Principles of Geology* was published in 1832, Darwin's *The Origin of Species* appeared in 1860, and Spencer's books began to be serialised in magazines after the Civil War. The impact of the last two, who frequently fused into a single person, proclaiming 'Social Darwinism', is hard to exaggerate. Even the pessimistic, like the young Henry Adams, bitter and confused from his brief diplomatic career during the war, were won over. In his review of his own education, written in a sceptical third person, Adams recalled that 'Unbroken Evolution under uniform conditions pleased everyone, except curates and bishops. It was the very best substitute for religion; a safe, conservative, practical, thoroughly Common-Law deity. Such a working system for the universe suited a young man who had [in administering the Union cause in the north] just helped to waste five or ten thousand million dollars and a million lives, more or less, to enforce unity and uniformity on people who objected to it; the idea was only too seductive in its perfection; it had the charm of art'. Such a system, indeed, suited everyone for whom the war had been a shattering experience, a scar on the innocence of the original America. It also seemed to some degree to resolve the difficulty in the Americans' puzzle about their history. An approximate perfection had indeed been achieved in 1776, but in a 'militant' and not an 'industrial' society. Spencer had shown that there could be progress from one level of perfection to another. It was clear, therefore, that America could recover its nearly perfect but militant past in a wholly perfect industrial future, and thus be assured of progress. Others again found solace in Spencer's solution of what an industrial proprietor identified as 'the problem presented to systems of religion and schemes of government': 'to make men who are equal in liberty, that is, in political rights and therefore entitled to the ownership of property, content with that inequality in its distribution which must inevitably result from the application of the law of justice'. The tributes made at the dinner given for Spencer at Delmonico's in New York on the last evening of his triumphant tour in 1882 indeed embarrassed even him, but in a rare burst of affection on the quay the next morning he clasped the hand of Andrew Carnegie and declared to the crowd that here were his best friends. Indeed. The sales of his books far exceeded those of others on similar subjects. Everyone spoke of him. He was quite extraordinarily well-suited to one part of the American consciousness in the 1860s, '70s and '80s, and indelibly pervaded popular beliefs for long afterwards.

One of the after-dinner speakers at Delmonico's was William Graham Sumner, who praised Spencer for having established the foundations of sociological method. Sumner was the child of an English immigrant whom he described as belonging to 'the class of men whom Caleb Garth in *Middlemarch* is the type'. He graduated from Yale, spent some time in Geneva, Göttingen and Oxford, and returned to a tutorship in New Haven in 1868. Four years later, he was appointed Professor of Social and Political Science there. He was perhaps the most compelling teacher in the entire history of American social thought. Every Yale man felt bound to attend his lectures, and few appear to have been reluctant to. With brilliance, brio and considerable bad temper, Sumner preached Spencer. He had come upon the Englishman's *Study of Sociology* in the year of his appointment to the chair at Yale. 'It solved the old difficulty about the relations of social science to history', he recalled, 'rescued social science from the dominion of cranks, and offered a definite and magnificent field to work, from which we might hope at last to derive definite results for the solution of social problems'. But he did not merely parrot evolutionism. In the most intense good faith, in the manner of the most relentless Calvinist, he repeatedly struck against what he regarded as the confused and sentimental advocates of reform in the name of a necessitarian evolution which, he believed, demonstrated beyond all reasonable doubt to all reasonable men that the only alternative to the survival of the fittest was the survival of the unfittest and the consequent extinction of all that was necessary to the maintenance of liberty and civilisation. The new millionaires, the Carnegies of the 1870s and 1880s, making a fortune in railways and oil and steel, epitomised the health of society. Inequality was not merely inevitable and pre-destined. It was the mark of freedom. *What Social Classes Owe to Each Other*, he believed and explained in a book of that name, was very little. Virtually all of those who came to describe what they were doing in the 1880s and 1890s as 'sociology' were thus to him objects of contempt and scorn. They had adopted the description in order to combine the virtues of practicality, evident in their interest in 'reform', with the virtues of reflective concern, evident in the prevailing phrase 'social ethics'. In this, they annoyed Sumner, but like him, they respected Spencer's strictly intellectual intent and needed also to justify themselves to the more hard-headed patrons of the new secular universities. He long refused to have anything to do with them, even though his *Folkways*, a late book in which he argued for a necessitarian acceptance of evolutionary changes (and thus, one might suppose, although wrongly, for an acceptance of the changes by then taking place in views about the desirability of unrestricted economic and social competition), became one of the first classroom classics of American sociology. His election to the presidency of the new American Sociological Society in 1907 appears to have been something of a mistake. Small could not think what he had to do with the *ethos* of the new subject. He died, however, in 1910, and left merely a memory of his inspiration, a few devotees in Yale, and a blandly reinterpreted *Folkways*.

Like Spencer himself in England, Sumner outlived widespread enthusiasm for his ideas. The very fact that so much of his work was directed against reformers is sufficient testimony of the mark that these people were making as far back as the early 1870s. The causes of the pressures for reform were complex, and the calls for reform were often confused and contradictory. But there were essentially two strains. The first came from the south and west, from those whose business was agriculture, the second from the north and east, from the cities. Both were articulated within the prevailing liberalism. The farmers' discontent derived from an eventually unbearable tension between their conception of themselves as the quintessential Americans, the embodiment of rural arcadia and the associated values of the primitively innocent eighteenth century, and their forced capitulation to economic change. Especially where they were growing crops for export, they suffered from the fall in world prices that persisted throughout the last thirty years of the century, and the Homestead Act, intended to provide more land to relieve their discontents, merely aggravated the situation, for in extending themselves the new homesteaders were forced to mortgage. With prices falling their debts increased in value, they were forced to sell to the railroad and other interests that had already been exploiting the Act for their own purposes, and their misery increased. 'In God we trusted', said one bitter wag, 'in Kansas we busted'. The enemy appeared to be the banks and the trusts in the east. The solution, to begin with, appeared to be to combine within the states and to demand the distribution of more money to stop the deflation, later, to work through a new national People's Party, and later still, after the rout in the presidential election in 1896, to combine in trusts as formidable as those which had been believed to be causing much of the trouble in the first place. But by then, the weaker farmers had gone to the wall, and thence to the cities. Chicago doubled in population in one decade, between 1880 and 1890, and over the whole period, from 1860 to 1910, the urban population increased nearly sevenfold. This was the source of the difficulties about which the middle classes, if one may use that term, came later to protest and tried to reform. And the Progressive movement, as it has come to be called, clearly was a middle-class one. Manual workers were in the main first-generation immigrants from the countrysides of middle and western America and of Europe. Poor but bewildered, they did not comprehend the reformers, and in the case of the foreign immigrants preferred such security as was offered by the city bosses, a framework of dependence and patronage more familiar to them from the structures they had left behind. They also joined the new combinations of labour against capital. Non-manual workers, on the other hand, were overwhelmingly native-born, very often mobile having come into precarious independence or white-collar employment from a manual past. Where the population of the country as a whole slightly more than doubled in the years between 1870 and 1910, and the manual groups tripled, white-collar employees increased no less than eight times. By 1910, there were over five million of them, and only three million of the hitherto more numerous independents. The interest of both groups appears above all to have been that of mobility, the realisation of the promise of the boom years, of the Gilded Age, of what has come to be called the American Dream. Discontent was thus confused and even contradictory. But it was rife, and there was a good deal of agreement about the enemy, the trusts, the combinations of capital so offensive to a liberal conscience. Monopolies, it was agreed, were against the interests of each and the interests of all, and had to be broken. Others were concerned to ameliorate the poverty and restore the morale of the oppressed.

The first reformers were from the urban churches and seminaries and theological colleges, men whose consciences were pricked and whose interests were threatened by evangelical revivals in the countryside and the spiritual indifference of urban migrants. Ministers made some of the first investigations of deprivation and despair, and the first recognisably sociological teaching in the country began to appear in their seminaries and colleges. They were soon joined, however, by increasingly co-ordinated groups of charitable and philanthropic associations and by the muckraking journalists. The example of the British Social Science Association provided the model for an American one in 1865, and although like the eventually very powerful National Conference of Charities and Correction this body was largely secular in tone its activities were in many respects similar to others, like the Institute of Christian Sociology, that had a more orthodox inspiration. They sponsored surveys, prepared reports, published journals, recruited influential men to their boards, and stimulated a climate of interest and concern that spread far beyond ministers and social workers eventually to generate the explosive demand for applied sociological instruction in secular colleges. In this they were helped by the fact that the increasingly large and literate urban populations for the first time provided a market for popular newspapers. The new editors realised that they could best compete with each other by publishing ever more shocking *exposés*. There was much to expose, and 'muckraking' rapidly became an established mode. Fortunes were made by proprietors whose subsequent interests were exactly those inveighed against by their writers and resented by their readers.

Meanwhile, changes were taking place in education. Before the Civil War, most colleges were either, as Hofstadter has described them, 'pathetic, libraryless little boardinghouses for drill masters and adolescent rioters living under the thumb of this or that sect', or relatively inert institutions of gentlemanly leisure for the pious, as Sumner for instance (once a minister himself) found out even in the 1870s when he crossed with President Porter at Yale over the use of Spencer's *Principles*. The first change had come in 1861. Congress, worried by the poor state of American farming, granted subsidies for the purchase of land on which to build new agricultural and mechanical colleges. Soon afterwards, private donors started competing with each other to finance colleges in the cities. The effect of this was a most remarkable overhaul and expansion of higher education. Cornell was opened in 1868, a reforming president was installed at Harvard in 1869, the first graduate school opened at Johns Hopkins and another reformer took charge at Ann Arbor in 1875, Minnesota, Wisconsin, Chicago, Clark and Stanford had all been established by 1891, and by 1900 Yale, Princeton and Columbia were changed beyond recognition. The number of students, which had been in relative decline up to 1869, increased five times in the next forty years.

This was the institutional framework of the development of sociology. The older colleges like Harvard were content to keep social inquiry within the established faculties, but the newer ones were not. Not all the new presidents were as energetic as the almost legendary William Harper, who when offered a million dollars to start a university in Chicago by his fellow-baptist John D. Rockefeller replied that he needed fifteen, and got thirty, and who hired Albion Small to start a sociology department in 1892; but within a few years there were more professors of sociology in America than in the whole of western Europe. These men came from almost everywhere, but rarely from more traditional subjects. Some went to Germany, whose pattern of graduate training had been imitated and made famous at John Hopkins in the 1870s, some, including the first professors at Yale, Chicago and Columbia, had had previous careers in the ministry, and some had ministers in their families. Others had written for the newspapers. Harper's energy drove an initially alarmed and anxious Small into starting the *American Journal of Sociology* in 1895, and in this, as well as in the new texts and the papers of the American Sociological Society which began to appear in 1906, one can trace the rapid transformation of the subject in America from an inchoate series of disparate speculations and inquiries into a more coherent body of doctrine with, despite what Small said in 1916, a reasonably distinct 'point of view'.

Lester Ward, who went from a career of over forty years as a botanist and museum curator to the first chair at Brown in 1906, remarked in the 1890s that all American sociologists were 'virtually disciples of Spencer'. Charles Cooley, a gentle and retiring man who easily resisted the temptation to start a separate department at Michigan but who taught sociology there from 1892 until 1929, put it more precisely when he wrote in 1920 that 'I imagine that nearly all of use who took up sociology between 1870, say, and 1890 did so at the instigation of Spencer'. Yet by the 1890s only William Sumner, briskly shunning his sentimental and misguided new colleagues, was in any sense still preaching Spencer. The others had all in various ways already departed from Spencer to intellectual destinations that quite subverted his original principles. They did so in two related ways. The first was Ward's. Like others of his generation (he was born in 1840) Ward was persuaded by the kind of enterprise that Darwin and Spencer were engaged upon. For most of his working life, after all, he was a working scientist. But he had an acute and compassionate sense of what had happened to American society after the Civil War, and was untypically well aware of the changes that were taking place in England, France and Germany. He realised, and said, that unrestricted laissez-faire was causing both misery and waste, and that those who saw no further than the end of Spencer's books were failing to appreciate the extent to which not only European but also American governments, even where they were not clear about the implications of what they were doing, were already beginning to control its effects. His intellectual reaction to this was vigorous. He argued initially in a perfectly straightforward manner. 'If social laws are really analogous to physical laws, there is no reason why social science may not receive practical applications such as have been given to physical science'. But later, and especially in his *Dynamic Sociology* (which he originally intended to call *The Great Panacea*), he leant more clearly towards a distinction between the 'genetic' and the 'teleological', between what inheritance, in the Lamarckian sense, had made of man and what man, thus educated, could make of himself. He came to place great faith in education, which is why he turned to an academic career, but he never satisfactorily resolved the tension in his thinking. In some ways rather like Hobhouse he could not abandon his belief that Spencer's sort of intellectual programme was desirable, but no more could he accept Spencer's own conclusions.

One might at first imagine that Ward would have gained something from Hegel, and be led to ask why he did not. One reason is that for even a widely read botanist working in museums in Washington, away from any university, Hegel would hardly have been the most obvious of pleasures. But another, more significant, is that even if Ward had read Hegel, and talked about it with others, he would have sensed and himself no doubt come to accept that Hegel's cast of thought was exactly what progressive thinking did not require. For one of the set of intellectual changes in America of which sociology was an instance, the changes that Morton White has described as 'the revolt against formalism', was a growing philosophical disinclination for the prevailing transcendental idealism of the older faculties, and thus among others for Hegel, who was taught, in so far as he was systematically taught at all, as a benevolent and comfortably diffuse republican of moderate views. The younger philosophers were instead coming gradually to adopt what William James popularised in a lecture in California in 1898 as a 'pragmatic' point of view and this, which thence affected others, constituted the second and much more thoroughgoing subversion of Spencer.

James was neither the first nor the most careful of the pragmatists. But it was he who introduced and popularised the philosophy among his contemporaries. He moved in both literary and scientific circles in Massachusetts, and took a degree at the Harvard Medical School. He was an enthusiastically religious man, but in a very personal way; he greatly disliked the pious abstractions of the Harvard theologians. He was also persuaded by biological accounts of human activity. Doubtless recalling his own youth, he later told the audiences in Cambridge and New York to whom he first gave his *Pragmatism* that 'you want a system that will combine both things, the scientific loyalty to facts and willingness to take account of them, the spirit of adaptation and accommodation...but also the old confidence in human values and resultant spontaneity, whether of the religious or the romantic type. And this is then', he guessed, 'your dilemma; you find the two parts of your *quaesitum* hopelessly separated. You find empiricism with inhumanism and irreligion; or else you find a rationalistic philosophy that indeed may call itself religious, but that keeps out of all definite touch with concrete facts and joys and sorrows'. His own solution, however, was not to provide a system at all. Instead, he extended Spencer to argue that since all human activity could be interpreted as the outcome of the instinct for survival, so therefore could thinking be. He broke completely with any form of monism by drawing the simple inference that what we think is what is useful to us. And he concluded that what we think may also only be *assessed* by its utility. What is true is what is useful, and if what is useful for one is what is not for another, so be it. For the one it is true and for the other it is not. 'I have lain awake several nights in succession', wrote Charles Peirce, a slightly older and far more careful man who wished to preserve some rational stability, and who had had a mild influence on an impatient James in Cambridge, 'in grief that you should be so careless of what you say'. But Peirce talked largely to himself. It was James who in his exuberant liberal inexactitude so exactly met the confusions of those who were caught between the broken monisms of theology and naturalism and wished to be able to justify their need to combine the two and yet retain as much practical and intellectual discretion as possible. The 'revolt against formalism' had reached its most extreme point.

An important fact about James's sort of pragmatism, of course, is that it is not in any ordinary sense of the term a doctrine at all. Having accepted it, one is virtually bound to abandon what anyone else derives from it. It is at best a 'point of view'. As such, it affected the sociologists. Ward was by 1900 too old to take much notice of new fashions, and Sumner was fixed in his firmament at Yale. But the others responded with enthusiasm. Cooley was perhaps the most direct. Like so many of his contemporaries, he was at once stimulated and repelled by Spencer, attracted to his 'general conception of the progressive organisation of life' but hostile to his heartless dogmatism and to his insufficient appreciation of the complexities of individual psyches. At about the time that Cooley began to teach sociology at Ann Arbor (where he was born and where he stayed for almost all his life) he read James, and he was at once attracted to James's conception of the self. In his more directly psychological essays James had distinguished between the 'I' and the 'me', the self as knower and the self as known, and of the latter had said that 'a man has as many social selves as there are individuals who recognise him and carry an image of him in their mind'. But 'although', Cooley wrote to himself in his journal, 'William James has insight into the social nature of the self, he [does] not develop this into a really organic conception of the relation of the individual to the social whole...a sociological pragmatism remains to be worked out'. Cooley himself attempted it. The result was a conception of individuals in sympathy and affection gaining a sense of others and of themselves as social in 'primary groups', like the family, a process which he optimistically extrapolated to a future state in which not merely communities or countries but indeed the whole world would be united by an organic bond of mutually sympathetic consciousness, a state in which the evils of 'formalism' and 'disorganisation', evils which caused the atrophy of individuals and the division of societies, would have disappeared. Cooley paid virtually no attention to institutions. He appears generally to have believed that conflict was due to misunderstanding. Albion Small, who somewhat bitterly remarked towards the end of his life that he had spent most of it 'insisting that there *is* something at the far end of the sociological rainbow', when he did so in the many programmatic articles he wrote to fill the early numbers of his *American Journal* tended in an even less direct way to insist upon the possibilities of active reform, upon the ability of individuals to fashion their social circumstances. And although there is virtually nothing of Simmel in his own papers, he did translate several of the German's essays for his journal, essays that in their *lebensphilosophische* spirit are very reminiscent of James's pragmatic speculations. Giddings, the irascible, dogmatic racist who studiously avoided Jewish colleagues at Columbia and surrounded himself with second-rate acolytes, a man whose moral and mental characteristics predisposed him to a most conventional sort of scientism, used to tell his students in a very pragmatic vein that 'if it isn't theory, it won't work'. In so far as he had a theory of the possibility of society, which was his general concern, he stressed what he called the 'interstimulation and response' that generated a 'consciousness of kind'. Even Edward Ross, a populist muckraker of the old school (he once wrote a book on *Sin and Society*) who established a forceful department in Wisconsin (the university most closely associated, through La Follette, with a progressive administration) but who remained relatively indifferent to the professionalisation of sociology, a man who in his autobiography recalled being in China before the collapse in 1911 and talking to Trotsky in Russia in 1917 more fondly than he did his days as a departmental chairman, a man who was not especially concerned to establish doctrines of any sort (but whose texts sold better than any of his peers') used to say that it was the 'social process', the creation of 'groups, relations, institutions, imperatives,...out of the actions and interactions of men' that sociologists should study.

Despite what Small had said, there was therefore a very distinct 'point of view' in the early sociology. It never departed, even in Ward, from its more general heritage. It paid virtually no attention to institutions in the European sense, implied, at the very least by omission, that society was to be understood as the creation of individuals, that it was truly a society, and not a mere aggregation, by virtue of the sense of community that individuals established with each other in their interactions, and (with the exception of Ross) that the past accumulation of institutional practices and their constraining conventions were largely irrelevant to an understanding of how people came to do what they did. In European terms, it started with something remarkably like a state of nature but then suggested that stable association arose not from rational deliberation but as a psychological consequence of practical relations. What Small also failed to see was that in this it repeatedly undermined the very possibility of a distinctive intellectual content or method. It arose in circumstances which those proposing it did not wish to take for granted, and in a popular philosophical culture, the culture of pragmatism, which precluded any sort of stable systematisation. It was the effect of an urgent wish to recover the original inspiration of American society. As such, it perpetually returned to first principles and so continually undermined itself. Only in this sense did it lack a distinctive intellectual content; but it had a very distinctive point of view.

The history of sociology in America in the 1920s is indeed the history of institutional rather than of intellectual success. To begin with, it is the history of the department at Chicago. For a variety of reasons, neither Sumner, Giddings, Cooley, Ward nor Ross had wished or was able to maintain the original pace of the departments in which they had taught. The Chicago department had before the war consisted of only four men. But one of these was W. I. Thomas, a renegade from the study of literature, who before he was fired for a minor peccadillo in 1919 was able to collaborate upon and finish what came to be taken to be a model study, of *The Polish Peasant in Europe and America*, and was able to attract to the department Robert Park, the man who was initially responsible for its subsequent élan. Park's career was an epitome of thinking progressivism. He went as an undergraduate to Ann Arbor, where he was attracted to John Dewey's pragmatic philosophy of reform. He worked as a muckraking reporter. Dissatisfied with this, and knowing that the careers of reporters could be mercilessly short, he enrolled at Harvard and studied under William James. He went to Berlin, where he listened to Simmel, and to Heidelberg, where he wrote a thesis under the direction of Windelband. Eventually frustrated by nothing but study, he took the job of secretary to Booker T. Washington and immersed himself in Negro causes. It was at Washington's Tuskegee Institute that he met Thomas. Once established at Chicago, he successfully promoted a large number of empirical studies of various social problems in the city. These were enthusiastically if loosely directed by his conception of Chicago as an ecological laboratory, a place in which (partly because it was flat) one could very clearly see the way in which social interactions sorted themselves into geographically distinct associations. This view was informed by a set of ideas that took in virtually all of the notions which Park had earlier acquired in Michigan, Harvard, Berlin, and Heidelberg, as well as on his feet as a reporter, a set of ideas that defies simple summary but which in its pragmatic premises much resembled those of the pre-war sociologists.

Small had already realised that to secure their subject's unquestioned acceptance in the universities, sociologists had to suppress their moral and political interests and insist instead upon the scientific status of what they were doing. Park too used this strategy, although his funds came from those still directly interested in local reform and social work. More than anything else, however, it was the arrival at Chicago in 1927 of W. F. Ogburn that transformed simple strategy into professional faith. Ogburn was one of the first of the generation whose entire education had been sociological. He had worked as a student and a teacher in Giddings' department at Columbia and acquired a competence in statistics as well as a firm belief in what he always referred to as 'scientific sociology'. These he deployed from Chicago in innumerable articles and books, in various professional associations, and on Present Hoover's Research Committee on Social Trends in the late 1920s. Ogburn was an extremely confident man. He once told a former colleague from Columbia that 'the problem of social evolution is solved and', he added, 'I have played a considerable part in solving it. By solving, I mean solving in the sense that Darwin solved the problem of biological evolution. Darwin did it by pointing out three factors: variation, natural selection and heredity...The problem of social evolution is solved by four factors: invention, exponential accumulation, diffusion and adjustment'. Of course, he concluded, 'there will no doubt be refinements in the analysis and measurements just as there have been in Darwin's three factors'. Indeed, although he is now recalled by American sociologists for his discussions of social change (in which he also introduced the somewhat simple notion of a 'cultural lag' behind the pace of technical developments), it was by his own view of methodological refinements that he most markedly affected American sociology. 'In the past', he explained in his presidential address to the American Sociological Society in 1928, 'the great names in sociology have been social theorists and social philosophers. But this will not be the case in the future...a scientific sociology will be quite sharply separated from social philosophy, for it will be recognised how much social philosophy is a rationalisation of wishes'. Indeed, he was sure that firmly to secure such a science 'it will be necessary to crush out emotion and to discipline the mind so strongly that the fanciful pleasures of intellectuality will have to be eschewed in the verification process'. Some sociologists did not accept this charter, not least because it was accompanied by a virtual hegemony of the Chicago department in the affairs of the Society, in the *American Journal*, and in the staffing of newer departments in the west and south. But many did. It promised an impeccably scientific legitimation.

Exactly what such a legitimation should consist of had at the same time been inferred by the same sociologists from Bridgman's *The Logic of Modern Physics*. Bridgman, bringing with him the prestige of the proper sciences, argued in the spirit of a ruthless positivism that the meaning of a proposition lay in the methods used to verify it; he implied, in the spirit of pragmatism, that truth is not independent of the operations by which it is secured. The decisive sociological connection between this formal case and Ogburn's general charter came later in the

1930s, and lay in splicing both onto the older tradition of the social survey. This was largely the achievement of Paul Lazarsfeld, a refugee to New York from National Socialism in Austria who had himself been educated in the fashionable atomistic positivism of post-war Vienna, and who managed in a period and in a city in which there was a growing enthusiasm for market research and for polls of public opinion on other matters to set up a bureau of applied social research. This was eventually attached to Columbia University, and from it, Lazarsfeld did much successfully to persuade sociologists that their distinctive instrument, and thus their most promising claim to scientific practice, lay in the statistical analysis of 'data' on sampled individuals. In a culture in which instruments have often served for ideas and often carried the same institutional force, this came more clearly than any more obviously theoretical idea to constitute professional practice.

The history of American sociology in the 1930s, however, is also the history of a more properly theoretical renaissance. This lay in the transformation of some European ideas into the distinctively American point of view, and started at Harvard. Harvard did not establish a separate sociology department until 1931, and then did so under the direction of a Russian immigrant. But the new ideas came less from this man, Pitirim Sorokin, than from younger ones, and especially from Talcott Parsons. Parsons had come to Harvard from Amherst College in 1927, persuaded that the interest he had acquired during a year in Heidelberg in Sombart and Max Weber's accounts of capitalism could better be pursued at the larger university. Parsons' motives were more narrowly academic than any of the earlier American theorists. He was interested more in theoretical reflection for its own sake. Nevertheless, he did begin, as he later recalled, from a certain anxiety about what he saw as the breakdown of Russian society after 1917 and about the growing enthusiasm for National Socialism in Germany. Theoretically, he started from the observation that although the historical economists in Germany and others like Alfred Marshall in England and Pareto in Italy had all realised that neither the pursuit of individual utility nor the simple fact of power (*Macht*) could account for the relative stability and indeed the very existence of society, none of them had properly developed their insight. He then read Durkheim's *The Division of Labour* (which he had at first rejected on hearing Malinowski's account of it in London) and realised that the key lay in Durkheim's point that there was a 'non-contractual element in contract', a normative order that was logically prior to the organisation and direction of economic activity. The essence of Parsons' case (which he set out at length in 1937 in *The Structure of Social Action*) was that the other theorists were also in different ways inclining toward the same idea, and that he had made what he called the 'convergence' clear. The question had been that of how society was possible. The answer was, by individuals' voluntary adherence to the social facts of the normative order, to a set of common values and a corresponding set of practical rules. But this answer was very ambiguous. If, as Parsons implied, the attachment was a rational one, then was it rational in Weber's uncertain sense of *wertrational* or in Durkheim's wholly different sense of corresponding to the facts of a particular society? And if it was rational at all, then how could Pareto's strict distinction between purely utilitarian rationality and *non*-logical action even be considered to contribute to the common solution? Parsons sensed the difficulty, for the problem of rationality worried him for the next fifteen years. But he seems never to have seen the force in this respect of the difference between Weber and Durkheim, and the issue became further confused when he read Freud and toyed with the possibility that the attachment was not perhaps rational at all. The outcome of this ambivalence was a disappointing set of essays in the early 1950s in which he simply said that at some times individuals associate because they have an interest in doing so, at others because they feel like it, and at others because they feel morally obliged to. This, while incontestable, did not answer the question, and it exposed the fragility of the 'convergence' which he thought he had shown in the first book.

Parsons always said that his main interest was in social integration, and this interest, of course, raises the question not only of how integration is possible in the first place but also of how it can continue. The answer was suggested to him by L. J. Henderson while he was still revising the manuscript of *The Structure of Social Action*. Henderson was a Harvard physiologist who took a great interest in social theory and ran a seminar in Pareto that greatly affected sociologists in Cambridge. He suggested to

Parsons that just as biologists regarded organisms as systems, self-maintaining sets of elements arranged in such a way that a change in one element induced a corrective change in all the others, and just as Pareto had regarded the economy as a system, so too could one look at societies in the same way. This inspired Parsons' next book, *The Social System*. There, he side-stepped the more interesting questions raised by the model of a system, of what sorts of changes cause what sorts of adjustments with what sorts of result, and concentrated instead upon the unremarkable inference that if when elements change they cause changes in other elements than when they do not they can be said to have the consequence, or 'function', of maintaining stability. He translated 'function' into 'imperative', thereby changing it from effect to cause, and proceeded to argue that social systems were stable because of the imperative to be so, an imperative, however, for which the only evidence was the stability it was supposed to explain. He completed the case by asserting against both his first book and arguments he was simultaneously publishing elsewhere that the imperative achieved its effect through the 'internalisation' in each individual of prevailing values and norms. It was not an impressive book.

Indeed, Parsons' theoretical enterprise was a failure even on its own terms. Yet it was remarkably influential. Few matched his classificatory diligence, but many purveyed his sense. 'Structural' (or 'normative') functionalism, as it came to be called, was in the 1950s and early 1960s virtually coextensive with theory among American sociologists. One reason for this was again institutional. In exactly the way in which the instruments of survey analysis served to constitute a professional technique, functionalism served to constitute a professional value. This was most apparent in introductory textbooks and on those occasions when the profession explained itself to the laity. But the need for professional identity does not explain why it was that functionalism, rather than some other sort of theoretical notion, became so popular. It is true that there were few competitors, yet it is at first sight strange (in view of what I have already said about the earlier point of view in America) that the most successful one should have been so explicitly based upon European ideas. However, Parsons not only eliminated all that was distinctive in the various Europeans whom he discussed in the first book (that was part of his intention); in so doing, he almost exactly re-established the point of view of the early American sociologists. These men, to whom he never referred, began from something approaching a state of nature and in general proceeded to account for the development of never very clearly defined social entities in terms of a cumulative sense of association between initially freely acting individuals. Parsons began from a similarly primitive state and proceeded to account for social cohesion in terms, to begin with, of a free commitment to values held in common and later also of affection. And as the earlier sociologists had wavered between regarding individual initiatives as instrumental and emotional so he wavered between regarding them as 'rational' and 'affective'. This is not to claim a convergence even more striking than his. On the contrary, it is to say that in excising the very different conceptions of rationality in the European thinkers in what he had in 1937 loosely described as 'effort', and in ignoring the political point and historical location of their arguments, Parsons had not merely not shown any convergence between them but had not shown anything about them as Europeans at all, except that by largely disregarding their point and selectively re-interpreting what they said they could unintentionally be made to look remarkably like Cooley, Ward, Small, Giddings and Ross.

Yet the problem had slightly changed. The reforming sociologists were almost wholly pre-occupied by the first of Parsons' two questions, of how to establish (in fact in conditions of change, demoralisation and dispute to re-establish) some social cohesion. The Pareto circle at Harvard, on the other hand, and their students, were increasingly exercised by the question of how once it had been established it could be secured. The difference lies in the political distance between 1890 and 1930. Parsons himself, as I have said, was concerned about events in central Europe. George Homans and Elton Mayo, who also went to Henderson's seminars, wanted a reply to the increasingly plausible and insistent Marxists and a way of averting industrial strife. Henderson himself is said to have been a conservative man. But each of these concerns was for a middle way between the anarchy of the market and arbitrary power. Each was liberal. Indeed, the common dismissal of functionalism and the other ideas generated at Harvard in the 1930s as simply 'conservative' quite misses the point about American sociology in particular and American social thought more generally. European social theory since the Enlightenment has in general been an attempt to secure a coherent liberalism on the ruins of a crumbling and decreasingly legitimate patriarchy. American social theory has been an attempt to secure a coherent liberalism on the basis of nothing at all. However, as a latter-day Lockean would be bound to point out, to try to secure a liberal theory and a liberal political practice upon little more than the premise of the unattached individual and the promise of the effects of unmediated social pressure, constrained only by the law, is extraordinarily difficult. Men may be epistemologically free, as free indeed as William James had said, but without constitutive institutions they are likely to undermine themselves in the most illiberal sort of constraint.

The making sacred of techniques and ideas within a profession leads to extreme formality. Yet these particular techniques and ideas had their origin in a 'revolt against formalism'. It was therefore not at all surprising when at the end of the 1950s the striking internality of American thought and practice once again turned full circle in a revived pragmatic attack. This came from another Columbia sociologist, Wright Mills, in *The Sociological Imagination*. In the spirit of the ideas he had so carefully documented in his doctoral dissertation on 'pragmatism and sociology', but affected also by the Marxist milieu in New York – *emigrés* from the Frankfurt School had been colleagues of his at Columbia some years before, Mills took apart Parsons' 'grand theory' and Lazarsfeld's 'abstracted empiricism' and in so doing went to the heart of the professional codes. He was prescient. The condition of American society in the 1960s and into the 1970s was to undermine these formalisms to a degree that he could not, in 1959, have hoped for. But meanwhile, some Europeans had been discovering themselves in *The Structure of Social Action*.

10

History unresolved

WHETHER OR NOT the First World War marked a decisive change in the course of European history, the Second certainly marked a change in the way in which Europeans regarded it. It was not merely that they at last came to see what had begun in the years before 1914. It was also that they began to wonder if the past connected to the present at all. They had good reason. Germans saw one part of their past cancel itself in the most appalling way and another reappear in the forced creation of a separate state to the east. Frenchmen saw their evolutionary optimisms turned upside down. Even Englishmen were faced with a decidedly sour outcome to their somewhat complacent gradualism. The result was in each case an erratic and confused but very evident reconsideration of the philosophies of history by which the course of events had previously been made intelligible. And since social theorising in Europe had been intimately linked to these philosophies it too was recast. Some, of course, continued to believe that continuity was still plain; others that it had been broken. Some argued that the future could be created independently of the past; others dismissed this. Some wished simply to ignore both past and future; others hesitated. And some looked to America.

It was however in France, where the influence of American ideas was negligible, that this was most clear. More exactly, it was in France that all the effects which appeared variously elsewhere occurred together. This was because of the extreme disjunction between French politics after the 1920s and the ways in which French intellectuals had by 1945 come to make sense of their history and its possibilities. In the period between the wars in France, parliamentary politics were precarious. The centre parties were divided and impotent, in the case of the Radicals, almost wilfully so. The left was concentrated in the large Communist Party. And by the early 1930s the right was veering towards fascism. Intellectually, or at least ideologically, the French were divided as they had been for a hundred years between the Catholic and still somewhat monarchist right, the republican centre with its solidaristic philosophy that had come down through men like Jaurès and Durkheim remarkably unchanged except in certain rhetorical respects from Saint-Simon, and the non-Marxist revolutionary left. But many of the first were unhappy with fascism, most of the second were unable to find any expression in the division between the Radicals and the S.F.I.O., and many of the third resisted the Communist Party, whose ideology was completely alien. There was by the 1930s, therefore, considerable pressure to redraw the ideological lines that had remained so suitable to the political battles of the years before 1920. This was increased by the shock of occupation in 1940 and by new alliances in the resistance to it. The pressure eventually became intolerable after the collapse of the socialist victory in the elections in 1945 and the subsequent relapse of parliamentary politics; the determinedly Stalinist stand of the Communist Party through the Soviet occupation of Prague in 1948 and the Soviet suppression of the Hungarian uprising in 1956; and the eventual paradox of the Fifth Republic in which an apparently conservative general (but a hero of the largely left-wing alliances of the resistance years) proceeded to encourage exactly the kind of progressive corporatism that had for so long been the dream of the Saint-Simonian centre.

In the years before 1940, the pressure would appear to have been equally great upon both republicans and revolutionaries. But the republicans had taken a position that was only to be found between the Radicals and the S.F.I.O., and since both of these parties were agreed to be disgracing themselves, the attractions of a *via media* were correspondingly reduced. For this reason, and because of the impending depression and the rumblings of fascism both at home and abroad, the political intellectuals turned back to their own revolutionary tradition and also to the Leninist Marxism that had come to France with the new Communist Party in 1920. But this presented another difficulty. The slogans of the first had been devised to bring about change in a non-industrial society, and the programme of the second, while obviously related to the facts of the depression and offering what was then regarded as a clear alternative to fascisms, put the Soviet Union before France. Thus, while some joined the Party, either in a spirit of misplaced practicality or, like some surrealists, simply because they were naive, others looked for an alternative. Within France itself, however, none was readily available. Hegel was in 1930 as unknown as Marx, so that there were no native grounds for the kind of solution that had been proposed in Germany by Korsch, Lukács or the members of the new Institute in Frankfurt. And the Cartesian rationalism upon which all the intellectuals had been raised in their *lycées* was conventionally supposed to refer to a regular external world whose existence, politically, was exactly what was in question. For the first time, therefore, French intellectuals began to take the Germans seriously, and in the years before the collapse of intellectual life in Germany in 1933 several went there not, like their predecessors, to compare, but to learn. Also, in 1933 a Russian immigrant, Alexandre Kojève, began to lecture on Hegel at the Ecole des Hautes Etudes. From all this, and from the translations into French of Marx's early manuscripts, which had appeared in Germany between 1927 and 1932, there developed what may without exaggeration be described as an intellectual revolution that was to transform French social theory.

It began in an almost entirely philosophical way. 'I [then] wondered', recalled Raymond Aron, 'whether one day it would be necessary to choose between the salvation of my country and the preservation of freedom'. This was the question that most of his contemporaries asked. Aron himself went to Germany wishing to believe Marx, found that he could not, and convinced of what he called Max Weber's 'tragic existentialism' returned to write about how one was to confront a history that offered no ready commitment. Others concentrated more particularly upon the idea of 'freedom' itself, and none more intensely than a friend of Aron's, Jean-Paul Sartre. Sartre began from Descartes' celebrated challenge to scholastic essentialism: 'cogito ergo sum'. This, Sartre argued, carried two distinct implications. One was that man was free to choose and decide; the other, that he was aware of the clear and distinct ideas in his consciousness by which he was able to do so. Descartes had himself claimed that man was completely free to deny what was false, but constrained in what he could accept, since what was right was what corresponded to rules which could not rationally be denied. (This of course was the philosophical foundation of Durkheim's sociology by which Aron, at least, had been repelled in his *lycée*.) Perfect freedom was God's alone. Sartre, however, would not accept the constraint. Leaning first upon Husserl and later upon Hegel, neither of whom, however, he entirely accepted, he argued that there was a distinction between Being-in-itself, Being-for-itself and Being-for-others. The distinction between the first two, he claimed, was equivalent to the distinctions between the unconscious and the conscious and the determined and the free. Descartes had been right in connecting the freedom of thought with conscious reflection, but wrong in the limits he had imposed upon the latter. This argument would appear to have committed Sartre to an extreme idealism, but since he was never very interested in things other than people, and since like the German phenomenologists he seems to have believed himself to have escaped from the old epistemological problems, this did not trouble or even much concern him. Instead, he turned to the question of the relationship between an intentional consciousness of others and the effect of this upon one's own intentions. Being-in-itself, he maintained, became being-for-itself when it actively apprehended other people as objects outside itself. But these others were themselves intending. 'We have observed', he wrote in *Being and Nothingness*, 'that the Other's freedom is the foundation of my being. But precisely because I exist by means of the Other's freedom I have no security; I am in danger in this freedom. It moulds my being and makes me be, it confers values upon it and removes it from me; and my being receives from it a perpetual passive escape from self. Irresponsible and beyond reach, this protean freedom in which I have engaged myself can in turn engage me in a thousand different ways of being'. That is to say, I act intellectually as an *I*, but to act for myself I have to act against others, and in so doing I become defined as a *me*. It is bad faith, a denial of one's freedom, to accept the definitions or purposes of others, but not to do so is perpetually to be thwarted in one's own freedom. Thus, in acting freely one's 'freedom will become conscious of itself and reveal itself in anguish, as the unique source of value, and the emptiness by which the *world* exists'. In the human world, there is no freedom but what one creates

oneself; in creating it, however, one is ineluctably confronted
with its denial. This, very crudely put, was the conclusion of
Being and Nothingness. Sartre had accepted Hegel's idea of
intellection as an activity; but he had rejected Hegel's dialectic,
the argument that in so acting slaves (to use Hegel's metaphor)
could comprehend masters and so enlarge their own freedom.
Masters too, if in good faith, were free, and they would again
deny the slave. By the time that he finished the book, however,
Sartre had already been affected by the occupation of France
and the exhilarating resistance to it, and in a then uncharacteristic aside in *Being and Nothingness* he wondered whether there
was not an alternative to what he had elsewhere argued to be the
only two moral possibilities, sadism and masochism, a possibility,
that is to say, of 'radical conversion' to an 'ethics of deliverance
and salvation'. He had begun to turn to Marx.

Those intellectuals in France who already had, however, and
they were few, had almost all done so on the assumption that
Marxism was to be taken as Marx himself in his later work and as
the Second International intended: as a determinate theory of
the past, present and future of capitalism. This was as true of
those who were sympathetic as of those, like Aron, who were
not. Virtually no-one had thought about the doctrine's Hegelian
basis and the worrying questions that this raised about the
possibility of a straightforwardly positive theory in the
nineteenth-century sense. Virtually none among them therefore
spoke to Sartre's concern. The exception was Maurice Merleau-
Ponty who, Sartre later said, 'revealed to me that I was making
history in the way that Monsieur Jourdain made prose'. Merleau-Ponty had himself been attracted to the German
phenomenologists, but he had also been to Kojève's lectures on
Hegel and had read Marx. He combined these ideas in 1947 in a
book on *Humanism and Terror*, and it was this that drew Sartre.
Replying in part to Arthur Koestler's condemnation in *Darkness
at Noon* of the Moscow trials in particular and of Stalin's oppres-
sions in general, Merleau-Ponty conceded that the Soviet Party
had committed enormous crimes. However, he continued,
drawing upon his own phenomenological thinking, humanity is
realised only when each man's freedom is recognised and conceded by the other, such a realisation is promised only in Hegel's
philosophy and in the proletariat's battle against the

bourgeoisie, and since the party is the instrument of this battle it has to be supported. It alone is on History's side. This argument connected to Sartre's own belief which he had set out in *Being and Nothingness* that the only moral possibilities were sadism and masochism, and that of these, only sadism could be in good faith: the necessary violence of the party corresponded to the necessary violence of the existentially free individual, and was the only alternative to masochistic capitulation.

Merleau-Ponty, however, had almost at once begun to have doubts. He published them seven years later in *Adventures of the Dialectic*. His mistake in 1947 he now thought had been 'to believe that the proletariat alone constituted the dialectic, and that the enterprise of putting it into power, temporarily divorced from any dialectical judgement, could put the dialectic itself in power'. It was of course necessary, he went on, to retain the notion of the dialectic, for without it there could be no conception of the sublime unity of self and other in thought and practice and thus no conception what to fight for. But it was likely that this unity could only be realised in the passing moment of the revolution itself, and that the post-revolutionary society would again be one in which man oppressed man. It was thus essential to give more thought to the structure of this new society, and particularly to its economics. Sartre's mistake after reading *Humanism and Terror*, Merleau-Ponty concluded, had been to confuse the revolution with its consequences. It had been, but Sartre persisted. Explaining that Stalin's death and Khruschev's speech to the Twentieth Congress of the Soviet Party in 1956 had at last facilitated a properly critical appraisal of the philosophy of *praxis*, Sartre published in 1960 the first part of a formidable *Critique of Dialectical Reason* (the second part of which has never appeared). In this, the most prolix and to many earlier enthusiasts for existentialism the most puzzling of his works, Sartre developed the aside he had made in *Being and Nothingness* and the enthusiasm he had felt for Merleau-Ponty's earlier book. He asserted that the economics of *Capital* were correct and beyond discussion, and argued that the question was how to realise the socialist society that they promised. His answer was a very extended one, but essentially rested upon a distinction between 'totality' and 'totalisation', between an objective whole and the more subjective whole, or wholes, that existentially free individuals could create in collective *praxis*. He concentrated upon the possibilities of the second. These lay, he argued, in individuals realising that as long as they constrained each other in social relations premised upon material scarcity they would remain alien to each other, mere aggregates, the 'practico-inert'. Only in *praxis* to abolish scarcity could they transcend their strictly individual inertia and become a 'group', thereby realising both theoretical and practical 'totalisation'. The contrast, as he put it, was between the queue of people waiting for the 'bus outside Saint-Germain-des-Près and the crowd storming the Bastille in July 1789. The *Critique* raised many questions of philosophical coherence and political strategy, and left much unclear. But one fact was apparent. Sartre had not taken Merleau-Ponty's point. Regardless of what might be possible in the revolution itself, and despite his anxiety that 'groups', as he put it, might 'degenerate', into 'series' and 'institutions', he did not ask how the new society might then be run. Except in Merleau-Ponty's detached and elusive faith, Hegel had still not realised himself in French philosophy.

Nevertheless, three things had happened. The Communist Party's continued belief in the possibility of a proletarian revolution had been shown to be incoherent by a philosophical argument that in part derived from the philosophical basis of Marxism itself. By what right, the existentialists had asked, could the Party lead the masses? Would it not thereby deny the freedom in whose name it acted? The Marxist philosophy of history had been broken. In what sense, if any, the existentialists also asked, could the party be justified by History if adherence to determinate historical laws was inconsistent with existentially free (if anguished and inert) individuals taking matters into their own hands? And lastly, Merleau-Ponty had conceded what only a very few had even suspected. The problems of a communist society might in certain crucial respects closely resemble those of a capitalist one. But these questions did not come from the existentialists alone. It was plain to more practical men that if it had ever existed the possibility of a proletarian revolution in France had by 1955 quite certainly disappeared. It was by the same time equally clear that the Soviet Union, the model of the French Party, was not in any way an instantiation of socialist freedoms. For radicals, these truths raised the question of what then could be done. Was any kind of revolution possible? If it was, then did the partial but alarming similarities between communist and capitalist countries mean that it would have to be a revolution against some other force than the old bourgeoisie? And if it would, did this mean that the proletariat would play no distinctive part? Indeed, who were the proletariat? Exactly what kind of society was it that one was living in?

The answers to these questions accumulated after 1958. In that year, de Gaulle had staged a virtual *coup d'état* and sociology was academically disconnected from philosophy. It was a coincidence, but an important one. De Gaulle's intention was to consolidate and promote the economic growth that had at last begun in France in the 1950s with an administrative politics that would rise above the squabbles of the Fourth Republic. The newly professional sociologists were in many cases refugees from the still stubborn Communist Party who had left it precisely because it did not concede the changes that the new growth was bringing about. A Saint-Simonian regime had begun with Marxist revisionists to make sense of it to the new sociology students. They did so by advancing one or other of three sorts of argument. The first and least radical was that sociology had a responsibility to the success of *le Plan*. It was a positive science with technical application. The second was that although no longer a classically capitalist society, France was still one in which men were exploited and oppressed. However, the new commercial and industrial structures, and the sectoral changes in the economy, meant that there was now a 'new working class' of technicians and of other people in new (although still lowly) occupations whose identity as a class was already becoming evident in their action to improve their situation. Whether this new class was in any sense revolutionary, however, remained open and in dispute. The third argument was that to continue to talk of working classes, old or new, drew attention from the fact that the effective controllers of the society were not now the capitalists but their technocratic and administrative agents, men applying new forms of technical knowledge. Alienation persisted, but it was now the less straightforwardly material alienation of what Alain Touraine came to call 'dependent participation'. The political implications of the first view were clear; those of the second and third, however, were not. What was to be done? The fact that even the revisionist sociologists were also professionals tended in the years before 1968 to deter them from political prescription. Lichtheim remarked at this time that 'if the role of Marxist doctrine in contemporary France can be reduced to a formula, it...[is]...that from the vision of a revolutionary future it has turned into the critical contemplation of an eternal and seemingly unchangeable present'. It was ironic but revealing that the only prominent and prolific sociologist who committed himself was Aron. Earlier in the decade, he had published some of his Paris lectures on the economic, social and political similarities between both capitalist and non-capitalist industrial societies. These had been criticised by Hegelians, Marxists and existentialists alike, but embraced by Americans who saw in them further evidence of a withering away of ideologies (that is to say, of Marxism) and of an international 'convergence' towards controlled market societies. Aron attacked all these people for having vulgarised his empirical arguments and for having assumed that the only alternative to Marxism was a mindless acceptance of the *status quo*, and attempted more clearly than he seemed to have been able to do before (in *The Opium of the Intellectuals*) to explain his sceptical and pessimistic liberalism.

But even Aron was not specific about what could be done. All the sociological intellectuals were therefore very surprised when something was done in the spring of 1968. To describe what happened in France in the April and May of that year is almost as difficult as to try to explain it. In essence, however, there was a revolt first of students and then of *lycéens* in Paris which spread to the provinces and to employees in many different sorts of enterprise. By the third week in May, ten million workers were on strike, and there were discussions everywhere on the organisation of work and the future of the regime. They even affected lawyers, doctors and parts of the police. There seems no doubt that the *praxis* of which a now delighted Sartre had written, Merleau-Ponty's sublime revolutionary fervour, was everywhere. The communists dismissed it as 'adventurism' and the government was at first equally contemptuous. But de Gaulle was eventually driven to consider using the army that he had so alienated in the withdrawal from Algeria in the later 1950s and

early 1960s. The army, however, said that it would only intervene if the communists did. In fact, the riot police proved
effective enough in putting down street demonstrations. The
students and workers had no strategy and no tactics beyond
occupation and discussion. The government allowed right-wing
counter-attacks. And the movement was over by 1 June. It had
begun in arguments for university reform from students whose
numbers had doubled in the previous eight years. Outside the
universities and the *lycées* it developed in arguments about both
money and control. Its causes were complex, but it is difficult to
resist the view that one of the less immediate ones was what
Trotsky might have recognised as the country's 'uneven
development'. French society had always been one of extreme
contrast and discontinuity, and this, together with the tensions
that accompanied it, had been exacerbated in the rapid
economic growth since the 1950s. In the most general way, the
discontent appeared in its multiple alliances and antagonisms to
vindicate those like Touraine who had been talking about a new
kind of society with new kinds of classes in it. Such indeed was
the ideology of many of those who took part, and especially of
the nucleus of *enragés* among the sociologists on the new campus
at Nanterre. And as many recognised, it appeared also to
vindicate the view that Sartre and Merleau-Ponty had shared of
the possibilities of revolutionary action. But no more than had
the existentialists or the new and more empirical revisionists did
it produce a coherent view of a practicable future. On the
contrary, it made it clear that French society, as Touraine put it a
year later, was 'having more and more trouble existing on the
level of historic action'. Nevertheless, it produced some consensus outside the Communist Party about what that action had to
be directed to. In a book on *Progress and Disillusion* that
appeared in 1968 itself Aron described this as 'the dialectic of
universality', the tension between the social pressure for control,
rationalisation and anonymity and the individual pressure for
autonomy and expression. Touraine, writing after the May,
talked of 'the contradictions between the impersonal control
exercised by technocracy and the revolt in the name of personal
and collective creativity'. Others wrote in the same vein. The
revisionists had discovered what Aron had known since the
1930s: that the real problem was Max Weber's.

The communists, of course, were in difficulties. In an account of *Everyday Life in the Modern World* published just before the May, the once sympathetic Henri Lefebvre drew their attention to 'a society tactically and strategically oriented towards the integration of the working class'. 'It succeeds in part', he argued, 'by a day-to-day life organised in a repressive way through restrictions and the persuasive ideology of consumer sovereignty rather than by the reality of consumption, but at the same time it loses the capacity to integrate its elements: youth, ethnic groups, women, intellectuals, sciences, cultures'. This was the Party's nightmare. Its traditional support was being incorporated into the new society, and anger remained only on the fringe, in the organisational embarrassments of the young, the foreign, the female and the intellectual. The old guard had been seeing it since 1950. It was simply that it had become horribly obvious in 1968 as the 'adventurists' outflanked the communists in their own preserves. Indeed, the Party came under great strain. There were fierce internal disputes between those who wished to take a gradualist stand against the madness in the streets and factories and offices, the few that wished to take advantage of it, and the old Stalinists. But much the most theoretically ingenious solution had already begun to be argued by Louis Althusser.

Althusser's intention was to rescue a scientific Marxism from the supposed deviations of the existentialist years without having to reassert a materialist philosophy of history. He attempted this by reconstituting Marxism as a science of objective structures. Sartre had already been attacked by another 'structuralist'. In 1966, Lévi-Strauss, of Sartre's own generation and himself claiming inspiration from Marx, had insisted in the final chapter of a book on primitive myth that history, as Sartre had conceived of it in the *Critique*, was itself a solipsistic myth. It was not merely that it consisted in a reconstruction of the past in terms of the principles of the present. It was also that these principles themselves, which in Sartre's account were the product of a fully conscious and intending *cogito*, were nothing but the predetermined expression of unconscious dispositions, dispositions, Lévi-Strauss insisted (drawing upon what he took to be the claims of structural linguistics) that were intelligible as structures of signs, structures that were both logically and empirically prior to the illusions of the *cogito*. Of course, Lévi-Strauss conceded, such illusions were a necessary part of making sense of society, and especially of a society with a recorded past, but they could not themselves be said to make proper sense of it. They *were* illusions. Only the anthropologist, standing outside the society, and furnished with a knowledge of the similar structures informing all other societies, could appreciate this, and appreciate, therefore, that what were claimed to be particular and particularly appropriate interpretations of a particular society were not such at all. Sartre's answer to this was curiously defensive. It raised philosophical difficulties even more acute than did his own work, not least in the supposed validity of the deliverances of the anthropologist's own *cogito*, but he merely replied that 'structures are created by activity which has no structure, but suffers its results as structure'. Indeed, the argument was scarcely an argument at all. Lévi-Strauss had simply asserted his case.

Althusser, however, did argue. He did not argue against Sartre until 1972, over ten years after he had begun to publish his own interpretation of Marx, but it was against Sartre's project, the project of an existential Marxism, that he did. He did so in two ways. The first was to insist upon and elaborate a distinction between science and ideology. Ideologies, he claimed, were always the expressions of a particular interest. In this sense, the young Marx, fighting the particular illusions of Germany before 1848, was as ideological as the existentialists who had been fighting the dialectical materialists in the French Party after 1945. Sciences, on the other hand, were true by virtue of being rationally constructed truths that served no interest at all except that of science itself. If Marx was right, and Althusser claimed that he was, at least in his later writings (which he first identified as having emerged after the 'epistemological break' in 1845, and then as not having emerged until after Marx finished the first volume of *Capital* in 1866), he was right regardless of where one's own, and his, ideological interest lay.

This was Althusser's second and more extended claim. Men were not subjects. The illusion of subjectivity was the illusion of the younger, and even the middle-aged, Marx. It was in the Marx of the later volumes of *Capital*, and of pieces like the *Critique of the Gotha Programme*, the Marx that Sartre, for instance, had quite taken for granted, that the truth lay. This truth, however, was analytical and structural, not predictive and historical. Marx's own earlier predictions were wrong, but he was right in suggesting how structures worked. He was right, that is, in pointing to a distinction between the material, the political, the ideological and the theoretical or scientific. He was right in pointing to the tripartite character of each, to the fact that each has an object of labour, a means of production, and a product. And he was right in suggesting that the material ultimately determines the others. Althusser put great weight on the qualification. Although the material will furnish the conditions of any structure, it is possible and indeed even probable that something else will be dominant within it. Consequently, structures are complex, endlessly variable conjunctures, and always in tension or contradiction. The theory, if it is such, is curiously ambiguous. Althusser conceded what many non-Marxists would concede, and have conceded since before Marx, that modes of production, if one wishes to use that phrase, furnish the limits within which institutions and individuals can act, and in that extremely weak sense determine that action. But he thereby conceded that in any place at any time anything may be more immediately determinant, or 'dominant'. He did not clearly define 'contradiction'. And he ran a great risk of undermining the validity of his own belief that there are sciences, as distinct from ideologies, by the vicious argument that they (including his own theory) are materially conditioned but that only he (from his theory) can tell what is and what is not. Indeed, it is difficult to take the scheme seriously as a theory at all. But it is clear how it was intended to secure what used to be called vulgar Marxism without committing anyone to anything at all. The material determines, except where it does not; and there is always a determinate set of contradictions, but no way of telling what they might lead to. Although it is not in any sense the official ideology of the French Communist Party (that remains much more orthodox), it was a measure of the desperation of communist ideologues. In its articulation, it was also (and in its more recent developments remains) a measure of the extremes of which French rationalism is still capable.

In the years between 1930 and 1970, therefore, French intellectuals veered from one pole to the other in attempting to comprehend the country's uneven development. By the beginning of the depression, the Durkheimian scheme, like its Jaurèsian counterpart, had ceased to be plausible. Wherever the country was going it was not towards an enlightened liberal solidarism. The rhetorics of 1789 and 1871 seemed equally empty. Yet there was no readily available alternative to the dogmatic Leninism of the communist party. There thus began a complete reconsideration of possibilities, at first in phenomenology and existentialism and later in a socialised existentialism that owed much to Hegel without ever firmly committing itself to the view of dialectical possibility that Lukács and others had taken in Germany in the 1920s. This, however, flowered just as the French Communist Party was becoming clearly anachronistic and the Soviet Union was being seen for what it was, and just as de Gaulle began his paradoxically Saint-Simonian Fifth Republic. It received accolade and defeat in 1968, and then died. Creating the future had been tried and found difficult. The present, however, corresponded to no known stage in any known philosophy of history. Saint-Simon himself had conceded that the reign of the *industriels* would pass, but he had not said to whom. And nothing in Marxism allowed for the kind of controlled corporate capitalism ushered in with *le Plan*. Only the historically terminal pessimism of Max Weber seemed to make sense. The communists were caught more severely than any by these changes, and some of them rewrote history by deliberately excising time. By 1970 it was reasonably clear what had happened. But it was not at all clear what it implied for the future.

There is a Promethean aspect to these French disputes. Ultimate issues appear to be at stake, and the nation seems to take sides. 'Do *les événements* refute structuralism?' asked *Le Monde* in 1968. But this is deceptive. Despite their rhetoric of hostility and even contempt, the protagonists shared the same parish, the same education, the same friends, the same experiences and much the same attitudes. Aron may have devoted whole books to criticising Sartre's *Critique*, Lévi-Strauss's argument against it may have read like ideological warfare of the most bitter kind, and Merleau-Ponty's subtle and elusive phenomenology may have seemed worlds away from Lévi-Strauss's almost mechanical structuralism. But each took pains to explain his respect and friendship for the other; all shared a culture within which they were easily able to exchange the abstractions that seem so dense to others. Even in the intellectual revolution that occurred there in the 1930s the French retained their own internality. What was far more remarkable, however, is that despite National Socialism, defeat and partition, West Germans also retained much of theirs.

The difficulties of Imperial Germany and its successor after 1919 were in the most general terms those of a society industrialising within institutions that belonged to a non-industrial past. The corrosions of the market were resisted, before 1914, by an authoritarian bureaucracy, and both before and afterwards, by politicians in contempt of parliament and by patriarchy everywhere. The ironical achievement of National Socialism was to have gone so far in demolishing these old allegiances that they could never again be properly revived. Local allegiances, however deferential and however themselves resistant to liberal notions, were a threat to the total state. But although this process of what an American might now call 'modernisation' was carried even further in the new Democratic Republic in the east, in the west, in the new Federal Republic, it faltered. The very description of the country revealed how: it was to be a federation of the old *Länder* whose autonomy the National Socialists had done much to reduce. And even though in the eventually startling economic growth in the 1950s and 1960s the effects of the market were to continue what had begun in that way even before 1914, older allegiances were allowed to revive and older attitudes not only persisted but were in some respects even encouraged. Thus, while some new universities were created, and although the bureaucratic models of university organisation in the United States were imported into some older institutions, many professional humanists were able to re-establish the insularity and prestige which they had had to abandon after 1933. The Federal Republic is markedly less 'modern' than the Democratic. It is still a somewhat uneven society, on the face of it open in the sense in which any flourishing market society must be, yet in many places still closed, local and hierarchical. This unevenness exists within academic life itself. The influence of American example has been considerable, yet there also persists much of the attitude of the old *Bildungsbürgertum*. In German sociology, therefore, there exists an uneasy mixture of American professionalism and the older German cultural criticism.

Looking back at the end of the 1950s over nearly fifteen years of West German sociology, Helmut Schelsky remarked that no-one had in that time attempted to characterise the society as a whole. Germans had lost their historical self-confidence. Instead, there was an increasing number of special studies which although professional and relying upon an eclectic mixture of the liberal sociologies of old Germany and the United States, in their very professionalism tended to obscure the assumptions upon which they rested. This is evident from a handbook that Schelsky himself helped to edit in 1955. This professionalism has continued, but in the 1960s there did appear two sets of arguments about the character and tendency of the whole society. Each consisted in a revival of questions that had been asked in the years between 1910 and 1930, but each departed from the answers that had been given then.

The first appeared in two forms, only one of which was directly sociological but both of which had a common starting point: the deficiencies of pre-war sociologies in general and of the apparently least deficient of them in particular, that of Max Weber. Unless one was a Marxist, and even if one was, and open-minded, it was difficult to resist the view that Weber's account of Imperial Germany and of the strangled development there of liberal capitalist precept and practice was the most illuminating. No-one had been so energetic; no-one had had such a fine institutional sense; and no-one had been more insistent about the dangers of what he had called 'traditional' domination. After the disaster of National Socialism, it seemed that if anything could be recovered from the older German social scholarship it had largely to be recovered from Max Weber. It is therefore easy to imagine the surprise and consternation caused by the publication in 1959 of a book which argued that Weber's politics and thus the historical and sociological questions that he had asked derived from his view that the overriding value was Germany's national greatness. This book, by Wolfgang Mommsen, did not go unchallenged, and the debate persists. But for liberals the accusation was sufficient for them to discard this, the most plausible of their ancestors. An account of German society from a liberal point of view had thus to be re-invented. This was largely the achievement of Ralf Dahrendorf, and Dahrendorf's liberalism together with his unqualified agreement with Mommsen's thesis explains why it is that in reading him one has the curious sensation of reading something by Weber from which the man's name has mysteriously vanished.

Dahrendorf's philosophical, or at least political, premise was clearest in his essay on 'homo sociologicus'. There, he simply argued that although there is much of individual behaviour which may only be explained by the ways in which any individual has been and continued to be defined by others, there is equally much which cannot. This is the residue of individuality, and the repository of freedom. Dahrendorf's question was what in modern conditions inhibits and facilitates this freedom? Having previously dismissed American accounts of a Parsonian kind as 'utopian', descriptions of a fantasy of social integration which ignored all the real difficulties, his first systematic answer to it was in a book in 1959 on *Class and Class Conflict in Industrial Society*. There, he argued with Marx's proposition (as he put it) that authority was a special case of property and concluded by asserting that it was exactly the other way round: property was a special case of authority. The most fundamental fact of modern social arrangements was the existence of and individuals' places in 'imperatively co-ordinated associations'. He reneged on this, however, in 1966, insisting now that he had been wrong in saying that classes derived from positions of super- and subordination and suggesting instead that in so far as there was a class-based conflict at all (the lecture was called *Conflict after Class*) it rested in a myriad of different situations which could not be captured in any one conceptual category. These conceptual abstractions, however, were less interesting than his answer to the question of how liberalism might be secured in the Federal Republic itself, an answer that appeared in 1965 in a book on *Society and Democracy in Germany*. His answer was remarkably Weberian, although less clear. He drew a distinction between patterns of 'authoritarianism' and 'totalitarianism' in twentieth-century Germany, the one characteristic of the pre-industrial past with which the country had entered the century and the other, antithetical to it, characteristic of Hitler's regime and of the new Democratic Republic. His argument was that Hitler had paradoxically done a service in removing many of the old authoritarian obstacles to liberally democratic beliefs, actions and institutions, and that the post-war market society in the Federal Republic had gone some way further by a different means. 'The chances of liberal democracy in a German society', he concluded, 'have never been as great as they are in the German Federal Republic'. But he did not think that they were overwhelmingly certain. Many of the old attitudes persisted. More important, on his account, was the persistence of an indifference to political participation, of a marked privacy. Yet he also conceded of the early 1960s that 'it is becoming increasingly difficult to formulate the main issues of political and economic conflict'. This would appear to raise three questions, none of which he answered. Can the apathy not be explained by the absence of clear issues? Is it anyway such a threat to liberal democracy if that democracy, as Dahrendorf claims, is working well? And if it is a threat, then is it not the case that it could only be removed either by more overt class conflict or by exactly the kind of *Wertrationalität* that Dahrendorf, remembering Max Weber, so feared? It may well be that as his own impressive account of the history of Germany showed, insufficient energy has always been shown there in safeguarding individuals from the encroachments of local institutions and the State. But if such securities are now more assured, it seems strange to have regarded their natural consequence (the kind of consequence, for example, that obtains in Britain) as a threat, perverse to have complained of a lack of debate about real issues.

It was exactly such a complaint, however, which came to characterise and continues to characterise the second sort of argument against the character of the Federal Republic. This derived from the newly- if somewhat loosely-named Frankfurt School. Many of the radical Marxists who had gathered at the new university in Frankfurt in 1924 had emigrated to the United States after 1934. Some, like Herbert Marcuse, remained there. Others, like Max Horkheimer (who had directed the Institute since 1930) and Theodor Adorno, returned to Frankfurt in 1950. Horkheimer and Adorno had been the main protagonists of the second of the two distinguishable views in the Institute in the 1920s, of the view that direct working-class action was not only impractical but also undesirable, the view that what was required was a more general and less directly political criticism of the very culture of bourgeois society. Both men had kept themselves remarkably aloof from American society in the 1930s and 1940s; it was a society they neither liked nor cared to try to understand. Accordingly, when they returned to Frankfurt in 1950, they were encumbered neither by any very substantial modification of their views nor by any opposing group of more straight-forwardly political Marxists. The new Frankfurt School was theirs, and it was in the 1950s virtually the only centre in the country of even putatively radical thinking.

Horkheimer and Adorno had crystallised this thinking in 1947 in a book on the Enlightenment. The triumph of reason in the eighteenth century, they argued, had in fact been its eclipse. The technical, so-called rational domination of nature, first intellectually, in the natural sciences, and then practically, in modern technology, had been accompanied by a parallel domi-nation of men: first, again intellectually, in the new and avowedly rational sciences of man, most especially classical economics, and then, again practically, in the so-called rational-isation of urban industrial life and its attendant social discipline. It had been a domination in the name of one kind of reason that vitiated the possibility of another, the glorification of technical means and the suppression of debate about ends, a preoccupa-tion with what men could be made to do at the expense of what they could make of themselves. But they offered no solution. Indeed, in his own writings, Adorno expressly despaired of any rational solution at all, and almost paralysed by what he regarded as the dreadful banality around him, talked only of art. Hegel might have remarked that he had lapsed into 'felt reason'. Ironically, however, a solution was suggested, not by anyone in Frankfurt, but by Marcuse, who although he has continued to live in the United States and was also for a time a hero of student visionaries both there and in western Europe between 1964 and 1968, has continued to think and write within the moral, political and intellectual conventions already estab-lished by the Institute's more Hegelian members in the late 1920s, and has indeed been taken seriously only in Germany itself.

In his own most extended account of his case, in *One Dimen-sional Man*, which was published in 1964, Marcuse started from two assumptions: that contemporary industrial societies were ones in which 'all counteraction is impossible' because of the pervasiveness of technical rationality, of the one-dimensional rationality of optimal means for given ends; and that such 'a specific historical practice [as this rationality] is measured against its historical alternative'. The latter at once marked him off from Horkheimer and especially from Adorno. Such an alternative was to them not even conceivable. Modern industrial societies, Marcuse claimed, had succeeded in satisfying the material needs of their members and in giving them a certain, very tightly constrained degree of liberty, of freedom from interference by others to enjoy the material rewards for their having acceded to the 'imperatives' of technical rationality. This satisfaction, however, was at the expense of 'true' needs. Marcuse identified these true needs on the basis of his reading of Hegel and Freud. They were the need for non-alienation, for an individual fulfilment that once achieved would *ipso facto* constitute a non-contradictory society, the old *Sittlichkeit*, and the need for not-repression, for a 'desublimation' that once achieved would enable individuals freely to express all of which they were capable. There was a difficulty even in this. There is no suggestion in Freud that although one civilisation may have exacerbated the pathologies he described a different civilisation would remove them. And a desublimated society would seem likely to be more anarchic than the Hegelian resolution of subject and object in the harmonious, because at last rational, *Sittlichkeit*. However, Marcuse concluded the argument by considering the possibilities for freedom in these two senses, and wavered. At one point, he committed himself to a straightforwardly historicist belief, suggesting that with the development of automation in the process of production men would eventually be made redundant and then constitute exactly the kind of negation that Marx considered the proletariat to be in entreprenurial capitalism, the refutation of the society and the liberated harbingers of the new universal order. At other points, however, he remained pessimistic. The success of the existing order, he here implied, is altogether too complete. Four years later, however, after hearing about what had gone on in Paris in the spring of 1968, he wrote a hurried *Essay on Liberation* in which although his diagnosis remained the same he was markedly more optimistic about the possibilities of 'negation' from outside the society, from the Third World, from the stubborn refusals of students and other rebels, not, or not yet, incorporated into the pervasive unidimensionality, from dropouts, from necessarily unconventional art, and from the 'unconscious', *ex hypothesi* immune to all social influence. But he never explained in what way any of these constituted or even pointed towards the positive promise of a new order. Indeed, what had happened in Paris in the June of 1968 should have given him pause. Altogether, the argument was superficial and even crude. His characterisation of industrial societies was rarely specific, and where it was it was arguably quite wrong. He seemed remarkably insensible to the differences between such societies, and especially to differences between capitalist and non-capitalist ones. He used Hegelian categories but did not seriously consider the extent to which the empirical premise of Hegel's own political philosophy, the existence of separate and autonomous property-owners in a *bürgerliche Gesellschaft*, differed from his and the extent, therefore, to which much more careful conceptual consideration had to be given to any argument for an Hegelian sort of transcendence in modern societies in which, as he himself claimed, autonomy was much reduced. And he was inexcusably ambivalent about his own philosophy of history. He used an historicist scheme to make his critical point but quite obsured the issue of whether his historically located alternative was predetermined or even, indeed, possible as a specifically historical alternative at all.

This last argument was the one made against him by Jürgen Habermas, an altogether more subtle man who although never in any proper sense part of the so-called Frankfurt School shared many of their beliefs and for a time taught at Frankfurt itself. Habermas has certainly been concerned with the one-sidedness of modern society, which like Marcuse he sees in its philosophy and in its social and political practices. But unlike Marcuse and indeed unlike all the members of the original group he is not an Hegelian. Hegel, he argued, 'could claim necessity for the progression of phenomenological experience only retrospectively from the standpoint of absolute knowledge', and it is such 'absolute' foundations that Habermas wishes to deny. Yet Habermas accepts, with Fichte and Hegel after him, that Kant's solution was no solution at all. Kant conceded that 'it is entirely impossible for we humans to explain how or why...morality [and knowledge] interests us', and as both Fichte and Hegel maintained (although offering different solutions), this amounts to saying that the foundations of reason are rationally indefensible. Marx, of course, had argued that there was an explaining interest, the interest of the species as a whole in controlling nature in such a way that the 'species-being' would not itself be violated by that control. This, Habermas contends, is partially right and partially wrong. It is right in so far as it recognises that the interest is a species interest, neither transcendent nor contingently empirical. It is wrong, however, in reducing this species interest to an interest merely in the control of nature. This is only one of three quite distinct species interests. A second, partially grasped by Dilthey, is an interest in communication, an interest in achieving consensus with others in order to realise the more 'anthropologically deep-seated' interests of 'autonomy' and 'consensus'. However, just as the first interest can be thwarted by the domination over men of particular forces and relations of production, so the second can be thwarted by the domination of past modes of communication, of languages, for instance, which serve (rather in Simmel's view) to constrain that which they were originally developed to free. Thus, there is pressure to reassert the 'deep-seated' interests in autonomy and consensus, and this is the pressure of what Habermas calls 'an emancipatory cognitive interest', an interest precisely in reflecting upon the ways in which the 'deep-seated' interests are constrained. The ego, he says, recalling Fichte, will have to escape its domination by 'self-reflection' in which it will make 'itself transparent to itself as action that returns into itself'. It will have critically to inspect the way in which it is constituted, that is to say, dominated, by the instrumental and communicative interests of others. Only then can it emancipate itself. However, and this for Habermas is crucial, it will not emancipate itself simply as an ego, whether of the empirical or (in Husserl's sense) the transcendental sort. It can only do so by recognising that its emancipation will be an emancipation of the species as a whole, that the emancipation of each ego is the emancipation of them all in autonomy and consensus.

It is clear what Habermas has tried to do. He has accepted

Kant's point that the highest interest is the interest in reason, and thus autonomy. He has accepted Hegel's point that this reason has itself to be grounded. He has accepted Marx's point that it cannot be grounded in the abstract presupposition of a comprehending *Geist.* He has accepted Dilthey's point that the interest in controlling nature is not the only human interest. He has accepted Husserl's point that in addition to instrumental and communicative interests there is the interest of *theoria,* the interest in actively comprehending the world in order not merely to grasp the phenomenal essence of that world but also to grasp the essence of one's own intentionality in so doing. And through the Fichtean reaction to Kant, and the Marxian, he has argued that this third interest, the 'emancipatory' one, is the interest of a self-reflecting species which in so reflecting will see that the realisation of its 'deep-seated' interests is at once a philosophical matter and a practical one. The interests cannot be realised without the right conditions, and the right conditions cannot be realised without the right philosophy. He is clearer, however, about how these conditions cannot be created than he is about how they can be. He is clear that the view (Marcuse's view) that the instrumental interest in technical domination, together with its ideological and institutional consequences, can be suppressed, is absurd. 'Technology', he argues, 'if based at all on a project, can only be traced back to a "project" of the human species as a whole, and not to one that could be histori-cally surpassed'. Habermas is not a confidently dialectical historicist, and for that, he suffered as much as Adorno at the hands of radical students in Frankfurt in 1967 and 1968. Yet he has declared that 'on the basis of industrial society and its technically mediated commerce, the inter-dependence of politic-al events and the integration of social relations have progressed so far beyond what was even conceivable two centuries ago that, within this overall complex of communication, particular his-tories have coalesced into the history of one world...at the same time, mankind has never before been confronted so sharply by the irony of a capacity to make its own history, yet still deprived of control over it...the immanent presuppositions of the philosophy of history have not by any means become invalid; on the contrary, it is only today that they have become true'. There is, in the Marxist phrase, a world-historical domination. It is clear, to Habermas as to more orthodox Marxists, that this domination cannot as it were be simply thought away. Yet it is not clear, as it has until recently been to orthodox Marxists, what specific action has to be taken to resolve the dilemma and emancipate the species.

Habermas's case, although original, is familiar. It recalls Horkheimer, Adorno and Marcuse, the Webers and Max Scheler. It shares the distinction that each made in some way between technical reason and a higher kind. But it rejects any Hegelian notion of historical transcendence, it rejects the view that reconciliation may only be achieved in philosophy, or indeed, in art, it rejects the Webers' relativism (and Max Weber's conviction that human interests are in their highest form strictly individual interests), and although like Scheler it suggests a third realm, above the practical and the phenomenological, it rejects any notion of this realm as transcendent or Platonic, accessible to men but not grounded in their 'species-being'. It recalls Herder's socialisation of Kant, but would fall under Kant's own charge that such a move at best blurs the task of reason. It explicitly recalls Parsons, but in its description of the interest in autonomy and consensus as 'deep-seated' and 'metalogical' it too blurs the critical question of whether the interest is rational or not. And it is sociologically naive. Habermas does not clearly explain how the domination is to be removed. Yet for all its weaknesses, or ambivalence, it does point to a real feature of modern industrial societies, a feature that preoccupied Max Weber, a feature that refugees from the Democratic Republic remark upon in the Federal Republic, a feature that worried Dahrendorf, the passivity of the population and the lack of discussion there.

This similarity is not superficial. Although Dahrendorf was asking about the fragility of liberal democracy in Germany and Habermas about the regimented passivity of the population, each connects with the other and with the discussions of 'the social question' in Germany from the 1890s. The connection lies in the preoccupation with domination. The earlier theorists had in general condemned the domination of the market and in a few cases of the Prussian bureaucracy, yet had looked from their patriarchal universities for another domination, another basis for legitimate authority, a value. So too does Habermas, and

Dahrendorf, who was far more sensitive to the realities of German society, was despite himself dismayed by the absence of issues which would raise the quality of German politics and in a Kantian sense the dignity of German society. It is an ironical connection. It cannot be explained by continuities in the status and organisation of universities, for although such continuities exist they are less remarkable than in France. It would seem to lie more in an enduring and particularly German conception of individual possibility, a conception that has survived very considerable institutional changes.

By the time that Wright Mills had published his attack upon 'grand theory' and 'abstracted empiricism' in America they had already come to be taught in France and Germany. They were the only available models of a properly professional practice, and in the confusion in each country in the 1950s about each society's historical location they appeared to offer an ahistorical solution. But no sooner had they been adopted in Germany in the early 1950s and after the academic separation of sociological instruction in France in 1958 than they began to be transformed in America itself. Both normative functionalism and the assumptions of conventional survey analysis presupposed a homogeneous population and ignored questions of institutional power and what some Americans had learnt to call class differences. Mills himself attacked Parsons' conception of power as legitimate authority rather than a zero-sum game in which the fact of people with it implied others without it, and had already written a book on what even President Eisenhower had described as the 'military–industrial complex' that ran America. But it was only after 1959 that there arose definite issues to which such anger could direct itself. The litany is now familiar: the Cuban revolution and the fiasco of the Bay of Pigs, the Organisation of American States, the at last apparent insecurity of civil rights in the south and black rebellion in the northern cities, the war in South East Asia, the failure of the poverty programme, the Democratic convention in Chicago in 1968, the nomination of Richard Nixon, and the undermining of Allende's regime in Chile. Each destroyed one or other of the familiar liberal assumptions, that Americans had achieved freedom and equality at home and stood virtually alone against the evident menace of organised communism abroad. Each led remarkably large numbers of college students to question what they were being taught.

In the early 1960s this was still a mixture of normative functionalism, pragmatist social psychology and techniques for analysing survey data. But for the theorists, at least, the question had again changed. Before 1914 it had been of the possibilities of integration. In the 1930s it had been of the likely persistence of integration. Now, it was of the possibilities of stable change, and once more, the answers were curiously soothing. Industrial societies, it was claimed, were all converging towards a common destination dictated by the technical and organisational imperatives of advanced industrialisation. The future, although more directed than Americans had been used to, would resemble the United States more than the Soviet Union as the latter succumbed to the impossibilities of managing itself without market mechanisms and the devolution of decisions. Non-industrial societies, on the other hand, would if they were not already doing so experience a differentiation of structures the more efficiently to meet the imperatives dictated by economic development, and their citizens would in turn come to abandon their 'traditional' constraints in the ineluctable evolution towards 'modernity' and 'rationality'. Any deviations from these patterns could be explained (as Chalmers Johnson explained the Chinese revolution) as externally-induced disequilibria or (as Edward Shils explained American intellectuals' hostility to the war in Vietnam) as partial failures of normative incorporation. In such a way, contemporary history was assimilated to the foreshortened historical understanding in American social thought so that the diverse peculiarities of other societies and the worrying features of America itself could always be explained away. Needless to say, however, even to those whose education had not given them the means with which to challenge the assumptions from which these accounts derived, the accounts did come to look a little thin in the face of the continual stream of extraordinary and appalling events throughout the 1960s and into the 1970s. They looked even thinner in the face of the professional sociologists' continued insistence upon the validity of the distinction between 'actionism' (as one called it) and the responsibilities of the scientist, and upon explanations of the

confused and angry students in terms of inadequate socialisation
or the functionalist view of deviance.

These students, and the relativity few (and usually young)
professional sociologists who could no longer accept the conventional liberal pieties, turned in one or more of four directions.
The first was towards the past. Drawing once again on the
conviction so useful to Americans in times of despair, the
pragmatic conviction that individuals are creative and free and
thus in principle capable of starting again, and idealising the
supposedly communal communities of the first settlers, many
turned towards what came to be described as a 'counter culture'
which stressed private invention and primitive communism. In
its purest form, this culture set itself not only against existing
reality but also against any attempt analytically to comprehend
it. A second group, however, stopped short of complete retreat.
These, convinced also that the once vaunted consensus was a
myth, and convinced therefore that the sociology which had
explained it was irrelevant, turned back as their precedessors
had done in the period before the First World War to the
question of how, if at all, society was possible. Once again, this
had become a pressing question, and once again, it was answered in terms of a pragmatic sociology or social psychology of
inter-personal association. In some forms, this recalled the old
distinction between the 'I' and the 'me' that had so fascinated
Cooley, and raised the question of the status of the first in the
face of pressures on the second. In others, it turned away from
this more general issue towards a more exact understanding of
how individuals did or did not manage to communicate with
each other and thus establish a relationship. But whether as
'symbolic interactionism' (which was a name often given to the
first) or as 'ethnomethodology' (which was a name often given to
the second), the assumption was the same: the very possibility of
any stable social relation and of some persisting individual
identity within it was in doubt. This doubt, however, extended
only to relations between individials, or at the most, to relations
between individuals and agencies charged with dealing with
them (like police departments). It did not extend to the structure of the society more generally. Indeed, although radical in
style, the second putative solution was in this respect extremely
conservative. The third, however, was not. This was towards the

kind of pragmatic and radical but populist criticism of the established institutions of authority that had already been revived by Wright Mills. Some were affected by Mills' own writing, which was always pointed and direct, and about the world, but by the end of the 1960s, most were affected by the world itself.

Finally, there was Marxism. America is a puzzle to Marxists. On the one hand, it is the most nearly perfect capitalist society, least encumbered with any of the conventions and beliefs of a patriarchal past and most permeated by market relations. On the other hand, precisely because of the absence of such a past it altogether lacks the ideological divisions so characteristic of European societies, divisions, indeed, which are there so characteristic that they have often wrongly been taken to be the products of capitalism itself. It is not therefore difficult to see why earlier Marxist arguments in America, such as they were, concentrated almost entirely upon Marx's more purely economic predictions. Equally, it is not difficult to see why attempts to make use of his more sociological and political arguments have always foundered. This is exactly what happened at the end of the 1960s. The dissensus and conflict of that decade had disposed many to Marxism, and in the middle of 1968 it was perhaps not unreasonable to believe with Norman Birnbaum (whose arguments had some purchase upon the American New Left in the Students for a Democratic Society) that 'the students' critique of their own society and their refusal of the roles assigned to them in it constitutes an anticipatory strike by a critical segment of the labour force'. But the middle of 1968 was a peculiarly heady time, and a bitterly transient one. It lay between the events in Paris and the election of Richard Nixon, as the war in South-East Asia was escalating still further. By 1969, the Students for a Democratic Society had come to despair even of such action as they were proposing, and in a series of manoeuvres in which faction after faction attempted to show that it was more radical than the other, victory went finally to the Weathermen (who were dedicated to fighting even the American working class). The New Left, which had by then managed successfully to organise political groups in some working class areas, collapsed. With it, there also collapsed the nascent radical sociology it had begun to inspire, and the victory of the Weathermen (who were only ever a very small group) reveals why. The left had argued itself into a most extreme and self-defeating sort of opposition precisely because there was in practice no part of American society outside itself to which it could attach its hopes and with which, therefore, it could hope successfully to act. The conditions which had fuelled the radicalism led most Americans to vote for Nixon. A native Marxism, generated in America to answer American questions, had been strangled, had even perhaps strangled itself, at birth.

If what I have said is correct, socially sensitive men in West Germany and the United States have since the Second World War generally responded to what they have variously described as pressing domestic problems by drawing upon intellectual models already available to them in their society. In France, they did so by transforming alien models into distinctively fresh syntheses that now, thirty years later, have acquired a native character. In these respects, England falls somewhere in between. It too of course has been seen to have problems, but problems of a less severe sort and problems that to begin with could still be formulated within the intelligentsia's prevailing liberal socialism. However, it has become clear to some that it is precisely this tradition which has failed to solve them, and for the first time since the 1880s men have begun to turn again to alien, and especially German, theories. This is partly the result of the introduction of alien conceptions of sociology into English universities, but like these conceptions themselves it has received its impetus from the failure of gradualist socialism in its first electoral triumphs.

Unlike the French socialists, who also won an election in 1945, the British Labour Party did not have to contend with either a communist party or large numbers of suspicious Catholic workers. Moreover, it had the advantage of the fact that the war had also convinced many liberals and liberal conservatives that after it there could be no return to the conditions that had made the depression possible, and no future possibility even if such a depression did recur of allowing working-class families to sink into extreme poverty. Accordingly, virtually all were committed to some degree of central economic management and to an overhaul of social policies. The war had in domestic matters thus played directly into the hands of the pre-war liberal socialists. When both middle- and working-class voters deserted the Labour Party, therefore, in 1950 and 1951, on the second occasion allowing a Conservative government, there was considerable heart-searching. This was more evident on the right of the party than the left. The extensive nationalisation of some basic industries and services between 1945 and 1950 had not evidently improved the situation of the working class, not least because of the external constraints on the economy, and since the left (not considering revolution) then had no other programme, they were reduced to a confused silence. The right of the Labour Party, on the other hand, were not. They took the view that the class composition of the country was changing, that the Labour Party had come to power just too late, and that if it was to remain a viable and successful alternative to the Conservatives it had to reconsider its policies. This was most clearly expressed in Anthony Crosland's *The Future of Socialism* in 1955 and in other essays of his that were later published as *The Conservative Enemy*. Crosland argued that the 1945 government had shown that nationalisation of some industries made economic sense, that the public administration of services removed people from the vagaries of the market and ensured that certain essential social rights could be exercised, and that the task of democratic socialism was thus to continue to remove the privileges of acquired status and to redress the inequalities produced and perpetuated by a still largely market economy. One of his premises was that nothing more could be done within the existing political arrangements even if it was thought desirable, since a significant proportion of the working class was acquiring middle-class incomes and aspirations. This view, reasonably representative of those on the right of the Labour Party, and of its leadership, came to be challenged in three ways.

Some argued that even if one accepted the view, inequalities and deprivations were not being adequately redressed. There was still poverty which the social services did not reach; in a society in which individual advancement depended even more than it had before upon education, the proportion of working-class children being selected for middle-class education and thus for middle-class occupations had not much changed since before the war; and many who were selected for some reason abandoned that education before they could make use of it. A second group articulated the assumption of the first by arguing that the working class was still distinctively working-class. This class lived in communities whose structure was quite different from those in middle-class areas and perhaps indeed still similar to those of previous periods, and although its weekly or monthly income might in certain cases have been the same as or even greater than that of white-collar workers, it was less secure, and the rise in real incomes did not in any marked way affect its attitudes, as Crosland had suggested that it had. A third group in turn extended the second. Consisting to begin with of a small number of intellectuals who had left or become very uneasy with the tiny communist party after the Soviet re-occupation of Budapest in 1956 and Khruschev's speech to the Twentieth Congress of the Soviet Party in the same year, it argued that since the working class was still the working class, and since democratic socialism had no effective policy to change this, socialism must be rethought. This was the origin in Britain of what at the beginning of the 1960s was elsewhere in Europe coming to be called the New Left.

At the same time, there began an expansion of higher education. It started from the view that on grounds both of equity and efficiency, for the nation needed graduates, there were too few university places, and that the existing curricula were unsuited to a modern society. There was too much classics and history and not enough social studies, too much pure science and not enough applied. New universities were planned, and in most of these as well as in almost all of the older ones sociologists were recruited. The historical conjunction was thus unfortunate. Just as the subject had become academically established, it fell into intellectual disarray. The three available models, which had been taught in a very small number of departments in the 1950s, were those of American functionalism and survey analysis and the British tradition of empirical inquiry into inequality and poverty. There were also several ex-anthropologists, but although their approach to research was different, they shared a general acceptance of functionalism. The newly professional sociologists required a professional code, and having at first found it in American work they were then almost at once faced with intellectual and political controversies of it. The empirical liberal socialists found themselves scorned by both conservative professionals and radical socialists. The result was confusion, but in it, there again emerged three strands.

First, the liberal socialists persisted. They were convinced that their political premises were correct, and because of these premises they were right in thinking that they alone were able to communicate their findings and inferences to the Labour Party and to public authorities. These premises were essentially identical to those that had prevailed in England since at least the turn of the century. These liberal socialists took the social structure largely for granted (which is not to say that they commended it), and concentrated instead upon the fate of individuals and groups within it. Second, the professionals too persisted, and facing more and more hostility from both colleagues and students to their American models they turned towards a consideration of the older European theorists. These theorists did not, of course, take social structures for granted, but the philosophical foundations and political point of their arguments were in England generally ignored in favour of the way in which what they said could be reconstituted as a strictly professional charter. For this reason, few connections were made between what they, now embalmed, had said and the condition of contemporary Britain. Those that were made, however, were both intrinsically interesting and historically so, for they consisted in connecting the European interest in the character of the social structure itself, as a structure, with the native liberal socialism. The result was an interest in England in what elsewhere in Europe has tended to be of lesser concern among both sociologists and socialists, the structure of inequality.

I said in a previous chapter that there was virtually no consideration before the war of the nature of social class. An exception, perhaps the only exception, were two essays by T. H. Marshall on class and on property and eventually a more considered reflection on the extension of social rights which emerged in 1950 as a discussion of *Citizenship and Social Class*. In this book, Marshall argued that the extension, first, of elementary civil rights, 'liberty of the person, freedom of speech, thought and faith, the right to own property and to conclude valid contracts, and the right to justice', second, of political rights, and third, of social rights, sometimes formal, sometimes not, rights to employment, health, housing, education and a minimal social security, the first in the eighteenth century, the second in the nineteenth and the third in the twentieth, marked both a progressive undermining of previously legitimate patriarchal authorities and of course, and more directly, a modification of, perhaps even, although not comprehensively, some alternatives to, the market. This essay has been said to be the single most important contribution since 1920 to the analysis of what all but Marxists call social stratification. Those who have said so, however, have been English or American; and it was about Britain that Marshall was writing.

Earlier theories, which were mostly German, had addressed themselves to the problem raised by the substitution of a more or less authoritarian state by the market, of the substitution, as they saw it, of one kind of domination by another, and to the question of how this could be redressed. Both Dahrendorf and Habermas, for instance, have continued to address themselves to it. But in England it was less the domination that exercised people than inequality itself. Most thinking Englishmen, being, even when nominally socialist, one or another sort of liberal, had by the early 1950s come to take it for granted that the market had long since replaced direct institutional domination, so that all that remained were questions of imperfection within that market, rather than questions about its very legitimacy. But there was, as I have said, some distance between 1950, when Marshall gave his lectures, and the end of the 1960s. There had been thirteen years of Conservative government and another four or five of Labour; but the inequalities had not gone away. And since they had not, then perhaps there was after all something to be said for the argument, the hitherto alien argument, that some sort of domination did after all exist and persist. Perhaps Marx and Max Weber and the others who had, in one way or another, pressed that argument did after all have something to say to the condition of Britain. For political reasons, therefore, as well as academic ones, the more far-reaching questions of power and authority were at last being asked.

It may seem that the lines which divided the groups that were asking these questions, the old liberal socialists, who had hoped for so much, indeed almost everything, from 1945, the newer professionals, and the New Left, were fine and difficult to see.

But to begin with, they were not. Those who wrote for the *New Left Review* in the 1960s were neither liberals nor professionals. They worked on the assumptions of Marxists in Weimar Germany and contemporary France, that Marxism was still the theory and the practice that could at once explain and transform the society. Accordingly, the *Review* included critical appraisals of men like Lukács and political and to some extent sociological (but also and more commonly historical) discussions of 'the present crisis', all revolving around the question of how this crisis had come about and how, in contemporary conditions, one could resolve it in the transformation to a properly socialist society. By the end of the decade, however, not only was it clear that the more diffusely liberal socialism of Keynes and Beveridge had not achieved all that its architects and its supporters had expected of it; it was also very clear that in France itself the more idealist or existentialist sorts of Marxism had, as *praxis*, failed, and were under attack from the communists and their stringent and increasingly insistent new ideologue, Althusser.

The *Review*'s interest in Althusser and in other similarly structuralist versions of Marxism was distant and critical. Like Gramsci, whom its editor, Perry Anderson, and others like him so admired, it was more concerned with the 'consciousness' of a working class which seemed to be paralysed by prosperity and what Gramsci had called ideological 'hegemony', the distinct and more elusive but no less consequential domination of the prevailing liberal parliamentarianism and the consensus on which that parliamentarianism was conventionally said to rest. But the professional sociologists, by contrast, were taken by Althusser's sort of structuralism and the 'materialism' which informed it. One of their reasons was purely professional. It provided a paradigm for their science. As Feyerabend once remarked of American sociologists, many in Britain had interpreted Kuhn's history of physics in *The Structure of Scientific Revolutions* as an argument for the view that to be a proper science, an intellectual practice has to have a set of dominating assumptions which constitute and define the domain of that practice. It was an interpretation, of course, like Popper's, with which it is in every other respect at odds, that betrayed an old-fashioned faith in the authority of 'science'. In fact, Althusser's structuralism, and variants of it, offered professional sociologists no more, but also no less, than what it offered the French communists for whom it was intended:

a rhetorically reassuring system which committed no one to anything at all. A second reason for its attraction to some of the sociologists, however, was not at all professional. Indeed, in its implications, it was a reason that actually undermined the desire for disciplinary distinctiveness that impelled the first.

This was the more purely economic condition of Britain itself and of other comparable countries in the later 1970s. All the western European economies which had received help in their post-War reconstruction, from the Marshall Plan, from other American investments, and from the United States' military presence, had grown very rapidly between the late 1940s and the early 1960s. But that growth had then begun to slow, and nowhere did it do so more than in Britain itself. By the middle of the 1970s, the country had the lowest rates of investment, of capital accumulation, and of growth of output per worker of any economy of its kind. The liberal socialists, who had put so much hope in growth and what it would allow for redistribution through public goods, had lost their ground. And presiding over the decline were, once again, Labour governments. By the end of the 1970s, the second of these, under Callaghan, had been forced to seek help from the International Monetary Fund, had had, as a result, to cut public expenditure, had thereby come into conflict with its own supporters in the public service unions, and in 1979, had collapsed in disarray. The party, in Crosland's words, was over. The Keynesian state, the state that had prevailed almost everywhere in western Europe since 1945, seemed to have failed. And with it, after the early 1970s, went the Bretton Woods agreement that Keynes had had a hand in putting together in 1944. The flow of dollars out of the United States, which had come to alarm more recent administrations there, the collapse of stable exchange rates, and the sudden rise in the price of oil in 1973, caused a fury of financial speculation that led many governments to take exactly the sorts of defensive measure that Bretton Woods had been intended to pre-empt.

Social theorists everywhere had almost all, for a very long time, been sanguine about what they usually called 'capitalism'. Either it was a fact of nature, and here to stay, or it was an awful and absurd but reassuringly self-destructing force that was bound, sooner or later, to issue in a new economic order which would be firmer and much more fair. But in Britain, as elsewhere in western Europe and in the United States too, the events of the

1970s came to change that view. The capitalist economies themselves were in difficulties; these, and the Soviet Union's refusal
to countenance the kinds of reform suggested in Czechoslovakia
in 1968, the failure of the reforms that Khruschev and Brezhnev
had attempted in the USSR itself, and China's gradual defection
from central direction after 1978, forced sociologists like others
to cease taking the two established alternatives as given.

Sociology, therefore, and even more social theory as that had
come to be understood, the examination of past, present and
possible social orders on one or another economic assumption
which could be taken for granted, was no longer enough.
Althusser's structuralism offered the subject a paradigm at exactly
the moment at which what it actually proposed, that the economic
was, in the last instance, primary, implied that the subject was
inadequate to that moment. The fundamental questions were
questions of economies and of the states that more or less
effectively controlled them. It might of course be the case, as
Habermas had argued in the middle of the decade, that the most
fundamental question about these states was the question of their
legitimacy, of the extent to which, where they were nominally
democratic, they could still command their citizens' support. But
even Habermas conceded that the answer to what he described
as this 'legitimation crisis' lay in the 'economic crisis', the 'crisis
of accumulation' as the more orthodox Marxists were calling it,
that the states were suffering. It lay in what everyone, after Marx
himself and the other classical economists, was now calling 'political economy'.

To any historian the more remote past will seem more determinate than the more recent. But even allowing for this, sociology
and its attendant social theory in France, Germany, the United
States and Britain since the Second World War has, by comparison with previous periods, been particularly confused and
confusing. First, there has in each of the European countries
been a general disillusion with both liberal and Marxist philosophies of history. The divergent optimisms of each have been
refuted by events, and yet the more particularly social theories
available to understand these events are largely a product of these
philosophies. The brief resort to a re-invented history in existentialist and phenomenological Marxisms proved as unsatisfactory

as the resort to ahistorical theories from the United States. And the even briefer resort to an abstract cancellation of history in forms of structuralism seemed to many to wish the problem away rather than to solve it. Second, despite the resultant intellectual failures of social theory in each of these countries, academic administrators had been successfully persuaded, or had successfully persuaded themselves, that sociology was an appropriately modern university subject in appropriately modern universities which could appropriately learn much from the United States. They reached this conclusion at the end of the 1950s, when in the country of its original and always most extreme professionalisation, sociology had come to seem a politically harmless and relatively self-contained pursuit. As a result, American sociology entered European universities in the 1950s and early 1960s to co-exist at first in mutual incomprehension with native traditions, with existentialism and Marxism in France, with a critical liberal history and varieties of Hegelian Marxism in Germany, and with pragmatic liberal socialism in England; later in the 1960s and in the 1970s, as events gave new force to these various traditions, it was in a more evident hostility to them; until, by the 1970s, both it and they too began to collapse in the face of what seemed to be more urgent and thus pre-eminent questions, questions of economies and of the politics of economies, which served further, as the events of the early 1920s had done, to erode the foundations of social theory.

Conclusion

To reconstruct the intentions of others, which is what I have tried to do in this history, presupposes the project in and for which these intentions were the intentions they were. Yet as Hegel said when he was preparing to publish his lectures on the *Philosophy of Right*, the Owl of Minerva flies only at dusk; the project is only clear when the reconstruction is done and the history completed. I began this history in supposing that there was something called 'social theory' which was as it was and had usually been presented. I conclude it by suggesting that the theory has not been so distinctive as even this vague and permissive description of it would imply; that in so far as it has been, it has finished, because it has failed; and that its failure reveals a fault in that larger project of which one can now see that it has been just one, relatively recent, part.

This is not to say that it has failed in what Aron decided was its 'specific intention of a science of the social'. Aron's accounts of the more well-known social theorists are as sensitive and intelligent as any. And he was correct to suggest that for many of them, producing a science did matter. But this was never a first intention, and in many, it was quite absent. Montesquieu and Rousseau never had it. Hegel did, but what he called his 'form of science' was very different from anything that would now be described in that way. Saint-Simon, Comte, Marx and Durkheim, like Hegel, were intending to secure much more with their 'sciences' than mere laws. And many of those writing in France and Germany in the years after 1919 turned against the idea altogether. As Popper himself has often said, it is not possible even in retrospect to see the history of social theory as the progressive falsification of risky conjectures and the substitution of better ones. Some theories, like Marx's, have produced false conjectures and survived. Others, like Rousseau's, have faded even though their conjectures have turned out to be true. But this is not instead to say that the history has consisted in the periodic overthrow of 'paradigms' after relatively settled periods of 'normal science'. Social theories certainly are, in the post-empiricists' now familiar formulation, more or less extensive sets of propositions, the meaning and truth of any one of which is often only intelligible in relation to the whole. But since the post-empiricists, although not Kuhn himself, have tended to extend their theoretical holism to all intellectual activities, much more has in any instance to be said to distinguish any such activity as a science. In any event, the guiding assumptions about our relations to nature and the status of our sociability have changed little in the last two hundred years. Different assumptions about each have often co-existed in the same places and even, occasionally, in the same man. There have been many normal social sciences and none. If social theory has been an instance of any one analytical project, this is not in any interesting and important sense 'science' at all, but the philosophy of history. Yet that, as I shall explain, says too much about it and too little.

Nor has social theory failed in not realising some other, more particular intention. It has not, as some have said, been an attempt to defend a 'conservatism' against commercial and industrial life. The only theorists intending to resurrect a patriarchy have been the ultramontane reactionaries like de Bonald and de Maistre, the defenders of slavery in the American South, and Othmar Spann. Comte did, it is true, think de Maistre 'eminent' and 'illustrious', a man of some insight. But de Maistre was a Catholic, in Comte's terms 'metaphysical', even 'theological', and archaic. It has not, as others have said, been an attempt to counter Marx. Marx was ignored by many Germans both before and after the First World War, was not taken seriously in France until the 1930s, was always read by few in England, and except to a few in the 1930s and again in the 1970s, has been incidental in the United States. Likewise, it has not simply been a series of attempts to come to terms with 'capitalism'. Durkheim, for example, seems never to have been very interested in the economics of capitalism, or even to have seen their relevance to much of what he was saying about the society in which they worked; Weber sidestepped them, and Marx, although he confronted them, was like the other two addressing himself to more fundamental questions about the nature and possibilities of all societies. And the history of social theory has never just been, as Hughes suggested in one of the more deliberately historical accounts, of the years between 1890 and 1930, a challenge to 'positivism' in the name of the creative autonomy of consciousness. Hughes did explore a pervasive loss of nerve at the end of the nineteenth century, a loss of nerve which others had missed and continue often to ignore. But positivism, in the sense in which he uses the term, had a less secure hold than he suggests on many before 1890, even in France, and both Durkheim and Max Weber were in part engaged in trying to rehabilitate the claims of science in the face of what each regarded as the degeneracy of his intellectual tradition.

The intention in social theory has been more general than any of these. It has been to answer the question of how to ground an ethical argument. It is the most recent of the kinds of answer there have been. But it has never, as others have sometimes done, replaced any other. After two hundred years or so of social theory, more kinds of answer now co-exist and compete than at any previous point. But this one has failed. Indeed, it has succeeded only in casting doubt on whether the question is the question to ask: on whether it makes sense to expect a general answer, and thus, on whether there can be any sort of ethical theory at all.

The idea of such a theory was established in what in Europe and North America became its defining form in Greece, in the fifth and fourth centuries BC. The Greeks' arguments were 'theoretical' in an extended sense. They were philosophical, made in abstract, general and rational reflection, and they were empirical, in that the reflection always bore back on real states of affairs. The general sense and reference of the 'ethical' was, in ancient Greek, to character, that of the 'moral', in Latin, to custom. A question in ethics and morals was accordingly a question which inclined anyone trying to answer it to give his answer in terms of one or another of these qualities. The way in which he would arrive at that answer, the philosophical way, would incline him to make it as abstract and general as he could. But it would nevertheless incline him to make it an answer that referred back to the ethically or morally desirable kind of character or of civic or political life.

This inclination was recovered in early modern Europe and in that recovery, the desirable kind of character and of public life came more and more to be cast, as in fact it had already begun to be in Rome, in what we would now see as historical terms. But between the end of the Roman empire and the reassertion of the classical arguments in the early modern period, the inclination had been denied and the classical sense of 'theory' narrowed. In this long interval, of a thousand years or so, men continued to incline to the general and the abstract, and in their own fashion, continued thus to argue philosophically. But the increasingly most influential of them were contemptuous of the contents and qualities of what Augustine called 'this temporal life'. A man should concentrate instead, Augustine argued, on 'the everlasting blessings that are promised for the future, using like one in a strange land any earthly and temporal things', but 'not letting them entrap him or divert him' from the path that leads to the city of God. There was nothing mundane, no earthly and temporal thing, he argued, certainly not the inherent sinfulness of character or the accordingly flawed nature of custom, which could meet the ethical standard. The Roman empire was the embodiment of the *civitas terrena*, and by the end of the fourth century, that enterprise was driven wholly by fear, pride and lack of gratitude. 'What are empires', Augustine asked, 'but great robberies?'

Augustine's arguments were directed to Pelagius's. Both men were Christians. The contrast, however, between them could not have been sharper. 'Whenever I have to speak of laying down rules for behaviour and the conduct of a holy life', explained Pelagius in one of his letters to Demetrias, 'I always point out, first of all, the power and functioning of human nature, and show what it is capable of doing ... lest I should seem to be wasting my time, by calling people to embark on a course which they consider impossible to achieve'. 'Since perfection for man is possible', he wrote when she asked him about becoming a nun, 'it is obligatory'. A Christianised Stoicism did reappear in Aquinas's distinction between a law for men as they were and the precepts of supernatural revelation. Men were less completely corrupt than Augustine had thought, and as the Protestants were again to insist, and could accordingly find goodness in following the natural law. But they had still, in Aquinas's view, to worship, have faith and hope, and exercise some charity. None of the later Christian arguments, even where they were proposed, like Aquinas's own, in circumstances which were incomparably more orderly and secure than those of the late fourth century, went back beyond Augustine to recover Pelagius's sort of optimism, the classical optimism, about what men could manage.

That recovery came only with a sense of the real possibility of deploying secular powers against those of the Church. The Roman empire, in Peter Brown's description, had been 'a landscape that was slowly veined and folded, from the third century onwards, by innumerable little earth tremors, welling up from deep inside the inner lives of its inhabitants'. So too was that of the succeeding *Imperium* of medieval Europe. The tremors in this were most evident in the Italian city states, and in hindsight, it is possible to detect them there even in the middle of the thirteenth century. But by far the most dramatic came at the start of the sixteenth, in Machiavelli. Machiavelli rejected Christianity as completely as Augustine had rejected the world; it had, he said, 'set up as the greatest good humility, abjectness and contempt for human things'; he revived the *virtus* of republican Rome; and with what is still an incomparable vigour, he argued that in the world, the world defined by the political community, it could, at a price, be had.

What this *virtù* consisted in exactly remained, in its details, obscure. Scholars still dispute it. But in all the arguments about it, there was the conviction that it could be realised in the world and sustained by what early modern theorists, now theorists of politics, came with increasing frequency to call 'the state'. And if it was to be sustained in the state, they came also to agree, then that state must be defended against external powers, like those of the Holy Roman Empire; and it must have no rivals within its territory as the object of allegiance and the authority for law. The arguments were often pointed, as they were by Machiavelli himself, most obviously in the *Discourses*, least so in *The Prince*, to an immediate and particular difficulty. But they were also always made in terms which were abstract and general and to that extent directed to the problems of politics more widely considered. In this, and in the rationality of the reflection with which they moved to their conclusions, they were made philosophically. They were at the very least implicit arguments in ethics, guided by the conviction that the question was, in the classical sense, an ethical question and that the answer to it had to be an answer about civic character. And after the Reformation and the Counter Reformation and the fighting in and over each, it seemed more than merely reasonable to insist on separating a defensible virtue from any Christian conception of it. Wars, remarked Bodin, were plainly 'made for matters of religion'. They did not concern the Prince's estate.

The elision of the ethical with the political and the exclusion of the supernatural, of course, was for long never so clean as this. And even if Bodin believed what he said about the grounds for war, few, except at their most abstractly and optimistically ethical, agreed with him. Nevertheless, ethical theory remained a task for philosophical argument and in this attempt at it, the beginning and the end of that argument were in politics. And yet the sphere of politics was not clear. If political theory has an ethical purpose, and an ethical purpose is a political purpose, a political purpose may itself be thought to exist for states of affairs, more generally social states of affairs, in which the good may flourish. But in early modern political thinking, like that of Greece and Rome, citizens tended to be thought of merely as real or potential members of an indivisible entity. The distinction between a state and its society was not deliberately drawn.

The distinction hovers in Locke and the eighteenth-century Scots and in Montesquieu and Rousseau. It is hinted at in the widening sense in the eighteenth century of 'the people'. It is there, almost stated, in Hegel's deliberate invocation of the *Sitten* which are the state's foundations. And it appears in Saint-Simon. But although Hegel, most clearly, did identify 'particular interests' which 'fall within civil society and lie outside the absolutely universal interest of the state proper', he did so only to go on to argue that without that 'absolutely universal interest', civil society was not complete. 'Hegel's profundity', Marx remarked, 'lies in his view of the separation of civil and political society as a contradiction. But he is wrong in contenting himself with a semblance of its resolution and passing off the semblance as the real thing. The fact is that the "so-called theories" which he despises require the separation of civil and political status; and rightly so, since they articulate one of the consequences of modern society which is that now the element of political stratification is nothing other than the factual expression of the actual relation between the state and civil society, that is, their separation.' In this argument of Marx's, but by then not only in Marx, the distinction is made.

But Marx, at least after his doctoral dissertation, always resisted the description of what he was doing as ethics. He would also, after the later 1840s, have resisted the suggestion that what he was doing in doing it was a philosophy of history. And indeed, that is not a good description. It fails to take account of the fact that the older political theory had already come by some to be described, as he was to describe his own, as a 'science'. And it overlooks the fact that a philosophy of history had long been deployed to defend some of the older and much more deliberate attempts at an ethics. This had not, as I said, been true of the Greeks' attempts. It is poetry, Aristotle explained in his *Poetics*, which 'tends to express what is universal, history relates particular events'; 'the historian relates what has happened, the poet represents what might happen, what is typical'. *Historia*, simple inquiry, was out of time and at best met mere curiosity. The past only had meaning beyond itself in that which we now call myth, of which the poets wrote. For the Jews and Christians too, the facts of that past had no more than an ethically incidental and as it happened, negative meaning. For the one, 'the relation between the historian and the prophet', as Momigliano puts it, 'is the Hebrew counterpart' to the Greek relation between the historian and the philosopher or poet. For the other, as Augustine remarked, 'the centuries of past history would have rolled by like empty jars if Christ had not been foretold by means of them'.

But between the conquest of Greece and the collapse of Rome, it did come to be thought that a philosophy of history, predicated on inquiry and referring to the world, could illustrate the universal and thus connect to ethical argument. The thought was prompted by the Roman conquests themselves. The first proponent of such a history, Polybius, regarded these as having effected the first true unity of the human world and thus, the first instantiation of the universal in it. 'The mere statement of a fact', Polybius agreed with Aristotle, 'may interest us, but it is of no benefit to us. But when we add the cause of it, the study of history becomes fruitful. For it is in the mental transference of similar circumstances to our own times', a more orderly and evidentially considered transfer than that which the poets made in myth, 'that gives us the means of forming presentiments of what is about to happen, and enables us at certain times to take precautions and at others by reproducing former conditions to face with more confidence the difficulties that menace us'. The example that Polybius set was exemplar history. Tacitus, one of the earliest advocates of this history, distinguished between learning right conduct by one's own lights and learning it by example, and thought the latter to be the more effective. Bolingbroke, one of its last, declared in 1738 'that he who studies History as he would study Philosophy will soon distinguish and collect examples, and by doing so will soon form to himself a general system of Ethicks and Politicks on the surest foundations, on the trial of those principles and Rules in all ages, and on the confirmation of them by universal experience'. This universal history had more or less disappeared in Christian Europe, reappeared with the humanists, and was almost always deployed to defend the attempt to ground an ethics in politics. In the fifteenth and sixteenth centuries, the model example was usually that of republican Rome itself. Later, there was the less assuredly universal but enviably stable and serene republic of Venice. But whatever was preferred, the conviction in exemplar history remained Polybius's own; events lent support to ethical argument, and they did so because they could be seen to move as *fortuna* herself moved and *virtù* and its corruption with her, in cycles. There were possibilities in history that were always still possibilities for it.

By the end of the eighteenth century, however, this conviction had collapsed. And it did so for the reasons that had at the same time begun to cause the move from attempts to ground an ethical theory in politics to attempts to ground it in 'society'. The new commercial and industrial activities and, after 1789, the revolution in France, seemed to have set events on a new course rather than to have started any discernible turn in the old. History, so it seemed to many, no longer moved in cycles. But it did not obviously follow that it was any the less universal. A universal could still be found within it, not, now, in any past instance, for there was no return, but in the future. And if the relation between the past and the future was linear and irreversible, it was tempting to cast that relation in terms of the causal laws which 'the incomparable Mr Newton' and others had shown to govern universal events in nature. But because the irreversible changes that seemed to be taking place seemed to be taking place in the political economy and in the 'political community' or 'commonwealth' which lay at the edge of the state, and which were more and more often moving against its rulers, taking place, that is, in civil society, the new universal was a subject for something that might better be thought of as a 'social' rather than a too partially political theory. This was how it nevertheless retained the Polybian project of revealing a universal in the world which it had always been the intention in an ethics to reveal.

The transition, however, was neither smooth nor complete. In Germany, indeed, where it was most dramatic and for that reason most clear, it was a transition to three connected but quite distinct arguments. The first of these arguments, which has since been taken by many exclusively to define what an argument in ethics must be, was Kant's. This abstracted more severely than any before it, grounded itself entirely in the rational reflection always held to be essential in the philosophical way of arriving at any such theory, and generated claims that must, Kant argued, be claims for every rational man. It was an argument that beyond Kant's thin acknowledgement of its possibility in 'Enlightenment', owed nothing to considerations of fact and history at all. I have elabroated on it in Chapter 2. In reaction to it, the other two arguments started from the premise that the ethical subject had to be grounded in something other than his pure reason, in the language he spoke, for example, or in the *Sitten* of his society. But each then went in a different direction. One was the direction of social theory itself. Hegel and Marx believed that having been so grounded, the subject of ethics could then be brought to a universal condition. The other was more insistently historical. Herder, and the proponents of a new historiography whom I did not discuss in Chapter 2, did not believe that he could.

Ranke furnished the motto of this new History. The historian, he insisted, should write only about what has happened: 'wie es eigentlich gewesen'. 'Eigentlich' has no exact equivalent in English. One can read it as 'actual' or 'true' or, departing rather from the simple empiricism that Ranke has often more recently been held to have been urging, 'essential' or 'intrinsic'. But what Ranke was objecting to is clear. 'To History has standardly been given the function of judging the past, of instructing men for the profit of future years. The present attempt does not aspire to such a lofty undertaking.' Young historians in a new profession of History were now to be directed to primary sources; they were to avoid praise and blame; they were to talk of causes rather than of moral qualities; and although the causes would doubtless reveal continuities, the historians were nevertheless to concentrate on the pastness of the past, its separation or at least its distinctiveness from the present.

The impulse in this move was by no means as purely professional as it has since been made by many (not least in modern Germany) to seem. It was a nationalist one. Even where the immediate point of historical writing had previously been very specific, even parochial, as it had been in Machiavelli's history of Florence, or in Bodin's of France, to define particularities it had always been cast in at least putatively universal terms. The virtues and vices of Florence and France were instances of some more general quality. But at the end of the eighteenth century and the beginning of the nineteenth, it came to be believed in Germany (even in Italy itself, where the ancient past was being recovered as a more particularly national past) that universal history had ended with Rome. Some conservatives continued to believe that the Church had continued what Rome had not. Others, as I have said, were excited by the thought that the revolution in France had introduced a new universal of a different kind. But an increasingly firm belief, in reaction to both (and soon in Britain as well as in Germany and Italy) was that the Histories that there were to be written were national histories. Accordingly history, the new History, was (outside Italy itself) to start after Rome, in the middle ages, and the professional historians were to define themselves by first working on the documents of that time.

In Germany, this had an influence in social and political thinking itself. Hegel, despite his insistence on starting from actual *Sitten*, lampooned the new enthusiasm for 'the conservation of Old German monuments and patriotic relics of all sorts, the song of the *Nibelungen*, Imperial treasures, King Roger's shoes, Albrecht Dürer's woodcuts', all the 'particularisms of *Deutschduum*'. He never lost his own enthusiasm for Napoleon and the absolute. Others, however, wished to conserve the *Kultur*. As I explained in Chapter 7, there was a move by the end of the nineteenth century (in opposition by then as much to the British, and especially to the arguments of J. S. Mill, as to France) to drive a distinction between the truths of Nature, timeless and unconditional and discoverable by the now time-honoured methods of the *Naturwissenschaften*, and the truths of culture. Rickert, for example, argued that the latter, if they could be called true at all, were true only for the culture in which they were seen. Yet as I explained, Rickert and the men who read him, like Max Weber, did wonder whether these truths might nonetheless be said to be truths not merely 'to' but also 'of', truths of an object, the culture itself, and so objective. And if they were objective, then they could perhaps after all be included, as the propagandists at the Ministry of War, Max Weber and the Frankfurt theorists all did come to include them, in a more general theory.

Nevertheless, Kant's transcendental defence of an ethics and the cultural historians' more implicit defence of a more particularly moral integrity do each stand to one side of the project which is marked by Hegel and then, and by no one more clearly, by Marx. It is in Marx, if not by any means only or even first in him, that the transition to social theory is complete. The project is still the project of ethics. Its ambition is universal and the universal is still to be expressed, although not now grounded, in a politics. But character, custom and the now distinctively and dependently political itself are replaced, in Marx and others, by 'laws of motion' which determine them, and it is the working through of these laws, and not mere reflection, which will solve 'the riddle of history', Marx' re-casting of the general good. One can see why Marx himself and Marxists and non-Marxists too dispute the argument as an ethics. But one can also see why it is difficult to see it as anything else. And having seen social theory in this way, it is easier to see how that theory has failed. It has failed in the face of the facts, and it has done so in a way which suggests a mistake in the idea of an ethical theory itself.

There are perhaps two points at which the first of these failures becomes especially clear. The more decisive of the two, because it was a point in European experience, was the outbreak of war in 1914, Lenin's coup in Russia in 1917, and the collapse of similar attempts to the west, in Austria, Hungary, Italy and above all in Germany, in 1918, 1919 and 1920. From at least the 1750s, theorists had come increasingly to believe that politics should be determined by interests in the society it was the politics of. And they had come increasingly to believe that it would be. An 'optimism of the intellect', in Gramsci's phrase, at least of the democratic intellect, was at one with an 'optimism of the will'. But as Gramsci reflected further, in Mussolini's prisons, on the defeats of the winter of 1919–20 in Turin and on the subsequent decimation of his Party, he came to think that a 'pessimism of the intellect' was perhaps more appropriate. What these events in Italy had suggested, like events elsewhere since 1914, was that politics was in large part its own cause, and that for this and other reasons unpredictable, or at least, not safely predictable from anything outside itself. The change in Gramsci's own thinking, his rejection of the purported laws of historical materialism and his reluctant concession to the directing task of the Party, the 'New Prince' as he called it, is one of the most dramatic. The changes in reflective Marxists more generally, into one or another form of Marxist-Leninism or into what were (except in Lukács) more open and less directly political sorts of idealism, were dramatic too. Marxists, as I have said, had taken the central tenets of social theory as seriously as any. But history was everywhere doubted. And events since the early 1920s, the rise of fascism in Germany and elsewhere, the depression, the Second World War, the hopes and fears and falterings of the post-War socialist governments in western Europe, the developing sense in socialists in the west of the Soviet Union, setbacks in Europe in the middle of the 1950s, and in both Europe and America towards the end of the 1960s, the apparent reversals of the later 1970s and 1980s, have done little to allay those doubts.

The liberal and socialist confidence which preceded these events, like the conservatives' fears, almost all turned on the belief that what was called 'capitalism' had irreversibly changed the course of European history, and had done so from below (or so it was thought by all but Max Weber, who nevertheless wished that in Germany it had). And this too, it now seems, was a mistake. Not only is it clearer than it was (except, one supposes, to those who were doing it) that the later developers, as they have come to be called, Germany itself and Japan, were being deliberately developed by their governments. It is also increasingly clear that the early developers, Britain, always the classic case, and perhaps others too, like the Netherlands, developed as they did in conditions created by their governments. The independent operation of the market, even, by the beginning of the twentieth century, in the United States, has always been a qualified and strictly conditional fact. And by the 1930s, as early and late developers alike, including now the Soviet Union, resorted to one or another kind of intervention to raise production, lower unemployment and (where they did not have overseas possessions) protect their economies, it became difficult to argue otherwise. There was always reason to doubt that the world had ever looked as the social theorists thought that it had. By the 1930s and 1940s, there was every reason to do so.

Faute de mieux, the old rhetorics continued to affect perceptions in the post-War period. Nevertheless, events in Europe and in America in this period, as I explained at the end of Chapter 10, have done much to reduce their force. And events beyond have done even more. This is the second of the two points at which the social theories, the repositories of the old rhetorics, have failed in the face of the facts. Many of the architects of what came to be described as the 'development' of the new nations had already abandoned the antimony between 'capitalism' and 'socialism' that more or less explicitly ran through almost all of these theories by the beginning of the twentieth century. Some, like the statistician and planner Mahalanobis in India, had little experience which might have led them to accept it. Others, like the economist Rodenstein-Rodan, who began by thinking in the early 1940s about the post-War development of south-eastern Europe, were determined to get away from it. Even those who met at Bretton Woods in 1944 were agreed that what had to be established were the conditions between nations for the kind of macro-economic management within them to which the western countries were already committed. There were then, of course, and have continued to be considerable differences in the ways in which this management has been done. In some western countries, like Britain, it has been minimal, restricted largely to fiscal controls by the central bank and the ministry of finance; in others, like Austria, France, Norway, Sweden and West Germany, it has been much more extensive. But in the more successful of the developing countries, the differences in this respect have not been so marked. If one truth is emerging about these countries, about Japan, the Republic of Korea, India, and others, as well as the Soviet Union, it is that despite their very different circumstances and strategies, the direction of the state, often acting independently of what can plausibly be described as the interests of any particular class, has been decisive. This direction, and attempts at it in many less successful countries too, has been reinforced, as I explained at the end of the last chapter, by the collapse of stable exchange rates, the cornerstone of the Bretton Woods agreement, at the beginning of the 1970s; by the increase in private lending which was already under way in the 1960s and was greatly accelerated by the rise in the price of oil after 1973; and in the 1980s, by the choice which governments in these countries now face between agreeing with more classically liberal advisers (and the International Monetary Fund) that they should cut public spending and raise prices to what are regarded in Washington as realistic levels, and listening to those who once again urge a more or less moderate increase in public spending and greater protection. It has meant that states, whether deliberately directing the economy or deliberately refusing to, have had and will continue to have a considerable impact on the nature and distribution of interests within their societies. And it has produced the irony of several western politicians, Mitterand in France, for example, and Kinnock in Britain, taking what have come to be called the 'newly industrialising countries' as models for the future of their own.

Intellectuals in the older societies, of course, in what after the Brandt Commission in the 1970s has come to be called 'the North', have striven to capture the transformations in the rest of the world in their existing models. They have been tempted to do so because these models are still, despite their deficiencies, the only general models there are, and also and more indirectly, because each of the two world powers is itself at least rhetorically guided by one of them. But in part because these models are promoted by the powers, and in part because each of them is transparently inadequate, the one, from twentieth-century Marxist-Leninism, cancelling history by claiming to conclude it, the other, from eighteenth-century liberalism, cancelling it by refusing to see it, intellectuals in the rest of the world are increasingly disposed to avoid them. 'In the colonial period', remarked Cabral before his country's independence from Portugal, 'it is the colonial state that commands history. When imperialism arrived in Guinea, it made us leave history – our history'. The impulse almost everywhere has been to recover that history and in so doing, to reject what many in these countries now call the 'universals' of the North. Northern intellectuals find themselves more and more often striving to sympathise with the South in languages from which the South itself wishes to escape.

The desire there to do so is in one way or another generated by the fact, the elusive and variable but almost everywhere causally decisive fact, of nationalism. The idea of nationhood was the idea with which independence was fought, the idea with which it was then given a form, and the idea with which it has then defended itself. The nation is the idea with which states, as the guarantors of the economy, the guardians of the society, and in many inst-ances the only clear entity in the territory, maintain themselves. Of course, it is not the only such idea. There are claims of ethnicity, language and religion too, claims which are sometimes woven into the idea of the nation and sometimes used against it. The character of 'nationhood' itself, however, is clear. It is a claim to what Benedict Anderson calls an 'imagined community', to a more or less abstract and fanciful notion created to make an often inchoate reality cohere. It is a claim also to a voice. The Bolívars at the beginning of the nineteenth century and the Cabrals at the end of the twentieth have been presented with the political independence of territories which were defined by their colonial power for largely external reasons, and which within themselves contained no obvious social cohesion, not even that cohesion conferred in conflicts of class.

A few of these countries have been able to draw on a history, a pre-colonial history, with which to fashion their nationhood. Like nineteenth-century Germans and Italians, they have been able to excavate an identity. Most, however, have not, and have accordingly been forced back into abstract ideas. In the fight against Spanish power in the Americas at the beginning of the nineteenth century, these tended to be the ideas of Enlighten-ment liberalism, ready weapons against Catholic absolutism. In the fight against British and French and other powers in the twentieth century, they have been the ideas of one or another sort of socialism, ready weapons against liberal capitalism. Yet as I have said, in part because each of these is a Northern notion, and in part because each is now deployed in and against the

Third World by the United States or the Soviet Union, there is as much interest in abandoning them as in continuing to use them. Indeed, 'interest' is far too weak a word with which to describe the impulse. For if there is one fact about the new nations which was not envisaged by those who looked at their prospective development in the 1940s, it is, as Hirschman says, that their 'passions' have turned out to be as decisive as their interests. Hirschman's contrast is an eighteenth-century one. The argument then, most completely perhaps, in Adam Smith, was that societies driven by interest would encourage prudence and mutual respect as well as prosperity, and thereby extinguish the passions of aristocracies bent on defending their honour with arms against each other and a dependent poor. Marx, in this respect conservative, inverted it by arguing that the dependent poor had to attack the new order of interests, and his doctrine has continued to speak to the passions of those, in the new nations and outside, who wish to resist that order.

The world has turned out to be very different from the one the social theorists expected. It is not, if ever it was, governed by social forces. It is governed by governments. These governments have in good part been their own causes. And they have themselves acted in ways which have done as much to mould their societies as they have to respond to them. In this, they have used ideologies and instruments which the nineteenth- and early twentieth-century social theorists rarely imagined and if they did, tended generally to abhor. The instruments have been more directive and the ideologies, expressing 'passions' as much as 'interests', have been different in kind and more varied. Yet what some call the world system (it is in fact rather unsystematic) impinges in a way which gives no nation and no financial authority a decisive power. And the fact that what have been the two most powerful states in the past forty years have at least rhetorically been informed by the old conceptions, is a fact that has served only to reinforce the further fact that the power which these two states have in the world, as distinct from their potential, because nuclear, power over it, is very far from complete, and that their attempts to increase it tend further to reduce it. In all these respects, the world resembles the Europe the social theorists thought had passed as much as the one they thought had arrived.

Social theorists, as it happens, have failed in the face of the facts. And most recent theorists have yet to see that the kind of failure that this is suggests a mistake in the more enduring idea of an ethical theory itself. As I have said, some Germans had already had some sense of this at the end of the eighteenth century. The mistake that in their view was being made about the human world was that it could and should be understood as one world. The truths of the new and more deliberately historical *Geisteswissenschaften* were truths of and for a particular *Geist*, and not general. This hinted at the possibility that the truths of public morality were themselves more partial. And yet, and with immediate authority and effect, Kant had insisted that they had by definition to be universal, the political theorists had long assumed that they had to be too, and the social theorists came later to agree. There was some agony, and it increased. If the truths of theoretical reason were particular truths, what sense, Nietzsche, for instance, and Max Weber came to ask, could there be in continuing to suppose that the truths of ethics were not particular, even perhaps arbitrary, too? Perhaps there were no truths of ethics at all? If, on the other hand, the truths of theoretical reason were general truths, how, the Marxists, but not only the Marxists, came increasingly to ask, should one explain the failures of practice? It was not just that something seemed to be wrong with social theory in relation to the facts. Something seemed more seriously to be wrong with what had for so long been taken in that theory to be the symmetry between theoretical and practical reason.

The agonies, as I have explained, were induced by events. But they were induced by ideas too. From the German historicisms, but also from American pragmatism, the Anglo-American analytical philosophy of language, and elsewhere, from ideas which are in many cases distinct from social theory if not historically separate from it, there has in the twentieth century been some convergence on the conclusion that there is no convergent conclusion to the questions which social theory and other sorts of ethics have asked. The arguments are the arguments I alluded to in the Preface against my ever having been able to write this history as I had wanted to. The more radical of them insist that no knowledge at all is now available to us. What we say about the world is merely what we *say* about the world, contained in and constrained by our projects. It is, as Wittgenstein called it, a 'game', the rules of which we construct. Indeed the concept of 'the world' itself is, in this view, either internal to our talk, making 'the very idea of a conceptual scheme', in Davidson's phrase, set against reality, a mistake; or it is in virtue of its externality, unspecified and unspecifiable and therefore blank. It is, in Rorty's farewell, a 'world well lost'. The more cautious agree that what we say about the world is internal to our scheme and so indeterminate. But they nevertheless insist that there are contents of the world, roughly speaking, those contents of the world which are not the contents of consciousness, for which realism is true. These contents are as they are independent of any scheme at all, and candidates still for an absolute although most now concede, a never indisputable conception. The second of these arguments is more plausible, perhaps, than the first, but whichever of the two one takes, the conclusion for what might once have been thought of as moral and political knowledge is the same. There is no fact of the matter which is not a fact of our own conceptions. As our conceptions, these are only accessible as the conceptions they are to us. And even to us, they are the conceptions they are in virtue of just one fact in the world, that we have these conceptions and not others. And if, which is obvious, we have conceptions at all because of some fact of our nature which is in some much more general sense 'ours', this nature almost always underdetermines any actual conceptions that 'we', more particularly, have.

If this is right, there are difficulties in the idea of an ethical theory. Some might say that there is a corresponding difficulty in the idea of a social or political theory, in the explanatory sense, too. But that goes too far. If the contents of consciousness are relative to a scheme, then there are, it is true, just schemes of them. But these schemes rule in rather than rule out the possibility of alternative and illuminating accounts in other schemes. The only difference is that we now have to think in a different way about the truth of such accounts, or more reasonably, have just to cease to worry about their truth at all. But the difficulties for ethics go deeper than this. Unseating any incontrovertible or as it used to be said, any 'objective' foundation for conceptions of the good, unseats the possibility of finding any firm and enduring foundation for an ethics which can be at once sufficiently full in any actual instance to provide a guide to practical reason, and yet immune to reflective revision. We are forced to retreat to higher and firmer but inevitably more general ground which can at best set the limits to such reflection. The irony is clear. History may appear first, as Marx said, as tragedy, the second time as farce. Intellectual history, he might have added, can repeat itself with a greater understanding of why it does. In so far as the convergence on the conclusion that there can be no convergence is brought about by the kind of reflection induced by social theory itself, we know now that this theory can no longer be a way of escaping from it. The dilemma that presented itself to Hegel and his contemporaries at the beginning of the nineteenth century reappears at the end of the twentieth. But the escape which they attempted to make from it is now closed.

This does much to explain why the most impressive of recent attempts have returned, as they have, to Kant. Rawls is one such attempt, Habermas another. Rawls is interested in justice, in the right, as he puts it, rather than the good, Habermas, it appears, in freedom. The one is rather more careful than the other, but their strategies are similar and together they make the *impasse* plain. Rawls concedes that to establish the principles of justice 'it is necessary to rely on some notion of goodness, for we need assumptions about the parties' motives'. But he also sees that these assumptions 'must not jeopardise the prior place of the concept of right'. He accordingly restricts 'the theory of the good' he uses to argue for the principles of justice to 'the bare essentials'. He calls it a 'thin theory'. This theory suggests that whatever thicker conceptions of the good there may be, and in any large and complex society there will almost certainly be many, many of them incompatible with each other, all individuals require for the advancement of their conceptions 'roughly the same primary goods, for example the same rights, liberties and opportunities, as well as certain all-purpose means such as income and wealth'. The theory further assumes that 'citizens are free and equal moral persons who can contribute to, and honour the constraints of, social co-operation for the mutual benefit of all'. 'Justice as fairness', as Rawls puts it, 'regards each person as someone who can and does desire to take part in social co-operation for mutual advantage'. But it does not in his view 'depend upon historical or social facts'. 'While the determination of primary goods invokes a knowledge of the general circumstances and requirements of social life, it does so only in the light of a conception', he emphasises, 'of the person given in advance'. Habermas argues similarly. It is a fact about persons as persons, he says, and as I elaborated in Chapter 10, that they have an interest in autonomy and consensus, in *Mündigkeit*. They are for him as they are for Rawls, potentially free and equal moral persons in whose nature it is to co-operate for the benefit of all. But as again for Rawls, they do need certain primary goods in order to be able to do so. These in Habermas's view are freedoms from what he sees as the coercions of 'labour' and 'communication', from the powers of production and from the impediments to free and perspicuous communication. Habermas has a conception of the general circumstances of social life, as Rawls puts it for himself, in the light merely of a conception of the person given in advance.

Both men, that is, start just from a conception of what people are and the general circumstances in which they find themselves, from what might once have been described as the absolute necessities of good character, and argue to a view of what societies which included such persons could be. They assume that people are committed to living together, that they are committed to come to do so through a 'reflective equilibrium', as Rawls calls it, a 'self-reflection', in Habermas's phrase, in conditions of 'communicative competence', in order to arrive at a consensus. They further assume (Rawls is much clearer about this than Habermas) that they will be willing, having arrived at this consensus, also to agree to explicit principles to maintain it; and that in any instance, they will be disposed to decide between these principles by an equally explicit procedure of decision. Lastly, they take it that all this can be done with the greatest 'publicity', as Rawls calls it, with what one might describe as the greatest practicable degree of social transparency. And the society which is to be thus public is, as they each sketch it, a society of the kind that we, as distinct from the medieval English or the citizens of modern Zaire, do inhabit. It is a society in which incomes and wealth are the 'all-purpose means', in which there are further constraints in practical life and in language too, and in which it might, just, make sense to imagine that there could be the will and the means to arrive at a reflective equilibrium between our intuitions and our reasons. But it is not at all clear how such a society might be held together by a mere understanding of a common interest in justice or in *Mündigkeit.* And it is above all unclear who are the 'we' for whom such a society is an option. Rawls, unlike Habermas, does see that there are innumerably many and particular loves and attachments and thick conceptions of the good, but having consigned them, as moral and political philosophers of a more or less liberal inclination tend often now to do, to the private realm, he leads us all too easily out to the empirically indeterminate constituency of all the rational agents there are.

Hegel would have appreciated this return, in one case *via* contractualism, in the other *via* Marxism, to Kant. He and his compatriots might have added that it shows that neither argument should have started where it has. But it is not now so clear how, even if either had started in a different, more particular, more limited, place, it could have gone on. Hegel's own solution, to start with the *Sitten,* insert a telos, and so emerge with a universal *Sittlichkeit,* will not now do. Nor, as he presented it, will Nietzsche's exhortation to mere will. We are presented with a state of affairs in which we have theories intended for us which do not do enough, if they do anything at all, for us as we are; or theories which if they are to be theories for us, as we are, require so much additional contingency as to cease in any strong sense to be theories at all. And even if we were to find against all present probability that 'we' were in fact members of an international community of rational, reflective and self-equilibrating agents, talking to each other in almost transcendental transparency, it would still be the case that since, as Williams puts it, 'the excellence or satisfactoriness of a life', individual, social, political, 'does not stand to beliefs involved in that life as premise stands to conclusion'; since it consists in actually having the beliefs and living the life; what we would be living, even in this international life, would not be what has usually been thought of as a *theory* at all. Rawls, in his later reflections on 'Kantian constructivism', and Habermas too, have retreated from their initial Kantianism. But neither has yet arrived at quite this conclusion.

It is a conclusion, however, that is encouraged by that more general turn in twentieth-century thought towards thinking of any particular 'us' as a particular us, the 'we' that we are and not otherwise in virtue of the life that we lead and the interests and commitments which we have in that life and which make it the life it is, ours, for us. But it is also a conclusion delivered by social theory itself, which in the course of trying to define a more general, even universal 'we', has in the anthropological, sociological and political reflection that it has encouraged, succeeded only in reinforcing the conviction that the interesting 'we' are many. And that qualification is crucial. For if the theory is to be a theory for us as we are, with the passions and the interests that we have and which impel us, in the particular circumstances in which we find ourselves, and for which any practical reason has to decide, it will, if it is general, not greatly interest us. And since the history of the twentieth century is one in which passions and interests have remained defiantly particular, and in so far as they are public, have remained so in good part for political rather than social reasons, it is scarcely surprising that as the theories they were intended to be these theories have failed us, have come in many cases to cease to connect to *us* at all.

They were intended to disenchant the world of older conceptions. 'That thou mayst understand aright', says Keats through Moneta in *The Fall of Hyperion*,

> 'I humanise my sayings to thine ear,
> Making comparisons of earthly things;
> Or thou mightst better listen to the wind,
> Whose language is to thee a barren noise,
> Though it blows legend-laden through the trees.'

Now themselves barren noises, legends on the wind, their turn, perhaps, has come.

Bibliographies

These consist of primary works that I refer to or discuss or draw upon in the book together with those secondary accounts (other than social and political histories) that I have used or would more or less enthusiastically recommend. I have starred those that I think are especially illuminating. For the second edition, I have provided a bibliography for the new Conclusion and added a few particularly useful items which have been published since 1975. Where I have not used an original edition, I have if possible given the year of first publication in parentheses after the author's name. I have used English translations except where I was aware that they were inadequate.

Preface

Bayley, John. *Tolstoy and the Novel*. London, 1966

Berlin, Isaiah. 'Introduction', Alexander Herzen, *My Past and Thoughts*. Vol. I. London, 1968

Davidson, Donald. 'Replies to David Lewis and W. V. Quine', *Synthèse*, 27 (1974), 345–9

Pocock, J. G. A. 'The state of the art', in *Virtue, Commerce and History: essays on political thought and history, chiefly in the eighteenth century*. Cambridge, 1985, 1–34

*Rorty, Richard. 'The historiography of philosophy: four genres', in Richard Rorty, J. B. Schneewind, Quentin Skinner (eds.). *Philosophy in History: essays on the historiography of philosophy*. Cambridge, 1984, 49–75

Williams, Bernard. *Descartes: the project of pure inquiry*. Harmondsworth, 1978

Introduction

Althusser, Louis. *Lenin and Philosophy*. London, 1971

Althusser, Louis, Etienne Balibar (1967). *Reading Capital*. London, 1971

Althusser, Louis. *Philosophie et philosophie spontanée des savants*. Paris, 1974

Bachelard, Gaston (1934). *Le Nouvel Esprit scientifique*. Paris, 1946

Bachelard, Gaston (1949). *The Philosophy of No.* New York, 1968

*Collingwood, R. G. *The Idea of History.* T. M. Knox (ed.). Oxford, 1946

Douglas, Mary (1970). *Natural Symbols.* Harmondsworth, 1973

*Dunn, John. 'The identity of the history of ideas', *Philosophy,* 43 (1968), 85–116. Also in Peter Laslett, W. G. Runciman, Quentin Skinner (eds.). *Philosophy, Politics and Society.* 4th series. Oxford, 1972, 158–73

Durkheim, Emile (1903). *Primitive Classification.* Rodney Needham (intro.). London, 1963

Durkheim, Emile (1912). *The Elementary Forms of the Religious Life.* London, 1915

Friedrichs, Robert. *A Sociology of Sociology.* New York, 1970

Goldmann, Lucien (1955). *The Hidden God.* London, 1964

Grice, H. P. 'Meaning', *Philosophical Review,* 66 (1957), 377–88

Grice, H. P. 'Utterer's meaning and intentions', *Philosophical Review,* 78 (1969), 147–77

Hacking, Ian. 'Five parables', in Richard Rorty, J. B. Schneewind, Quentin Skinner (eds.). *Philosophy in History: essays on the historiography of philosophy.* Cambridge, 1984, 114–24.

Hampshire, Stuart. *Thought and Action.* London, 1959

Kuhn, T. S. *The structure of Scientific Revolutions.* Chicago, 1962

Kuhn, T. S. 'Reflections on my critics', in Imre Lakatos, Alan Musgrave (eds.). *Criticism and the Growth of Knowledge.* Cambridge, 1970, 231–78

Lecourt, D. (1972). *Marxism and Epistemology: Bachelard, Canguilhem, Foucault.* London, 1975

Lévi-Strauss, Claude (1949). 'History and anthropology', in *Structural Anthropology.* New York, 1963, 1–27

MacIntyre, Alasdair. *A Short History of Ethics.* London, 1966, 1–4

Marx, Karl, Friedrich Engels (1932). *The German Ideology.* New York, 1947, 3–78

Popper, K. R. *Objective Knowledge.* Oxford, 1972

Quillet, P. *Bachelard: présentation, choix de textes, bibliographie.* Paris, 1970

Runciman, W. G. *Social Science and Political Theory.* Cambridge, 1963

*Skinner, Quentin. 'Understanding and explanation in the history of ideas', *History and Theory,* 8 (1969), 3–53

Strawson, P. F. 'Intention and convention in speech acts', *Philosophical Review,* 73 (1964), 439–60

Taylor, Charles. 'Interpretation and the sciences of man', *Review of Metaphysics,* 25 (1971), 3–51

Toulmin, Stephen. *Human Understanding.* Vol. 1. Oxford, 1972

Wolin, Sheldon S. *Politics and Vision.* Boston, 1960

Chapter 1. Enlightenment and doubt

D'Alembert, Jean le Rond (1750). *Preliminary Discourse to the Encyclopedia.* Indianapolis, 1963

Annales de la société Jean-Jacques Rousseau. passim

Becker, Carl. *The Heavenly City of the Eighteenth-Century Philosophers.* New Haven, Conn., 1932

Berlin, Isaiah. 'Montesquieu', *Proceedings of the British Academy*, 41 (1956), 267–96

Berlin, Isaiah (ed.). *The Age of Enlightenment.* New York, 1956

Buchdahl, Gerd. *The Image of Newton and Locke in the Age of Reason.* London, 1961

Bury, J. B. *The Idea of Progress.* London, 1920

Cassirer, Ernst (1932). *The Question of Jean-Jacques Rousseau.* Bloomington, Ind., 1954

*Cassirer, Ernst (1932). *The Philosophy of the Enlightenment.* Boston, 1951

Cassirer, Ernst. 'Kant and Rousseau', in *Rousseau, Kant, Goethe.* Princeton, 1945, 1–60

Charvet, J. *The Social Problem in the Philosophy of Rousseau.* Cambridge, 1974

Crocker, Lester G. *The Age of Crisis.* Baltimore, 1959

Diderot, Denis (1762, 1769). *Rameau's Nephew and D'Alembert's Dream.* Harmondsworth, 1966

Diderot, Denis (1772). *Supplement to the Voyage of Bougainville.* Baltimore, 1935

Diderot, Denis. *Selected Philosophical Writings.* J. Lough (ed.). Cambridge, 1953

Foucault, Michel (1966). *The Order of Things.* London, 1970

Frankel, Charles. *The Faith of Reason.* New York, 1948

Gay, Peter. *The Party of Humanity.* London, 1954

Gay, Peter. *The Enlightenment: an interpretation*, 2 vols. London, 1967, 1970

Guyenot, Emile. *Les Sciences de la vie aux XVIIe et XVIIIe siècles.* Paris, 1941

Helvétius, Claude Adrien. *A treatise on Man, his intellectual faculties and his education.* London, 1777

Holbach, P. H. d'. (1770). *The System of Nature.* London, 1796–7

Hubert, René. *Les Sciences sociales dans l'Encyclopédie.* Lille and Paris, 1923

Hubert, René. *Rousseau et l'Encyclopédie.* Paris, 1928

Lough, J. (ed.). *The Encyclopédie of Diderot and D'Alembert.* Cambridge, 1954

Lough, J. *The Encyclopédie.* London, 1971

Lovejoy, Arthur O. (1923). 'The supposed primitivism of Rousseau's Discourse on Inequality', in *Essays on the History of Ideas.* Baltimore, 1948, 14–37

Lovejoy, Arthur O. *The Great Chain of Being.* Cambridge, Mass., 1936

MacIntyre, Alasdair. *A Short History of Ethics.* London, 1966, 121–89

Manuel, Frank E. *The Eighteenth Century Confronts the Gods*. Cambridge, Mass., 1959

Montesquieu, Charles Louis (1721). *Persian Letters*. C. J. Betts (ed. and intro.). Harmondsworth, 1973

Montesquieu, Charles Louis (1748). *The Spirit of Laws*. New York, 1949

Montesquieu, Charles Louis. *Complete Works*. London, 1777

Mornet, Daniel. *Les Origines intellectuelles de la Révolution Française: 1715–87*. Paris, 1933

Naville, Pierre (1943). *Paul Thiery d'Holbach et la philosophie scientifique au 18e siècle*. Paris, 1967

Roche, K. F. *Rousseau: stoic and romantic*. London, 1974

Rockwood, R. O. (ed.). *Carl Becker's Heavenly City Revisited*. Ithaca, N.Y., 1958

Rousseau, Jean-Jacques (1755). *Discours sur l'origine et les fondements de l'inégalité parmi les hommes*. F. C. Green (ed. and intro.). Cambridge, 1941

Rousseau, Jean-Jacques (1762). *The Social Contract*. Maurice Cranston (intro.). Harmondsworth, 1968

Rousseau, Jean-Jacques (1762). *Emile, ou de l'éducation*. F. and P. Richard (intro.). Paris, 1951

Rousseau, Jean-Jacques (1782). *Confessions*. London, 1938

Rousseau, Jean-Jacques. *Oeuvres complètes*. Paris, 1967

Schochet, G. J. *Patriarchialism in Political Thought*. Oxford, 1975

*Shackleton, R. M. *Montesquieu: a critical biography*. Oxford, 1961

*Shklar, Judith. *Men and Citizens: a study of Rousseau's social theory*. Cambridge, 1969

Smith, D. W. *Helvétius*. Oxford, 1965

Starobinski, Jean. *Jean-Jacques Rousseau*. Paris, 1957

Trevor-Roper, Hugh. 'The historical philosophy of the Enlightenment', *Studies on Voltaire and the Eighteenth Century*, 27 (1963), 1668–76

Vartanian, Aram. *Diderot and Descartes*. Princeton, 1953

Vyverberg, Henry. *Historical Pessimism in the French Enlightenment*. Cambridge, Mass., 1958

Wagar, Warren. 'Modern views of the origin of the Idea of Progress', *Journal of the History of Ideas*, 28 (1967), 55–70

Wahl, Jean. 'La bipolarité de Rousseau', *Annales*, 33 (1953–5), 49–55.

Chapter 2. History resolved by mind

Avineri, Shlomo. *Hegel's Theory of the Modern State*. Cambridge, 1972

Barnard, F. M. *Herder's Social and Political Thought*. Oxford, 1965

Beck, Louis W. *Early German Philosophy*. Cambridge, Mass., 1969

Berlin, Isaiah. *Two Concepts of Liberty*. Oxford, 1958

Berlin, Isaiah. 'Herder and the Enlightenment', in Earl R. Wasserman (ed.), *Aspects of the Eighteenth Century*. Baltimore, 1965, 47–104

Bruford, W. H. *Germany in the Eighteenth Century.* Cambridge, 1935

Bruford, W. H. *Culture and Society in Classical Weimar, 1775–1806.* Cambridge, 1962

Bryson, Gladys. *Man and Society: the Scottish Inquiry of the Eighteenth Century.* Princeton, 1945

Butler, E. M. *The Tyranny of Greece over Germany.* Cambridge, 1935

Clark, Robert T. *Herder.* Berkeley and Los Angeles, 1955

Fackenheim, Emil L. 'Kant's concept of history', *Kant-Studien*, 48 (1957), 381–98

Fackenheim, Emil L. *The Religious Dimension of Hegel's Thought.* Bloomington, Ind., 1967

Ferguson, Adam (1767). *An Essay on the History of Civil Society.* Duncan Forbes (ed. and intro.). Edinburgh, 1966

Harris, H. S. *Hegel's Development.* Oxford, 1972

Hegel, Georg Wilhelm Friedrich (1807). *The Phenomenology of Mind.* London, 1931

Hegel, Georg Wilhelm Friedrich (1812–16). *Science of Logic.* London, 1969

Hegel, Georg Wilhelm Friedrich (1817). *Philosophy of Mind.* London, 1971

Hegel, Georg Wilhelm Friedrich (1817). *The Philosophy of Right.* Oxford, 1942

Hegel, Georg Wilhelm Friedrich. *Political Writings.* T. M. Knox (ed.). Oxford, 1964

Hegel, Georg Wilhelm Friedrich (1923–55). *Lectures on the Philosophy of History.* New York, 1956

Hegel, Georg Wilhelm Friedrich. *Aesthetics.* Oxford, 1975. [I relied for this chapter on translations made for classes at Essex University by Stanley Mitchell]

Herder, Johann Gottfried von (1784–91). *Reflections on the Philosophy of History of Mankind.* Frank E. Manuel (ed. and intro.). Chicago, 1968

Herder, Johann Gottfried von. *Herder on Social and Political Culture.* F. M. Barnard (ed. and intro.). Cambridge, 1969

Hont, Istvan, Michael Ignatieff. 'Needs and justice in "The Wealth of Nations"', in Istvan Hont, Michael Ignatieff (eds.), *Wealth and Virtue: the shaping of political economy in the Scottish Enlightenment.* Cambridge, 1983, 1–44

Hume, David (1739–40). *A Treatise on Human Nature.* Oxford, 1896

Hume, David. *Essays, moral, political and literary.* Oxford, 1963

Kant, Immanuel (1781). *Critique of Pure Reason.* London, 1929

Kant, Immanuel (1799). *Anthropology from a Pragmatic Point of View.* M. J. Gregor (intro.). The Hague, 1974

Kant, Immanuel. *On History.* Louis W. Beck (ed. and intro.). Indianapolis, 1963

Kant, Immanuel. *Kant's Political Writings.* H. Reiss (ed. and intro.). Cambridge, 1970

Kaufmann, Walter. *Hegel: a re-interpretation.* Garden City, N.Y., 1965

Kaufmann, Walter (ed.). *Hegel: texts and commentary.* Garden City, N.Y., 1966

Kaufmann, Walter (ed.). *Hegel's Political Philosophy.* New York, 1970

*Kelly, George A. *Idealism, Politics and History: Sources of Hegelian Thought.* Cambridge, 1969.

Kettler, David. *The Social and Political Thought of Adam Ferguson.* Columbus, Ohio, 1965

Knox, T. M. 'Hegel's attitude to Kant's ethics', *Kant-Studien,* 49 (1957), 70–81

Kojève, Alexandre (1947). *Introduction to the Reading of Hegel.* New York, 1963

Lovejoy, Arthur O. (1916). 'The meaning of "romantic" in early German Romanticism', in *Essays on the History of Ideas.* Baltimore, 1948, 183–206.

Lovejoy, Arthur O. (1920). 'Schiller and the genesis of German romanticism', in *Essays on the History of Ideas.* Batimore, 1948, 207–27

Lovejoy, Arthur O. 'Herder and the enlightenment philosophy of history', in *Essays on the History of Ideas.* Baltimore, 1948, 166–82

Löwith, Karl (1941). *From Hegel to Nietzsche.* London, 1965

Lukács, Georg (1954). *The Young Hegel.* London, 1975

MacIntyre, Alasdair. *A Short History of Ethics.* London, 1966, 190–214

MacIntyre, Alasdair (ed.). *Hegel.* New York, 1972

Mainland, W. F. *Schiller and the Changing Past.* London, 1957

Manuel, Frank E. *Shapes of Philosophical History.* Stanford, Calif., 1965

Millar, John. *The Origin of the Distinction of Ranks.* London, 1779

Miller, R. D. *Schiller and the Idea of Freedom.* Oxford, 1970

Mure, G. R. G. *A Study of Hegel's Logic.* Oxford, 1950

Pascal, Roy. *The German Sturm und Drang.* Manchester, 1953

Pelczynski, Z. (ed.). *Hegel's Political Philosophy.* Cambridge, 1971

Pelczynski, Z. A. (ed.). *The State and Civil Society: studies in Hegel's political philosophy.* Cambridge, 1984

Popper, K. R. (1954). 'Kant's critique and cosmology', in *Conjectures and Refutations.* London, 1963, 175–83

Rabel, G. (ed.). *Kant.* Oxford, 1963

Regin, D. *Freedom and Dignity: the historical and philosophical thought of Schiller.* The Hague, 1965

Rosen, Michael. *Hegel's Dialectic and its Criticism.* Cambridge, 1982

Schiller, Johann Cristoph Friedrich von. *The Philosophical and Aesthetic Letters and Essays.* London, 1845

Schneider, Louis (ed.). *The Scottish Moralists on Human Nature and Society.* Chicago, 1967

Simon, Walter M. *Friedrich Schiller: 1759–1805*. Keele, 1966

Solomon, Robert C. *In the Spirit of Hegel: a study of G. W. F. Hegel's 'Phenomenology of Spirit'*. New York, 1983

*Taylor, Charles. *Hegel*. Cambridge, 1975

Taylor, Charles. *Hegel and Modern Society*. Cambridge, 1979

Ward, K. *The Development of Kant's View of Ethics*. Oxford, 1972

Wells, G. A. *Herder and After*. The Hague, 1959

Williams, T. C. *The Concept of the Categorical Imperative*. Oxford, 1968

Chapter 3. History resolved by men

Acton, H. B. *The Illusion of the Epoch*. London, 1955

Althusser, Louis. (1966). *For Marx*. London, 1969

Althusser, Louis, Etienne Balibar (1967). *Reading Capital*. London, 1971

*Avineri, Shlomo. *The Social and Political Thought of Karl Marx*. Cambridge, 1968

Berlin, Isaiah (1939). *Karl Marx*. London, 1963

Blumenberg, Werner (1962). *Karl Marx*. London, 1972

Bober, Mandell M. *Karl Marx's Interpretation of History*. Cambridge, Mass., 1948

Cohen, Gerald A. 'Bourgeois and Proletarians', in Shlomo Avineri (ed.). *Marx's Socialism*. New York, 1973, 101–25

Cohen, G. A. *Karl Marx's Theory of History: a defence*, Oxford, 1978

Elster, Jon. *Making Sense of Marx*. Cambridge, 1985

Feuerbach, Ludwig (1843). *The Essence of Christianity*. New York, 1957

Freedman, Robert (ed.). *Marx on Economics*. Harmondsworth, 1962

Kamenka, Eugene. *The Ethical Foundations of Marxism*. London, 1962

Kamenka, Eugene. *The Philosophy of Ludwig Feuerbach*. London, 1970

Kolakowski, Leszek. *Marxism and Beyond*. London, 1969

*Kolakowski, Leszek. *Main Currents of Marxism*. Three volumes. Oxford, 1978

Korsch, Karl (1923). *Marxism and Philosophy*. London, 1970

Korsch, Karl. *Karl Marx*. London, 1938

Lange, Oscar. *On the Economic Theory of Socialism*. Minneapolis, 1938

Lichtheim, George. *Marxism*. London, 1961

Lichtheim, George. 'The origins of Marxism', *Journal of the History of Philosophy*, 3 (1965), 96–105

Löwith, Karl. 'Max Weber und Karl Marx', *Archiv für Sozialwissenschaft und Sozialpolitik*, 67 (1932), 53–99, 175–214 [translation forthcoming]

Lukács, Georg (1923). *History and Class Consciousness*. London, 1971

MacIntyre, Alasdair (1953). *Marxism and Christianity*. New York, 1968

MacIntyre, Alasdair. *A Short History of Ethics*. London, 1966, 227–48

McLellan, David. *The Young Hegelians and Karl Marx*. London, 1969

Marx, Karl (1927–32). *Early Writings*. Lucio Coletti (ed.). Harmondsworth, 1975

Marx, Karl (1927). *Critique of Hegel's Philosophy of Right.* Joseph O'Malley (ed. and intro.). Cambridge, 1970

Marx, Karl (1932). *The German Ideology.* New York, 1947

Marx, Karl (1847). *The Poverty of Philosophy.* London, n.d.

Marx, Karl. *The Revolutions of 1848: Political Writings vol. 1.* David Fernbach (ed.). Harmondsworth, 1973

Marx, Karl (1848). 'Wage labour and capital', in *Karl Marx and Frederick Engels: selected works.* London, 1968, 72–94

Marx, Karl (1850). 'The class struggles in France, 1848–50', in *Karl Marx and Frederick Engels: selected works.* vol. 1. London, 1962, 139–227

Marx, Karl (1852). 'The eighteenth Brumaire of Louis Bonaparte', in *Karl Marx and Frederick Engels: selected works.* London, 1968, 95–180

Marx, Karl (1939). *The Grundrisse.* Martin Nicolaus (intro.). Harmondsworth, 1973

Marx, Karl (1898). 'Wages, price and profit', in *Karl Marx and Frederick Engels: selected works.* London, 1968, 186–229

Marx, Karl (1867). *Capital.* Vol. 1. London, 1961

Marx, Karl. *Surveys from Exile: Political Writings vol. 2.* David Fernbach (ed.). Harmondsworth, 1973

Marx, Karl. *The Civil War in France.* London, 1871

Marx, Karl (1885). *Capital.* Vol. 2. London, 1907

Marx, Karl (1893–4). *Capital.* Vol. 3. London, 1962

Marx, Karl. *The First International and After: Political Writings vol. 3.* David Fernbach (ed.). Harmondsworth, 1974

Marx, Karl, Friedrich Engels (1927–32). *Selected Correspondence.* Dona Torr (ed.). London, 1934

Marx, Karl, Friedrich Engels (1848). 'Manifesto of the Communist Party', in *Karl Marx and Frederick Engels: selected works.* London, 1968, 31–63

Ollman, Bertell. *Alienation: Marx's conception of man in capitalist society.* Cambridge, 1971

Rubel, Maximilien. *Bibliographie des oeuvres de Karl Marx.* Paris, 1956

Rubel, Maximilien. *Karl Marx.* Paris, 1957

Schumpeter, Joseph. *Capitalism, Socialism and Democracy.* New York, 1942

Stein, Lorenz von (1850). *History of the Social Movement in France.* Totowa, N.J., 1964

Sweezy, Paul. *The Theory of Capitalist Development.* New York, 1942

Tucker, Robert C. *Philosophy and Myth in Karl Marx.* Cambridge, 1961

Chapter 4. History resolved by laws I

Anschutz, Richard P. (1953). *The Philosophy of J. S. Mill.* Oxford, 1963

Bryson, Gladys. 'Early English positivists and the Religion of Humanity', *American Sociological Review,* 1 (1936), 343–62

Charlton, Donald G. *Positivist Thought in France during the Second Empire, 1852–70.* Oxford, 1959

*Collini, Stefan, Donald Winch, John Burrow. *That Noble Science of Politics: a study in nineteenth-century intellectual history.* Cambridge, 1983

Comte, Auguste. *The Crisis of Industrial Civilisation: the early essays of Auguste Comte.* Ronald Fletcher (ed.). London, 1974

Comte, Auguste. *Cours de Philosophie Positive.* Paris, 1830–42

Comte, Auguste (1851–4). *System of Positive Polity.* London, 1875–7

Cowling, Maurice. *Mill and Liberalism.* Cambridge, 1963

Evans-Pritchard, E. E. *The Sociology of Comte.* Manchester, 1970

Holthoon, F. L. van. *The Road to Utopia: a study of John Stuart Mill's social thought.* Assen, 1971

Hubert, René. 'Comte', *Encyclopedia of the Social Sciences.* Vol. 3. New York, 1930, 151–3

Iggers, George S. *The Cult of Authority.* The Hague, 1958

Lévy-Bruhl, Lucien. *La Philosophie d'Auguste Comte.* Paris, 1900

*Manuel, Frank E. *The New World of Henri Saint-Simon.* Cambridge, Mass., 1956

Manuel, Frank E. *The Prophets of Paris.* Cambridge, Mass., 1962

Martineau, Harriet. *Autobiography.* Boston, 1877

Mill, John Stuart (1843). *A System of Logic.* London, 1875

Mill, John Stuart (1848). *Principles of Political Economy.* Donald Winch (ed. and intro.). Harmondsworth, 1970

Mill, John Stuart (1859). *On Liberty.* G. Himmelfarb (ed. and intro.). Harmondsworth, 1974

*Mill, John Stuart (1865). *Auguste Comte and Positivism.* Ann Arbor, Mich., 1961

Mill, John Stuart (1869). *The Subjection of Women.* Cambridge, Mass., 1970

Mill, John Stuart. *Autobiography.* London, 1873

Mueller, Iris. *John Stuart Mill and French Thought.* Urbana, Ill., 1956

Packe, Michael St. J. *The Life of John Stuart Mill.* London, 1954

Robson, J. M. *The Improvement of Mankind: the social and political philosophy of John Stuart Mill.* Toronto, 1968

*Ryan, Alan. *The Philosophy of John Stuart Mill.* London, 1970

Saint-Simon, Henri. *Oeuvres complètes.* Paris, 1966

Simon, Walter M. *European Positivism in the Nineteenth Century.* Ithaca, N.Y., 1963

Stephen, Leslie. *The English Utilitarians.* London, 1900

Whewell, W. (1837). *History of the Inductive Sciences.* London, 1967

Whittaker, T. *Comte and Mill.* London, 1908

Chapter 5. History resolved by laws II

*Abrams, Philip. *The Origins of British Sociology, 1834–1914.* Chicago, 1968

Annan, Noel. *The Curious Strength of Positivism in English Thought.* London, 1959

Booth, Charles. 'The inhabitants of Tower Hamlets (School Board Division), their condition and occupations', *Journal of the Royal Statistical Society*, 50 (1887), 326–91

*Burrow, J. W. *Evolution and Society.* Cambridge, 1966

*Collini, Stefan. *Liberalism and Sociology: L. T. Hobhouse and political argument in England 1880–1914.* Cambridge, 1980

Duncan, David. *The Life and Letters of Herbert Spencer.* London, 1908

Galton, Francis. *Natural Inheritance.* London, 1881

Galton, Francis. *Essays in Eugenics.* London, 1909

Green, T. H. *Lectures on the Principles of Political Obligation.* London, 1907

Hobhouse, L. T. *Mind in Evolution.* London, 1901

Hobhouse, L. T. *Morals and Evolution.* London, 1906

Hobhouse, L. T. *Social Evolution and Political Theory.* New York, 1911

Hobhouse, L. T. *Development and Purpose.* London, 1913

Hobhouse, L. T. *Social Development.* London, 1924

Hobson, J. A., Morris Ginsberg. *L. T. Hobhouse, his life and work.* London, 1931

Huxley, T. H. *Evolution and Ethics.* London, 1893

*Medawar, P. B. (1963). 'Herbert Spencer and the Law of General Evolution', in *The Art of the Soluble.* Harmondsworth, 1969, 45–67

Moore, G. E. *Principia Ethica.* Cambridge, 1903

Pearson, Karl. *The Groundwork of Eugenics.* London, 1909

*Peel, J. D. Y. *Herbert Spencer.* London, 1971

Richter, Melvin. *The Politics of Conscience: T. H. Green and his age.* London, 1964

Rowntree, B. S. *Poverty: a study of town life.* London, 1901

Schlipp, P. A. (ed.). *The Philosophy of G. E. Moore.* New York, 1942

Sidgwick, Henry. 'Economic science and statistics', *Journal of the Royal Statistical Society*, 48 (1885), 595–616

Simey, T. S. and M. B. *Charles Booth.* Oxford, 1960

Spencer, Herbert. *Social Statics.* London, 1851

Spencer, Herbert. *The Principles of Psychology.* London, 1855

Spencer, Herbert (1862). *First Principles.* London, 1910

Spencer, Herbert (1862). *Reasons for Dissenting from the Philosophy of M. Comte, and other essays.* Berkeley, 1968

Spencer, Herbert (1873). *The Study of Sociology.* London, 1894

Spencer, Herbert. *Descriptive Sociology.* David Duncan *et al.* (compiled and abstracted). London, 1873–1934

Spencer, Herbert. *The Data of Ethics.* London, 1879

Spencer, Herbert (1884). *Man versus the State.* Donald MacRae (ed. and intro.). Harmondsworth, 1969

Spencer, Herbert. *Autobiography*. London, 1904

Webb, Beatrice. *My Apprenticeship*. London, 1936

White, Alan (1958). *G. E. Moore: a critical exposition*. Oxford, 1969

Warnock, Geoffrey. *Contemporary Moral Philosophy*. London, 1967

Chapter 6. History resolved by laws III

[This bibliography owes much to the excellent one in Lukes, *op. cit.*, 561–615]

Barnes, J. A. 'Durkheim's Division of Labour in Society', *Man* (N.S.), 1 (1966), 158–75

Besnard, Philippe (ed.). *The Sociological Domain: the Durkheimians and the founding of French sociology*. Cambridge and Paris, 1983

Bouglé, Célestin (1896). *Les Sciences sociales en Allemagne*. Paris, 1912

Bourgin, H. *De Jaurès à Léon Blum: l'Ecole Normale et la politique*. Paris, 1938

Clark, Terry N. 'Emile Durkheim and the institutionalisation of sociology in the French university system', *Archives Européennes de Sociologie*, 9 (1968), 37–71. See also Anthony Oberschall (ed.). *The Establishment of Empirical Sociology*. New York, 1972, 152–86

Clark, Terry N. 'The structure and functions of a research institute: the Année sociologique', *Archives Européennes de Sociologie*, 9 (1968), 72–91

Cuvillier, Armand. 'E. Durkheim et le socialisme', *Revue socialiste*, 122 (1959), 33–43

Davy, Georges. 'Emile Durkheim: l'homme', *Revue de métaphysique et de morale*, 26 (1919), 181–98

Durkheim, Emile. 'La science positive de la morale en Allemagne', *Revue philosophique*, 24 (1887), 33–58, 113–42, 275–84. Pp. 40–3, 138–40 and 276–8 are translated in Anthony Giddens, (ed. and intro.). *Emile Durkheim: Selected writings*. Cambridge, 1972, 94–5, 92–4, 90–2

Durkheim, Emile. 'F. Tönnies: Gemeinschaft und Gesellschaft', *Revue philosophique*, 27 (1889), 416–22. Pp. 421–2 are translated in Anthony Giddens (ed. and intro.), *op. cit.*, 146–7.

Durkheim, Emile (1893). *De la division de la travail social*. Paris, 1902.

Durkheim, Emile (1892). 'Montesquieu's contribution to the rise of social science', in *Montesquieu and Rousseau*. Ann Arbor, Mich., 1960, 1–64

Durkheim, Emile (1895). *The Rules of Sociological Method*. Glencoe, Ill., 1950

Durkheim, Emile (1897). *Suicide*. London, 1952

Durkheim, Emile. 'Antonio Labriola: Essais sur la conception matérialiste de l'histoire', *Revue philosophique*, 44 (1897), 645–51. Pp. 648–51 are translated in Anthony Giddens (ed. and intro.), *op. cit.*, 159–62

Durkheim, Emile (1898). 'Individualism and the intellectuals', Steven Lukes (intro.), *Political Studies*, 17 (1969), 14–30.

Durkheim, Emile (1900). 'Sociology and its scientific field', in Kurt H. Wolff (ed.), *op. cit.*, 354–75

Durkheim, Emile (1903). *Primitive Classification*. Rodney Needham (intro.). London, 1963

Durkheim, Emile (1912). *The Elementary Forms of the Religious Life*. London, 1915

Durkheim, Emile (1914). 'The dualism of human nature and its social conditions', in Kurt H. Wolff (ed.), *op. cit.*, 325–40.

Durkheim, Emile (1918). 'Rousseau's Social Contract', in *Montesquieu and Rousseau*. Ann Arbor, Mich., 1960, 65–138

Durkheim, Emile. 'Introduction à la morale', *Revue philosophique*, 89 (1920), 79–97

Durkheim, Emile (1922). *Education and Sociology*. Glencoe, Ill., 1956

Durkheim, Emile (1924). *Sociology and Philosophy*. London, 1953

Durkheim, Emile (1925). *Moral Education*. New York, 1953

Durkheim, Emile (1928). *Socialism and Saint-Simon*. A. W. Gouldner (ed. and intro.), London, 1959

Durkheim, Emile (1950). *Professional Ethics and Civic Morals*. London, 1957

Durkheim, Emile (1955). *Pragmatism and Sociology*. J. B. Allcock, A. Cuvillier (eds. and intro.). Cambridge, 1983

Giddens, Anthony. 'The suicide problem in French sociology', *British Journal of Sociology*, 16 (1965), 1–18

Giddens, Anthony. 'The "individual" in the writings of Durkheim', *Archives Européennes de Sociologie*, 12 (1971), 210–28

LaCapra, Dominic. *Emile Durkheim*. Ithaca, N.Y., 1972

Lacombe, Roger. *La Méthode sociologique de Durkheim*. Paris, 1926

Lourau, René. 'La société institutrice, Durkheim et les origines de la science de l'éducation', *Les Temps modernes*, 24 (1969), 1648–64

*Lukes, Steven. *Emile Durkheim: his life and work*. London, 1973

Neyer, Joseph. 'Individualism and socialism in Durkheim', in Kurt H. Wolff (ed.), *op. cit.*, 32–76

Poggi, Gianfranco. *Images of Society: essays on the sociological theories of Tocqueville, Marx and Durkheim*. Stanford, 1972

Richter, Melvin. 'Durkheim's politics and political theory', in Kurt H. Wolff (ed.), *op. cit.*, 170–210

Seger, Imogen. *Durkheim and his Critics on the Sociology of Religion*. New York, 1957

Smith, W. Robertson (1889). *The Religion of the Semites*. London, 1956

Tarde, Gabriel. 'Questions sociales', *Revue philosophique*, 35 (1893), 618–38

Tarde, Gabriel. 'La realité sociale', *Revue philosophique*, 52 (1901), 457–79

Wolff, Kurt H. (ed.) (1960). *Emile Durkheim et al.: essays on sociology and social philosophy.* New York, 1964

Wolin, Sheldon S. *Politics and Vision.* Boston, 1960, 352–434

Worms, René. 'Emile Durkheim', *Revue internationale de sociologie*, 25 (1917), 561–8

Worms, René. *La sociologie, sa nature, son contenu, ses attaches.* Paris, 1921

Worsley, Peter. 'Emile Durkheim's theory of knowledge', *Sociological Review* (N.S.), 4 (1956), 47–62

Chapter 7. History resolved by will

Antoni, Carlo (1940). *From History to Sociology.* London, 1962

Aron, Raymond, 'Max Weber', in *Main Currents of Sociological Thought.* Vol. 2. London, 1968, 177–252

Baumgarten, Eduard (ed.). *Max Weber: Werk und Person.* Tübingen, 1964

*Beetham, David. *Max Weber and the Theory of Modern Politics.* London, 1974

Bendix, Reinhard. *Max Weber: an intellectual portrait.* London, 1966

Bendix, Reinhard, Gunther Roth. *Scholarship and Partisanship: essays on Max Weber.* London, 1971

Dilthey, Wilhelm (1883 ff.). *Meaning in History.* H. P. Rickman (ed. and intro.). London, 1961

Dilthey, Wilhelm (1907). *The Essence of Philosophy.* New York, 1969

Falk, Werner. 'Democracy and capitalism in Max Weber's sociology', *Sociological Review*, 27 (1935), 373–93

Giddens, Anthony. *Politics and Sociology in the Thought of Max Weber.* London, 1972

Hodges, H. A. *Wilhelm Dilthey: an introduction.* London, 1944

Hodges, H. A. *The Philosophy of Wilhelm Dilthey.* London, 1952

Kluback, William. *Wilhelm Dilthey's Philosophy of History.* New York, 1956

Löwith, Karl. 'Max Weber und Karl Marx', *Archiv für Sozialwissenschaft und Sozialpolitik*, 67 (1932), 53–99, 175–214 [translation forthcoming]

Lindenlaub, Dieter. *Richtungskämpfe im Verein für Sozialpolitik.* Wiesbaden, 1967

Marx, Karl (1891). 'Critique of the Gotha Programme', in *Karl Marx and Frederick Engels: selected works.* London, 1968, 315–41

Mayer, J. P. *Max Weber and German Politics.* London, 1944

Mitzman, Arthur. *The Iron Cage: an historical interpretation of Max Weber.* New York, 1970

Mommsen, Wolfgang J. (1959). *Max Weber und die Deutsche Politik, 1890–1920.* Tübingen, 1974

Mommsen, Wolfgang J. 'Max Weber's political sociology and his philosophy of world history', *International Social Science Journal*, 17 (1965), 23–45

Mommsen, Wolfgang J. *The Age of Bureaucracy: perspectives on the political sociology of Max Weber.* Oxford, 1974

Palmer, R. E. *Hermeneutics.* Evanston, Ill., 1968

Rickert, Heinrich (1899). *Science and History: a critique of positivist epistemology.* Princeton, 1962

*Ringer, Fritz K. *The Decline of the German Mandarins: the German academic community, 1890–1933.* Cambridge, Mass., 1969

Runciman, W. G. *A Critique of Max Weber's Philosophy of Social Science.* Cambridge, 1972

Samuelson, Kurt (1957). *Religion and Economic Action.* London, 1961

Schelting, Alexander von. *Max Weber's Wissenschaftslehre.* Tübingen, 1934

Schluchter, Wolfgang. *Aspekte bürokratischer Herrschaft: Studien zur Interpretation der fortschreitenden Industriegesellschaft.* Munich, 1972

Schmitt, Gustav. *Deutscher Historismus und der Übergang zur parliamentarischen Demokratie.* Lübeck and Hamburg, 1964

Schmoller, Gustav. *Die Soziale Frage.* Munich, 1918

Sombart, Werner. (1902). *A History of the Economic Institutions of Modern Europe.* F. L. Nussbaum (ed.). New York, 1933

Sombart, Werner (1911). *The Jews and Modern Capitalism.* London, 1913

Sombart, Werner (1913). *The Quintessence of Capitalism.* London, 1915

Stammer, Otto (ed.) (1965). *Max Weber and Sociology Today.* Oxford, 1971

Tenbruck, Friedrich H. 'Die Genesis der Methodologie Max Webers', *Kölner Zeitschrift für Soziologie und Sozialpsychologie*, 11 (1959), 573–630

Turner, Bryan S. *Weber on Islam.* London, 1974

Weber, Marianne (1926). *Max Weber: a biography.* Harry Zohn (ed.). New York, 1975

Weber, Max (1893). 'Die ländliche Arbeitsverfassung', in *Gesammelte Aufsätze zur Sozial- und Wirtschaftsgeschichte.* Tübingen, 1924, 444–69

Weber, Max (1894). 'Entwickelungstendenzen in der Lage der ostelbischen Landarbeiter', in *Gesammelte Aufsätze zur Sozial- und Wirtschaftsgeschichte.* Tübingen, 1924, 470–507

Weber, Max (1895). 'Der Nationalstaat und die Volkwirtschaftspolitik', in *Gesammelte Politischen Schriften.* Tübingen, 1958, 1–25

Weber, Max (1904). '"Objectivity" in sociology and social policy', in Edward Shils, Henry A. Finch (eds.). *The Methodology of the Social Sciences.* Glencoe, Ill., 1949, 49–112

Weber, Max (1905). *The Protestant Ethic and the Spirit of Capitalism.* London, 1930

Weber, Max (1906). 'Zur Lage der bürgerlichen Demokratie in Russland', in *Gesammelte Politische Schriften.* Tübingen, 1958, 30–65

Weber, Max (1906). 'Russlands Übergang zum Scheinkonstitutionalismus', in *Gesammelte Politische Schriften.* Tübingen, 1958, 66–108

Weber, Max (1906). 'The Protestant sects and the spirit of capitalism', in H. H. Gerth, C. W. Mills (eds.). *From Max Weber*. London, 1948, 30^-22

Weber, Max (1916). *The Religion of China: Confucianism and Taoism*. New York, 1964

Weber, Max (1916–17). *The Religion of India: the sociology of Hinduism and Buddhism*. Glencoe, Ill., 1958

Weber, Max (1917). 'Russlands Ubergang zur Scheindemokratie', in *Gesammelte Politische Schriften*. Tübingen, 1958, 192–210

Weber, Max (1917). 'Wahlrecht und Demokratie in Deutschland', in *Gesammelte Politische Schriften*. Tübingen, 1958, 233–79

Weber, Max (1917). 'Parliament und Regierung im neugeordneten Deutschland', in *Gesammelte Politische Schriften*. Tübingen, 1958, 294–431

Weber, Max (1917). 'National character and the Junkers', in H. H. Gerth, C. W. Mills (eds.), *op. cit.*, 386–95

Weber, Max (1917). 'The meaning of "ethical neutrality" in sociology and economics', in Edward Shils, Henry A. Finch (eds.), *op. cit.*, 1–47

Weber, Max (1917–19). *Ancient Judaism*. New York, 1952

Weber, Max (1918). 'Der Sozialismus', in *Gesammelte Politische Schriften*. Tübingen, 1958, 492–518

Weber, Max (1919). 'Politics as a vocation', in H. H. Gerth, C. W. Mills (eds.), *op. cit.*, 77–128

Weber, Max (1919). 'Science [Wissenschaft] as a vocation', in H. H. Gerth, C. W. Mills (eds.), *op. cit.*, 129–56

Weber, Max (1920). 'Author's introduction' [written for *Gesammelte Aufsätze zur Religionssoziologie*. Tübingen, 1920–1], in *The Protestant Ethic and the Spirit of Capitalism*. London, 1930, 13–31

Weber, Max (1922). 'The economy and the arena of normative and de facto powers', in Gunther Roth, Claus Wittich (eds. and intro.). *Economy and Society*. New York, 1968, 311–1461

Weber, Max (1922). 'Conceptual exposition', in Gunther Roth, Claus Wittich (eds. and intro.) *op. cit.*, 3–307

Weber, Max (1923). *General Economic History*. London, 1927

Chapter 8. History doubted

Abel, Theodor. *Systematic Sociology in Germany: a critical analysis of some attempts to establish sociology as an independent science*. New York, 1929

*Aron, Raymond (1935). *German Sociology*. Glencoe, Ill., 1964

Bayet, A. *Le suicide et la morale*. Paris, 1923

*Benoît-Smullyan, E. *The Development of French Sociologism and its Critics in France*. Thesis deposited in the Widener Library, Harvard University, Cambridge, Mass., 1937

Benoît-Smullyan, E. 'Sociology in the French language', in H. E. Barnes and H. Becker (eds.). *Social Thought from Lore to Science.* Boston, 1938, 815–77

Benoît-Smullyan, E. 'The sociologism of Emile Durkheim and his school', in H. E. Barnes (ed.), *An Introduction to the History of Sociology.* Chicago, 1948, 499–537

Blondel, C. *Le Suicide.* Strasbourg, 1933

Bouglé, Célestin. *Humanisme, Sociologie, Philosophie: remarques sur la conception française de la Culture générale.* Travaux de l'Ecole Normale Supérieure (Lettres). Paris, 1938

Bowley, A. L. *The Nature and Purpose of the Measurement of Social Phenomena.* London, 1915

Bowley, A. L., A. R. Bennet-Hurst. *Livelihood and Poverty.* London, 1915

Branford, V. V., Patrick Geddes. *The Coming Polity.* London, 1921

Branford, V. V., Patrick Geddes. *On Social Inheritance.* London, 1923

Caine, S. *The History of the Founding of the London School of Economics.* London, 1963

Caradog-Jones, D. 'Evolution of the social survey in England since Booth', *American Journal of Sociology*, 46 (1940–1), 818–25

Cassirer, Ernst. 'Neo-Kantianism', *Encyclopaedia Britannica*, 14th ed. (1930), 215–16

Collingwood, R. G. 'Oswald Spengler and the theory of historical cycles', *Antiquity*, 1 (1927), 311–25, 435–46

Coser, Lewis A. 'Georg Simmel 1858–1918', in *Masters of Sociological Thought.* New York, 1971, 177–215

Davy, Georges (1931). *Sociologues d'hier et d'aujourd'hui.* Paris, 1950

Davy, Georges, A. Moret. *Des Clans aux empires.* Paris, 1923

Duprat, Guillaume L. 'La psycho-sociologie en France', *Archiv für Geschichte der Philosophie und Soziologie*, 37 (1926), 133–60

Fletcher, Ronald (ed.). *The Science of Society and the Unity of Mankind: a memorial volume for Morris Ginsberg.* London, 1974

Freyer, Hans. *Soziologie als Wirklichkeitwissenschaft.* Leipzig, 1930

Geddes, Patrick. *Cities in Evolution.* London, 1915

Ginsberg, Morris. *Studies in Sociology.* London, 1932

Ginsberg, Morris. 'Recent tendencies in sociology', *Economica*, 13 (1933), 22–39

Ginsberg, Morris. *Sociology.* London, 1934

Ginsberg, Morris. *Reason and Unreason in Society.* London, 1948

Ginsberg, Morris. *On Justice in Society.* London, 1965

Grünwald, Ernst. *Das Problem der Soziologie des Wissens.* Vienna and Leipzig, 1934

Halbwachs, Maurice. *Les Causes du suicide.* Paris, 1930

Hobson, J. A. *Free Thought in the Social Sciences.* London, 1926

Holborn, Hajo. 'Der Deutsche Idealismus in sozialgeschichtlicher Beleuchtung', *Historische Zeitschrift*, 174 (1952), 359–84

Hubert, René. 'Essai sur les origines et des progrès de la sociologie en France', *Revue de l'histoire de la philosophie et d'histoire générale de la civilisation* (N.S.), 6 (1938), 111–55, 281–310

Hughes, H. Stuart. *Oswald Spengler*. New York, 1952

Husserl, Edmund (1907). *The Idea of Phenomenology*. The Hague, 1964

Husserl, Edmund (1910). 'Philosophy as a rigorous science', in *Phenomenology and the Crisis of Philosophy*. New York, 1965

Husserl, Edmund. 'Phenomenology', *Encyclopaedia Britannica*, 14th ed. (1927), 699–702

Institute of Sociology, *The Social Sciences: their relations in theory and in teaching*. London, 1936

Institute of Sociology. *Further Papers on the Social Sciences*. London, 1937

Jay, Martin. *The Dialectical Imagination: a history of the Frankfurt School and the Institute of Social Research, 1923–50*. Boston, 1973

Jay, Martin. *Adorno*. Cambridge, Mass., 1984

Korsch, Karl (1923). *Marxism and Philosophy*. London, 1970

Landheer, Barth. 'Othmar Spann's social theories', *Journal of Political Economy*, 39 (1931), 239–48

Lenk, K. 'Das tragische Bewusstsein in der deutschen Soziologie der zwanziger Jahre', *Frankfurter Hefte*, 18 (1963), 313–20

Leroy, Maxime. *Histoire des idées sociales en France*. Paris, 1946–54

Lévi-Strauss, Claude. 'French sociology', in Georges Gurvitch, W. E. Moore (eds.). *Twentieth-Century Sociology*. New York, 1945, 503–37

Lichtheim, George. *Lukács*. London, 1970

Lukács, Georg (1923). *History and Class Consciousness*. London, 1971

Lukács, Georg (1953). *Die Zerstörung der Vernunft*. Berlin, 1954

Mannheim, Karl (1929). *Ideology and Utopia*. London, 1936

Mannheim, Karl. *Rational and Irrational Elements in Contemporary Society*. London, 1934

Mannheim, Karl. *Essays on the Sociology of Knowledge*. P. Kecskemeti (ed.). London, 1952

Mauss, Marcel. 'Division et proportions des divisions de la sociologie', *Année sociologique* (N.S.), 2 (1927), 95–176

Mauss, Marcel. 'Fragment d'un plan de sociologie générale descriptive', *Année sociologique*, sér. A. fasc. 1 (1934), 1–56

Neumann, S. 'Alfred Weber's conception of a historico-cultural sociology', in H. E. Barnes (ed.). *An Introduction to the History of Sociology*. Chicago, 1948, 353–61

Oppenheimer, Franz. 'Tendencies in recent German sociology', *Sociological Review*, 24 (1932), 1–13, 125–37, 249–60

Remmling, G. W. *The Sociology of Karl Mannheim*. London, 1975

*Ringer, Fritz K. *The Decline of the German Mandarins: the German academic community, 1890–1933*. Cambridge, Mass., 1969

Rumney, Jay. 'British Sociology', in Georges Gurvitch, W. E. Moore (eds.). *Twentieth-Century Sociology.* New York, 1945, 562–85

Scheler, Max (1912). *Ressentiment.* Lewis A. Coser (ed.). New York, 1961

Scheler, Max (1913). *The Nature of Sympathy.* London, 1954

Scheler, Max (1921). *On the Eternal in Man.* London, 1960

Scheler, Max. 'Weltanschauungslehre, Soziologie und Weltanschauungssetzung', in *Schriften zur Soziologie und Weltanschauungslehre.* Leipzig, 1923, 1–25

Scheler, Max. *Philosophical Perspectives.* Boston, 1958

Schelting, Alexander von. 'Karl Mannheim: Ideology and Utopia', *American Sociological Review*, 1 (1936), 666–73

Schmitt, Richard. 'Phenomenology', *Encyclopedia of Philosophy.* New York, 1967

Sidgwick, Henry (1874). *The Method of Ethics.* London, 1962

Simey, T. S. 'The contribution of Sidney and Beatrice Webb to sociology', *British Journal of Sociology*, 12, (1961), 106–23

Simmel, Georg (1908). *Sociology.* Kurt H. Wolff (ed.). Glencoe, Ill., 1950

Simmel, Georg. *Philosophische Kultur: gesammelte Essays.* Leipzig, 1911

Simmel, Georg. *Brücke und Tür: Essays des Philosophen zur Geschichte, Religion, Kunst und Gesellschaft.* M. Landmann, M. Susman (eds.). Stuttgart, 1957

Sociological Review, 13–25 (1921 to 1933), *passim*

Spann, Othmar. *Gesellschaftslehre.* Leipzig, 1923

Spann, Othmar. *Gesellschaftsphilosophie.* Munich and Berlin, 1928

Spengler, Oswald (1918). *The Decline of the West.* London, 1923

Spiegelberg, Herbert (1960). *The Phenomenological Movement.* The Hague, 1965

Spykman, Nicholas J. (1925). *The Social Theory of Georg Simmel.* New York, 1966

*Staude, John R. *Max Scheler.* New York, 1967

Tönnies, Ferdinand (1887). *Community and Association.* East Lansing, Mich., 1957

Tönnies, Ferdinand (1909). *Custom.* New York, 1961

Tönnies, Ferdinand. *Geist der Neuzeit.* Leipzig, 1935

Tönnies, Ferdinand. 'The concept and law of human progress', *Social Forces*, 19 (1940), 23–9

Vierkandt, A. (ed.). *Handwörterbuch der Soziologie.* Stuttgart, 1931

Vierkandt, A. (1931–7). *Sociology.* New York, 1941

Vörlander, K. *Kant und Marx.* Tübingen, 1926

Watnick, Morris. 'Relativism and class consciousness: Georg Lukács', in Leopold Labedz (ed.). *Revisionism.* London, 1962, 142–65

Webb, Beatrice and Sidney (1932). *Methods of Social Study.* T. H. Marshall (intro.). Cambridge, 1975

Weber, Alfred (1920). *Fundamentals of Culture-Sociology.* New York, 1939

Weber, Alfred. *Deutschland und die europäische Kulturkrise.* Jena, 1924

Weber, Alfred (1943). *Farewell to European History.* London, 1948

Weingartner, Rudolph H. *Experience and Culture: the philosophy of Georg Simmel.* Middletown, Conn., 1962

Wells, A. F. *The Local Social Survey in Great Britain.* London, 1935

Wiese, Leopold von (1924–9). *Systematic Sociology.* Howard Becker (ed.). New York, 1932

Wiese, Leopold von (1931–7). *Sociology.* Franz Mueller (ed.). New York, 1941

Wiese, Leopold von. 'The social, spiritual and cultural elements of the inter-human life', *Sociological Review*, 24 (1932), 125–37, 249–60

Wolff, Kurt H. (ed.). *Georg Simmel, 1858–1918.* Columbus, Ohio, 1959

Wolin, Sheldon S. *Politics and Vision.* Boston, 1960, 352–434

Chapter 9. History ignored

Allen, G. W. *William James.* London, 1967

Arieli, Yehoshua. *Individualism and Nationalism in American Ideology.* Cambridge, Mass., 1964

Bernstein, Richard J. *Praxis and Action.* Philadelphia, 1971, 165–229

Bramson, Leon. *The Political Context of Sociology.* Princeton, 1961

Bridgman, P. W. *The Logic of Modern Physics.* New York, 1927

Borkenau, Franz. *Pareto.* New York, 1936

Broom, Leonard, Philip Selznick. *Sociology.* New York, 1955

Calhoun, John. *Life, and selections from speeches.* New York, 1843

Chugerman, Samuel. *Lester F. Ward: The American Aristotle.* New York, 1965

Cooley, Charles Horton. *Human Nature and the Social Order.* New York, 1902

Cooley, Charles Horton. *Social Organisation.* New York, 1909

Cooley, Charles Horton. *Social Process.* New York, 1918

Cooley, Charles Horton. 'Reflections on the sociology of Herbert Spencer', *American Journal of Sociology*, 26 (1920–1), 129–45

Coser, Lewis A. 'Robert Ezra Park, 1864-1944', in *Masters of Sociological Thought.* New York, 1971, 357–84

Dunn, John. 'The politics of Locke in England and America in the eighteenth century', in J. W. Yolton (ed.). *John Locke: problems and perspectives.* Cambridge, 1969, 45–80

Faris, Robert E. *Chicago Sociology, 1920–32.* San Francisco, 1967

Fitzhugh, George (1854). *Sociology for the South, or The Failure of Free Society.* New York, 1965

Fitzhugh, George (1857). *Cannibals All! or Slaves without Masters.* C. Vann Woodward (ed. and intro.). Cambridge, Mass., 1960

Giddings, Franklin. *The Principles of Sociology.* New York, 1896

Giddings, Franklin. *Inductive Sociology*. New York, 1901

Giddings, Franklin. *The Responsible State*. Boston, 1918

*Hartz, Louis. *The Liberal Tradition in America*. New York, 1955

Henderson, L. J. *Pareto's General Sociology*. Cambridge, Mass., 1935

Heyl, Barbara. 'The Harvard Pareto Circle', *Journal of the History of the Behavioural Sciences*, 4 (1968), 316–34

*Hofstadter, Richard. *Social Darwinism in American Thought, 1860–1915*. Philadelphia, 1945

Hofstadter, Richard. *The Age of Reform*. London, 1956

Hofstadter, Richard. *The Progressive Historians*. New York, 1969, 437–66

Homans, George. *Sentiments and Activities*. London, 1962

Homans, George, Charles P. Curtis. *An Introduction to Pareto*. New York, 1934

James, William. *Pragmatism*. New York, 1907

Jandy, E. C. *Charles Horton Cooley*. New York, 1942

Johnson, Harry M. *Sociology*. New York, 1960

Kolakowski, Leszek. *Positivist Philosophy*. New York, 1968

Lundberg, George A. *Trends in American Sociology*. New York, 1929

Mayo, Elton. *The Human Problems of an Industrial Civilisation*. New York, 1933

Merton, Robert K., L. Broom, L. C. Cottrell (eds.). *Sociology Today*. New York, 1959

Mills, C. Wright. *The Sociological Imagination*. New York, 1959

Mills, C. Wright. *Power, Politics and People*. I. L. Horowitz (ed. and intro.). New York, 1963

Mills, C. Wright. *Pragmatism and Sociology*. I. L. Horowitz (intro.). New York, 1964

*Oberschall, Anthony. 'The institutionalisation of American sociology', in Anthony Oberschall (ed.). *The Establishment of Empirical Sociology*. New York, 1972, 187–251

Odum, Howard. *American Sociology*. New York, 1951

Ogburn, W. F. 'The folkways of a scientific sociology', *Papers and Proceedings of the American Sociological Society*, 24 (1930)

Ogburn, W. F. *William F. Ogburn on Culture and Social Change*. Otis Dudley Duncan (ed. and intro.). Chicago, 1964

Papers and Proceedings of the American Sociological Society, 1 (1906), and subsequent volumes, *passim*

Park, Robert E., E. W. Burgess (eds.). *Introduction to the Science of Sociology*. Chicago, 1921

Park, Robert E., *et al. The City*. Chicago, 1925

Parsons, Talcott, '"Capitalism" in recent German literature: I, Werner Sombart', *Journal of Political Economy*, 36 (1928), 641–61

Parsons, Talcott. *The Structure of Social Action*. New York, 1937

Parsons, Talcott. *The Social System*. Glencoe, Ill., 1951

*Parsons, Talcott. 'On building social system theory', *Daedalus* [*Proceedings of the American Academy of Arts and Sciences*, 99] (1970), 826–81

Parsons, Talcott, Edward Shils (eds.). *Toward a General Theory of Action.* Cambridge, Mass., 1951, 47–243

Perry, Ralph Barton. *The Thought and Character of William James.* Boston, 1936

Quine, W. V. O. 'Two dogmas of empiricism', in *From a Logical Point of View.* Cambridge, Mass., 1961, 20–46

Ross, Edward A. *Foundations of Sociology.* New York, 1905

Ross, Edward A. *Sin and Society.* New York, 1907

Ross, Edward A. *Seventy Years of It: an autobiography.* New York, 1936

Schwendinger, Herman, and Julia R. *Sociologists of the Chair: a radical analysis of the formative years of North American sociology, 1883–1922.* New York, 1974

Small, Albion W. 'Fifty years of sociology in the United States', *American Journal of Sociology*, 21 (1915–16), 721–864. See also other papers by Small in the *Journal*, 1–30 (1895–6 to 1924–5)

Sumner, William Graham. *What Social Classes Owe to Each Other.* New York, 1883

Sumner, William Graham. *Folkways.* Boston, 1906

Sumner, William Graham. *Essays.* New Haven, Conn., 1934

Thomas, William I., Florian Znaniecki. *The Polish Peasant in Europe and America.* Chicago, 1918

*Tocqueville, Alexis de (1836). *Democracy in America*, Vol. 2. New York, 1945

Ward, Lester F. *Young Ward's Diary.* Bernhard J. Stern (ed. and intro.). New York, 1935

Ward, Lester F. *Dynamic Sociology.* New York, 1883

Ward, Lester F. *Outlines of Sociology.* New York, 1898

Ward, Lester F. *Pure Sociology.* New York, 1903

White, Morton. *Social Thought in America.* New York, 1952

Wirth, Louis (1947). 'American sociology, 1915–47', *American Journal of Sociology*, Index to Vols. 1–52

Chapter 10. History unresolved

Albert, Hans. *Theorie und Realität.* Tübingen, 1964

Althusser, Louis (1966). *For Marx.* London, 1969

Althusser, Louis. *Lenin and Philosophy.* London, 1971

Anderson, Perry. *Passages from Antiquity to Feudalism.* London, 1974

Anderson, Perry. *Lineages of the Absolutist State.* London, 1974

Anderson, Perry. *In the Tracks of Historical Materialism.* London, 1983

Aron, Raymond. *Introduction à la philosophie de l'histoire: essai sur les limites de l'objectivité historique.* Paris, 1938

Aron, Raymond (1955). *The Opium of the Intellectuals.* Garden City, N.Y., 1957

Aron, Raymond (1963). *18 Lectures on Industrial Society.* London, 1969

Aron, Raymond. *La Lutte des classes.* Paris, 1964

Aron, Raymond. *Democratie et totalitarianisme.* Paris, 1965

Aron, Raymond (1965). 'The end of ideology and the renaissance of ideas', in *Industrial Society.* London, 1967, 92–183

Aron, Raymond. *Progress and Disillusion: the dialectics of modern society.* New York, 1968

Aron, Raymond. *La Révolution introuvable.* Paris, 1968

*Aron, Raymond. *Histoire et dialectique de la violence.* Paris, 1973

Attewell, Paul. 'Ethnomethodology since Garfinkel', *Theory and Society,* 1 (1974), 179–210

Barnes, J. A. 'Time flies like an arrow', *Man* (N.S.), 6 (1971), 537–52

Barry, Brian. *Sociologists, Economists and Democracy.* London, 1970

Beauvoir, Simone de. *Force of Circumstance.* New York, 1964

Bell, Daniel, *et al. The End of Ideology.* New York, 1960

Belleville, Pierre. *Une nouvelle classe ouvrière.* Paris, 1963

Birnbaum, Norman. 'The Sociological study of ideology, 1940–60', *Current Sociology,* 9 (1960)

Birnbaum, Norman. *The Crisis of Industrial Society.* New York, 1969

Blum, Alan F. *Theorising.* London, 1974

Blumer, Herbert. 'Society as symbolic interaction', in Arnold Rose (ed.). *Human Behaviour and Social Process,* London, 1962, 179–92

Bras, Gabriel le, *et al. Aspects de la sociologie française.* Paris, 1966

Caute, David. *Communism and the French Intellectuals, 1914–60.* London, 1964

Cicourel, Aaron V. *The Social Organisation of Juvenile Justice.* New York, 1968

Cicourel, Aaron V. *Cognitive Sociology.* Harmondsworth, 1973

Connerton, Paul. *The Tragedy of Enlightenment: an essay on the Frankfurt School.* Cambridge, 1980

Crosland, Anthony. *The Future of Socialism.* London, 1955

Crosland, Anthony. *The Conservative Enemy.* London, 1962

Crosland, Anthony. 'Socialism now', in *Socialism Now.* London, 1974, 15–58

Dahrendorf, Ralf (1958). 'Out of utopia', in *Essays in the Theory of Society.* London, 1968, 107–28

Dahrendorf, Ralf (1958). 'Homo sociologicus', in *Essays in the Theory of Society.* London, 1968, 19–87

Dahrendorf, Ralf (1959). *Class and Class Conflict in Industrial Society.* London, 1963

Dahrendorf, Ralf (1965). *Society and Democracy in Germany.* London, 1968

Dahrendorf, Ralf. *Conflict after Class*. London, 1967

Desan, Wilfred. *The Marxism of Jean-Paul Sartre*. New York, 1965

Deutsch, Karl W. 'Social mobilisation and political development', *American Political Science Review*, 55 (1961), 493–515

Douglas, Jack D. (ed.). *Understanding Everyday Life*. London, 1971

Feyerabend, P. K. 'Consolations for the specialist', in Imre Lakatos, Alan Musgrave (eds.). *Criticism and the Growth of Knowledge*. Cambridge, 1970, 197–230

Floud, J. E., A. H. Halsey, F. M. Martin. *Social Class and Educational Opportunity*. London, 1956

Frankenberg, Ronald. *Communities in Britain*. Harmondsworth, 1966

Gadamer, Hans-Georg (1960). *Truth and Method*. London, 1975

Gehlen, Arnold, Helmut Schelsky. *Soziologie*. Dusseldorf and Cologne, 1955

*Geuss, Raymond. *The Idea of a Critical Theory*. Cambridge, 1981

Giddens, Anthony. *The Class Structure of the Advanced Societies*. London, 1973

Giddens, Anthony (ed.). *Positivism and Sociology*. London, 1974

Glass, D. V. (ed.). *Social Mobility in Britain*. London, 1954

Godelier, Maurice (1966). 'System, structure and contradiction in "Capital"', in Michael Lane (ed.). *Structuralism*. London, 1970, 340–58

Goldthorpe, John H., David Lockwood, Frank Bechhofer, Jennifer Platt. *The Affluent Worker*. Vol. 3. Cambridge, 1969

Gorz, André (1964). *Strategy for Labor*. Boston, 1967

Gorz, André. *La Socialisme difficile*. Paris, 1967

Gramsci, Antonio. 'The modern prince', in *The Modern Prince and other writings*. New York, 1957

Habermas, Jürgen (1965–8). *Knowledge and Human Interests*. London, 1972

Habermas, Jürgen (1963–71). *Theory and Practice*. Boston, 1973

Habermas, Jürgen (1967). *Zur Logik der Sozialwissenschaften*. Tübingen, 1970

Habermas, Jürgen (1968–9). *Toward a Rational Society*. London, 1971

Habermas, Jürgen. 'A postscript to "Knowledge and Human Interests"', *Philosophy of Social Science*, 3 (1973). 157–89

Habermas, Jürgen. *Zur Rekonstruktion des Historischen Materialismus*. Frankfurt, 1976

Habermas, Jürgen. 'Towards a reconstruction of historical materialism', *Theory and Society*, 2 (1975), 287–300

Habermas, Jürgen, Niklas Luhmann. *Theorie der Gesellschaft oder Sozialtechnologie*. Frankfurt, 1971

Habermas, Jürgen (1973). *Legitimation Crisis*. London, 1976

Hauser, Philip M. 'On actionism in the craft of sociology', *Sociological Inquiry*, 2 (1969), 139–47. Also in J. David Colfax, Jack L. Roach (eds.). *Radical Sociology*. New York, 1971, 425–29

Heath, Anthony. *Rational Choice and Social Exchange.* Cambridge, 1976

Hirst, Paul Q. 'The uniqueness of the West' [review of Anderson, 1974], *Economy and Society,* 4 (1975), 446–75

Horkheimer, Max. *The Eclipse of Reason.* New York, 1947

Horkheimer, Max, Theodor Adorno (1947). *Dialectic of the Enlightenment,* New York, 1972

Horowitz, Irving L. (ed.). *The Rise and Fall of Project Camelot.* Cambridge, Mass., 1971

Horowitz, Irving L. *Professing Sociology.* Chicago, 1968

Inkeles, Alex. 'Industrial man', *American Journal of Sociology,* 66 (1960–1), 1–31

Inkeles, Alex. 'The modernisation of man', in Myron Weiner (ed.). *Modernisation.* New York, 1966, 138–50

Jackson, Brian, Dennis Marsden. *Education and the Working Class.* London, 1962

Jeanson, F. *Le Problème moral et la pensée de Sartre.* Paris, 1947

Johnson, Chalmers. *Peasant Nationalism and Communist Power.* London, 1963

Johnson, R. *The French Communist Party versus the Students.* New Haven, Conn., 1972

Kerr, Clark, *et al. Industrialism and Industrial Man.* New York, 1964

Kerr, Clark. *Marshall, Marx and Modern Times.* Cambridge, 1969

Klein, Josephine. *Samples from English Cultures.* Vol. 1. London, 1965

Kojève, Alexandre. *Introduction to the Reading of Hegel.* New York, 1963

Kolakowski, Leszek. 'Althusser's Marx', in *The Socialist Register 1971.* London, 1971, 111–28

Kornhauser, William. *The Politics of Mass Society.* London, 1960

Krausz, Ernest. *Sociology in Britain: a survey of research.* London, 1969

Lefebvre, Henri. *La Vie quotidienne dans le monde moderne.* Paris, 1968

Lévi-Strauss, Claude. *Tristes Tropiques.* Paris, 1955

Lévi-Strauss, Claude. *La Pensée sauvage.* Paris, 1962, 324–57

Lichtheim, George. *Marxism in Modern France.* New York, 1966

Lichtheim, George. *From Marx to Hegel, and other essays.* London, 1971

Lipset, Seymour Martin. *Political Man.* London, 1960, 45–76

Lipset, Seymour Martin. *The First New Nation.* London, 1963

Lipset, Seymour Martin, Neil J. Smelser (eds.). *Sociology: progress of a decade.* New York, 1962

Lockwood, David. 'For T. H. Marshall', *Sociology,* 8 (1974), 363–7

Lourau, René. 'Sociology and politics in 1968', in Charles Posner (ed.). *Reflections on the Revolution in France: 1968.* Harmondsworth, 1970, 225–38

Macciochi, M. A. *Letters from Inside the Italian Communist Party to Louis Althusser.* London, 1973

MacIntyre, Alasdair. *Marcuse.* London, 1970

Macintyre, Stuart, Keith Tribe. *Althusser and Marxist Theory.* Cambridge, 1975

Mallet, Serge. *La Nouvelle Classe ouvrière.* Paris, 1963

Mann, Michael. *Consciousness and Action in the Western Working Class.* London, 1973

Marcuse, Herbert (1932–69). *Studies in Critical Philosophy.* London, 1972

Marcuse, Herbert (1941). *Reason and Revolution.* London, 1954

Marcuse, Herbert. *Eros and Civilisation.* Boston, 1955

Marcuse, Herbert. *One-Dimensional Man.* London, 1964

Marcuse, Herbert. *Negations.* London, 1968

Marcuse, Herbert. *An Essay on Liberation.* Boston, 1969

Marshall, T. H. 'Social class: a preliminary analysis', *Sociological Review*, 26 (1934), 55–76

Marshall, T. H. *Citizenship and Social Class.* Cambridge, 1950. Also in T. H. Marshall, 1964, 71–134

Marshall, T. H. *Class, Citizenship and Social Development.* Garden City, N.Y. 1964

Mendès-France, Pierre. *La République moderne.* Paris, 1962

Merleau-Ponty, Maurice. *Humanisme et terreur.* Paris, 1947

Merleau-Ponty, Maurice (1955). *Adventures of the Dialectic.* Evanston, Ill., 1973

Mills, C. Wright. *The Power Elite.* New York, 1956

Naville, Pierre. *Le Nouveau Leviathan I: De l'alienation à la jouissance.* Paris, 1957

Naville, Pierre, Georges Friedmann. *Traité de sociologie de travail.* Paris, 1961–2

New Left Review, 1 (1960), and subsequent volumes, *passim*

Nicolaus, Martin. 'The professional organisation of sociology: a view from below' in J. David Colfax, Jack L. Roach (eds.). *Radical Sociology.* New York, 1971, 45–60

Offe, Claus. 'The abolition of market control and the problem of legitimacy', *Kapitalstate*, 1 and 2 (1973), 109–16, 73–5

Parkin, Frank. *Class Inequality and Political Order.* London, 1971

Parsons, Talcott. 'The distribution of power in American society', *World Politics*, 10 (1957), 123–43

Poster, Mark. *Existential Marxism in Post-War France: from Sartre to Althusser.* Princeton, 1975

Pouillon, J. 'Sartre et Lévi-Strauss', *L'Arc*, 26 (1965), 55–60

Poulantzas, Nicos. *Political Power and Social Classes.* London, 1973

Poulantzas, Nicos. *Classes in Contemporary Capitalism.* London, 1975

*Rabil, Albert. *Merleau-Ponty.* New York, 1967

Reynaud, J.-D. (ed. for the French Sociological Society). *Tendances et volontés de la société française.* Paris, 1966

Rosen, Lawrence. 'Language, history and the logic of inquiry in Lévi-Strauss and Sartre', *History and Theory*, 10 (1971), 269–74

Rostow, W. W. *The Stages of Economic Growth.* Cambridge, 1960

Sartre, Jean-Paul (1943). *Being and Nothingness.* London, 1957

Sartre, Jean-Paul. *Critique de la raison dialectique: I, théorie des ensembles practiques.* Paris, 1960

Sartre, Jean-Paul (1964). *Situations IV: Merleau-Ponty.* London, 1965

Schelsky, Helmut. *Ortsbestimmung der Deutschen Soziologie.* Dusseldorf and Cologne, 1959

Shils, Edward A. *The Intellectuals and the Powers.* Chicago, 1972

Smelser, Neil J. 'Mechanisms of change and adjustments to change', in Bert F. Hoselitz, W. E. Moore (eds.). *Industrialisation and Society.* Paris, 1963, 32–54

Touraine, Alain. *La Conscience ouvrière.* Paris, 1966

Touraine, Alain. *Le Mouvement de mai ou le communisme utopique.* Paris, 1968

Touraine, Alain (1969). *The Post-Industrial Society.* New York, 1971

Townsend, Peter (1968–74). *Sociology and Social Policy.* London, 1975

Turner, Roy (ed.). *Ethnomethodology.* Harmondsworth, 1974

Warnock, Mary. *The Philosophy of Sartre.* London, 1965

Weinberg, Ian. 'The problem of the convergence of industrial societies', *Comparative Studies in Society and History,* 12 (1969), 1–15

Wellmer, Albert. *Critical Theory of Society.* New York, 1971

Wolff, Robert Paul, *et al. A Critique of Pure Tolerance.* Boston, 1965

Conclusion

Anderson, Benedict. *Imagined Communities: reflections on the origin and spread of nationalism.* London, 1983

Aron, Raymond. 'Preface', in *Main Currents of Sociological Thought,* Vol. 2. London, 1968, v–viii

Bann, Stephen. *The Clothing of Clio: a study of the representation of history in nineteenth-century Britain and France.* Cambridge, 1984

Blumenberg, Hans (1966). *The Legitimacy of the Modern Age.* Cambridge, Mass., 1983

Brown, Peter. *Augustine of Hippo: a biography.* Berkeley and Los Angeles, 1967

Brown, Peter. *Religion and Society in the Age of St Augustine.* London, 1972

Burrow, J. W. *A Liberal Descent: Victorian historians and the English past.* Cambridge, 1981

Castro, Luis. *La Gran Colombia: una ilusion ilustrada.* Caracas, 1984

Chabal, Patrick. *Amilcar Cabral: revolutionary leadership and people's war.* Cambridge, 1983

Davidson, Donald. 'On the very idea of a conceptual scheme', *Proceedings and Addresses of the American Philosophical Association,* 67 (1974), 5–20

Dunn, John. *Western Political Theory in the Face of the Future.* Cambridge, 1979

Evans, Peter B., Dietrich Rueschemeyer, Theda Skocpol (eds.). *Bringing the State Back In.* Cambridge, 1985

Finley, M. I. 'Myth, memory and history', *History and Theory*, 4 (1964–65), 279–302.

Franklin, Julian H. *Jean Bodin and the Sixteenth-Century Revolution in the Methodology of Law and History.* New York, 1963

Gellner, Ernest. *Nations and Nationalism.* Oxford, 1983

Gilbert, Felix. 'European and American historiography', in John Higham *et al.* (eds.). *History.* Englewood Cliffs, N.J., 1965, 317–87

Gilbert, Felix. 'Machiavelli's "Istorie Fiorentine"', 'The historian as guardian of the national consciousness; Italy between Guiccardini and Muratori', in *History: choice and commitment.* Cambridge, Mass., 1977, 135–53, 387–409

Gramsci, Antonio. *Selections from the Prison Notebooks.* Quentin Hoare, Geoffrey Nowell-Smith (eds.). London, 1971

Hegel, G. W. F. (1952–81). *The Letters.* Clark Butler (ed.). Bloomington, Ind., 1984

Hirschman, Albert O. *The Passions and the Interests*: *political arguments for capitalism before its triumph.* Princeton, 1977

Hirschman, Albert O. 'The rise and decline of development economics', 'The turn to authoritarianism in Latin America and the search for its economic determinants', in *Essays in Trespassing*: *economics to politics and beyond.* Cambridge, 1981, 1–24, 98–135

Hughes, H. Stuart (1958). *Consciousness and Society*: *the reorientation of European social thought, 1890–1930.* New York, 1963

James, Susan. *The Content of Social Explanation.* Cambridge, 1984

Keats, John. *The Complete Poems.* John Barnard (ed.). London, 1973

Kelley, Donald R. *Foundations of Modern Historical Scholarship*; *language, law and history in the French Renaissance,* New York, 1970

Lakatos, Imre, Alan Musgrave (eds.). *Criticism and the Growth of Knowledge.* Cambridge, 1970

MacIntyre, Alasdair. *A Short History of Ethics.* London, 1966

Meier, G. M., Seers, D. (eds.). *Pioneers in Development.* New York, 1984.

Momigliano, Arnaldo. 'Time in ancient historiography', *History and Theory*, Beiheft 6 (1966), 1–23

Momigliano, Arnaldo. 'Tradition and the classical historian', *History and Theory*, 11 (1972), 279–93

Momigliano, Arnaldo. 'Greek historiography', *History and Theory*, 17 (1978), 1–28

Nadel, George H. 'Philosophy of history before historicism', *History and Theory*, 3 (1963–64), 291–315

Nisbet, Robert A. *The Sociological Tradition.* London, 1967

Pelczynski, Z. A. (ed.). *The State and Civil Society: studies in Hegel's political philosophy.* Cambridge, 1984

Pocock, J. G. A. 'The origins of the study of the past', *Comparative studies in Society and History,* 4 (1962), 209–46

Pocock, J. G. A. *The Machiavellian Moment: Florentine political thought and the Atlantic Republican tradition.* Princeton, 1975

Rawls, John. *A Theory of Justice.* Cambridge, Mass., 1971

Rawls, John. 'A well ordered society', in Peter Laslett, James Fishkin (eds.). *Philosophy, Politics and Society.* Fifth series. Oxford, 1979

Rawls, John. 'Kantian constructivism in moral theory', *Journal of Philosophy,* 77 (1980), 515–72

Rawls, John. 'Social unity and primary goods', in Amartya Sen, Bernard Williams (eds.). *Utilitarianism and Beyond.* Cambridge, 1982, 159–85

Rorty, Richard. *Philosophy and the Mirror of Nature.* Princeton, 1979

Rorty, Richard. *Consequences of Pragmatism: essays 1972–80.* Minneapolis, 1982

Scanlon, T. M. 'Contractualism and utilitarianism', in Amartya Sen, Bernard Williams (eds.). *Utilitarianism and Beyond.* Cambridge, 1982, 103–28

Shklar, Judith. *After Utopia: the decline of political faith.* Princeton, 1957

Skinner, Quentin. *The Foundations of Modern Political Thought.* Two volumes. Cambridge, 1978

Skinner, Quentin. *Machiavelli.* Oxford, 1981

Walzer, Michael. *Spheres of Justice.* Oxford, 1983

*Williams, Bernard. *Ethics and the Limits of Philosophy.* London, 1985

Zeitlin, Irving M. *Ideology and the Development of Sociological Theory.* Englewood Cliffs, N.J., 1968

Index

Catholicism: and Enlightenment, 10–14; and French thinking, 11–12, 77–9, 85, 114–15, 117, 128, 172–3; and medieval thought, 8–10; and Scheler, 181–3; *see also* Protestantism

class: Durkheim on, 125, 129, 169; eighteenth-century Scots on, 29; Hegel on, 48–9; in American sociology, 196–8; in English sociology, 169–70, 246–52; in French sociology, 169, 224–7; in German sociology, 169, 233–4; T. H. Marshall on, 248–9; Marx on, 52–9, 249; Rousseau on, 21–3; Saint-Simon on, 71–2; Spann on, 185; Max Weber on, 151–5, 249; *see also* capitalism

Cole, G. D. H., 168

Collingwood, R. G., 6

communism: criticised, 67–8, 126, 153, 187, 227, 242; defended, 53–4, 57–8, 186–8; defined, 53–4, 57–8, 63, 126; Durkheim on, 126; in France, 114, 169, 171–2, 175, 225–30 *passim*, 250; in Germany, 153, 176–7, 188, 231–4, 240; Lukács on, 186–8; Marx on, 57–8, 63; Merleau-Ponty on, 222–3; social conditions of, 55, 67–8, 225–30; Max Weber on, 153; *see also* revolution, Russia, socialism, sociology and communism

Comte, Auguste, 72–9; and De Bonald and De Maistre, 255; and Branford, 167; and Durkheim, 121–2, 123, 124, 170; and Hobhouse, 107; and J. S. Mill, 77, 79–85, 115; and Saint-Simon, 72–5, 78, 114, 121–2, 170, 255; and Spencer, 93; arguments, 74–8; assumptions, 74; career, 72–3, 115; contemporary reception, 79; *Course of Positive Philosophy*, 73–7, 79; intentions, 73, 114, 170, 254; 'Plan for re-organising society', 73; *System of Positive Polity*, 77–8, 83

Condillac, Etienne de, 69–70

conservatism: criticised, 67, 147, 154, 157–8, 192, 194–6; defended, 67, 184–5, 197–8; defined, 184–5, 197–8; Fitzhugh on, 197–8; in United States, 192, 195, 197–8, 243–4; Locke on, 192; social conditions of, 17–18, 67, 243–4; Spann on, 184–5; Max Weber on, 147, 154, 157–8; *see also* sociology and conservatism

Cooley, Charles Horton, 204–5, 207–8, 209, 215, 243

Copernicus, Nicholas, 9

Coulanges, Fustel de, 132

'critical theory', 188–9, 216, 219, 234–40, 264

Crosland, Anthony, 246–7, 251

Dahrendorf, Ralf, 233–4, 240–1, 249

D'Alembert, Jean le Rond, 10, 13, 14

Darwin, Charles; and Ogburn, 211; and Spencer, 91, 96–7, 101–2, 104; arguments, 96; assumptions, 97; contemporary reception of, 104, 198; *see also* social darwinism

Davidson, Donald, 271

Davy, Georges, 174

Descartes, René; and Durkheim, 220; and Kant, 33; and Rousseau, 21; and Sartre, 219–20; arguments, 21; supposed effects, 66

Dewey, John, 210; *see also* pragmatism

D'Holbach, Paul Henri, 10, 13

Dickinson, Lowes, 168

Diderot, Denis, 20, 21

Dilthey, Wilhelm, 143–4, 145–7, 187, 238–9; *see also* hermeneutics

Douglas, Mary, 3

Dreyfus, Alfred, 117

Dunn, John, 6

Durkheim, Emile, 116–36; and Aron, 220; and Comte, 121, 123, 170; and Descartes, 220; and Ginsberg, 168; and Hobhouse, 168; and Kant, 118–19, 120–1; and Marx, 118, 122; and Parsons, 213, 215; and Rousseau, 118–19, 126, 135–6; and Saint-Simon, 121–2, 126, 170, 172, 218; and Schäffle, 122, 127; and Sidgwick, 166, 168; and Spann, 185; and Spencer, 118, 123, 124, 126, 129; and Tönnies, 123, 126; and Max Weber, 166; arguments, 118–36, 255; assumptions, 116, 119, 121, 128, 143, 195, 220, 230; career, 116, 122, 132, 135; *Division of Labour*, 120, 122–9, 130, 131, 136; *Elementary Forms of Religious Life*, 2–3, 122, 133, 135; 'Individualism and the intellectuals', 118–22, 125, 128, 195; intentions, 121, 128, 135, 139, 166, 170–1, 253–6; *Professional Ethics and Civic Morals*, 122; 'Sociology and pragmatism', 122, 134; 'Some primitive forms of classification', 2, 133–4; *Suicide*, 122, 129–32

Scheidemann, Philipp, 176
Scheler, Max, 181–3, 186, 240
Schelling, Friedrich von, 42, 141, 142, 187
Schelsky, Helmut, 232
Schiller, Johann Christoph Friedrich von, 36, 37, 41, 42, 137
Schlegel, August Wilhelm, 37
Schmoller, Gustav, 155, 178
Schweitzer, Johann Baptist von, 139
Scotland, theorising in, 12, 28–31, 80
Shils, Edward A., 242
Sidgwick, Henry, 109, 165–6, 168
Simmel, Georg, 181, 186–7, 188, 208, 210
Skinner, Quentin, 6
Small, Albion, 191, 201, 204, 208, 209, 215
Smith, Adam, 29, 31, 56, 269
social anthropology, *see* anthropology
social darwinism, 104, 198–201, 204–9, 211; *see also* Darwin, evolution, Spencer, Sumner
social policy, *see* sociology and social policy
social psychology, *see* ethnomethodology, pragmatism, psychology, symbolic interactionism
socialism: absence in United States, 194–5, 197–8; criticised, 114, 152, 154, 178–9, 197–8, 247; defended, 126, 246, 268–9; defined, 126, 246; Durkheim on, 126; in England, 164–70, 245–52 *passim*; in France, 66–7, 114, 125, 170–2, 175, 217–19; in Germany, 139, 175–9, 188; social conditions of, 66–7, 152–3, 194–5, 226; Max Weber on, 152–3, 154, 175; *see also* communism, marxism, political parties, revolution, sociology and socialism
Sociological Society, 111, 166
sociology: and communism, 126, 171–2, 178–9, 180–1, 187–9, 219–30, 241–2, 265; and conservatism, 153–5, 178–9, 184–5, 215–16, 243; and ethics, 256 ff.; and liberalism, 92, 99–111, 115, 117, 153–5, 164–75, 178–9, 244–52; and socialism, 105–8, 115, 117, 125, 164–75, 178–9, 215–16, 219–30, 244–53, 265; and social policy, 105, 110–13, 165, 175, 189, 202–4, 209–10, 244–53; compared with natural sciences, 4–6, 69–70, 81–2, 141–9, 210–11, 251, 261–2; criticised, 109, 117–18, 243–7; defended, 70, 135, 173; defined, 28,

70, 81–2, 111, 149; demand for, 111, 165, 175, 191, 202–3, 247–8, 253; difficulties in explaining, 1–7; in England, 79–111, 112–13, 164–70, 174–5, 190, 245–53; in France, 70–89, 115–36, 170–5, 190, 219–30, 252–3; in Germany, 112–13, 142, 150, 163, 175–90, 231–41, 252–3; in United States, 5, 163, 191, 196–216, 241–5, 252–3; of knowledge, 1–7, 180–4; professionalisation of, 5, 111, 115, 122, 170, 173, 189, 191, 202–3, 209–12, 214–16, 224, 242–3, 247–8, 251, 253; *see also* universities; project of, 28, 70, 111, 112–13, 163, 170, 202–3, 216, 253; term coined, 70; *see also* surveys
Socrates, 43
Sombart, Werner, 141, 158, 175, 178, 189
Sorokin, Pitirim, 212
Spann, Othmar, 184–5, 255
Spencer, Herbert, 90–100; and Cooley, 207–8; and Darwin, 91, 198! and Durkheim, 118, 123, 124, 126, 129; and Hobhouse, 106–8, 168; and James, 206–7; and J. S. Mill, 91–3, 109–10; and Moore, 109–10; and Sumner, 199–201, 203; and Ward, 204–5; arguments, 91–100, 109, 256; assumptions, 90; *Autobiography*, 90, 96–7; career, 91, 92, 96–7, 98, 199; contemporary reception, 100–8, 111, 116, 198–201, 204–9; *First Principles*, 92, 94–6, 97, 107; intentions, 90–1, 256; *Principles of Psychology*, 92–3; *Social Statics*, 91–2
Spengler, Oswald, 175, 179, 183
Stalin, Joseph, 221, 222
State, the: Dahrendorf on 233–4; distinguished from society, 47, 259, 266–7; Durkheim on, 123; French sociologists on, 224–5, 229–30; Freyer on, 185; Hegel on, 46–9; Hobhouse on, 105; Kant on, 34–5; Marx on, 52–4; Montesquieu on, 17–19; Rousseau on, 24–7; Scheler on, 182–3; Spann on, 185; Spencer on, 99–100; Max-Weber on, 154; *see also* communism, conservatism, liberalism, revolution, socialism
Stein, Lorenz von, 55
Stephen, Leslie, 92
Stewart, Dugald, 29–30, 40
stratification, *see* class